Hawthorne,
Melville,
Stephen Crane

A CRITICAL BIBLIOGRAPHY

Hawthorne, Melville, Stephen Crane

A CRITICAL BIBLIOGRAPHY

by THEODORE L. GROSS
and STANLEY WERTHEIM

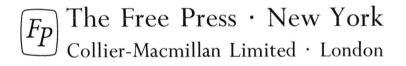

The Free Press · New York
Collier-Macmillan Limited · London

Contents

Preface

COMMENTARIES ON AMERICAN literature have grown so numerous that the student needs careful guidance in reading them. Bibliographies and checklists are no longer sufficient; they must be annotated so that the quality of scholarly studies can be distinguished from one book to another. The student who wishes to know more about an author's life or literature would be wise to follow Thoreau's advice about reading in general: "Read the best books first, or you may not have a chance to read them at all." The annotated bibliographies in this volume aim to help the student in discovering the finest and most representative scholarship dealing with the literature of Nathaniel Hawthorne, Herman Melville, and Stephen Crane.

Each of these writers has had a distinctly different reception from his critical audience. The history of Hawthorne scholarship is perhaps the most traditional. Like many classical American authors, Hawthorne was first presented by members of his family. Mrs. Hawthorne edited her husband's notebooks and eliminated or emended those remarks that seemed to her undignified; Julian Hawthorne published a two-volume biography of his father, *Hawthorne and His Wife* (1884), which created the image of a devoted parent and husband, a dedicated artist, and a loyal American. Early biographies and critical studies continued to regard Hawthorne with the respect accorded a major American writer, and they emphasized certain qualities which became associated with the author for more than half a century: his introspective character, his tendency to shun society and create a fiction of isolation, sin, and guilt. But in the 1930's, scholars re-evaluated Hawthorne in the light of scrupulous research into his life and work and drew the portrait of a more social, "normal" man who successfully opened, in Hawthorne's own words, "an intercourse with the world." Although his work has been interpreted differently at different times since the mid-nineteenth century, Hawthorne has always enjoyed the reputation of a major author; his stature has never seriously declined. From the late 1930's until the present day, critics have examined Hawthorne's fiction in the greatest detail and from almost every approach known to modern criticism: explication, myth, psychology, cultural history, symbolism, and linguistics.

Melville was less fortunate than his friend. His work received almost no serious consideration before the appearance of Raymond Weaver's biography in 1921. Contemporary reviewers commented upon his novels as they appeared, but most of them valued his early, less complicated books—*Typee* and *Omoo*—more highly than *Moby-Dick*, *Pierre*, and *The Confidence Man*. Melville's fear that he would be remembered "as a 'man who lived among the cannibals'" was not without justification, and his struggle to be understood by the public of his time is one of the more bitter commentaries on the state of nineteenth-century literary criticism in America. His recognition in the 1920's is, in turn, a tribute to modern scholarship, for a neglected author of the first rank was finally appreciated and made available to a wide reading audience. Raymond Weaver realized that *Moby-Dick* was Melville's masterpiece, and with the publication of *Herman Melville: Mariner and Mystic* (1921) and the later printing of *Billy Budd* (1924), the Melville revival began. The full recognition of Melville's stature as a major American author was established in 1938 by Willard Thorp, when he published *Herman Melville: Representative Selections*, a sound estimation and presentation of this complex author, which stimulated a subsequent scholarship that has examined Melville's language, religion, reading, mythology, philosophy, economics, orienda, and tragic sensibility as well as many aspects of his life. Both Hawthorne and Melville—with their irony and ambiguity, their tragic and symbolic vision, their tendency to say "No, in thunder!" and to record the inner life of man—have seemed especially pertinent to modern scholars.

Although Stephen Crane achieved fame among his contemporaries with the publication of *The Red Badge of Courage*, he suffered serious neglect after his death in 1900. It was not until Thomas Beer glamorized Crane's life, in his highly impressionistic biography *Stephen Crane: A Study in American Letters* (1923), that interest in Crane was revived. By 1927, Alfred Knopf had published a twelve-volume collected edition of Crane's works. Yet, in the thirties and forties Crane scholarship and criticism rarely transcended its emphasis upon the realism and naturalism of his fiction, while his poetry was virtually ignored. With the publication of John Berryman's biography (1950), William M. Gibson's *Stephen Crane: Selected Prose and Poetry* (1950), R. W. Stallman's *Stephen Crane: An Omnibus* (1952), and Daniel Hoffman's *The Poetry of Stephen Crane* (1957), Crane's true complexity and sophistication were recognized, and in the past decade his stature as an important American author has been secured.

Our primary intention in these bibliographies is to present the scholarship of Hawthorne, Melville, and Crane in a lucid, reliable, and stimulating manner, and to measure its quality against the highest contemporary standards. Any selective bibliography obviously reflects the taste of the bibliographer, and we know that we have omitted individual essays that others might include. But we trust that we have not forgotten any work which has contributed to our fundamental understanding of Hawthorne, Melville, and Crane.

THEODORE L. GROSS
STANLEY WERTHEIM

December, 1970

Hawthorne, Melville, Stephen Crane

A CRITICAL BIBLIOGRAPHY

Nathaniel
• Hawthorne

by Theodore L. Gross

CONTENTS ❧ *Nathaniel Hawthorne*

I. Introduction

As a man and as an artist, Hawthorne has compelled important writers and critics to return to the roots of their native culture. A nineteenth-century author whose best work is in the American grain, Hawthorne explores the moral dimensions of the Puritan heritage as well as the New England society of his own time. In criticizing his work, Americans have discovered and come to understand the complexity of their common past.

Hawthorne's contemporaries recognized certain distinctive qualities of his genius. Edgar Allan Poe, who had formulated his famous definition of the short story by using *Twice Told Tales* as his example, indicated his reservations about Hawthorne's originality and fondness for allegory; but he recognized that the structure, language, and moral perceptions of the tales were unmatched by any other American writer of his time. Herman Melville, who had become a friend of Hawthorne in the early 1850's, admired Hawthorne's tragic vision, his ability to say "No, in thunder," his "great power of blackness" that "derives its force from its appeal to that Calvinistic sense of Innate Depravity and Original Sin." Other nineteenth-century authors responded to Hawthorne's work; and in the remarks of James Russell Lowell, Henry David Thoreau, George Whipple, and James T. Fields runs the common assumption that Hawthorne is one of the two or three major American authors before the Civil War.

The critics and writers of Hawthorne's own time were, for the most part, commendatory. They praised Hawthorne for his moral vision, his skepticism, and his sense of tragedy. The first important author to measure Hawthorne's life and literature fully was Henry James. In 1879, as he approached the flowering of his own artistic development, James published a critical biography in the English Men of Letters series. In James's view, Hawthorne was a deeply gifted author—the "greatest imaginative writer we have," as he wrote to Hawthorne's son Julian—who was victimized by the thin social texture of nineteenth-century America. Because he had so little society to draw upon, Hawthorne was compelled to use an allegoric framework for much of his work which, for the realistic James, was "quite one of the lighter exercises of the imagination." James viewed Hawthorne through his own sense of how memorable fiction should be created, and his estimate is not wholly tolerant of an author whose sensibility was different from his own; but James analyzes the novels and stories with subtlety and sophistication, and he underscores Hawthorne's keen historical consciousness, his ability to give artistic credence to the Puritan past he understood so well.

This view of Hawthorne as a solitary artist who lived apart from the world and wrote dark allegories of man's inhumanity to man persisted until the early 1930's. George Woodberry, Herbert Gorman, Lloyd Morris, and Newton Arvin emphasized Hawthorne's loneliness, his tendency to brood over the Puritan legacy that informed his fiction; but in 1932, Randall Stewart published Hawthorne's *American Notebooks* and, in addition to correcting Mrs. Hawthorne's sentimentalized version which had helped to form the image of her husband as a withdrawn man, Stewart emphasized the social, "normal" aspects of Hawthorne's life. Stewart followed the *American Notebooks* with many articles which concentrated upon Hawthorne's public life; in 1942 he brought out an edition of Hawthorne's *English Notebooks*; and in 1948 he published *Nathaniel Hawthorne: A Biography*, which is still the most reliable treatment of the author's life. Other biographers and scholars studied Hawthorne in his social and historical milieu as well as through his work, and by the 1940's critics were exploring the fiction in great detail—particularly those novels and tales that were rich in symbolism, myth, linguistic ambiguities, and formal aesthetic problems.

Since the time of Stewart's pioneering work, critics have sought to establish Hawthorne as a far more complex author than his contemporaries imagined him to be. D. H. Lawrence had anticipated this criticism by stressing, in *Studies in Classic American Literature* (1923), the "perfect duplicity of *The Scarlet Letter*"; but it was not until F. O. Matthiessen analyzed Hawthorne's work in *American Renaissance* (1941) that its richness and tragic design were fully appreciated. Critics then followed by treating Hawthorne's work in terms of its social and political observation; its theological significance and Gothic elements; its many sources, ranging from Spenser to Swift and William Godwin; its relationship to various myths and archetypes; its profound psychology, artistry, humor, and connections with folklore. Finally—one might say inevitably—some contemporary critics have reacted against these diverse interpretations of Hawthorne and sought to return him to the nineteenth century in which he lived, presenting Hawthorne's life and work in terms of his cultural milieu.

In 1964, a group of some of the finest American scholars contributed to the *Hawthorne Centenary Essays* (40)[1], a volume which reflects the current state of Hawthorne studies and attempts to show Hawthorne and his work "as they presently confront us." Philip Young examined the book in a lengthy review and whimsically concluded that he was convinced we really understand Hawthorne now, that indeed

---

[1] Numbers in parentheses refer to other entries.

"he is profoundly an American writer, relevant to us, and the Great Society and all, as seldom if ever before, and finally to be understood, perhaps, only by modern Americans." There seemed to be little more to say about this great American author.

Six years have passed since Philip Young asked for a moratorium on Hawthorne scholarship, and critics have not heeded his suggestion. Hawthorne criticism still flourishes with the greatest intensity and interest, as each new scholar returns to those compelling novels and stories to discover Hawthorne's American past—and his own.

II. Chronology

Hawthorne's first American ancestor was William Hathorne, who emigrated from England to America in 1630. William Hathorne's son, John, was one of the three judges in the Salem witchcraft trials of 1692. Hawthorne recalls both men in "The Custom House," the preface to *The Scarlet Letter*. Other ancestors were Joseph, a Salem farmer; Daniel, a seaman who commanded a privateer in the Revolutionary war; and Nathaniel, born in 1775, also a seaman. In 1801 Nathaniel Hawthorne married Elizabeth Clarke Manning, with whom he had three children: Elizabeth Manning, born in 1802; Nathaniel, born in 1804; and Maria Louisa, born in 1808.

1804   Nathaniel Hawthorne born on July 4 in Salem, Massachusetts.

1808   Hawthorne's father died in Surinam, Dutch Guiana, while on a long voyage.

1816   Hawthorne's mother took her family to Raymond, Maine, where her brother owned land. The Hawthornes lived there for three years.

1819   Hawthorne attended Mr. Archer's School in Salem. In March, 1820, he left and studied under the lawyer, Benjamin C. Oliver, in preparation for college.

1821–1825   Hawthorne attended Bowdoin College until his graduation in 1825. He was not an exceptional student, graduating eighteenth in a class of thirty-eight. His closest friends in college were Horatio Bridge, Franklin Pierce (who later became President of the United States), and Jonathan Cilley. Henry Wadsworth Longfellow was a classmate.

1825   Hawthorne lived in his mother's house in Salem until 1837 in what he called his "haunted chamber."

1828   *Fanshawe: A Tale* published anonymously. Hawthorne grew dissatisfied with the novel and attempted to suppress its circulation.

1832   Hawthorne began to publish his stories anonymously or pseudononymously. "The Gentle Boy," "The Wives of the Dead," "Roger Malvin's Burial," and "My Kinsman, Major Molineux" appeared in *The Token* (1832), a Christmas annual. In 1835 "The Gray Champion," "The Ambitious Guest," and "Young Goodman Brown" were published in *New England Magazine*.

1836 From March to August, Hawthorne edited the *American Magazine of Useful and Entertaining Knowledge*.

1837 *Twice-Told Tales* published under Hawthorne's name. Eighteen of his thirty-six stories were included in the volume. Thus Hawthorne, in his own phrase, "opened an intercourse with the world."

1838 Hawthorne became engaged to Sophia Peabody.

1839–1840 Hawthorne was a measurer of salt and coal at the Boston Custom House.

1841 *Grandfather's Chair*, a collection of New England stories for children, was published. This volume presents a history of New England through the Revolution.

1841 From April to November, Hawthorne lived at Brook Farm in West Roxbury, Massachusetts. He bought $1,000 worth of stock in the co-operative but withdrew by the end of the year.

1842 Hawthorne married Sophia Peabody, July 9.

1842 Expanded edition of *Twice-Told Tales* published.

1842–1845 Hawthorne lived at the Old Manse, Concord, Massachusetts, and met Emerson, Thoreau, Ellery Channing, and other New England figures of importance.

1844 Hawthorne's daughter, Una, born.

1845 *Journal of an African Cruiser*, edited from Horatio Bridge's manuscript.

1846 *Mosses from an Old Manse*, Hawthorne's second collection of short stories. "Roger Malvin's Burial" and "Young Goodman Brown," written before 1837, were first included in this volume. Other prominent stories published were "Rappaccini's Daughter" and "The Hall of Fantasy."

1846 Hawthorne's son, Julian, born.

1846–1849 Hawthorne was a surveyor in the Salem Custom House.

1850 *The Scarlet Letter* published on March 16.

1850–1851 Hawthorne lived in Lenox, Massachusetts, and became friendly with Herman Melville.

1851   *The House of the Seven Gables* published in April; *The Snow-Image and Other Twice-Told Tales; True Stories from History and Biography.* A daughter, Rose, born on May 20. Hawthorne spent the winter at West Newton.

1852   In May, Hawthorne moved to the Wayside in Concord, Massachusetts. *The Blithedale Romance; A Wonder-Book for Girls and Boys,* which is a retelling of the classical myths; *Life of Franklin Pierce* (a campaign biography written for his friend and college classmate).

1853   *Tanglewood Tales for Girls and Boys* published in August.

1853–1857   President Franklin Pierce appointed Hawthorne as United States Consul at Liverpool; he served until 1857.

1854   *Mosses from an Old Manse* (revised edition).

1858–1859   On January 5, Hawthorne left London to travel to Paris and ultimately to Italy. He stayed in Rome until May 24, 1858, and then went to Florence.

1859   Hawthorne returned to England.

1860   *Transformation* published in London on February 28. In Boston, the novel appeared as *The Marble Faun.* Hawthorne returned to the Wayside.

1862–1963   Hawthorne published a number of sketches of English life and manners in the *Atlantic* as well as "Chiefly About War Matters." He also struggled to complete several romances: *Dr. Grimshawe's Secret, The Ancestral Footstep, Septimius Felton,* and *The Dolliver Romance.*

1863   *Our Old Home,* a book dealing with Hawthorne's experiences in England, published on September 18.

1864   Hawthorne died on May 19 at Plymouth, New Hampshire.

1868–1871   Mrs. Hawthorne published *Passages from the American Notebooks* (1868), *Passages from the English Notebooks* (1870), and *Passages from the French and Italian Notebooks* (1871).

III. Editions, Other Primary Materials, and Bibliographies

Editions:

1. *The Complete Works of Nathaniel Hawthorne*, with Introductory Notes. 12 volumes. Edited by G. P. Lathrop. Boston: Houghton Mifflin, 1883.

This edition is still standard, although it will soon be superseded by *The Centenary Edition of the Works of Nathaniel Hawthorne* (2).

    Lathrop added another volume, *Dr. Grimshawe's Secret*, but published it in an unreliable form.

2. *The Centenary Edition of the Works of Nathaniel Hawthorne*. Edited by William Charvat, Roy Harvey Pearce, and Claude Simpson. Textual editors: Fredson Bowers and Matthew Bruccoli. Columbus: Ohio State University Press, 1962–.

The following volumes have been published: I. *The Scarlet Letter*, 1962, 189 pp.; II. *The House of the Seven Gables*, 1965, 417 pp.; *The Blithedale Romance* and *Fanshawe*, 1964, 501 pp.; and IV. *The Marble Faun*, 1968, 610 pp. The short stories will soon appear. This edition will be standard for all students of Hawthorne's work.

    In *The Scarlet Letter*, the editors use printed editions "to establish the text in as close a form, in all details, to Hawthorne's final intentions as the preserved documents of each separate work permit." William Charvat provides a lengthy historical introduction to *The House of the Seven Gables*; Fredson Bowers notes 112 differences in the words of the text and three to four thousand variations in accidentals. Roy Harvey Pearce offers a valuable introduction to *The Blithedale Romance* and *Fanshawe; The Blithedale Romance* contains 2,000 accidentals and 49 variants. Claude M. Simpson creates the background to the writing of *The Marble Faun* in a sensible introduction; Fredson Bowers analyzes, in his 88-page textual introduction, the difficulties in establishing an accurate text.

    These texts are models of modern critical editing and present Hawthorne's work in a truly accurate form for the first time.

(7)

Other Primary Materials:

3. *The American Notebooks by Nathaniel Hawthorne.* Edited by Randall Stewart. New Haven: Yale University Press, 1932. 350 pp.

Modern Hawthorne studies can be dated from the reprinting of *The American Notebooks* by Randall Stewart, which is in effect a restoration of Mrs. Hawthorne's earlier publication, *Passages from the American Notebooks* (1868). Stewart points out in his lengthy and informative introduction that Mrs. Hawthorne's changes of her husband's work consisted of grammatical alterations and revisions; modifications of sexual allusions; expressions that seemed too realistic; awkward diction; and passages that commented upon certain living people. Stewart discovered that in the process of altering her husband's language, Mrs. Hawthorne often lost its "idiomatic tang" or gave Hawthorne's expression a forced, unnatural elegance. Furthermore she suppressed passages that tended toward pessimism, or cynicism, or heterodoxical religious views. In her editing, as Stewart notes in his biography (22), "Mrs. Hawthorne . . . took great liberties with the original manuscripts. She strove by omission and revision to give to the text the form which she thought Hawthorne himself would have given to it had he prepared the manuscript for publication." By presenting the original notebooks—he also edited *The English Notebooks* (5) in 1941— Stewart indicates that Hawthorne was not nearly so seclusive or morbid as previous biographers had pictured him.

In the introduction to this volume, Stewart analyzes Mrs. Hawthorne's revisions of the notebooks; Hawthorne's use of the notes in his fiction; and the dominant character types and recurrent themes in Hawthorne's work. He prints only entries based on available manuscripts, beginning his transcription in 1837. Stewart's edition is marked by clarity and simplicity; his text is reliable; and his introduction is an excellent guide for students who wish to understand Hawthorne's basic ideas and techniques.

4. *Hawthorne's Dr. Grimshawe's Secret.* Edited with an Introduction and Notes by Edward H. Davidson. Cambridge: Harvard University Press, 1954. 305 pp.

Davidson reproduces the novel "with photographic, and pedantic, minuteness"; the first and second drafts; and Hawthorne's copious notes. His edition is the only accurate text of the novel that we have. It reveals the trouble Hawthorne had in writing this last novel and the degree to which he was attracted to European Gothicism.

5. *The English Notebooks by Nathaniel Hawthorne.* Edited by Randall Stewart. New York: Modern Language Association of America, 1941. 667 pp.

Stewart points out that "Mrs. Hawthorne's expurgations and revisions were even more extensive in the English notebooks than in the American. The discussion of these alterations in the first chapter of the Introduction to the present work serves the double purpose of demonstrating the necessity of the new text and of bringing into strong relief certain traditionally obscured characteristics of Hawthorne himself. The second chapter of the Introduction attempts to present Hawthorne's complex and conflicting reactions to England. . . . The notes on the text describe peculiarities of the manuscript, identify quotations, persons, and obscure references, and indicate the uses of the notebooks in Hawthorne's other writings."

Because Mrs. Hawthorne revised her husband's notebooks so extensively, Randall Stewart's edition presents Hawthorne's work before the reader for the first time as Hawthorne virtually wrote it. These journals demonstrate Hawthorne's patriotism whenever America was attacked, his love of England, and his keen insight into well-known Englishmen (the Tennysons, the Disraelis, and the Royal Family). The journals reveal a shrewd New England provincial who views England with deep perception.

Like Stewart's edition of *The American Notebooks* (3), this volume is meticulously edited and invaluable to the student of Hawthorne. Both volumes are largely responsible for the subsequent image of Hawthorne: "a more virile and a more human Hawthorne," in Stewart's words; "a more alert and (in a worldly sense) a more intelligent Hawthorne; a Hawthorne less dreamy, and less aloof, than his biographers have represented him as being."

Stewart's own complete portrait of Hawthorne is his biography (22).

6. *Hawthorne as Editor: Selections from His Writings in The American Magazine of Useful and Entertaining Knowledge.* Edited by Arlin Turner. Baton Rouge: Louisiana State University Press, 1941. 290 pp.

Turner includes a good deal of Hawthorne's hack work. He reprints "the most significant of Hawthorne's writings for *The American Magazine of Useful and Entertaining Knowledge* during his six months as editor. . . . In the choice of selections for this book, the plan has been to include those essays and briefer items which have some intrinsic merit or throw light on what Hawthorne was reading and thinking; also those reflecting his interest in the world about him or bearing some relation to his other writings."

Although this volume does not add to our knowledge of Hawthorne the artist, it does suggest Hawthorne's descriptive skill, his concern with history and the social scene. The Hawthorne who wrote the early sketches is clearly presented here. The volume is directed to the specialist in Hawthorne.

Bibliographies:

7. Blair, Walter. "Hawthorne," *Eight American Authors: A Review of Research and Criticism.* New York: Modern Language Association of America, 1956, pp. 100–152. Reprinted in paperback, with a supplement (1955–1962) by

J. Chesley Mathews. New York: The Norton Library, 1963, pp. 100–152, 428–434.

Blair's estimate of Hawthorne criticism and scholarship is sensible and perceptive, but because of its form—it is written as a critical essay—the bibliography is difficult to use.

This essay should be supplemented by the annual bibliography which appears in *Publications of the Modern Language Association of America* and the bibliographies in *American Literary Scholarship*, an annual, edited by James Woodress. Durham: Duke University Press, 1963–. See also Buford Jones' *A Check List of Hawthorne Criticism, 1951–1966*, with a Detailed Index. Hartford: Transcendental Books, 1967. 91 pp. Jones' bibliography is briefly annotated.

8. Leary, Lewis, ed. *Articles on American Literature, 1900–1950*. Durham: Duke University Press, 1954, pp. 128–134.

These entries are not annotated, but the volume is an indispensable checklist for all students of American literature.

9. Spiller, Robert E. et al. *The Literary History of the United States*. Bibliography, Volume III, prepared by T. H. Johnson. New York: Macmillan, 1948, pp. 544–553. Supplement, ed. Richard M. Ludwig. New York: Macmillan, 1959, pp. 61–76.

These bibliographies are good introductory surveys of the standard works.

IV. Biographies and Critical Biographies

10. Arvin, Newton. *Hawthorne.* Boston: Little Brown, 1929. 303 pp.

Newton Arvin was a major critic of American literature, and his studies of Melville, published in 1950, and Longfellow, published in 1962, are classics of their kind. Arvin did some of the pioneering work in modern Hawthorne studies, His edition. *The Heart of Hawthorne's Journals* (1929), was an interesting selection of Hawthorne's most notable observations, although it was naturally superseded by Randall Stewart's edition of *The American Notebooks* (3) and *The English Notebooks* (5). *Hawthorne*, written early in his career and early in the history of modern Hawthorne scholarship, follows the general direction of previous biographies by emphasizing Hawthorne's predisposition to solitude; but Arvin examines the work from a psychological point of view and brings a subtle critical intelligence to his analysis of Hawthorne's fiction. He concentrates on Hawthorne's concern with sin, particularly the sin of pride, and concludes that there "was a tragic element in his life as well as in his death." This tragedy was that "of every life in which the self is not brought into the right relation with what lies beyond it, the essential tragedy of pride . . . The best that Hawthorne wrote is the reflection of his tragic adventure."

Arvin relied exclusively on published source material and, as a consequence, the biographical elements in his book are not completely accurate; subsequent studies of Hawthorne, particularly the work of Randall Stewart, have established Hawthorne as a more balanced, sociable man than Arvin suggests.

11. Cantwell, Robert. *Nathaniel Hawthorne: The American Years.* New York: Rinehart & Company, Inc., 1948. 499 pp.

Cantwell emphasizes Hawthorne's relationship to his environment, especially before 1850. In his eagerness to view Hawthorne as a socially well-adjusted New Englander, Cantwell neglects the inner man who created the fiction. This book is perhaps the most extreme attempt to re-create Hawthorne's social world: all the people who came into contact with the writer are identified; the various experiences of Hawthorne are documented at length; the places in which Hawthorne lived are

(*11*)

fully described. Cantwell draws portraits of some of Hawthorne's classmates at Bowdoin—Longfellow, Cilley, and Pierce; he recreates the political scene as a backdrop to Hawthorne's life; and he narrates the movement of Hawthorne's acquaintances as well as that of Hawthorne himself. The portrait of Hawthorne that emerges is one of more social equability and solidity, a man among his contemporaries.

Cantwell's study, however, must be used with great care. Without offering any lengthy criticism of its ungraceful style, its heavy-handed accumulation of unselected detail, we should note that the author often assumes that an anecdote is fact, that certain possible occurrences in Hawthorne's life were actually events. Sometimes Cantwell's conclusions can be rather startling: he claims, for example, that Hawthorne might have been a secret agent for the Treasury Department in 1838, but the evidence he offers is by no means convincing.

12. Conway, Moncure D. *Life of Nathaniel Hawthorne.* New York: Scribner and Welford, 1890. 224 pp.

This is an illuminating critique, especially when one considers how early in the study of Hawthorne's fiction it was written. In general, it views Hawthorne as a man whose temperament forbade a close relationship with people. Conway, an Emersonian, makes some interesting observations on the relationship between Emerson and Hawthorne. Although Emerson recognized Hawthorne's power, he could not enjoy his writings. "There was not enough sunshine in them for so devout an optimist. Himself brought up among liberal people—his youth passed at the feet of Channing—he [Emerson] knew little of the Puritan nightmare that haunted every pillow in the Salem of Hawthorne's boyhood. The tales of secret sin, of veiled wrong, of inherited dooms, were to him too pathological." Conway makes perceptive comments on Hawthorne's ideas as they are dramatized in his work and presents a well-balanced account of Hawthorne's life and fiction.

13. Hawthorne, Julian. *Nathaniel Hawthorne and His Wife.* 2 volumes. Boston: J. R. Osgood, 1884. 371 pp.

As the title indicates, Hawthorne's son has written a family biography which is really a reminiscence. "Of Hawthorne as an author I have had little or nothing to say; literary criticism had no place in my present design. His writings are a subject by themselves; they are open to the world, and the world during the past thirty or forty years has been discussing them—not to much purpose as a rule. Originality remains a mystery for generations."

Julian Hawthorne includes factual information and correspondence that have been helpful to later biographers. See also his *Hawthorne and His Circle.* New York: Harper & Bros., 1903, for some anecdotes and sketches of Hawthorne's American and English friends.

14. Hoeltje, Hubert H. *Inward Sky: The Mind and Heart of Nathaniel Hawthorne.* Durham: Duke University Press, 1962. 579 pp.

This volume, which is the product of years of devotion to its subject, is similar to Wagenknecht's biography (25) in that it is written in protest to much contemporary criticism of Hawthorne. "Here, let me say at once, is no book of criticism in which the writer wishes to demonstrate how much more clever he is than his subject. Here is no surgeon's dissecting knife, nor even the anteroom of the psychoanalyst. My reader will be content, I trust, with a modest attempt to lift that veil of which Hawthorne wrote, and to look with the respect due such a privilege, into the recesses of a human mind and heart."

Hoeltje intends to deal with the "two worlds" of Hawthorne—"the world of fact and the world of dream or imagination. . . . To look through the whole range of Hawthorne's writing (his letters, his journals, his fiction) in order to discover the pattern of the thought there, and to correlate this pattern with the facts of the outward life—to disclose, as far as possible, the whole man—is my endeavor in this book." Hoeltje sees Hawthorne as a more affirmative, less morbid person than most recent critics and scholars. But Hawthorne always seems at a certain distance to him; he avoids a consideration of the complexity of Hawthorne's mind, and thus the author of *The Scarlet Letter*, "Young Goodman Brown," "My Kinsman, Major Molineux," and "Roger Malvin's Burial" appears far more sanguine than in fact he was. Although biographies like those of Stewart (22) and Cantwell (11) also insist upon the "normal" aspects of their subject. Hoeltje transfers those external characteristics to the "inward" contours of Hawthorne's mind and thus mitigates the tension one feels in Hawthorne's best work. Perhaps this is the reason that throughout this book, he emphasizes Hawthorne's affinity to Emerson and under-values his relationship to Melville. As Frederick C. Crews points out in his recent study, *The Sins of the Fathers* (29), the "belief that the 'man and writer were one'—healthy, pedestrian, moral—is the sign of a simplistic psychology that looks only at surfaces—an especially drastic weakness in approaching Hawthorne."

15. [Jackson] Edward Mather. *Nathaniel Hawthorne, A Modest Man.* New York: Thomas Y. Crowell Company, 1940. 356 pp.

Jackson's intentions are to treat "the biography of Hawthorne as that of a man rather than that of an author, as that of a man with a peculiar history, a history which constitutes a study in human behavior. As an Englishman I have been particu-larly interested in his years of residence in England and in his violent opinions concerning the English." Hawthorne, Jackson suggests, "had been brought up to distrust the English." He was "shocked by the institutions of England" and by the co-existence of a privileged class and Liverpool slum dwellers. Because of his approach, which seems unnecessarily exclusive, Jackson has little to say about Hawthorne's work or his literary attitudes. He does, however, comment rather fully upon the author's connections with the transcendentalists and with other writers—European as well as American—of his own time. He points out that though Hawthorne had great predilections toward isolation, he was nevertheless a socially aware and active person. One can feel the influence of Randall Stewart's editing of the *American Notebooks* upon the biographer. Much of his work, as a consequence, has been superseded by Stewart's briefer but more dependable biography.

16. James, Henry. *Hawthorne*. London: Macmillan, English Men of Letters, 1879, 177 pp. Reprinted by Great Seal Books, Ithaca, New York: Cornell University Press, 1956, and by Edmund Wilson, ed., *The Shock of Recognition, The Development of Literature in the United States Recorded by the Men Who Made It.* New York: Farrar Straus and Cudahy, 1943, pp. 427–565.

This volume is of particular importance not only for its specific commentaries on Hawthorne's work and upon the cultural conditions that influenced Hawthorne but also for its revelation of James's own attitudes toward nineteenth-century America. James sees Hawthorne as a victim of a provincial country, with little past and little social texture. At the outset, he warns the reader that "the moral is that the flower of art blooms only where the soil is deep, that it takes a great deal of history to produce a little literature, that it needs a complex social machinery to set a writer in motion. American civilization has hitherto had other things to do than to produce flowers, and before giving birth to writers it has wisely occupied itself with providing something for them to write about." In a famous passage James enumerates "the items of high civilization, as its exists in other countries, which are absent from the texture of American life, until it should become a wonder to know what was left. No State, in the European sense of the word, and indeed barely a specific national name. No sovereign, no court, no army, no diplomatic service, no country gentlemen, no palaces, no castles, nor manors, nor old country houses, nor parsonages, nor thatched cottages, nor ivied ruins, no cathedrals, nor abbeys, nor little Norman churches; no great universities nor public schools—no Oxford, nor Eton, nor Harrow; no literature, no novels, no museums, no pictures, no political society, no sporting class—no Epsom nor Ascot!"

In spite of the cultural limitations that confronted him, Hawthorne was, in James's view, surprisingly successful. He used his Puritan background with great sensitivity, and though James has no sympathy for allegory—"allegory is one of the lighter exercises of the imagination"—he recognizes the accomplished artistry of *The Scarlet Letter*. The novel that most appealed to James, however, was *The Blithedale Romance*; one can see quite clearly its influence on James's own novel, *The Bostonians*.

Hawthorne is of no real value from the biographical point of view—it depends almost exclusively upon Lathrop's study (17) for its information—and as a work of criticism it is limited by James's condescension, his need to justify his own expatriation, his unwillingness to appreciate artistic techniques different from those that he practiced himself. Furthermore, the book is marked by judgments that have to be understood in terms of James's own developing intelligence, his concern about his own career as a writer of realism. James was fully conscious, as he wrote to Julian Hawthorne, that Hawthorne "was the greatest imaginative writer we had," even though he felt "that his principle was wrong."

In spite of these various limitations, James had a sophistication uncommon for an American of his day, and he measured Hawthorne's provincialism and narrow tradition against his own liberalized life. As a cultural document, *Hawthorne* is invaluable; as a work of criticism—despite its obvious shortcomings—it contains perceptions still worth noting.

17. Lathrop, George Parsons. *A Study of Hawthorne*. Boston: James R. Osgood, 1876. 482 pp.

This volume was the first full-length study of Hawthorne, which, as Lathrop admits at the outset, "was not designed as a biography" but rather as "a portrait." Written by his son-in-law, *A Study of Hawthorne* denies Hawthorne's tendencies towards Gothicism, romance, and mysticism, and presents a man who is more realistic, who does not really doubt or question theological concepts, and who remains faithful to a fundamental idealism. At his best, Lathrop reminds us that Hawthorne was rooted to the social present and was not merely a mythmaker; at his worst, he eulogizes Hawthorne to absurd proportions, placing him "on a plane between Shakespeare and Goethe." This biography served as the source for Henry James's *Hawthorne* (16), published in 1879.

18. Loggins, Vernon. *The Hawthornes, The Story of Seven Generations of an American Family*. New York: Columbia University Press, 1951. 365 pp.

Loggins traces Hawthorne's family from the fifteenth century to the death of the author's daughter-in-law in 1949. Loggins' work is particularly useful in his development of family relationships during the seventeenth and eighteenth centuries, and in his treatment of the great significance that Hawthorne's family had upon his sensibility. Loggins purposely considers Hawthorne as only one member of his family—he does not emphasize his individual importance.

19. Martin, Terence. *Nathaniel Hawthorne*. New York: Twayne Publishers, Inc., 1965. 205 pp.

This general survey of Hawthorne's life and work is an excellent introduction. Martin is fully aware of the criticism and scholarship that preceded his own work, and his wide knowledge lends substance to his own sensible judgments of Hawthorne's fiction. In his attempt to "introduce the reader to the nature of Hawthorne's achievement," Martin has "sought, first (in chapter one), to establish the contours and issues of his career as a writer; second (in chapters two and three), to explore the method of imaginative creation by means of which his fiction as we know it came into being . . . Third (in chapter four), I have tried to define the pervasive thematic concerns of Hawthorne's tales; fourth (in chapter five), the individual literary accomplishment of six representative tales. The final four chapters are devoted to Hawthorne's major romances: assuming a knowledge of his method of imaginative creation, these chapters assess the achievement, the difficulties, and the inevitable limitations of Hawthorne's art at its expansive best."

Martin's short volume is a fine presentation of a difficult subject, and his analyses of "The Minister's Black Veil," "The Maypole of Merrymount," "Young Goodman Brown," "Rappaccini's Daughter," "Ethan Brand," and "My Kinsman, Major Molineux"—as well as critiques of the novels—are rewarding. He offers an extensive, briefly annotated bibliography of more than one hundred items. Of all the general treatments of Hawthorne, the student would do well to begin with this introductory work, for it will orient him in terms of Hawthorne's fiction and the vast amount of critical attention that has been paid to it.

20. Morris Lloyd. *The Rebellious Puritan: Portrait of Mr. Hawthorne.* New York: Harcourt, Brace and Company, 1927. 369 pp.

Morris has set out to answer the question that Emerson put to himself the day after Hawthorne's burial: "What had been Hawthorne's secret?" Emerson characterized Hawthorne as a man who "had deliberately chosen to observe life rather than participate in it . . . Hawthorne had been unsparing in his criticism of Puritan America, but he had been its child. His incessant preoccupation, as a writer, with sin and with evil; his perception of life as a moral experience with a tragic meaning; his emphasis upon the invincible loneliness of the human soul: these were Puritan traits." Although Morris emphasizes Hawthorne's tendency toward solitude, he is aware of the social ambience of New England. He brings a certain scholarly attitude to his material, for he knows that both Hawthorne's wife and son took liberties in preparing the notebooks and the correspondence. But generally this biography is a rather impressionistic, sentimental work in which Hawthorne emerges as the recluse that Emerson imagined him to be.

21. Page, H. A. [pseudonym for Alexander Japp]. *Memoir of Nathaniel Hawthorne.* London: Henry S. King & Co., 1872. 301 pp.

Japp's intentions are "to throw light on Hawthorne's life and character, and to render his writings yet more familiar to English readers." Japp does not throw too much light on Hawthorne's life, but he does comment intelligently upon Hawthorne's fiction, concluding that "this man, with his 'awful in-sight,' and his morbid melancholy, yet held firmly by the spiritual world, [refused] to surrender the inmost citadel. Here he takes his position with the most commonplace of men;

and in this lies one element of his greatness. His works, while they may sometimes raise question as to conventional judgments on this or that action, always encourage the deepest reverence for the spirit of man itself."

22. Stewart, Randall. *Nathaniel Hawthorne, A Biography*. New Haven: Yale University Press, 1948. 279 pp.

In the 1930's Stewart published a series of articles, all drawn from primary sources, which established Hawthorne's public personality: "Hawthorne and Politics," *The New England Quarterly*, V (April, 1932), 237–263; "Hawthorne's Contributions to *The Salem Advertiser*," *American Literature*, V (January, 1934), 327–328; "Hawthorne in England: The Patriotic Motive in the Notebooks," *The New England Quarterly*, VII (March, 1935), 3–13; "Hawthorne's Speeches at Civil Banquets," *American Literature*, VII (January, 1936), 415–423; "Recollections of Hawthorne by His Sister Elizabeth," *American Literature*, XVI (January, 1945), 316–331; and "Hawthorne and the Civil War," *Studies in Philology*, XXXIV (January, 1947), 91–106.

Stewart's conception of Hawthorne's character, first formulated in these essays and in his editions of *The American Notebooks* and *The English Notebooks*, was given permanent expression in *Nathaniel Hawthorne: A Biography*. This volume is the most reliable biography of Hawthorne and is authoritative in all its information. It attempts to correct the previously imbalanced appraisals of Hawthorne that had portrayed him as a retiring author who shunned involvement in the external world. But Stewart's book is not a definitive biography—not even a completely balanced biography—for in making the necessary modifications upon previous scholarship, the biographer exaggerates Hawthorne's "normal" aspects.

Nathaniel Hawthorne: A Biography lacks the fullness of a major work. One senses the absence of those colorful details that make an author and his times especially memorable; one regrets the cursory treatment of Hawthorne's methods, techniques, and accomplishments as a writer; one feels the biographer's desire to tone down the complexities of his author's sensibility.

Stewart underscores Hawthorne's attempt to understand the most profound philosophical and theological problems: it was this attempt that gives Hawthorne's character the quality of gloom. Stewart reminds us that Hawthorne's tendency toward skepticism was a result of the age in which he lived. In a perceptive, though brief, analysis of Hawthorne's work, he claims that if "the emphasis of *The Collected Works*, the sum and synthesis of Hawthorne's knowledge and understanding of the world, seems to fall on the somber side, the explanation may be found in his sense of the stark realities, which he was unwilling to falsify or gloss over, and his critical reaction against an age which seemed to him to brush the human difficulties aside with too easy an optimism, and to put an extravagant and unrealistic faith both in man's abilities and in the new scientific and social machinery. From the perspective of today we can see that Hawthorne touched his times at point after point with admonitory finger, giving to his age the more earnest purpose, the deeper moral, and the closer and homelier truth which it seemed to him to require."

Stewart's treatment of Hawthorne's inner life is regrettably limited. The author avoids any profound interpretation of Hawthorne's character, his artistic accomplishment, or the cultural milieu in which he functioned.

One should read the excellent review of this book by Stephen Whicher, in *American Literature*, XXI (November, 1949), 354–357. Whicher notes that "the deliberate and serious limitation of this biography is that it minimizes, and seems to wish to reject, all questions that cannot be answered by factual research." Whicher reminds us that it was Hawthorne's "pronounced difference that made him one we write lives of today"; he feels that Stewart has not explored "the 'secret space' within" Hawthorne, "preoccupied with its darker imaginings, from which proceeded his strongest writings." To get close "to the special configuration of Hawthorne's personality "must be the ultimate aim of any study of his life."

23. Turner, Arlin. *Nathaniel Hawthorne, An Introduction and Interpretation*. New York: Barnes & Noble, Inc., 1961. 149 pp.

As an important critic of American literature, Turner has written about Hawthorne from various points of view. In "Hawthorne's Literary Borrowings," *PMLA*, LI (March, 1936), 543–562, he offers an extensive account of Hawthorne's use of other authors; in "Hawthorne as Self-Critic," *South Atlantic Quarterly*, XXXVII (April, 1938), 132–138, he draws attention to the keen estimates that Hawthorne was capable of making in regard to his own work; in *Hawthorne as Editor* (6) he reprints some of the contributions that Hawthorne made to *The American Magazine of Useful and Entertaining Knowledge*; in "Hawthorne and Reform," *The New England Quarterly*, XV (September, 1942), 700–714, he emphasizes the social aspects of Hawthorne's character.

Nathaniel Hawthorne, An Introduction and Interpretation is naturally comprehensive. Turner wants to produce "a brief history" of Hawthorne's mind, "stepping off its development from his boyhood onward, all along keeping a view in one direction to the available records of what existed in actuality and in another direction to the products of his mind." Within the limitations of his study, Turner is successful. One will find conservative, reliable interpretations of *The Scarlet Letter* and some of the better known tales, which Turner concludes, "achieve, through the management of materials and language, a unity of theme, action, mood, and tone rarely equaled in our literature."

The chief limitation of this study is that Turner uses too many of the works to illustrate his main ideas rather than analyze Hawthorne's fiction for its own sake. Thus Turner's book is more an "interpretation" than "an introduction," and the student would be wise to turn to the criticism of Terence Martin (19), Randall Stewart (22), or Mark Van Doren (24) for his initial orientation to Hawthorne's work.

24. Van Doren, Mark. *Nathaniel Hawthorne*. New York: William Sloane Associates, American Men of Letters, 1949, 285 pp.

This volume, written in Van Doren's characteristically graceful prose, does not add measurably to our knowledge of Hawthorne; but it does offer a distinctive, sensible point of view and intelligent readings of Hawthorne's fiction. Van Doren keeps the "balance between narrative and comment" that is his intention, and he offers a reliable survey of the man and his works.

Van Doren views Hawthorne as an author of contradictions: someone who was a naturally taciturn and shy man yet "talked more than he thought he did"; who retired from the world for periods of his life but who, as his wife pointed out, "liked crowds"; who had a natural tendency toward sentimentality but who checked it by his countervailing tendency towards skepticism. Hawthorne "anticipated every critic he will ever have. For this person, intricate though he appears, was devoted to nothing so much as to the truth." Van Doren's judgments are sound, and only in his evaluation of *The Blithedale Romance* does he state his case in opposition to the general opinion of Hawthorne critics; this novel, he feels, "has no outstanding virtue of any kind."

Van Doren considers allegory Hawthorne's greatest and poorest device. He argues that "Young Goodman Brown," "Rappaccini's Daughter," "The Birthmark," *The Scarlet Letter*, *The House of the Seven Gables*, and *The Marble Faun* are Hawthorne's finest achievements, and largely because of the heightened meaning of allegory; but too often Hawthorne did not keep "his significations always solid, always clear. Hawthorne knew Dante, but he knew Spenser and Bunyan better, and they are masters of the second class."

Although Van Doren underrates the value of *The Blithedale Romance*, he writes perceptively of Hawthorne's other works.

25. Wagenknecht, Edward. *Nathaniel Hawthorne: Man and Writer*. New York: Oxford University Press, 1961. 233 pp.

Wagenknecht has written a psychograph, a critical biography in opposition to much of the criticism of the 1950's, which tends to view Hawthorne only in terms of his art and finds in this author what happens to be presently fashionable. Wagenknecht does not deny that an intelligent understanding of Hawthorne's art needs to concentrate on symbolism, ambiguity, and myth, but he feels that the exclusive concern with these matters distorts the nineteenth-century Hawthorne. He sets out to place Hawthorne in context with the writers of his time—Longfellow, Lowell, and other New Englanders—and concludes that "there was a dark side to him, but he faced the light. If there was a potential Ethan Brand in him or a young Goodman Brown, he watched him and guarded against him and strangled him."

Although Wagenknecht's volume is perhaps a sensible corrective to many of the ingenious and often tedious analyses of Hawthorne's work, it neglects those darker aspects of Hawthorne's character that in fact distinguish him from Long-fellow and Lowell. In trying to emphasize the outgoing and healthy aspects of Hawthorne's character, Wagenknecht distorts the essential truth of his subject as much as those critics who see Hawthorne as fundamentally a recluse.

26. Woodberry, George E. *Nathaniel Hawthorne.* Boston: Houghton Mifflin, American Men of Letters Series, 1902. 302 pp.

This biography was the first one written by a reputable scholar. Although Wood-berry tends to write in the impressionistic manner of his time, his portrait of Hawthorne is substantially accurate, and he succeeds in evoking the past and present of New England that helped to shape Hawthorne's imagination. His natural emphasis—and this is true of most Hawthorne criticism until the 1930's—is upon the solitude that pervaded Hawthorne's life. From 1825 to 1837, when Hawthorne remained in his "haunted chamber," he "lived in an intellectual solitude deepened by the fact that it was only an inner cell of an outward seclusion almost as complete, for the house had the habits of a hermitage." Later, when he lived with his wife and children in the Berkshires, life "had a still deeper seclusion, as of a place of retreat and inviolable privacy; there was an atmosphere of solitude about it, wrapping round a sense of life with nature, and only slight and distant contact with the world."

Woodberry distorts this tendency toward loneliness, but he does not neglect other aspects of Hawthorne's life: his practical necessities; his relationships with other writers; his affiliation with the Democratic party. There are intelligent, conservative estimates of Hawthorne's most significant work, for Woodberry was a critic of great common sense; but he uses the work fundamentally to illustrate the writer. His real interests are biographical; as such, his book has been superseded by later, more authoritative studies, but it is still an interesting record of a Victorian's sophisticated reaction to a writer for whom he had the highest regard.

V. Criticism

Books:

27. Bell, Millicent. *Hawthorne's View of the Artist.* New York: State University
of New York, 1962. 214 pp.

Mrs. Bell emphasizes the social background of Hawthorne, suggesting that Hawthorne never really presents the artist as someone integrated in his society. "He saw
the artist's isolation not as a becoming pose, but as the very real result of some new
dislocation between the one and the many, the artist and the audience. He felt that
the idealist philosophies which diverted his contemporaries widened this gap."
Mrs. Bell maintains that Hawthorne held two divergent views of art, one "ideal"
and the other generally derogatory, an ambivalence that he never really resolved
in his own mind.

In creating this picture of the alienated artist, Mrs. Bell notes that Hawthorne
himself "was probably closer to the gritty substance of American history than most
of the cause-joiners of Concord. He was close to politics and politicians throughout
his life, and he really knew better than most men what the odds were in his time
against candor, idealism, and beauty." Mrs. Bell has written an important and
enlightening study. One wonders, however, whether it is possible to speak authoritatively about Hawthorne's view of art. Mrs. Bell analyzes Hawthorne's classical
tendencies and applies Morse Peckham's concept of negative romanticism—"the
expression of the feelings and ideas of a man who has left the static mechanism of the
eighteenth-century world behind, but has not yet arrived at the transcendentalist
reintegration." This approach, as Richard Jacobson points out in *Hawthorne's
Conception of the Creative Process* (37), is "wrongheaded because it desperately
struggles to find a neat category into which Hawthorne can be placed." Nevertheless
Mrs. Bell's conclusion seems justified. "In Hawthorne, art was not its own justification; all his life he would resolutely call upon himself to put writing aside for
better-salaried work—chiefly because he had to, but also (as has not generally been
realized) because he suspected the morality of self-absorbed artistic activity."

(*21*)

28. Bridge, Horatio. *Personal Recollections of Nathaniel Hawthorne.* New York: Harper & Brothers, 1893. 200 pp.

Bridge was a college classmate of Hawthorne's and a friend throughout their later life. His volume contains some important correspondence.

29. Crews, Frederic. *The Sins of the Fathers: Hawthorne's Psychological Themes.* New York: Oxford University Press, 1966. 279 pp.

Crews notes that the two recent manifestations of Hawthorne scholarship are the emphasis on Hawthorne's normalcy and the insistence "upon his *symbolism* and his *didactism.*" He feels that "these two developments are not only unfortunate and misleading but also closely related; they are expressions of the same cultural phenomenon. For in differing ways both the biographers and the critics have been anxious to depart from the emotional texture of Hawthorne's imagination. The religious-didactic Hawthorne of the symbolic critics is already implicit in the biographies, which—having disposed of psychological speculation by declaring it unscientific—deftly skip from a sober and debunking rehearsal of evidence to awe at Hawthorne's inspirational value." Furthermore, Crews believes that the "normalization springs . . . from a failure of intuition"; and he wishes to make a distinction between the public Hawthorne, who appeared quite healthy and outgoing, and the private Hawthorne, who had a much greater complexity. That complexity rests upon the contradictory qualities of the author, his tendency toward doubt, his fundamental ambivalence. "In short, Hawthorne was emotionally engaged in his fiction, and the emotions he displays are those of a self-divided, self-tormented man."

In his own critical study, Crews intends to "investigate the nature of Hawthorne's antiquarianism; ask whether his historical themes are really separable from his psychological ones; study the nature of family relationships, both literal and symbolic, in certain early plots; and begin to prove that a definable, indeed classic, conflict of wishes lies at the heart of Hawthorne's ambivalence and provides the inmost configuration of his plots."

Crews's work is valuable in its insistence upon Hawthorne's psychological ambiguity; and it is an important corrective to many recent studies—Hoeltje's *Inward Sky* (14) and Edward Wagenknecht's *Nathaniel Hawthorne: Man and Writer* (25) for example—that tend not to explore the inner complexities of Hawthorne's imagination. By considering the way in which Hawthorne's characters repress the truth, Crews is able to establish the central tension that makes Hawthorne's work fascinating; by emphasizing psychological rather than moral themes, he illuminates a significant aspect of Hawthorne's sensibility.

30. Davidson, Edward H. *Hawthorne's Last Phase.* New Haven: Yale University Press, 1949. 172 pp.

This study is the definitive work on Hawthorne's last period. Davidson points out the many difficulties Hawthorne confronted in attempting to complete his last romances. He indicates that Hawthorne wrote "twenty-two experimental studies: a draft of *The Ancestral Footstep*, six for *Doctor Grimshawe's Secret*, eight for *Septimius Felton*, and eight for *The Dolliver Romance*. In so far as any evidence remains, Hawthorne never before employed this technique in planning his novels of the major phase."

Davidson's intentions are clearly defined at the outset: "The first chapter traces Hawthorne's life and writings in the last phase. . . . In the second chapter I show how Hawthorne while residing in England as United States Consul to Liverpool, stored his notebooks and imagination for the time when he could return home to Concord. The latter half of this chapter investigates *The Ancestral Footstep*, in itself hardly more than a preliminary study for *Doctor Grimshawe's Secret*, which Hawthorne undertook in 1860. Each succeeding chapter treats a single romance—*Doctor Grimshawe's Secret*, *Septimius Felton*, and *The Dolliver Romance*—and each one demands a different approach and reveals different facets of Hawthorne's craftsmanship. The last chapter attempts to weave together all of these diverse threads into some general conclusions on Hawthorne's art-method."

Davidson's research is indispensable, and his portrait of Hawthorne struggling to complete a last romance is compelling. He never adequately explains, however, why Hawthorne was unable to complete a satisfactory novel. He suggests that "the tight world of New England society, together with its moral themes, was gone and he [Hawthorne] discovered that his world was in ruins"; he suspects that Hawthorne had "lost interest in the question of right and wrong." But these theories are never completely convincing as Davidson presents them.

31. Fairbanks, Henry G. *The Lasting Loneliness of Nathaniel Hawthorne, A Study of the Sources of Alienation in Modern Man.* Albany, N.Y.: Maji Books, Inc., 1960. 244 pp.

Fairbanks has written extensively on Hawthorne. In "Hawthorne Amid the Alien Corn," *College English*, XVII (February, 1956), 263–268, he concentrates upon the alienation of Hawthorne from his place in the community and traces the theme in "The Seven Vagabonds, Passages from a Relinquished Work," "The Artist of the Beautiful," and "Drowne's Wooden Image." "The life of the artist in America had severed" Hawthorne "from society and from reality." In "Sin, Free Will, and 'Pessimism' in Hawthorne," *PMLA*, LXXI (December, 1956), 975–989, Fairbanks suggests that the very fact that sin exists implies the existence of free will as well. "It was frustrating, indeed, for Hawthorne to sustain a traditional religious outlook in an increasingly secular society. That he partially succeeded, however, is attested by his unremitting concern with the reality of sin and human responsibility." In "Hawthorne and Confession," *Catholic Historical Review*, XLVII (April, 1957), 38–45, Fairbanks notes Hawthorne's interest in the Catholic confession.

Fairbanks indicates his general approach to Hawthorne in the final statement of *The Lasting Loneliness of Nathaniel Hawthorne*. He is disturbed that Hawthorne has been judged only in terms of aesthetic canons by "the ivory tower of English departments"; and he seeks to explore what he considers Hawthorne's pervasive theme—separation. "Hawthorne speaks the *lingua franca* of separation and *suffering*" which Fairbanks takes to be "the common malaise of his country men." In this sense, Hawthorne has a great appeal to the common reader. He wrote about "the four dislocations of the times: man separated from God, from Nature, from man, and from self."

Some of Fairbanks' interpretations of individual works are provocative, but in general his style is overwrought and rhetorical, and his concentration on one theme tends to be too exclusive.

32. Fick, Leonard. *The Light Beyond: A Study of Hawthorne's Theology.* Westminister, Md.: The Newman Press, 1955. 184 pp.

Fick attempts a schematization of Hawthorne's treatment of guilt and penance in terms of such constants as Augustianism, Thomism, and Arminianism. "Nathaniel Hawthorne's theological thinking is Arminian rather than Calvinistic," Fick asserts. "In contrast to the recognized teachers of Puritanism he [Hawthorne] insisted upon each individual's role in the important business of working out his happiness... The keystone, then, of Hawthorne's theology is an unshakable belief in an inscrutable Providence; and it is from the vantage point of this belief that he reconciles man to the problem of evil." According to Fick, Hawthorne struggles to "reconcile the incongruity of Divine Omnipotence and outraged, suffering humanity."

Fick's book is worth examining, but the critic forces his thesis excessively and tends to be fond of categorizing Hawthorne's theological beliefs too rigidly. The study is most valuable in its refutation of the oft-repeated theory that Hawthorne was attracted to skepticism or Roman Catholicism. In Fick's view, Hawthorne "was not a pagan. He was not a Catholic. He was a Protestant, though affiliated with no specific Protestant sect. . . . Hawthorne very early in his life evolved a theology that was personal to him, yet at the same time fundamentally Christian and, more often than not, decidedly orthodox."

33. Fogle, Richard Harter. *Hawthorne's Fiction: the Light and the Dark.* Norman: University of Oklahoma, 1952. 219 pp.

This study is written in the technique of the new criticism. Fogle is not concerned with history or biography; he looks only at the literature, examining carefully six tales—"Young Goodman Brown," "The Minister's Black Veil," "Ethan Brand," "The Maypole of Merry Mount," "The Artist of the Beautiful," and "Rappaccini's Daughter"—and the four major novels. The light in Hawthorne is his clarity of design, his classic balance, and his lucid language. The dark refers to Hawthorne's "tragic complexity," which involves Hawthorne's ambiguous use of allegory and symbolism, his tendency to cast doubt upon interpretations that at first seem clear, and the complexity of his characterization. Fogle maintains that Hawthorne's philosophy is a "broadly Christian scheme which contains heaven, earth, and hell— man forgets his limits, thinks of himself as all good or all bad and then falls into spiritual isolation and pride." Although Hawthorne's symbols are used in an allegoric way, they tend toward the specific and are "broadly traditional, drawn from the main stream of Western thought." Allegory and symbol cannot really be dissociated in Hawthorne's work—they are "organically united."

Fogle's general formulations are convincingly demonstrated and apply to some of Hawthorne's other successful tales as well. However, Fogle tends to categorize Hawthorne's work too rigidly, to belabor his thesis, and at times to make artificial distinctions between form and content.

See Leon Howard, "Hawthorne's Fiction," *Nineteenth-Century Fiction*, VII (March, 1953), 237–250, for a dissenting point of view. Howard is "disturbed, as a teacher of literature, at the current tendency to consider literary documents solely as self-sufficient works of art, with or without references to their author's possible intentions. This tendency is unfortunate, I believe, for at least two reasons. The first is that it leads to the leveling of the great individual literary works of the past and the reduction of them to the intellectual capacities and interests of a particular type of critic. The second is that the difficulty of abstracting a writer's art from his larger self is so great that this partial approach to his work subtly attributes to the writer a precocity which he does not generally possess . . ."

34. Folsom, James K. *Man's Accidents and God's Purposes: Multiplicity in Hawthorne's Fiction*. New Haven: College and University Press, 1963. 178 pp.

Folsom suggests that Hawthorne finds Oneness inscrutable and thus reverts to a concept of "multiplicity" in the tales and romances. "Hawthorne himself once used a phrase for his philosophical beliefs, 'Man's accidents are God's purposes,' a phrase more significant than might at first appear. The conventional Platonist, the philosopher in the grand tradition of Platonic thought, would have put it just the other way around: 'God's purposes are Man's accidents.' For him the accent would be on God and purpose; for Hawthorne it is on Man and accident." To Hawthorne, reality was unknowable, and he sought to understand it far less than an author like Melville. He concentrated, instead, on the world of multiplicity which he could measure with his finite intelligence."

Folsom's study, which is marred only by its tendency toward over-statement, is especially rewarding in its emphasis on Hawthorne the writer rather than Hawthorne the philosophical thinker. In chapters devoted to romance, allegory, plot, and comedy, Folsom discusses the aesthetic purposes that inform Hawthorne's ambiguity and his intricate use of symbolism. He concludes that Hawthorne's "emphasis is on the Many, not on the One" and that only rarely did he "attempt to synthesize them into a unity."

35. Gorman, Herbert. *Hawthorne, A Study in Solitude*. New York: George H. Doran Company, 1927. 179 pp. Reprinted, New York: Biblo Tannen, 1966. 179 pp.

This volume is the fullest treatment of Hawthorne's tendency toward isolation. Gorman views Hawthorne as "a man whose mood was essentially dark, who was visited by small daemons, who was haunted by spectres, who saw in Time the horrors of eternity and yet who, in himself, was a dull, shy, quiet relic of iron-minded Puritan forebears. . . . He was a painfully shy young man almost antagonistic because of an acute realization of his accursed bashfulness. . . . Nathaniel Hawthorne walked arm in arm with solitude."

Gorman has intelligent readings of the novels, but they are always set against the background of Hawthorne's retiring character. This conception is reiterated so often that Gorman inevitably distorts the meaning of Hawthorne's work. He also writes impressionistically about Hawthorne's life, mixing romantic impressions with biological facts until it is difficult to distinguish between them.

36. Hall, Lawrence Sargent. *Hawthorne, Critic of Society*. New Haven: Yale University Press, 1944. 200 pp.

Hall intends "to deal only with those aspects of Hawthorne's life and work which bear directly on his social thought." Encouraged by the work of Stewart and Matthiessen, Hall portrays Hawthorne as a writer who was intimately conscious of the society in which he lived. "Hawthorne belonged to an excitable, irrepressible, altruistic generation which took for granted the validity and importance of democracy as a social faith, and the mission of the United States as the champion of that faith. And he went in for social thinking more thoroughly than many of his contemporaries. He joined Brook Farm for one thing, while Emerson preferred to stay a house-holder in Concord and Thoreau retired to the woods. Hawthorne's social consciousness has been less obvious to critics than that of his fellow writers because it was less blatant. And a surreptitious habit of thought and expression has caused him to be improperly set forth for years as a romantic in art, and in life a reticent spook."

This study is a valuable corrective to those works which concentrate upon Hawthorne's mysticism, solitary habits, and romantic qualities. Hall demonstrates quite convincingly Hawthorne's Jacksonian tendencies and his attachment to the Young American group of the time. "Hawthorne," he concludes, "conscientiously faced the positive and negative elements in the American equation. In the Puritans he found bleak evidence of the contrast between man's forward-looking and his back-sliding. In the society of his own day, and in himself as a member of that society, he observed the same discrepancy in newer guises between what life is and what man would have it."

37. Jacobson, Richard J. *Hawthorne's Conception of the Creative Process.* Cambridge: Harvard University Press, 1965. 51 pp.

Jacobson's interesting essay was a LeBaron Russell Briggs Prize Honors Essay in English at Harvard University in 1965. As the title indicates, Jacobson "aims at an examination of the processes of mind that Hawthorne viewed as underlying creativity." He finds that Hawthorne's conception of the creative process was a "fusion of classic and romantic attitudes," and he makes connections between Hawthorne's theory of art and that of Coleridge in the *Biographia Literaria.* After offering brief but suggestive analyses of those stories concerned with the artist— "Drowne's Wooden Image," "The Artist of the Beautiful"—as well as the novels, he concludes: "Hawthorne's allegory of the heart as cavern comes closest to expressing his sense of the creative character. . . . Life is initially seen only in terms of its surface veneer of happiness. A more mature and deeper vision reveals misery and sin. But in the calm center, where good and evil are blended in a unified impression of life, the artist reaches his most penetrating understanding."

38. Lundblad, Jane. *Nathaniel Hawthorne and the European Literary Tradition* (Essays and Studies on American Language and Literature, No. 6). Upsala and Cambridge: Harvard University Press, 1947. 196 pp.

In this work, which is an expansion of her earlier study, *Nathaniel Hawthorne and the Tradition of Gothic Romance* (Essays and Studies in American Language and Literature, No. 4; Upsala, 1946), Jane Lundblad offers a methodical examination of Hawthorne's use of Gothic devices. Although she relates Hawthorne to the "European Literary Tradition," the author is mainly interested in the Gothicism of Hawthorne's fiction. The first three chapters of the book are devoted to "The Cultural and Literary New England Background Before 1820" and to Hawthorne's life and reading. The substance of the study and its most valuable part are Jane Lundblad's close attention to fifteen tales and four romances in terms of the Gothic elements Hawthorne uses. The author concludes that Gothic devices are most often employed in the early and the late work, and are least present in the fiction of Hawthorne's middle period. She also notes that Hawthorne's pictures of exotic, passionate women is influenced by Mme de Stael; his ideas on art, architecture, and the image of the cold-blooded villain derive from Balzac.

This study is valuable in its emphasis on an important aspect of Hawthorne's work; but it reads too often like a catalogue, a mere listing of the many Gothic devices which Hawthorne adapted for his own use.

39. Male, Roy R. *Hawthorne's Tragic Vision.* Austin: University of Texas Press, 1957. 187 pp.

Male is an important Hawthorne critic. Before the publication of his book, he wrote a number of articles, such as "Hawthorne and the Concept of Sympathy," *PMLA,*

LXVIII (March, 1953), 138–149, in which he distinguishes between the ideas concerning the concept of sympathy that Hawthorne accepted and rejected from the German and English Romanticists; "'From the Innermost Germ': The Organic Principle in Hawthorne's Fiction," *Journal of English Literary History*, XX (September, 1953), 218–236, in which he underscores the significance of this principle— "justly held to be the very root of Romanticism in America"—in Hawthorne's work; and "The Dual Aspects of Evil in 'Rappaccini's Daughter,'" *PMLA*, LXIX (March, 1954), 99–109, in which he emphasizes Hawthorne's treatment of the dual aspects of human nature.

In *Hawthorne's Tragic Vision* Male notes that Hawthorne's "accomplished work is a rare combination of poetry and fiction: poetry in that each image functions as part of a larger design; fiction in that the narrative is woven in a 'humble texture' that preserves some degree of verisimilitude. . . . Hawthorne possessed what one of his friends called 'the awful power of insight,' and his fiction remains valuable chiefly because of its penetration into the essential truths of the human heart. His one fruitful subject was the problem of moral growth." The author relates the idea of tragedy to the Miltonic concept of the Fall and the idea of original sin to the love of man and woman.

Male offers perceptive readings of "The Gentle Boy" and "My Kinsman, Major Molineux" as examples of "the quest for a home, the search for a parent." He also treats "Rappaccini's Daughter" extensively as a "complex story that directly anticipates *The Scarlet Letter*"; "Young Goodman Brown" as a tale in which "Faith's ambiguity is the ambiguity of womanhood," and where "the dark night in the forest is essentially a sexual experience, though it is also much more"; and finally "Ethan Brand" as a tale in which "Brand becomes transfixed by the vision of evil and ultimately embraces its destructive power." He then adds extensive and illuminating analyses of the four major novels. "In *The Scarlet Letter*," Male suggests, "the quest for truth is an effort to know Pearl." Hester offers solace to Dimmesdale through Pearl—the child is the ceaseless reminder that "truth cannot be perceived outside its temporal context." Both Hester and Dimmesdale ascend toward the truth that life must be grasped concretely before it can be lived fruitfully; and in their ascension they achieve spiritual union. In *The House of the Seven Gables* the union between woman and man is symbolized in the house and the inhabitants of the street; the invasion of the house by Phoebe and Holgrave dramatizes the interpenetration of the present and the past. "*The Blithedale Romance* is Hawthorne's dark comedy, his most passionate book . . . because the characters attain no tragic understanding"; it is, in Male's perceptive phrase, a "pastoral wasteland." In *The Marble Faun* the conflict is centered on a man who possesses "timeless freedom" and a woman "who is already fallen"; this novel confirms that Hawthorne's "tragic vision in the romance eventually leads back through *Paradise Lost* to Ecclesiastes and Genesis."

Hawthorne's Tragic Vision is a rewarding interpretation of Hawthorne's major work, defining as it does the pattern of tragedy that gives the fiction its lasting significance.

40. Pearce, Roy Harvey, Editor. *Hawthorne Centenary Essays*. Columbus: Ohio State University Press, 1964. 480 pp.

This collection of essays is intended "to commemorate the centenary of Hawthorne's death with a volume of studies which would show him and his work as they presently confront us"; as such, it serves as a dependable reflection of current critical attitudes toward Hawthorne.

There are analyses of the individual works: Terence Martin examines "The Method of Hawthorne's Tales"; Charles Feidelson, Jr. interprets *The Scarlet Letter*; Marcus Cuncliffe analyses *The House of the Seven Gables*; Robert C. Elliot finds *The Blithedale Romance* limited because Hawthorne chose "romance as the form to incorporate his material." There are also treatments of Hawthorne's "art and substance" by critics who have written extensively on Hawthorne: Hyatt Waggoner, Daniel Hoffman, Roy Harvey Pearce, and R. W. B. Lewis. In general these critics do not depart from the perceptions of their earlier work—their wish is to be comprehensive rather than distinctively original.

The third section, entitled "Discovery and Rediscovery," summarizes the attitudes and work of previous critics and scholars: Edwin H. Cady examines Hawthorne scholarship from 1864–1900; Seymour L. Gross and Randall Stewart take account of "The Hawthorne Revival"; Roger Asselineau measures the impact of "Hawthorne Abroad"; and Fredson Bowers studies the present state of "Hawthorne's Text." In an Afterword, Lionel Trilling writes about "Our Hawthorne," and estimates Hawthorne's significance to modern readers. Trilling suggests that the new criticism, with its intense examination of Hawthorne texts, has in many ways limited our ability to see Hawthorne as he presented himself in the nineteenth century; and when we read him as the tragic author, whose tales of isolation and morbidity, of guilt and sin, seem so relevant today, we find him lacking the ultimate power of Blake or Kafka, an author who "has no great tyrant-dream in which we can take refuge."

This volume, as enlightened as it is, suggests the difficulty that the modern critic faces in trying to establish an original relationship to Hawthorne. Philip Young, in a humorous and perceptive survey of the book which appeared in *Kenyon Review*, XXVII (Spring, 1965), pp. 215–234, asks for a moratorium on Hawthorne scholarship: "I am convinced we really understand him [Hawthorne] now, and I rationalize the attraction by telling myself he is profoundly an American writer, relevant to us, and the Great Society and all, as seldom if ever before, and finally to be understood, perhaps, only by modern Americans. But in truth I have been accidently savoring all the while a remark about our Hawthorne that I will at last put down: 'There is something unhealthy about his writings which one does not notice at first, but which in the long run will work upon you like a very weak and very slow poison.'

The observation is Emile Montegut's; the translation from the French is M. Asselineau's; the date, 1852."

41. Reid, Alred S. *The Yellow Ruff and The Scarlet Letter*, A Source of Hawthorne's Novel. Gainesville: University of Florida Press, 1955. 150 pp.

Reid maintains that the source of the novel is the murder of Sir Thomas Overbury in 1613, and he documents his theory by drawing comparisons between the account of the murder and incidents, characters, and the style of *The Scarlet Letter*. "The numerous parallels between the novel and accounts of the murder indicate not a mere chance borrowing of a few details, but a major creative operation that assimilated a group of materials into a new and vastly superior poetic arrangement."

Some of the parallels Reid establishes are Chillingworth's friendship with a Dr. Forman; Mistress Hibbens' acquaintance with Anne Turner, who was hanged for Sir Thomas Overbury's murder; the conscience-ridden Jervaise Helwyse and Dimmesdale—Helwyse had plotted the poisoning of Overbury and was tortured by guilt.

Reid's evidence is convincing so long as one does not attend to other possible influences on the novel.

See also Charles Ryskamp's essay, "The New England Sources of *The Scarlet Letter*," *American Literature*, XXXI (November, 1959), 257–272. Ryskamp concentrates upon what he considers the chief American source of *The Scarlet Letter*—Dr. Caleb H. Snow's *History of Boston*. This book gives information on the houses of the early settlers and the landmarks in the city. The time of *The Scarlet Letter* is 1650. Snow describes Boston in great detail. Hawthorne draws upon Snow for his description of Governor Bellingham's house; the characters of his novel—Hester, Pearl, Chillingworth, and Dimmesdale—were actual historical figures. Hawthorne was a thorough reader of Puritan history, and he was particularly interested "in the unusual, obscure fact."

42. Schubert, Leland. *Hawthorne, the Artist: Fine-Art Devices in Fiction*. Chapel Hill: The University of North Carolina Press, 1944. 181 pp.

Schubert boldly limits himself by treating Hawthorne's work only in terms of its form and not in terms of its content. "While these two elements of a work of art are rarely separated—and usually should not be separated—they are nevertheless separable. For the sake of analysis, and consequently better understanding, the separation is desirable . . . We shall analyze Hawthorne's writing and criticize it as we would the work of any other artist, whether a painter, a sculptor, or even a musician."

Schubert confesses that his "study is *art* criticism, perhaps, rather than literary criticism." In his treatment of *The Scarlet Letter*, for example, he finds the novel "falling into a structural pattern of seven parts (exclusive of the frame), as many of Hawthorne's stories tend to do"; and he supplies a chart to clarify his point. He emphasizes the rhythm and repetition of certain words, the use of color—particularly of red and black—, and the sound-patterns of the book. By making analogues between art, music, and literature, by exaggerating the significance of form, Schubert reminds us of Hawthorne's conscious artistry. Schubert concludes his volume by asserting that judged by formal criteria "the novels can be ranked *The Scarlet Letter, The House of the Seven Gables, The Blithedale Romance,* and lastly *The Marble Faun*—the order in which the books were published. In other words, Hawthorne's skill in handling form in art seems to have diminished."

Schubert's work is valuable in its analysis of line, rhythm, and color in Hawthorne's art. But surely we do not read Hawthorne for only formal reasons, nor can the technical considerations of other art forms be brought successfully to bear on expression as discursive as literature. When we remember Hawthorne's deep concern with sin, guilt, and the effects of isolation, we realize that form must always be of ancillary interest in the examination of his work; and even within the category of form itself, Schubert stresses fine-art devices to the exclusion of point of view and plot.

43. Stein, William Bysshe. *Hawthorne's Faust, A Study of the Devil Archetype.* Gainesville: University of Florida Press, 1953, 172 pp.

This volume "seeks to reveal the organic nature of Hawthorne's accomplishment by applying the Faustian contract . . . He reverts to the covenant which fomented strife in the world: Eve's costly bargain with the serpent in the Garden of Eden. This ritual of the selling of the soul to the devil is thus an inevitable addition to Hawthorne's myth." The story of Faust "provides Hawthorne with the medium of inquiring into the riddle of good and evil." Hawthorne's chief sources for the myth are the versions by Marlowe; the Mathers; Gothic writers like Beckford, Lewis, Godwin, and Maturin; and, most significantly, Goethe. Stein deals with the "Five Fausts"—Aylmer (of "The Birthmark"), Rappaccini, Warland (of "The Artist of the Beautiful"), Drowne, and Ethan Brand.

The application of Stein's thesis to several works—notably *The Scarlet Letter,* "Young Goodman Brown," and "Rappaccini's Daughter"—is successful, but when forced upon the total body of Hawthorne's work, it seems excessively rigid.

44. Taylor, J. Golden. *Hawthorne's Ambivalence Toward Puritanism.* Logan, Utah: Utah State University Press, 1965. 69 pp.

This work, based upon Taylor's Ph.D. dissertation, shows "how as an artist Hawthorne drew freely upon whatever facets of Puritan life and thought that suited his artistic needs, and how he evoked through his creative conversions of seventeenth-century New England historical sources unusually effective symbols for his nineteenth-century values." Taylor offers interesting examinations of "two stories that best reflect Hawthorne's ambivalence toward Puritanism: 'The Maypole of Merry Mount' and 'The Gentle Boy.'" These stories, he concludes, "look to the future and not to the past. They transcend their setting and speak to mankind of his most besetting weakness, his inability to guide his life by an harmonious balance between the head and the heart."

45. Tharpe, Joe. *Nathaniel Hawthorne: Identity and Knowledge.* Carbondale: Southern Illinois Press, 1967. 180 pp.

Tharpe berates American critics for being "insular if not chauvinistic" and claims that "Nathaniel Hawthorne's work needs reinterpretation, and it needs to be seen in the context of Western literature." With this enlarged perspective, Tharpe connects Hawthorne's work with that of Homer; Sophocles; Goethe and other Germans; LeSage and other French authors. He suggests that Hawthorne may have influenced Dostoevsky and Robert Musil, and he views Hawthorne as an author who prefigured the stream of conscious technique in the novel.

Tharpe's comparisons and references are many, but few are convincing because they are so circumstantial and conjectural. The influence of one author upon another is a matter of fruitless speculation if it does not illuminate the literature one reads; and Tharpe's work is more confusing than clarifying. The student should read sections of F. O. Mattheissen's *American Renaissance* (98), in which the critic draws analogues between Hawthorne and Milton, James, and Eliot, to see how the significance of literary influence can be provocatively explored.

46. Von Abele, Rudolph. *The Death of the Artist: A Study of Hawthorne's Disintegration* (Internation Scholars Forum, Volume II). The Hague: Martinus Nijhoff, 1955. 111 pp.

Von Abele considers Hawthorne's attitude towards the artist in a democratic society and explores his views of art and sex. Hawthorne, Von Abele believes, felt that the artist was alien to democracy and thus his work "appeals to an elite." Von Abele attempts to demonstrate the reasons for Hawthorne's disintegration as an artist, claiming that "the excellencies and faults of" Hawthorne's art "can be directly attributed to the state . . . of the inner life"; that inner life is essentially morbid. Hawthorne never admitted his trouble and only in *The Scarlet Letter* did he find the proper symbol—in the character of Dimmesdale—for his own tensions. Von Abele makes too close a connection between the work of art and the mind that created it; he makes no distinction between the man and the work of art he has created. His book, as a consequence, is provocative but not entirely reliable.

47. Waggoner, Hyatt. *Hawthorne, a Critical Study.* Cambridge: Harvard University Press, 1955. 268 pp.

Waggoner finds four fundamental aspects to Hawthorne's character: the light-hearted author of "The Snow Image," "Little Daffydowndilly"; the man who, like Miles Coverdale of *The Blithedale Romance*, observed others and passed negative judgments; the man who saw into the complexity of human nature; and, lastly, the older writer who, after 1850, found it difficult to write anything worthwhile and who ultimately found excuses for not writing at all. Waggoner views Hawthorne as a man of many paradoxes. Because there are so many conflicting qualities within Hawthorne's character, Waggoner believes that even reliable and definitive biographies do not ultimately reveal the works; indeed the impression one is likely to get "is that there is little connection between the man and his works." Waggoner therefore chooses to devote himself exclusively to the art itself, and he presents very close readings, especially of imagery: in *The Scarlet Letter*, light and color, flowers, names, and mirror imagery predominate; in *The House of the Seven Gables*, curves and circles are important; in *The Blithedale Romance*, fire and mask imagery control the meaning of the book; in *The Marble Faun*, nature, light and dark, towers, and heart imagery are pervasive.

Waggoner offers close and perceptive readings of "My Kinsman, Major Molineux," "The Canterbury Pilgrims," "Alice Doane's Appeal." "Earth's Holocaust," "Roger Malvin's Burial," and "Rappaccini's Daughter," finding that they exist "in a realm somewhere between symbolism and allegory, as those terms are used today." Waggoner also analyses the major novels and strikes a proper balance between formal considerations and thematic significance.

Hawthorne, Waggoner maintains, "learned his craft as he learned what to do with the past—the Gothic tale changed into the moral tale (though the Gothic elements are still present)." Hawthorne thrived "on the past—it was part of him. The present was not usable as art. The present became 'sketches' not tales—and if it appeared in the tales, Hawthorne's art suffered." Waggoner concludes his book by suggesting that Hawthorne's "work looks back to epic and romance and forward to such writers as James, Conrad, Kafka, Faulkner." Like these authors, he achieved some of his finest effects by portraying "the truth of the human heart" through indirection. When considered in relationship to writers like Emerson and Thoreau, Hawthorne seems more modern—and basically because of his keen sense of the past.

Hawthorne, a Critical Study is a fine appraisal of Hawthorne's fiction, one of the best works of its kind in modern Hawthorne criticism. Its chief limitation lies in Waggoner's complete unwillingness to take into effect matters of biography and social background.

Waggoner has also published an excellent introduction to Hawthorne's fiction: *Nathaniel Hawthorne*. Minneapolis: University of Minnesota Press, 1962 (University of Minnesota Pamphlets on American Writers, No. 23).

General Critical Essays:

48. Anderson, D. K., Jr. "Hawthorne's Crowds," *Nineteenth-Century Fiction*, VII (June, 1952), 39–50.

Anderson calls attention to Hawthorne's "instinctive interest in crowds" and points out that he "also makes them an important vehicle of his art." Generally, in Hawthorne's groups, individual members lose their identity; in *The Scarlet Letter*, however, he finds the golden mean and "individualizes a few of its voices." The crowds in Hawthorne's work have many functions: they furnish light ("The Gray Champion"), motion (*Dr. Grimshawe's Secret*), composition (*The Scarlet Letter*), and sound (*The Marble Faun*). Anderson goes on to point out the many psychological functions of crowds: their intensification of loneliness, bewilderment, indignation, and sadness.

49. Astrov, Vladmir. "Hawthorne and Dostoevski as Explorers of the Human Conscience," *The New England Quarterly*, XV (June, 1942), 296–319.

Astrov suggests that Dostoevski might have been aware of Hawthorne's writings, and he indicates the similarities of the two authors. Both men created psychological novels; both explored the human conscience; both were cut off from their "initial religious moorings"; both were filled with doubt; both were attracted to German romantic idealism and to French socialist conceptions; both pleaded "for the rights of the spiritual, and stressed the power of the irrational and the abysmal in soul and life." Astrov goes on to trace the similar treatment of guilt in *Crime and Punishment* and Hawthorne's major novels. The influence of Hawthorne on Dostoevski is highly dubious, but there is no question, as Astrov states at the conclusion to his article, that "an ideological kinship" existed between them.

50. Baxter, Annette. "Independence or Isolation: Hawthorne and James on the Problem of the Artist," *Nineteenth-Century Fiction*, X (December, 1955), 225–231.

Miss Baxter deals with the authors' varying attitudes toward art and compares their treatment of isolation. James felt the artist's need for independence; Hawthorne saw the artist as someone "threatened by the spectre of isolation." Hawthorne's artists bear their isolation with difficulty whereas James's creative protagonists view their partial isolation as a challenge. "James located the satisfactory equilibrium of the artist somewhere between the demands of art and the need for human relationships. . . . For Hawthorne, any satisfactory equilibrium must be consonant with the strictures of art and the overruling requisite of the artist's humanity."

51. Bewley, Marius. *The Complex Fate: Hawthorne, Henry James and Some Other American Writers*. London: Chatto and Windus, 1952. 247 pp.

Bewley is particularly concerned with the American qualities present in Hawthorne's work, and he makes interesting comparisons between *The Blithedale Romance* and Henry James's *The Bostonians*, between *The Marble Faun* and *The Wings of the Dove*. He calls attention to the social texture of Hawthorne's fiction and indicates the New Englander's concern with indigenous materials, his interest in evil, and his treatment of Americans in Europe. "Hawthorne literally gave James a tradition." Bewley believes that Hawthorne influenced James far more than the European novelists whom James met.

In a later volume, *The Eccentric Design: Form in the Classic American Novel.* New York: Columbia University Press, 1959, Bewley tries to define the inner "sphere of reality" in Hawthorne's short stories and novels, concluding that "Hawthorne's approach . . . is impersonal and moralistic with a minimum of interest in the psychology of the individual." In his attempt to discover the "profoundest meaning" of Hawthorne's reaction against the existing cultural poverty, Bewley is not especially convincing. His arguments are more illuminating, more cogently rendered, in *The Complex Fate.*

52. Bier, Jesse. "Hawthorne on the Romance: His Prefaces Related and Examined," *Modern Philology,* LIII (August, 1955), 17–24.

Bier analyzes Hawthorne's conception of the romance and his literary theory, as stated in the prefaces to "Rappaccini's Daughter," *The Scarlet Letter, The House of the Seven Gables, The Blithedale Romance,* and *The Marble Faun.*

Hawthorne's prefaces are characterized by a good deal of self-evaluation and an apologetic or even adverse criticism of Hawthorne's own work. He speaks of his own shortcomings, his "inveterate love of allegory," and the "dehumanized quality of many of his characters." In the prefaces—especially to *The House of the Seven Gables* and *The Blithedale Romance*—Hawthorne differentiates between the romance and the novel: "he sought to get away from realism or mere literal story."

For a more extensive examination of Hawthorne's attitudes toward romance, see Richard Chase, *The American Novel and Its Tradition* (59).

53. Blair, Walter. "Color, Light, and Shadow in Hawthorne's Fiction," *The New England Quarterly,* XV (March, 1942), 74–94.

Blair traces recurrent images through Hawthorne's work and indicates how Hawthorne uses color for three major purposes—"to characterize, to mark important changes in the narrative, and to stand for moral meanings." After a brief examination of stories like "The Minister's Black Veil" and "Rappaccini's Daughter," Blair analyzes *The House of the Seven Gables* and *The Scarlet Letter* in detail.

Blair also contributed the valuable bibliographical essay on Hawthorne to *Eight American Authors, A Review of Research and Criticism,* ed. Floyd Stovall. New York: Modern Language Association of America, 1956 (7).

54. Brownell, W. C. "Hawthorne," in *American Prose Masters.* New York: Scribner's, 1909, pp. 63–130.

Brownell considers *The Scarlet Letter,* which he terms "the Puritan Faust," a great work of art; Hawthorne's other fiction is conceived by his fancy rather than by his imagination. Brownell views Hawthorne as a fatalist who does not know how to make his allegory "imaginatively real"; only when he considers his Puritan past—as in *The Scarlet Letter*—is Hawthorne able to create convincing fiction. Brownell states that "a great deal of Hawthorne would be the better for the extraction of the allegorical and symbolic elements combined with it. . . . Oftenest his intrusion of symbolism, that parasite on allegory itself, is a crying abuse of a perfectly superficial and trivial expedient. He was, in fact, allegory-mad."

Writing in the age of realism, Brownell suspected Hawthorne's tendency toward romanticism and didacticism; but he did not really appreciate many of Hawthorne's intentions and techniques and thus underrated him. Most modern critics view Hawthorne's allegory as a modified symbolism which grows rich the less it is bound by the technical demands of allegory.

55. Buitenhuis, Peter. "Henry James on Hawthorne," *The New England Quarterly*, XXXII (June, 1959), 207–225.

Buitenhuis measures James's various estimates of Hawthorne's work in his early reviews, his critical study, *Hawthorne* (1879), and his *Notes of a Son and Brother* (1914). Whenever James "discussed Hawthorne's work, he dwelt on the relationship to his native land of the man whom he once called, 'that best of Americans.'" In his review of Hawthorne's *Notebooks*, James found Hawthorne uninformed, incurious, and unappreciative of France and Italy, although the volumes were absorbing because of their purity and charm. In 1872, James felt that Hawthorne's loyalty to a simpler civilization and his strong national flavor were advantages in his work; in 1879, when he published *Hawthorne: A Critical Study*, James thought of these qualities as limitations, blaming Hawthorne's failings almost entirely on his parochial *milieu*.

Twenty years later, in an introduction to some selections by Hawthorne, James's appreciation of Hawthorne grew considerably. He noted that Hawthorne's "distinguished mark" was "the feeling for the latent romance of New England," and that "alienation was the vital principle of all of Hawthorne's art." James experienced a sense of nostalgia for America toward the end of the nineteenth century and this feeling caused a renewed respect for Hawthorne's own attachment to his native land. He concluded that in Hawthorne's time it was possible "for an artist to be one of the greatest without going outside his environment: before, in effect, it had been necessary for him to become aware of the complex fate of an involvement with Europe."

56. Carpenter, Frederic I. "Puritans Preferred Blondes: The Heroines of Melville and Hawthorne," *The New England Quarterly*, IX (June, 1936), 253–272.

Carpenter concentrates upon Melville's *Mardi* and *Pierre* and Hawthorne's *The Blithedale Romance* and *The Marble Faun*. "In these novels," he suggests, "blondness is an ideal virtue and darkness a servile and sometimes unforgivable sin." In *The Blithedale Romance*, Zenobia is the dark and full-blooded heroine, "the very embodiment of experience"; Priscilla is "the familiar blonde maiden, clothed entirely in white," and clearly preferable to Zenobia. In *The Marble Faun*, Miriam is the dark-haired heroine and Hilda the light-haired figure; Carpenter concludes that Hawthorne seeks "the celestial white wisdom of Hilda" and renounces "the dark but deeper wisdom of earth." Carpenter believes that Hawthorne's sense of sin inhibited his characters from acting upon their instincts, from expressing their desire and need for freedom.

57. Chandler, Elizabeth L. "A Study of the Sources of the Tales and Romances Written by Nathaniel Hawthorne before 1853," *Smith College Studies in Modern Languages*, VII, No. 4 (1926), 1–64.

Miss Chandler writes a "biography" of Hawthorne's works. She traces the sources of Hawthorne's early fiction in his letters and notebooks and then relates his life to his work. Her biographical sketch of Hawthorne tends to see him, especially in the years from 1825–1837, as a "gloomy spectre"; but she does view the works sensibly. Miss Chandler takes Hawthorne's work through *The Blithedale Romance*.

58. Charney, Maurice. "Hawthorne and the Gothic Style," *The New England Quarterly*, XXXIV (March, 1961), 36–49.

Charney traces the influence of the Gothic novel, Gothic art, and especially Gothic architecture on Hawthorne's work. Some of the comparisons between Gothic architecture and Hawthorne's work are too forced, and he concentrates on Hawthorne's romanticism to the neglect of classical elements; but his central point that Hawthorne was most deeply impressed by the "multitudinousness" of the Gothic style is sound. Hawthorne, Charney suggests, saw that Gothicism could organically control many details in his fiction.

59. Chase, Richard. *The American Novel and Its Tradition*. Garden City, New York: Doubleday Anchor Books, 1957, 266 pp.

In this study Chase is interested in assessing "the significance of the fact that since the earliest days the American novel, in its most original and characteristic form, has worked out its destiny and defined itself by incorporating an element of romance. . . . I am interested mainly in defining the leading characteristics of the American romance-novel, as it may be called—that freer, more daring, more brilliant fiction that contrasts with the solid moral inclusiveness and massive equability of the English novel." Chase devotes twenty pages to "Hawthorne and the Limits of Romance" and explores the romantic qualities in *The Scarlet Letter* and *The Blithedale Romance*. He concludes that "although Hawthorne was a superb writer of romance and a considerable novelist from any point of view, he was aware that his romances, as he himself insisted on calling them, proceeded in part from his failure to take a place among the great novelists." Chase is always an interesting critic, and his distinctions between *The Scarlet Letter* and *Moby-Dick* in terms of their symbolic structure are illuminating.

60. Clark, Harry Hayden, "Hawthorne: Tradition *versus* Innovation," in *Patterns of Commitment in American Literature*, ed. Marston LaFrance. Toronto: University of Toronto Press, 1967, 19–37.

Clark explores Hawthorne's "attitude toward the sum of human experience in the past versus a free-willed departure from the past in the name of innovation or progress." Hawthorne's view of the past is conditioned by four assumptions: Hawthorne thought the myths of the Golden Age contained all that is abhorrent to the Christianized moral sense; he viewed the Fall of Man as "antecedent corruption and decay"; he preferred Jacksonian democracy; he gained from his classical studies a "balance between the head and the heart."

Hawthorne's hostility toward Puritanism is really an attack on "the later spokesmen who upheld 'petrified' beliefs" and who were guilty of political tyranny. He had, however, a great respect for tradition. "Most of Hawthorne's fiction involves the circular or mythic theme of withdrawal or alienation, initiation, and return with a steadying emphasis on the 'constants' which he thought were essentially common to most human experience and to the builders of the winnowed tradition of excellence who combined allegiance to both the head and the heart."

61. Cowley, Malcolm. "Hawthorne in the Looking Glass," *Sewanee Review*, LVI (Autumn, 1948), 545–563.

This essay develops the significance of mirror images in Hawthorne's fiction. "His readers come to feel that this continual mention of mirrors is something more than a writer's mannerism. We might describe it as a compulsive habit, and it is one that helps to explain his literary personality." Cowley concludes that Hawthorne "developed the habit of looking into mirrors for the truth" and used them as a symbolic bridge between the outer and inner world.

————., ed. *The Portable Hawthorne*. New York: The Viking Press, 1948.

Cowley concentrates on Hawthorne's preparation as a writer and emphasizes, once again, Hawthorne's use of mirror imagery. He notes that "for all his decorum" Hawthorne was "a man of strong passions who liked to write about women of strong passions." In *The Portable Hawthorne* Cowley includes the entire text of *The Scarlet Letter* as well as some of the famous stories: "My Kinsman, Major Molineux," "Young Goodman Brown," and "The Artist of the Beautiful." He also adds one of Hawthorne's adaptations of Greek myths for children, full selections from the notebooks, and a dozen letters.

62. Cronin, Morton. "Hawthorne on Romantic Love and the Status of Women," *PMLA*, LXIX (March, 1954), 89–98.

There are three types of women in Hawthorne's work: fragile creatures like Alice Pyncheon and Priscilla; self-reliant girls like Ellen Langton, Phoebe, and Hilda;

tragic heroines like Hester Prynne, Zenobia, and Miriam. Although Hawthorne is a critic of Puritanism, he advocates a traditional morality whenever he discusses women in society; he does not sympathize with the one who breaks the law nor does he sanction individual ethical freedom. "In his subtle conservatism, Hawthorne is the T. S. Eliot of the nineteenth century."

63. Davidson, Frank. "Hawthorne's Hive of Honey," *Modern Language Notes,* LXI (January, 1946), 14–21.

Davidson traces the influence of Shakespeare and Milton on "Earth's Holocaust," "The New Adam and Eve," and "Rappaccini's Daughter." The title of his essay is taken from a letter that Hawthorne's new bride wrote in December, 1842: "At present we can only get along with the old English writers, and we find that they are the hive from which all modern honey is stolen."

Davidson notes the influence of *Measure for Measure* on "Earth's Holocaust," and *Paradise Lost* on "The New Adam and Eve" and "Rappaccini's Daughter."

————. "Thoreau's Contribution to Hawthorne's *Mosses,*" *The New England Quarterly,* XX (December, 1947), 535–542.

Thoreau's engaging conversations with Hawthorne in the early 1840's may have affected Hawthorne's short stories. The two men were neighbors in Concord from the summer of 1842 until the autumn of 1845. Davidson suggests that Thoreau and Hawthorne were similar in temperament, but the influence of Thoreau on Hawthorne's work in the 1840's can only remain conjectural.

64. Donohue, Agnes McNeill. *A Casebook on the Hawthorne Question.* New York: Thomas Y. Crowell Company, 1963. 347 pp.

The purpose of this casebook is to "stimulate critical attention . . . to an awareness of the many 'questions' in Hawthorne." Mrs. Donohue concentrates on ambiguity, ambivalence, and man's moral nature. "The often conflicting feelings that Hawthorne has about men's moral nature are expressed obliquely in allegory, myths, archetypes, symbols, and images. He uses recurrently the light and the dark, the red and the black, the forest and the clearing, the head and the heart, the garden and the labyrinth, the prison and the grave, the journey and return. Hawthorne avoids the literal by asking rhetorical questions or offering through various characters contradictory explanations of events."

Mrs. Donohue reprints "The Haunted Mind," "Fancy's Show Box," "The Maypole of Merry Mount," "The Minister's Black Veil," "My Kinsman, Major Molineux," "Roger Malvin's Burial," "Wakefield," "The Gentle Boy," "The Birthmark," and "Young Goodman Brown." The last six stories are followed by critical essays. Mrs. Donohue also reprints some of the "classic Hawthorne criticism" by Poe, Melville, James, Lawrence, Winters, Matthiessen, and Q. D. Leavis.

65. Doubleday, Neal. "Hawthorne's Criticism of New England Life," *College English*, II (April, 1941), 639–653.

Doubleday demonstrates convincingly that *The House of the Seven Gables* and *The Blithedale Romance* indicate Hawthorne's concern with society. His social criticism is present in the former novel and his criticism of reformers and their delusions in the latter. In *The House of the Seven Gables*, he "compares two strains in New England—the lineal descendants of Puritan aristocracy in the Pyncheons and the rising, new, confusedly liberal or radical class, as represented by Holgrave." In *The Blithedale Romance*, Hawthorne "is not so much interested in attacking or satirizing or portraying the actuality of Brook Farm as he is in appraising the general tendency of his generation toward altruistic but unrealistic reform."

————. "Hawthorne's Inferno," *College English*, I (May, 1940), 658–670.

The author makes connections between Dante and Hawthorne and concentrates on Hawthorne's use of intellectual pride as the worst sin in many of the stories—his reading of "The Celestial Railroad" is especially useful. "Because man's life falls between two mysteries, and because his nature must develop only under the conditions of mortality, it is the part neither of wisdom nor of virtue, Hawthorne thinks, to deny, or to attempt to transcend, the limits of human possibility."

————. "Hawthorne and Literary Nationalism," *American Literature*, XII (January, 1941), 447–453.

Doubleday emphasizes Hawthorne's knowledge that writers of his time were eager to use native themes in their work. These writers were not transcendentalists like Emerson or Alcott; they wanted American authors to create an indigenous literature in the way that Scott had celebrated Scottish literature. "For Hawthorne, historical background relieves, and at the same time gives perspective to, an ethical or spiritual theme. . . . Hawthorne may indeed have cherished Scott, for much of his work is to be regarded as a development in an American tradition which nourished itself on Scott."

————. "Hawthorne's Satirical Allegory," *College English*, III (January, 1942), 325–337.

This essay also relates Hawthorne's work—the eight tales and sketches that he wrote while living in the Old Manse—to the events of his time. Doubleday underscores the fact that the tales included in *Mosses from an Old Manse* are far more satirical in intent than those of *Twice-Told Tales*. He discusses briefly "A Select Party," "The Intelligence Office," "The Hall of Fantasy," "The Christmas Banquet," "The Celestial Railroad," and "Earth's Holocaust" in detail. Doubleday believes that "The Celestial Railroad" has been underrated by critics—"it is a clever, consistent, and well-sustained allegory."

66. Eisinger, Chester E. "Hawthorne as Champion of the Middle Way," *The New England Quarterly*, XXVII (March, 1954), 27–52.

Eisinger feels that too many critics, in concentrating upon pride, Puritanism, solitude, and the haunted mind, have emphasized "the bleak and gloomy aspects of [Hawthorne's] work." Hawthorne, Eisinger maintains, "was a champion of the middle way which was for him the norm," and he examines the short stories accordingly. Hawthorne believed that the human being is prey to the antithetical forces of the mind and the heart and is aware of the good and evil in life. "This man's task is to hold these forces in balance," even though he will yearn for perfection or seek a "Promethean kind of knowledge." To "deny the passions, to live in isolation, to become a victim of imbalance—all these are crimes against the normal, healthy way of life that follows nature to love and marriage. Fortified by this inspiriting relationship, man must go out to participate in society." From Eisinger's point of view, "Too many critics have confused the picture of Hawthorne the solitary with the intent of Hawthorne the artist. . . . Narrow as his experience was, Hawthorne made use of it all to write, as T. S. Eliot has said, a moral criticism of life."

This essay is a sensible corrective to much Hawthorne criticism, but it tends to repeat its rather obvious perception. For a modification of Eisinger's interpretation of several stories, see Sherwood R. Price, "The Head, The Heart, and 'Rappaccini's Daughter,'" *The New England Quarterly* (September, 1954), 399–403.

67. Erskine, John. "Hawthorne," *Cambridge History of American Literature*, ed. by William P. Trent, John Erskine, Stuart P. Sherman, and Carl Van Doren. New York: G. P. Putnam's Son, II, pp. 16–31.

Erskine relates Hawthorne's ideas to those of the Transcendentalists, but in doing so he exaggerates the influence of Emerson and Alcott. It is true, as Erskine states, that Hawthorne was concerned with some of the problems which confronted the Transcendentalists and it is also true that "it was not in his disposition to suggest answers to them." But he was far more critical of the Transcendentalists than Erskine indicates. See the work of F. O. Matthiessen (98) and Stewart (22) for a modification of Erskine's view.

For an earlier version of Erskine's attitudes, see "Nathaniel Hawthorne," *Leading American Novelists*. New York: Henry Holt & Co., 1910, 179–275. "Hawthorne has no rival in his own country for literary skill—for sustained excellence on a large scale, for the management of plot, and for the magic of language that denotes the master of style." Hawthorne approached all experience with a mental reservation and his temperament was largely his mother's: a brooding, philosophizing attitude toward experience. "In his special field Hawthorne has no rivals, nor even competitors; it is therefore hard to indicate his place in American literature. He is concerned chiefly with the inner life of the soul, and at his best he ranks high among all masters of spiritual tragedy. In so far as his preoccupation with spiritual things distinguishes

him, he represents American Puritanism; he does not, however, represent it completely. He fails to portray its energy in action and its cheerfulness—the elements of
character that Mrs. Stowe delights in and illustrates. That Hawthorne did not himself lack these human qualities is proved by his journals and home records, which
show him to have been a true man, courageous and lovable and lighted with the
divine fire."

68. Faust, Bertha. *Hawthorne's Contemporaneous Reputation: A Study of Literary
Opinion in America and England, 1828–1864.* Philadelphia: University of
Pennsylvania Press, 1939. 163 pp.

This volume is a valuable source for Hawthorne's reputation from 1828 to 1864.
"It is based chiefly upon notices and articles in the magazines and reviews of the
period, in America and Great Britain. Criticism of Hawthorne's work found in
contemporaneous books is also included. To this are occasionally added the opinions
of Hawthorne's readers and acquaintances as they appear in letters and memoirs,
and some newspaper comment where it seems significant. The material is arranged
in chronological order except for a few instances where the desire for coherence
has suggested a slight deviation; and it is elucidated, where necessary, by biographical and literary references.

"The aim of the study is to show Hawthorne as he appeared to the eyes of his
contemporaries, to trace the progress of his literary reputation during his lifetime,
and also, in a measure, to give a general impression of the state of critical thought in
America and England, and to reveal the spirit of the age as it is reflected in a particular
facet."

Bertha Faust reproduces a total of 161 items, only 38 of which appeared before
1850. Reviewers considered Hawthorne patriotic, moral, or impressionistic. Others
compared him with Pope, Goldsmith, Scott, and Dickens. Melville and Lowell
made favorable comparisons with Shakespeare. "At the time of his death," Mrs.
Faust concludes, "no one, in America at least, questioned his classic status." The
ranking of the books, while Hawthorne was alive, was *The Marble Faun*, *The
House of the Seven Gables* and *The Scarlet Letter*, but Mrs. Faust maintains, Hawthorne
was not affected by the criticism of his contemporaries.

69. Feidelson, Charles, Jr. *Symbolism and American Literature.* Chicago: The
University of Chicago Press, 1953. 355 pp.

Feidelson treats Hawthorne together with Whitman, Melville, Emerson, Thoreau,
and Poe. He praises Matthiessen's *American Renaissance* (98) as "the first large-scale
attempt to define the literary quality of American writing at its best," but he
considers that Matthiessen emphasizes politics and society too much, and he wishes
to focus his attention upon the devotion that these authors brought "to the possibilities of symbolism."

Feidelson thinks that Hawthorne's conscious philosophy belonged to the eighteenth century, his symbolic imagination to the nineteenth. As a man, Hawthorne was both a solitary and an intellectual; his lack of confidence in reality and the subjective and his "inability to come to grips with the solid earth" caused him to evolve his conception of the "romance." His fiction is symbolic, not allegoric, as he seeks "to open an intercourse with the world." In his brief section on Hawthorne, Feidelson concentrates upon the relationship of "The Custom House" to *The Scarlet Letter* as well as upon the novel itself. He feels that "Every character [in *The Scarlet Letter*] re-enacts 'The Custom House' scene in which Hawthorne contemplated the letter, so that the entire 'romance' becomes a kind of exposition of the nature of symbolic perception."

70. Fiedler, Leslie. *Love and Death in the American Novel.* New York: Criterion Books, 1960. 603 pp.

This book expresses more fully ideas that were first presented in the well-known essay, "Come Back to the Raft Ag'in Huck, Honey." Fiedler emphasizes what he considers "the neglected contexts of American fiction, largely depth-psychological and anthropological, but sociological and formal as well." The treatment he uses is "thematic rather than strictly historical, selective rather than exhaustive." He is interested in making certain connections between "sentimental life in America and the archetypical image, found in our favorite books, in which a white and a colored American male flee from civilization into each other's arms." He finds, as he deals extensively with classics like *The Scarlet Letter*, *Moby-Dick*, and *Huckleberry Finn*, that the American novelist has failed to deal maturely with "adult heterosexual love," that his work reveals an "obsession with death, incest and innocent homosexuality."

Fiedler applies these notions to Hawthorne's work and especially to *The Scarlet Letter*, in an essay which he calls "*The Scarlet Letter*: Woman as Faust." He finds that "duplicity and irony are the hallmarks of" Hawthorne's work, that Hawthorne evokes "the ambiguity of moral choice." Although *The Scarlet Letter* "is the only eminent American book before the modern period to have made—or to have seemed to make—passionate love its center," the treatment of passion is really "shadowy and sterilized." Nevertheless Fiedler finds suggestive relationships among various characters—for example, an equivocal mother, an evil father, and between them, Dimmesdale, who is described at first as "child-like" and at last as "childish." Thus the incest theme, although in the disguise of adultery, is in the background of the novel. Fiedler also underscores the relationship between Dimmesdale and Chillingworth as one which is compounded of "the intolerable intimacy of doctor and patient, analyst and analysand, husband and wife, father and son, cuckold and cuckolder," and, of course, the relationship between Dimmesdale and Hester, in which Dimmesdale is the "secondary sinner" and Hester the true Faustian protagonist who "considers that damnation bliss!"

The analysis of *The Scarlet Letter* is particularly successful because Hawthorne's novel is the kind of text that contains the Gothic overtones, the sexual themes, the oblique and suppressed relationships that yield to Fiedler's ingenious sensibility.

71. Fields, James T. "Hawthorne," *Yesterdays with Authors.* Boston: J. R. Osgood, 1871, pp. 41–124.

Fields was Hawthorne's publisher and offers some interesting reminiscences, especially in relation to the difficulties Hawthorne had in the composition of *The Dolliver Romance*. At one point, on January 17, 1864, Hawthorne wrote him that his mind had "for the present, lost its temper and its fine edge" and that he "had better keep quiet." Hawthorne had deteriorated so greatly that he did not have the physical strength to complete the romance of his last years.

72. Flint, Allen. "Hawthorne and the Slavery Crisis," *The New England Quarterly,* XLI (September, 1968), 393–408.

Flint studies Hawthorne's views of Negroes, slavery, and the Civil War. Hawthorne referred to himself as "more of an abolitionist in feeling than in principle. For the most part, he accepted the "stereotype of the buffoonish minstrel-show Negro" and had a bigoted, narrow view of black people. The reason for his attitudes was largely the result of an extremely limited exposure to Negroes.

In terms of the Civil War, Hawthorne was strongly in favor of preserving the nation. His campaign biography of Franklin Pierce and especially his essay, "Chiefly About War Matters," reveals his attitude. Once the war began, Hawthorne became increasingly convinced that a genuine Union might be impossible. In the end, he was filled with "anger, bewilderment, and the critical curiosity so typical of his mind. He felt and perceived the problems, denied the solutions that others proposed, and was unable to formulate better solutions."

73. Foster, C. H. "Hawthorne's Literary Theory," *PMLA,* LVII (March, 1942), 241–254.

This is an early attempt to focus upon Hawthorne's art and thought. As Foster notes, his article was accepted before F. O. Matthiessen's *American Renaissance* (98) could be considered. Although Matthiessen treats the same subject more fully, Foster's essay is still worth reading.

Hawthorne's belief, Foster suggests, was that art idealizes life and thus provides greater truth than reality itself. The artist, as well as living within his age and coming to terms with it, must take account of the possible effects of inspiration. Hawthorne's work is the meeting ground of "several tendencies in seventeenth-century English literature: the melancholy tinged with beauty characteristic of Sir Thomas Browne, the love of nature found in the lyric poets and Izaak Walton, the severe and lofty classicism of Milton, and the allegoric attitude and art of John Bunyan."

See also Harry Hayden Clark's essay, "Hawthorne's Literary and Aesthetic Doctrines as Embodied in His Tales," *Transactions of the Wisconsin Academy of Sciences, Arts, and Letters*, L (1961), 251–275. Clark gives a chronological listing of those tales that deal with artists.

74. Fussell, Edwin. "Hawthorne, James and 'The Common Doom,'" *American Quarterly*, X (Winter, 1958), 438–454.

Fussell indicates how James made artistic use of Hawthorne's concern with isolation "from the common life"; the "common doom" is the individual's vulnerability to sorrow and death. The comparisons between Hawthorne and James are illuminating, particularly the way in which both authors suggest methods of eluding the "common doom." Fussell has some interesting comments on *Septimius Felton*.

75. Green, Martin. "The Hawthorne Myth: a protest," *Re-Appraisals: Some Commonsense Readings in American Literature*. New York: W. W. Norton and Co., pp. 61–85.

This is a severe downgrading of Hawthorne's value as a writer. Green feels that Hawthorne's work has little verisimilitude; he insists that "we have had nearly a century of anti-Emersonianism, and Hawthorne's reputation is one of the major forms it has taken."

Hawthorne's own definition of romance in his various prefaces and notes should be taken at face value: he was not "an intellectual writer in any sense," and the intellectual analyses of his work have been excessive. Hawthorne was a dreamer who never fully explored the meaning of his themes; he had an imprecise mind, which is reflected in stories such as "The Artist of the Beautiful" and "Ethan Brand." Green analyzes "Young Goodman Brown" and concludes that it is "not an allegory because it allegorizes nothing. There is no experience embodied in its language, and consequently no reason to construct elaborate meanings for its oddities. The critics' profound interpretations express their own reflections on religion and morality and doubt. Hawthorne's prose sufficiently indicates the intensity of imagination *he* put into the story." Green has harsh comments on the "historicity" and "the inconsistencies" of *The Scarlet Letter*. Hawthorne states that characters like Chillingworth change; but he never really shows us their change. "There is no development" in *The Scarlet Letter*. The irony that so many critics admire really amounts to no more than the confusions and inconsistencies in Hawthorne's own mind. "For the last thirty years or more, all the brightest minds in American literature have been guided by an aversion from the self-consciously noble and expansive in art, the uplifting, simplifying, energising; and a corresponding enthusiasm for irony and obscurity in the method, and tragedy, pessimism, a sense of evil, in the material."

76. Gross, Theodore L. "Nathaniel Hawthorne: The Absurdity of Heroism," *The Yale Review*, CVII (Winter, 1968), 182–195.

This essay emphasizes Hawthorne's skepticism about the heroic ideal of Emerson and Whitman. Hawthorne had a keen sense of the absurd in life and a "tough literal-mindedness" that prevented him from creating completely tragic works of art. "There is a sense of whimsy, of comic attitudes, of absurdity" in Hawthorne's unremembered sketches and tales of the 1830's and '40's; but these elements are present in the great stories as well. The author traces Hawthorne's use of absurdity in "Roger Malvin's Burial," "My Kinsman, Major Molineux," "Young Goodman Brown," "The Minister's Black Veil," and then offers analyses of *The Scarlet Letter*, *The House of the Seven Gables*, and *The Blithedale Romance*. His conclusion is that "the passion of heroism—whether it take the form of the Reverend Hooper's self-appointed judgment of his congregation; the ambition of Robin Molineux; the distorted idealism of Arthur Dimmesdale; the aristocratic pretension of the Pyncheon family; or the absurd idealism of Hollingsworth and Zenobia—is forever the object of Hawthorne's earthy criticism. In an age of transcendental idealism, of Whitmanesque optimism and self-conviction, of a broad belief in democracy on the part of popular writers, Hawthorne is the first serious and artistic critic of the possibilities of heroism. He was persistently aware of man's limitations—those limitations that reduce the hero to human proportions, that make him real rather than the creation of a concept, the projection of a hope or of a dream—and his awareness prevented him from ever creating his characters in truly tragic terms."

77. Hawthorne, Manning. "Hawthorne and Utopian Socialism," *The New England Quarterly*, XII (December, 1939), 726–730.

Manning Hawthorne reproduces two letters which Hawthorne wrote to a Massachusetts man who had considered living in Brook Farm. These letters were written on July 18, 1841, and May 25, 1842. The later letter expresses Hawthorne's unwillingness to join the Utopian community in Northampton: "I confess to you, my dear Sir, it is my present belief that I can best attain the higher ends of my life by retaining the ordinary relation to society."

————. "Nathaniel Hawthorne at Bowdoin," *The New England Quarterly*, XIII (June, 1940), 246–279.

Manning Hawthorne examines Hawthorne's experiences at Bowdoin in detail and concludes that the author's college life was normal and fruitful. Unlike his classmates, who "were going eagerly forward, ready to seize opportunity and make a place for themselves in the outside world, [Hawthorne] turned from it; and entering the seclusion of his chamber, he shut the door."

————. "Parental and Family Influences on Hawthorne," *Essex Institute Historical Collection*, LXXVI (January, 1940), 1–13.

This essay refutes the assertions by Elizabeth Peabody and George Woodberry that Hawthorne was a recluse. Manning Hawthorne produces statements by Hawthorne's relatives who speak of the author's activities with his family and friends.

78. Hayford, Harrison. "Hawthorne, Melville, and the Sea," *The New England Quarterly*, XIX (December, 1946), 435–453.

Hayford makes some interesting comparisons of the attitudes that Hawthorne and Melville had toward the sea and suggests that their conversations were sometimes merely "yarning" about the sea. Hawthorne's family had been seafaring men and Hawthorne himself had an extensive acquaintance with ships and things of the sea.

79. Hicks, Granville. *The Great Tradition. An Interpretation of American Literature Since the Civil War.* New York: The Macmillan Company, 1933. 341 pp.

Hicks attributes Hawthorne's deterioration to the fact that he did not come to terms with the society around him. Of the mid-nineteenth century writers, "Hawthorne kept himself most remote from his own period, and it is his work that has suffered most with the passage of time."

Hicks's view is marred by his preoccupation with the social and economic reality of literature. As subsequent critics have noted, Hawthorne was not so seclusive nor so indifferent to social concerns.

80. Hoffman, Daniel. *Form and Fable in American Fiction.* New York: Oxford University Press, 1961. 368 pp.

Hoffman devotes approximately one third of his critical study to Hawthorne and examines closely "My Kinsman, Major Molineux," "The Maypole of Merry Mount," "Young Goodman Brown," *The Scarlet Letter,* and *The Blithedale Romance.* His intention is to trace the "shaping role" of folklore in nineteenth-century American writing. He takes certain archetypes like the Yankee bumpkin and the Yankee con man, certain tall tales and stories of witchcraft, and illuminates Hawthorne's work by showing how these traditional materials have given it a special and distinctive form. Hoffman is also concerned with traditional myths like "initiatory rites, dead gods and resurrections, the scapegoat king and the Prince of Darkness." In his analysis of "My Kinsman, Major Molineux," for example, Hoffman discovers a "conflict between an aristocratic past and a demotic future. . . . Inextricably welded to the political conflict (the plot of rebellious colonists against their royal governor) is the psychological conflict of young Robin's coming of age. The action conforms doubly to ancient patterns of ritual: the ceremony of a youth's initiation into knowledge, and the expunging of evil through the sacrifice of a scapegoat king." Thus Hoffman illuminates the specific texts he examines and approaches them from this interesting point of view: in our best literature "allegory was transformed into symbolism; the Gothic mode (despite its melodrama) assumed a seriousness unusual elsewhere by virtue of the communal values represented in supernatural folklore; and the transcendental aesthetic gave the whole work metaphoric consistency."

81. Honig, Edwin. *Dark Conceit: The Making of Allegory.* Evanston: Northwestern University Press, 1959. 210 pp.

Hawthorne's allegorical technique stems from the Protestant evangelical tradition of Spenser and Bunyan. Honig compares Hawthorne's allegory with that of Melville, Kafka, and D. H. Lawrence, and analyzes allusion, analogy, irony, and ambivalence in "Rappaccini's Daughter" and *The Scarlet Letter*.

82. Howard, Leon. *Literature and the American Tradition.* New York: Doubleday and Co., 1960, pp. 114–128.

Howard sets out to answer the question, "Does the literary history of America reveal the existence of an attitude of mind consistent and durable enough to be called an aspect of the national character?" The question was prompted largely by Howard's experiences as a teacher of foreign students, and his answer, affirmative in nature, leads him to a general survey of our literature.

Literature and the American Tradition is a practical though necessarily cursory treatment of individual writers, which tends to view the literature in terms of its national significance. Thus Howard believes that Hawthorne "had to find within himself the means of adapting the popular materials of a literature in English to the attitudes of mind characteristic of people who were not English but who were sharing with the English a cultural heritage which had begun to diverge into separate ways."

83. Howe, Irving. *Politics and the Novel.* New York: Horizon Press, Inc., 1957, pp. 163–175.

Howe includes in this critical study a brief chapter entitled "Hawthorne: Pastoral and Politics." He sees Hawthorne as "a man who could not summon larger enthusiasms nor pledge himself to any social movement; his prevalent temper was skeptical though a powerful impulse within him worked to assault and deride his skepticism. . . . His mind was sluggish, mild, rationalistic; his creative self was passionate, warmly receptive, sometimes even sensual." Howe explores Hawthorne's dualistic nature as expressed in *The Blithedale Romance*, and he finds that the book, Hawthorne's most political novel, does not "live up to the promise of the opening pages. . . . Between the serious matter, confined mostly to the first fifty pages, and a tedious gim-crack plot there is seldom any vital relation."

Howe's presentation is intelligent and provocative. See also his "Hawthorne and American Fiction," *American Mercury*, LXVIII (March, 1949), 367–374, in which he suggests that Hawthorne's "finest work was done when he steered a course between allegory and surface realism, blending aspects of both but subordinating them to . . . his 'moral realism.'"

84. Kariel, Henry. "Man Limited: Nathaniel Hawthorne's Classicism," *South Atlantic Quarterly*, LII (October, 1953), 528–542.

Kariel suggests that Hawthorne's works "gracefully expose and delineate the implications of modern tempers and ideologies. His works face the problems of ethics and politics, of morals and power, which trouble man today."

Kariel's view of Hawthorne's critical theory is too narrow; he sees Hawthorne almost exclusively as a classicist, whereas his views of art were in fact eclectic. See Jacobson's *Hawthorne's Conception of the Creative Process* (37) for an opposing view.

85. Kaul, A. N. "Nathaniel Hawthorne: Heir and Critic of the Puritan Tradition," *The American Vision: Actual and Ideal Society in Nineteenth-Century Fiction.* New Haven: Yale University Press, 139–214.

"The main object of this book is to show how these novelists [Cooper, Hawthorne, Melville, and Twain] were deeply concerned with both the society of their times and an ideal conception of social relationships, and how the consequent interplay between actual and ideal social values constitutes at least a partial source of their continuing vitality. . . ."

Hawthorne's central place in the history of the American imagination is a result of his complex treatment of certain central problems of American civilization, particularly of the alienation of the individual and the possibility of social regeneration. From one point of view, Hawthorne was not a social novelist at all—he "was not interested in portraying realistically the everyday life of his time"; but he chose, unlike many European novelists, to explore the society of Puritan New England because he knew that "the seventeenth century was decisive in fostering the essential American attitudes, character types, and ideals."

Kaul discusses stories which deal with individuals alienated from society ("Wakefield," "The Minister's Black Veil," "The Man of Adamant," "Egotism; or, The Bosom Serpent," "Rappaccini's Daughter," and "Ethan Brand"); the fellowship of all men ("Lady Eleanore's Mantle," "The Christmas Banquet," and "Young Goodman Brown"); and those tales which consider the possibility of achieving a regenerated society in this world ("The New Adam and Eve"). He then examines *The Scarlet Letter*, *The House of the Seven Gables*, and *The Blithedale Romance* rather extensively. In *The Scarlet Letter*, the society which persecutes Hester Prynne "is revealed as not only bigoted and joyless but essentially evil"—the novel is a commentary on the breakdown of human relationships. In *The House of the Seven Gables,* Hawthorne "explores the cultural past of the country in economic terms." In *The Blithedale Romance,* Hawthorne "presents the utopian experiment of Brook Farm as an extension of the Puritan tradition."

86. Kesselring, Marion L. *Hawthorne's Reading,* 1828–1850. New York: New York Public Library, 1949. 64 pp.

This is a listing of the titles of books that Hawthorne borrowed, as recorded in the Charge-Books of the Salem Athenaeum library, 1826–1839, 1848–1850. Kesselring is authoritative for the period he covers. His table of contents reads as follows: Analysis of Hawthorne's Reading; Transcription of the Salem Charge-Book Records for Mary Manning and Nathaniel Hawthorne; Transcription of Mary Manning's Entries in Salem Athenaeum Charge-Books, 1826–1828; Transcription of Nathaniel Hawthorne's Entries in Salem Athenaeum Charge-Books, 1828–1839 and 1848–1850; Identification of Books, Charged to Nathaniel Hawthorne and Mary Manning.

87. Kimbrough, Robert. "'The Actual and the Imaginary': Hawthorne's Concept of Art in Theory and Practice," *Transactions of the Wisconsin Academy of Sciences, Arts, and Letters,* L (1961), 277–293.

Kimbrough examines Hawthorne's imagination and the way in which he created his fiction. He feels that the critical assumption that "allegory is organic" to Hawthorne's work can be misleading, and he attempts to determine how "organic" to "Hawthorne's artistic purpose was his 'inveterate love of allegory.'" Hawthorne repeatedly affirmed that man, above the animals, "has *soul, intellect,* and *heart.*" He is a great writer "not because he attempted allegory, but because he did not."

Kimbrough's emphasis on Hawthorne's moral meaning is sensible but he evades the technical significance of allegory to Hawthorne's fiction.

88. Lang, H. J. "How Ambiguous is Hawthrone?" *Geister Einer Freien Gesellschaft.* Heidelberg: Queele and Meyer, 1962. Reprinted in *Hawthorne: Twentieth Century Views,* ed. A. N. Kaul. Englewood Cliffs, N.J.: Prentice Hall, Inc., 1966, pp. 86–98.

Lang analyzes "The Wives of the Dead," "Young Goodman Brown," "The Minister's Black Veil," and "Rappaccini's Daughter" in terms of "three sorts of ambiguity: the ambiguity inherent in language, especially language used for poetic purposes; . . . the ambiguity of human conduct, or, rather, the inescapable doubt we encounter once we try to get beneath the surface of the obvious in motivations"; and the "ambiguity of external action [in which] external action is paradoxically ambiguous only, since it should not give rise to real doubt at all, as far as essentials are concerned."

Lang makes a connection between the Salem witchcraft trials of 1692, Hawthorne's fiction, and James's "The Turn of the Screw," claiming that of the three

"Hawthorne, with his firm sense of values, was the least ambiguous." This judgment may be finally sound, but it seems doubtful that the witchcraft trials of Hawthorne's fiction had very much to do with James's creation of "The Turn of the Screw."

89. Laser, Marvin. "'Head,' 'Heart,' and 'Will' in Hawthorne's Psychology," *Nineteenth-Century Fiction*, X (September, 1955), 130–140.

Laser elucidates the psychology of Thomas C. Upham and shows its influence on Hawthorne's themes. In the use of favorite terms like "head, heart, and will," Hawthorne was indebted to the work of a now forgotten psychologist, Thomas C. Upham. Upham was a professor at Bowdoin when Hawthorne was there. He published *Elements of Mental Philosophy* in 1831; *Practical Treatise on the Will* in 1834; and *Outlines of Imperfect and Disordered Mental Action* in 1841. These works served as a "solid underpinning" for Hawthorne's own stories of intellectually or emotionally disoriented human beings.

90. Lawrence, D. H. *Studies in Classic American Literature*. New York: T. Seltzer, 1923. Reprinted by Doubleday Anchor Books, 1953, pp. 92–120, and by Edmund Wilson, ed. *The Shock of Recognition*. New York: Farrar, Straus and Cudahy, 1943, pp. 907–1077.

Lawrence's volume is of great significance, not only because of its own illuminating and at times brilliant revelations of our classical literature but because of its influence on subsequent criticism. Leslie Fiedler, for example, prefaces his *Love and Death in the American Novel* (70) by suggesting that Lawrence attempted "for the first time the kind of explication which does not betray the complexity or perilousness of its theme."

Lawrence was distressed at the increased mechanization of the modern world, and in the southwest of America and in Mexico he found a life that was more primitive, more compatible with his own notions. His examination of Cooper, Hawthorne, Melville, Whitman, and other writers is in part an attempt to measure the original passion that our nineteenth-century writers brought to the New World. He notes that there is a fundamental "split in the American art and art-consciousness. On the top it is as nice as pie, goody-goody and lovey-dovey . . . Serpents they [the classical American writers] were. Look at the inner meaning of their art and see what demons they were. You *must* look through the surface of American art, and see the inner diabolism of the symbolic meaning. Otherwise it is all mere childishness."

Lawrence examines *The Scarlet Letter* which, he believes, "gives the show away," and points out that "you have your pure-pure young parson Dimmesdale. You have the beautiful Puritan Hester at his feet. And the first thing she does is to seduce him. And the first thing he does is to be seduced . . . Of course the best part of the game lay in keeping up pure appearances." By calling attention to the tension that exists between the passion of these lovers and their external behavior, Lawrence successfully indicates the "perfect duplicity" of the novel. He also underscores the shift in attitudes in the New World: Chillingworth and Hester represent an attrition of the aristocratic mode of life whereas Dimmesdale and Hester of the New World suggest democratic people controlled by their puritan consciousness. The purest symbol of the dualistic nature of American life is of course Pearl, who seems innocent but who in fact is demonic.

The extreme style that Lawrence uses is well suited to his perceptions, although, as Edmund Wilson suggests, "*Studies in Classic American Literature* have shots that do not hit the mark and moments that are quite hysterical." Still they remain, as Wilson also points out, "one of the few first-rate books that have ever been written on the subject."

91. Leavis, Q. D. "Hawthorne as Poet," *Sewanee Review*, LIX (April, June, 1951), 179–205 and LIX (July, September, 1951), 426–458.

Mrs. Leavis extends the formulations first suggested by D. H. Lawrence in *Studies in Classic American Literature:* she too maintains that Hawthorne is concerned with a shift in values that resulted from the emigration to the New World, She feels that critics have obscured the essential aspects of Hawthorne's art by concentrating on allegory. Hawthorne was primarily concerned with American society and in his varied social commentaries he employed the devices of symbolism and not of allegory. Mrs. Leavis calls attention to the poetic techniques that Hawthorne uses in his work: images, symbols, and linguistic peculiarities. Her treatment is provocative and often illuminating, particularly her interpretation of "The Maypole of Merry Mount," "Young Goodman Brown," and "My Kinsman, Major Molineux."

In her reading of "My Kinsman, Major Molineux," Mrs. Leavis suggests that Hawthorne presents an historical parable of America's coming of age, viewed through a ritual drama of "the conquest of the old king by the new." Too often, however, in this long and valuable essay, Q. D. Leavis is exclusive rather than comprehensive, suggestive more than absolutely convincing.

92. Leibowitz, Herbert A. "Hawthorne and Spenser: Two Sources," *American Literature*, XXX (January, 1959), 459–466.

Leibowitz focuses on two particularly significant parallels: a comparison of "Young Goodman Brown" with Book I of *The Faerie Queene*, and one between "Rappaccini's Daughter" and Book II, with emphasis on Rappaccini's garden and the Bower of Bliss.

In the first parallel, Leibowitz finds Hawthorne's opinion of man's fate more pessimistic than Spenser's. In "Young Goodman Brown," "the mediating power of the church as the instrument of bringing divine favor to man to strengthen and purify his moral will is repudiated." In the second parallel, both Rappaccini's garden and the Bower of Bliss are "perversions of Nature," of "artificiality and death."

93. Levin, Harry. *The Power of Blackness*. New York: Alfred A. Knopf, Inc., 1958. 263 pp.

Levin's study is an impressionistic examination of Hawthorne, Poe, and Melville, the three nineteenth-century writers most dedicated to the exploration of the tragic vision. The title is taken from Melville's essay (150) in which the younger author admired Hawthorne's ability to invest his work with "the power of blackness." In his introduction Levin promises that "our theme will concretely link two broad assumptions: the symbolic character of our greatest fiction and the dark wisdom of our deeper minds. Together they constitute what I would rather describe as an antithesis than as a thesis, since they act in opposition to more publicized influences, blandly materialistic." He naturally emphasizes the brooding quality of Hawthorne's work in tales like "The Minister's Black Veil" and "Young Goodman Brown," and in novels like *The Scarlet Letter* and *The House of the Seven Gables*. But the emphasis on color imagery in Hawthorne has been considered many times before—see Hyatt Waggoner's *Hawthorne, A Critical Study* (47) Richard Harter Fogle's *Hawthorne's Fiction: The Light and the Dark* (33), Walter Blair's "Color, Light, and Shadow in Hawthorne's Fiction," *The New England Quarterly*, XV (March, 1942), 74–94 (53)—and to greater effect. Levin offers many perceptions that are illuminating, but his general treatment of Hawthorne does not seem especially original.

94. Lewis, R. W. B. "The Return into Time: Hawthorne," *The American Adam: Innocence, Tragedy, and Tradition in the Nineteenth Century*. Chicago: University of Chicago Press, 1955. 205 pp.

Lewis views Hawthorne as an author who is freed from history but who feels the insistent and repeated demands of the past. "Hawthorne was perhaps the first American writer to detect the inevitable doubleness of the tribal promise. For he was able by temperament to give full and fair play to both parties in the *agon*: to the hero and to the tribe as well. . . . In addition, Hawthorne felt very deeply the intimacy between experience and art . . . Finally, it was Hawthorne who saw in American experience the re-creation of the story of Adam and who, more than any other contemporary, exploited the active metaphor of the American as Adam—before and during and after the Fall. These are the three aspects of Hawthorne that I shall consider."

Lewis's essay, part of one of the more important studies of American literature in our time, is particularly perceptive in regard to *The Scarlet Letter* and *The Marble Faun*. "The opening scene of *The Scarlet Letter* is the paradigm dramatic image in American literature." The solitary individual is set against the inimical society and the action that ensues suggests that "the society's estimate of the moral structure of the universe may be tested and found inaccurate." In *The Marble Faun*, the agony that the characters of *The Scarlet Letter* experience is echoed. Once again, the main characters (Miriam and Donatello) flee from the city to the woods and discover that they must return to the city, Rome, and to the responsibility for their crime. "*The Marble Faun* is a novel explicitly about the hero as Adam; but it is no less a novel about the heroine as artist." Lewis underscores the Edenic imagery in the novel as it appears in Rome, the setting of evil. "The action has to do with the discovery of *time* as a metaphor of evil"—*after* the sin, Donatello grows aware of his own ancestry. "Hilda, and all the world, may call Donatello's action a crime or a sin. But his fall was in many serious respects an upward step—an entrance into that true reality which, for Hawthorne, is measured by time."

95. Lohmann, Christoph. "The Burden of the Past in Hawthorne's American Romances," *The South Atlantic Quarterly*, LXVI (Winter, 1967), 92–104.

Lohmann explores "the relationship between Hawthorne's use of the past and his treatment of sin, guilt, and expiation." He maintains that "the past of Hawthorne's works often assumes a moral, ethical, and theological function, so that its treatment is frequently identical with his treatment of sin and guilt." These ideas are traced in *The Scarlet Letter, The House of the Seven Gables,* and *The Blithedale Romance.*

96. Lueders, E. G. "The Melville-Hawthorne Relationship in *Pierre* and *The Blithedale Romance,*" *Western Humanities Review*, IV (August, 1950), 323–334.

Lueders offers an interesting comparison of these two novels, both of which were published in 1852. He points out that the books are more autobiographical than the authors' previous works; they criticize transcendentalism; and they compare light and dark women.

97. Marx, Leo. *The Machine in the Garden.* Technology and the Pastoral Ideal in America. New York: Oxford University Press, 1964, 1–33, 265–281.

Marx calls attention to the eight pages of notes which Hawthorne took on the morning of July 27, 1844. Hawthorne described in detail the setting of "Sleepy Hollow" and then shifted to reflections of the nearby train: "What begins as a conventional tribute to the pleasures of withdrawal from the world—a simple pleasure fantasy—is transformed by the interruption of the machine into a far more complex state of mind. . . . Hawthorne's notes mark the shaping (on a microscopic scale to be sure) of a metaphoric design which recurs everywhere in our literature."

In his specific treatment of Hawthorne, Marx examines closely "Ethan Brand," in which there broods "a sense of loss, anxiety, and dislocation." The fire in "Ethan Brand" is a surrogate for the machine and suggests the historical reasons for the fall from grace in America. "'Ethan Brand' conveys Hawthorne's inchoate sense of the doom awaiting the self-contained village culture, not the institutions alone, but the whole quasi-religious ideology that rests, finally, upon the hope that Americans will subordinate their burning desire for knowledge, wealth, and power to the pursuit of rural happiness."

98. Matthiessen, F. O. *American Renaissance: Art and Expression in the Age of Emerson and Whitman.* New York: Oxford University Press, 1941, pp. 179–368.

This book is perhaps the most significant and impressive critical study of nineteenth-century American literature. Matthiessen treats Hawthorne in relation to four writers of this period—Emerson, Thoreau, Melville, and Whitman—and to authors like James and Eliot, who share some of Hawthorne's aesthetic attitudes. More than any other critic, Matthiessen has placed Hawthorne in his historical context. He notes, for example, Hawthorne's contempt for transcendentalism in a tale like "The Celestial Railroad"; his democratic beliefs as expressed in a novel like *The House of the Seven Gables;* his use of New England materials in so much of his work; his concern with the artistic sensibility in stories like "The Prophetic Pictures" and "The Artist and the Beautiful" and in all of the novels.

Matthiessen is also intent upon examining the works of Hawthorne as literature, realizing that the common reader "does not live by trends alone; he reads books, whether of the past or present, because they have an immediate life of their own." Thus *American Renaissance* helps to modify the tradition that was suggested by Vernon Parrington (105), in which individual novels or poems are used to serve some predetermined thesis and in which belletristic writers like Hawthorne are often neglected or underrated. Matthiessen considers Hawthorne in terms of allegory and symbolism, and demonstrates how Hawthorne's "tragic vision" is artistically conveyed. He also offers superb readings of *The Scarlet Letter, The House of the Seven Gables, The Marble Faun,* "Young Goodman Brown," and most of the other famous tales. Matthiessen has separate chapters devoted to "The Crucial Definition of Romance," "Hawthorne and James," "Hawthorne and Milton," "From Hawthorne to James to Eliot," and "Hawthorne's Politics."

Matthiessen's book has encouraged subsequent critics to be more sensitive to language, to symbolism, to form—in short, to all artistic considerations.

99. Maxwell, Desmond E. S. "The Tragic Phase: Melville and Hawthorne," *American Fiction: The Intellectual Background.* New York: Columbia University Press, 1963, pp. 151–191.

Hawthorne was obsessed with sin, crime, natural human depravity, punishment, atonement, and the "fated" renunciation of Old World Power. He relinquished the pastoral mood for a vision of the forest as a dark moral wilderness that freed man of evil.

Maxwell surveys Hawthorne's fiction, with remarks on "The Great Carbuncle," *The Scarlet Letter,* "The Maypole of Merry Mount," "My Kinsman, Major Molineux," and *The Blithedale Romance.*

100. Miller, James E. "Hawthorne and Melville: The Unpardonable Sin," *PMLA,* LXX (March, 1955), 91–114.

Miller deals with the differentiation between the head and the heart in the fiction of both writers. He explores "the motives of Hawthorne's characters in committing the unpardonable sin, the fateful steps which constitute its commission, and the existence of these identical motives and steps in *Moby Dick.*" The unpardonable sin, in Hawthorne's work, originates "in a seemingly justifiable cause, in an apparent good." Thus Chillingworth, Aylmer, Ethan Brand, and Hollingsworth demand perfection and become "over-intellectualized and evil, wreaking havoc among [their] fellow-humans." Miller traces this idea in other works by Hawthorne—*The House of the Seven Gables, The Blithedale Romance,* "The Birthmark," "The Great Stone Face," and "Lady Eleanore's Mantle"—and then offers a close examination of *Moby-Dick.*

101. Mills, Barriss. "Hawthorne and Puritanism," *The New England Quarterly,* XXI (March, 1948), 78–102.

This article is valuable for the precise way in which it distinguishes between what aspects of Puritanism Hawthorne accepted and what aspects he rejected. While Hawthorne believed in innate depravity and the futility of political reforms, he censured the Puritans for their intolerance and their acceptance of absolute sovereignty. He admired the Puritans' democracy and justice as well as their courage and their seriousness. "Certainly Hawthorne did not swallow Puritanism whole. . . . His is an emotional philosophy, based on sympathies and antipathies of the heart, not the mind, and along with theology, he discarded the whole Puritan exegesis as too wildly intellectual."

In this sense Hawthorne escapes being labeled because he was more of an artist than a philosopher.

102. O'Connor, William Van. "Hawthorne and Faulkner: Some Common Ground," *Virginia Quarterly Review,* XXXIII (Winter, 1957), 105–123.

The works of the two writers, especially in relation to their mutual concern with the past, are compared. O'Connor considers their preoccupation with "gloomy wrongs." He juxtaposes *The Scarlet Letter* and *Light in August,* admitting the obvious differences between the two novels but insisting that the characters have at least one aspect in common: "their minds and imaginations are thoroughly moralized." In *The House of the Seven Gables, Absalom, Absalom!,* and *The Sound and the Fury* both writers are "concerned with the way the past lives on into the present." In *The Marble Faun, The Sound and the Fury,* and *Absalom, Absalom!,* the incest motif is used to symbolize "ingrownness." Both writers have a "will to rhetoric"; both are concerned with legendary and imaginative as much as with realistic material; and both deal with regional areas.

103. Orians, G. Harrison. "Hawthorne and Puritan Punishments," *College English,* XIII (May, 1952), 424–432.

This is a valuable source of punishments, historically traced, that were used by Hawthorne in his work. Punishment was a topic Hawthorne "associated with the grimness and gloom of old Puritan communities which had the roaring sea before them and the howling wilderness back of them." Orians notes the various punishments of Hawthorne's tales: the cleft stick (used in "Endicott and the Red Cross"); imprisonment and the pillory (in *The Scarlet Letter*); whipping and ear-cropping (in *The Maypole of Merry Mount*). He then discusses the punishments related to the Scarlet A.

104. Parkes, H. B. "Poe, Hawthorne, Melville: An Essay in Sociological Criticism," *Partisan Review*, 2 (February, 1949), 157–165.

Parkes feels that "what is lacking in [Hawthorne's] framework of experience is any sense of the society as a kind of organic whole to which the individual belongs and in which he has his appointed place. And lacking the notion of social continuity and tradition, [he] lacks also the corresponding metaphysical conception of the natural universe as an ordered unity which harmonizes with human ideals." Hawthorne deals basically with people who suffer from isolation and sexual immaturity.

For an explicit refutation of this idea, see Q. D. Leavis, "Hawthorne as a Poet," *Sewanee Review*, LIX (April, June, 1951), 179–205; (July, September, 1951), 426–458 (91).

105. Parrington, Vernon L. "Nathaniel Hawthorne, Skeptic," *Main Currents in American Thought*. New York: Harcourt, Brace, and Company, 1927. Volume I, 442–450.

Parrington is generally unsympathetic to purely belletristic writers, and he thinks of Hawthorne as an author who was indifferent to "political and metaphysical speculation." He underscores the intellectual limitations of Hawthorne: "The intellectual poverty that resulted from his long immuring himself in a void is sufficiently revealed in his *American Notebooks*. In the somewhat tedious volume covering the eighteen years between 1835 and 1853—the most vigorous years of the renaissance—there is no suggestion of interest in the creative ideas of the time, in metaphysics or politics or economics or humanitarianism, and it makes but a paltry showing when set beside the journals of Emerson for the same years. Few books are referred to; systems of thought lie beyond his ken. Compared with the thinkers and scholars of the time he is only an idler lying in wait for such casual suggestions as he may turn into stories. . . . He was the extreme and finest expression of the refined alienation from reality that in the end palsied the creative mind of New England. Having consumed his fancies, what remained to feed on?"

This unsympathetic portrayal has been modified by many subsequent critics, most notably Randall Stewart (22) and F. O. Matthiessen (98). For an extended consideration of Parrington's volume see Lionel Trilling, "Reality in America," *The Liberal Imagination*. New York: The Macmillan Company, 1948; reprinted in Doubleday Anchor Books, 1957, pp. 1–19. Trilling challenges Parrington's low estimate of Hawthorne, which develops from the historian's assumptions about reality: "The man [Hawthorne] who could raise those brilliant and serious doubts about the nature and possibility of moral perfection, the man who could keep himself aloof from the 'Yankee reality' and who could dissent from the orthodoxies of dissent and tell us so much about the nature of moral zeal, is of course dealing exactly with reality."

106. Pochmann, Henry A. "Nathaniel Hawthorne," *German Culture in America*, Philosophical and Literary Influences. Madison: The University of Wisconsin Press, 1957, pp. 381–389.

Pochmann estimates Poe's statements that Tieck deeply influenced Hawthorne's work. He synopsizes a tale of Tieck, "The Friends," which appeared in the *Democratic Review* (May, 1845, XV, 496–501), and suggests the similarities between it and Hawthorne's fiction: the allegory, tone, style, and psychology. He also notes Hawthorne's affinity to Hoffmann and Chamisso. The most important Germanic influence on Hawthorne, however, was Goethe's *Faust*, for the Faustian motif is to be found frequently in Hawthorne's work: Aylmer, Rappaccini, Brand, and Chillingworth bear a resemblance to Dr. Faustus. "By and large," Pochmann concludes, "the influence of German literature on Hawthorne is relatively inconsequential. Most of Hawthorne's tales which suggest outside influence are traceable less to Germanic sources than to his peculiar temperamental inheritance."

107. Poirier, Richard. "Visionary to Voyeur: Hawthorne and James," *A World Elsewhere*, The Place of Style in American Literature. New York: Oxford University Press, 1966, pp. 93–143.

Poirier studies the style of James' book on Hawthorne and notes that the style comes across more strongly than the subject of Hawthorne itself. Poirier has high praise for "My Kinsman, Major Molineux," and examines it as an example of "stylistic struggle." This struggle "is not only to reveal the limitation of Puritan allegory; it is also to cast off the restraints of literary and social artificiality."

Poirier then turns to *The Blithedale Romance*, which he considers Hawthorne's "greatest achievement," and offers a lengthy treatment of the novel. Coverdale is a sort of Emersonian man turned a Dandy. Hawthorne "shows how the romantic dream of creating an environment for the self rather than submitting to the environment authorized by 'artificial systems' becomes a form of aestheticism." In many ways Coverdale anticipates the figure of Strether in *The Ambassadors*. "The connection between Strether and Coverdale is of a significance greater than anything it tells us about the relationship of Hawthorne and James. Coverdale the poet, Strether the man who is busy "converting" life into artistic still-lifes, illustrate the fact that an indifference to social reality, even a solipsistic one, is not to be taken as a sign that such characters or their creators are socially deprived. Quite the reverse. They retreat from society into a sort of aesthetic dandyism."

108. Ragan, James. "Hawthorne's Bulky Puritans," *PMLA*, LXXV (September, 1960), 420–423.

Ragan shows, in a treatment of *The Scarlet Letter, The House of the Seven Gables,* and *The Blithedale Romance,* Hawthorne's use of the human body to represent "the progressivism of American democracy." Characters like the substantial Puritan matrons gathered around the scaffold in *The Scarlet Letters*; the bulky Colonel Pyncheon in *The House of the Seven Gables*; the slim Priscilla all reveal in their bodily make-up distinct moral and social qualities.

109. Rahv, Philip. "The Dark Lady of Salem," *Partisan Review*, VIII (September, October, 1941), 362–381. Reprinted in *Image and Idea.* New York: New Directions, 1949, pp. 22–41.

Rahv analyzes, from a psychological point of view, the dark lady in Hawthorne's work: Hester Prynne, Zenobia, Miriam, and Beatrice (of "Rappaccini's Daughter"). He finds that Hawthorne's fiction contains "a submerged intensity and passion—a tangled imagery of unrest and longing for experience and regret at its loss . . . He was haunted not only by the guilt of his desires but also by the guilt of his denial of them." Hawthorne had "no genuine passion nor a revival of dogma but a fear of life induced by narrow circumstances and morbid memories of the past."

Rahv believes that Hawthorne is an interesting writer because he did not free himself completely from Puritanism; he views him as an author struggling between the past and the future, between the moribund religious tradition of old New England and the "newborn secular imagination."

110. Randel, William. "Hawthorne, Channing, and Margaret Fuller," *American Literature*, X (January, 1939), 472–476.

Randel refutes Oscar Cargill's thesis (in "Nemesis and Nathaniel Hawthorne," *PMLA*, LII, September, 1937, 848–862) that Hawthorne disliked Channing and punished him by slandering his sister-in-law, Miss Fuller, in *The Blithedale Romance.* "For this rash step Hawthorne was punished twofold: his sister was drowned, and his creative powers were atrophied for six years. Thus he himself fell victim to one of his favorite themes, divine retribution for sin."

Randel points out that Hawthorne did not dislike Miss Fuller very much and that his relations with Channing were also more favorable than Cargill allows.

111. Ringe, Donald L. "Hawthorne's Psychology of the Head and Heart," *PMLA*, LXV (March, 1950), 120–132.

Ringe considers the consequences of the conflict between the head and heart, especially in terms of *The Scarlet Letter.* He feels that Hawthorne solves the problem of sin and the Fall of Man in two ways: by striking a balance between the forces of the mind and of the heart (in, for example, the character of Holgrave); or by indicating the superiority of the heart (as in the case of Hester). Man is in a constant conflict between these two aspects of his character, and they center upon a critical and irreconcilable theme in his life—the problem of life in an evil world.

112. Rohenberger, Mary. *Hawthorne and the Modern Short Story*. The Hague and Paris: Mouton and Co., 1966, 148 pp.

Mary Rohenberger's primary purpose in this study is "to describe genre" and she uses Hawthorne as a primary example "because his importance as a writer of short stories is generally recognized"; Hawthorne occupies three of her eight chapters. She traces Hawthorne's literary theory, as developed in his various prefaces, and relates it to his short stories. "Roger Malvin's Burial," in her view, "presents graphically Hawthorne's conviction that truth is an inner reality"; "My Kinsman, Major Molineux" is a study in conflict—"political, social, and personal." These two readings, together with her interpretation of "Young Goodman Brown," are worth noting.

113. Rourke, Constance. *American Humor: A Study of the National Character*. New York: Harcourt, Brace and Company, Inc., 1931. Reprinted by Doubleday Anchor Books, 1953, pp. 150–154.

Miss Rourke, in her classic study of American humor, notes that "Hawthorne was on the outlook for odd and salient characters; he often enveloped them with humor in his brief notes; he had a gift for slight inflation in drawing, and even for the touch of caricature." In her brief treatment of Hawthorne, Miss Rourke suggests that Hawthorne turned toward the legend, a form of comedy then shaping itself within the popular consciousness. Miss Rourke concentrates on *The Scarlet Letter*, concluding that "Hawthorne at his finest never used the abstract formulations of the Puritan: he chose the direct and earthy mode . . . and there at least he slipped into an irreverent rude comedy far from the conscious Puritan habit."

114. Schneider, H. W. *The Puritan Mind*. New York: Henry Holt and Co., 1958, pp. 256–264.

Schneider emphasizes Hawthorne's belief that no amount of virtue can eliminate the malevolent aspects of human nature. For Hawthorne "sin is an obvious and conspicuous fact, to deny which is foolish. Its consequences are inevitable and to seek escape from them is childish. The only relief from sin comes from public confession. Anything private or concealed works internally until it destroys the sinner's soul." Schneider's remarks relate particularly to works like "Young Goodman Brown" and *The Scarlet Letter*. He believes that Hawthorne "saw the empirical truth behind the Calvinistic symbols. He recovered what Puritanism professed but seldom practiced—the spirit of piety, humility, and tragedy in the face of the inscrutable ways of God." Schneider's book is valuable in relating Hawthorne to other writers of Puritan themes.

115. Schwartz, Joseph. "Three Aspects of Hawthorne's Puritanism," *The New England Quarterly*, XXXVI (June, 1963), 192–208.

The three aspects that Schwartz discusses are Hawthorne's theology, his attitude toward the Puritan social life, and his view of Puritan politics. Hawthorne felt that "the religious system of Puritanism was hard, cold, and confined"; he thought that "Puritanism as a way of life . . . was gloomy, joyless, and rigid"; and he perceived that while the Puritans "demanded liberty of conscience and freedom in law from their British rulers, they were not willing to extend this same freedom to those who dissented from the Puritan pattern of life."

116. Shroeder, John W. "'That Inward Sphere'; Notes on Hawthorne's Heart Imagery and Symbolism," *PMLA*, LXV (March, 1950), 106–119.

This essay traces heart symbolism, which Hawthorne uses complexly, in reference to a revelation of the author's attitudes toward sin and guilt. Shroeder defines the nature of the symbol and explains its consequences in terms of Hawthorne's fiction.

117. Spiller, Robert E. "The Artist in America: Poe, Hawthorne," in *The Cycle of American Literature*. New York: The New American Library of World Literature, Inc., 1957, pp. 61–76.

"The purpose of this volume," Spiller writes in his preface, "is to provide its own historical context for the study of the literature of the United States." Spiller, who was an editor of *The Literary History of the United States*, has written in this volume a book that is an essay toward "a singleness of vision." His short treatment of Hawthorne concludes that "the agency" of Hawthorne's "perspective was allegory which, because it is used primarily for aesthetic rather than moral purposes, serves to supply a symbolic level of meaning for morality as the major force in human affairs. Hawthorne, like Poe, achieved in his best work an aesthetic detachment that made it possible for him to give to American life, at the moment of its first cultural renaissance, a critical presentation in literary art."

118. Stanton, Robert. "Dramatic Irony in Hawthorne's Romances," *Modern Language Notes*, LXXI (June, 1956), 420–426.

Stanton believes that irony is used by Hawthorne to illuminate the contrast between appearance and reality. "Hawthorne's dramatic irony has two main effects: first, it emphasizes the idea that moral values and laws have a real existence independent of their physical contexts; second, within each romance it helps to define the particular central theme."

———. "Hawthorne, Bunyan, and the American Romances," *PMLA*, LXXI (March, 1956), 155–165.

Stanton makes comparisons between the moral worlds of the two writers and concentrates on *The Scarlet Letter*, *The House of the Seven Gables*, and *The Blithedale*

Romance. He discusses three episodes which echo *The Pilgrim's Progress* several times: the forest scene between Hester and Dimmesdale (Chapters XVI–XX); the chapter, "The Flight of Two Owls," in *The House of the Seven Gables,* XVII; and the chapter, "A Modern Arcadia," in *The Blithedale Romance,* VIII. In each of these scenes, two or more characters try to cast off the evil of the past, seeking happiness and a simple, more natural life by rejecting convention. All three episodes end in discouragement or despair.

119. Stewart, Randall. *American Literature and Christian Doctrine.* Baton Rouge: Louisiana State University Press, 1958, 73–89.

In his chapter, "Guilt and Innocence," Stewart considers Hawthorne and Melville as counter-romantics who stood in opposition to Emersonian philosophy. In Hawthorne's work the concept of Original Sin is pervasive. Stewart examines "The Birthmark" as an example of Hawthorne's concern with sin and concludes that the "profounder wisdom" which Aylmer could not acquire was the acceptance of human imperfection. "Rappaccini's Daughter" and "Young Goodman Brown" illustrate the positive force of the evil principle which "is always at work in Hawthorne's fictions." *The Scarlet Letter* dramatizes another theme in Hawthorne's work: the tension between the Puritan and the romantic tendencies. "The *Scarlet Letter* is a criticism of Puritanism as well as of romanticism."

Stewart's essay is reliable but not very profound or original.

120. Trollope, Anthony. "The Genius of Nathaniel Hawthorne," *North American Review,* CXXIX (September, 1879), 203–222.

Trollope praises Hawthorne for the more mysterious aspects of his work, but the Victorian novelist is obviously controlled by his realistic approach to literature, and his treatment of Hawthorne's work is largely in those terms. He knows that he ought to like this Romantic writer, but he finds it difficult to accept Hawthorne's symbolic habit of mind.

121. Warren, Austin. *Rage for Order, Essays in Criticism.* Chicago: University Press, 1948, pp. 84–103.

Warren first demonstrated his ideas about Hawthorne in a valuable introductory essay to *Nathaniel Hawthorne: Representative Selections.* New York: American Book Company, 1934 (American Writers Series). He includes in this volume an excellent annotated bibliography. The perceptive introduction deals with "The Man, Theology, The Problems of Sin, Anti-Transcendentalism, Politics, European Influences, and Hawthorne as Artist." Warren is particularly illuminating in terms of Hawthorne's Puritanism.

In *Rage for Order, Essays in Criticism,* Warren includes an essay on Hawthorne which is an intelligent estimate of Hawthorne's character and work. He relates the fiction to that of subsequent authors like Pater, James, and Proust—"writers of the psychological novel concerned with the mysteries of the human soul. Hawthorne was possessed, surely, by a belief that our mysteries are more important than our knowledges. Once, in *The Scarlet Letter*, he trusted to find inadequate mystery in 'The Interior of a Heart.' He never again felt that confidence in the power of character to unfold its own plots."

122. Wegelin, Christof. "Europe in Hawthorne's Fiction," *Journal of English Literary History*, XIV (September, 1947), 219–245.

Wegelin demonstrates, rather convincingly, that Hawthorne could not describe Europe in any compelling way until he had traveled abroad. He concentrates upon *The Marble Faun* and Hawthorne's use of the European past in the novel. Unlike Irving's use of the English past, Hawthorne often evokes the "idea-complex of decay, guilt, and death." In comparison, his depiction of the English countryside in *Doctor Grimshawe* is filled with wonder and awe.

123. Whipple, Edwin P. "Hawthorne," *Character and Characteristic Men*. Boston: Houghton Mifflin, 1866, pp. 218–242.

Hawthorne had higher regard for Whipple than for any other nineteenth-century American critic; in fact, he remarked that this essay, first printed in *The Atlantic Monthly* in 1860, was "a really keen and profound article." Whipple sees Hawthorne's special vision as moral, and he praises his contemporary for his originality and his characterization. He calls attention to Hawthorne's skepticism and tragic outlook.

124. Williams, Stanley. "Nathaniel Hawthorne," *The Literary History of the United States*, Volume I. New York: The Macmillan Company, 1948. 3 vols. 1456 pp.

The Literary History of the United States is the most comprehensive survey of American literature in our time, although it is inevitably uneven in quality because the chapters are written by individual experts. The bibliography, which comprises the entire third volume, is excellent.

The essay on Hawthorne is a sensible treatment of Hawthorne's work. Williams notes that "in any study of Hawthorne's art, his life story must be regarded as causative"; and he draws the reader's attention to the way in which Hawthorne used his own past for literary purposes. He concludes that "in the Puritan experience, so austere that it still moved men to fear or anger, he [Hawthorne] discovered, with his artist's eyes turned inward, the enduring fabric of art."

125. Winters, Yvor. *Maule's Curse: Seven Studies in the History of American Obscurantism*. Norfolk, Conn.: New Directions, 1938. 240 pp.

In his essay, "Hawthorne and the Problem of Allegory," Winters points to the conflicting views of Puritanism and the consequent tendency toward allegory. New England Puritans involved themselves in a "Manicheistic struggle between Absolute Good and Absolute Evil" which inevitably produced the allegorical sensibility. Winters' general formulations seem sensible, but when he applies them to an individual novel like *The Scarlet Letter*, which he feels is perfect because it is pure allegory, he is not so persuasive. Thus his insistence that Hester represents the repentant sinner, Dimmesdale the half-repentant sinner, and Chillingworth the unrepentant sinner destroys whatever novelistic elements there are in the book and makes it seem like a religious tract.

Winters has little regard for Hawthorne's shorter works—the "sketches and short stories are at best slight performances"—and he feels that after *The Scarlet Letter* Hawthorne declined because he attempted to write novels. In rejecting his American heritage and becoming increasingly influenced by English romanticism, Hawthorne lost control of his material. Winters' ideas are stimulating precisely because they are so aggressively stated, but too often he is interested in judgment rather than interpretation, and he sacrifices the nuances of a text to the central thesis he is pursuing.

126. Wright, Nathalia. "The Language of Art: Hawthorne," *American Novelists in Italy*. Philadelphia: University of Pennsylvania Press, 1965, pp. 138–167.

Miss Wright traces Hawthorne's movements from his appointment in 1853 as American consul at Liverpool and notes that Italy was Hawthorne's favorite foreign country.

Hawthorne traveled "from January to June 1858 in Rome, from June to October in Florence, and from October 1858 to May 1859 in Rome again"; and he drew heavily on what he saw for *The Marble Faun*. Miss Wright offers a perceptive analysis of the novel and concludes that "In Italy Hawthorne found abundant confirmation of his conception of the moral weakness and the limited powers of man. Yet his stay there gave him a more hopeful view of human nature than he ever before entertained. There, as nowhere else, he saw its weaknesses and limitations in perspective: beside a long series of catastrophes survived by the spirit, as recorded in beautiful and enduring works of the imagination."

127. Yates, Norris. "Ritual and Reality: Mask and Dance Motifs in Hawthorne's Fiction," *Philological Quarterly*, XXXIV (October, 1955), 56–70.

"Aesthetically, masking and the dance appealed to Hawthorne because such relatively stiff and formal pageantry furnished the perfect means of objectifying and dramatizing—as in a morality play—one of his favorite themes, irresponsible illusion shattered by the harsh but solid realities of duty and the need for responsibility."

Yates notices the recurrence of these motifs in the minor tales and then examines their presence in *The Blithedale Romance*, where they "become a major element in the unfolding of both narrative and moral," and in *The Marble Faun*. The mask and dance motifs "appealed to Hawthorne because, in the Puritan tradition with which he was so familiar, they stood for collective evil, particularly devil-worship, pagan sensuality, and lack of restraint."

Fanshawe:

128. Bode, Carl. "Hawthorne's *Fanshawe*: The Promise of Greatness," *The New England Quarterly*, XXIII (June, 1950), 235–242.

Bode admits the artificial and histrionic qualities of *Fanshawe*, and he is aware of Hawthorne's "literary and historical derivations." He also notes the "stilted, melodramatic character of much of the writing"; the factitious action; and the simplicity of the volume in general. He feels, nevertheless, that "Hawthorne's greatness is foreshadowed through his superior handling of character. The best in *Fanshawe* lies in its characters, and the most memorable character is Hawthorne himself." Hawthorne permits the characters to change in accordance with circumstances rather than impose a determined future on them. In devoting himself to character at the expense of plot, Hawthorne reveals the future trend of his work.

129. Goldstein, Jesse Sidney. "The Literary Source of Hawthorne's *Fanshawe*," *Modern Language Notes*, LX (January, 1945), 1–8.

Charles Robert Maturin's *Melmouth the Wanderer* provided the plot outline and the major characters of *Fanshawe*. Goldstein traces the many parallels of character and plot. Both stories "concern themselves with the trials of an innocent maiden"; both have a designing villain. In both novels the fathers are merchants who write letters concerning their return home. Hawthorne altered *Fanshawe* in devising a happy ending for Ellen and in dividing "the characteristics and actions of Melmouth between two of his own characters, Butler and Fanshawe."

130. Gross, Robert Eugene. "Hawthorne's First Novel: The Future of a Style," *PMLA*, LXXVII (March, 1963), 60–68.

Gross emphasizes Hawthorne's Gothicism and indicates how it is used in his later fiction. He analyzes *Fanshawe* in terms of its theme, setting, language, and symbolism, concluding that "the balanced and concessive syntax, the abstract and general diction, the alienation theme, the whole arsenal of moralizing devices, the portentous tone, the grotesquery, the wise announcements, the imagic play, and the static plotting which appear in *Fanshawe* in 1828 appear not only in *The Scarlet Letter in* 1850, but also in *The Marble Faun* in 1860."

131. Orians, G. Harrison. "Scott and Hawthorne's *Fanshawe*," *The New England Quarterly*, XI (June, 1938), 388–394.

Orians establishes Hawthorne's debt to Scott, suggesting that when Hawthorne was at college, from 1821 to 1825, Scott was at the height of his power, issuing seven of his Waverley novels and influencing the important American writers. "Scott's influence and example not only directed Hawthorne's attention to historical narratives but, by virtue of the parallels between Scotland, the real subject of Scott's earlier novels, and New England, apparent in both topography and religious atmosphere, led him to turn to Colonial life, local legend, and tradition for his own particular field of effort."

Orians turns his attention to Scott's influence on *Fanshawe*. In his use of character, scene, and method, Hawthorne emulated the Waverley novels. Hawthorne's retrospective mood, his love of accidental meetings, his interest in topography, his fondness for verse epigraphs, lyrical interludes, tavern scenes—these elements recall those of Scott.

The Short Stories:

132. Adams, Richard P. "Hawthorne: The Old Manse Period," *Tulane Studies in English*, VIII (1958), 115–151.

Adams offers an illuminating treatment of that time in Hawthorne's life when he wrote some of his most significant tales. Adams points out the significant themes and ideas that recur in those stories which were finally included in *Mosses from an Old Manse* (1846). Light and darkness "connote the young man's knowledge and his ignorance. Coldness signifies isolation." Heat suggests relatedness, but in various ways. The largest group of stories consists of satirical sketches like "The New Adam and Eve," "The Hall of Fantasy," "The Procession of Life," "The Celestial Railroad," and "Earth's Holocaust." A second group includes stories devoted to the artist and his place in society: "The Birthmark." "The Artist of the Beautiful," "Rappaccini's Daughter" belong with Hawthorne's great early fiction and with *The Scarlet Letter*—it is an allegory of the highest order.

————. "Hawthorne's Provincial Tales," *The New England Quarterly*, XXX (March, 1957), 39–57.

Adams analyzes this collection of stories, which Hawthorne never published in a separate volume; he traces the themes that appear throughout the tales and interprets, perceptively, "Young Goodman Brown," "The Maypole of Merry Mount," "My Kinsman, Major Molineux," and "Roger Malvin's Burial."

Adams finds that the common theme of *The Provincial Tales* "is not basically a question of good versus evil but rather of boyish dependence and carelessness versus manly freedom and responsibility." The transition from one state to the other or failure to do so is dynamic.

133. Askew, Melvin W. "Hawthorne, The Fall and The Psychology of Maturity," *American Literature*, XXXIV (November, 1962), 335–343.

The fall is the central theme in Hawthorne's fiction, even in those works which do not "initiate the matter of Eden Adam," and though his characters "do not fall from God's grace, or into a theologically conceived hell or heaven," they fall into the "worldly, humanistic, and realistic equivalent of those; that is to say, they fall into inhumanity or humanity."

Askew maintains that the characters in Hawthorne's work "fall" into the human condition and not ino any formal religious conception of hell. He analyzes "The Maypole of Merry Mount," "Rappaccini's Daughter," and "The Minister's Black Veil," concluding that "this psychological pattern of Love, Acceptance-responsibility-maturity, and Life, as it figured forth in the myth of the fall in Hawthorne, adds a new dimension to the other readings to which the dense texture of his fiction so readily lends itself."

134. Bell, Millicent. "Hawthorne's 'Fire-Worship': Interpretation and Source," *American Literature*, XXIV (March, 1952), 31–39.

Mrs. Bell observes that Hawthorne saw "fire as an appropriate symbol for God as the Puritans were wont to conceive Him." This essay is an illuminating interpretation of a critically neglected story. "In the modest dissertation on the vanishing fireplace," Mrs. Bell notes, "we see hints of Hawthorne's views of the new style of religious thinking, his skepticism as to their value, and his conviction of the superior moral service performed by the older Christian beliefs." For a refutation of this article see Roy B. Male, Jr., "Criticism of Bell's Hawthorne's 'Fire-Worship': Interpretation and Source," *American Literature*, XXV (March, 1953), 85–87.

135. Boewe, Charles. "Rappaccini's Garden," *American Literature*, XXX (March, 1958), 37–49.

Whenever flowers appear in Hawthorne's work, they have a symbolic meaning. "Beatrice is identified with the gorgeous but deadly purple-blossom shrub which dominates the garden and which Beatrice embraces . . . Both are supremely beautiful: the touch of either is lethal to an ordinary human being." The wickedness in the garden is brought about by Rappaccini's "unholy manipulation of the static forms of God's Creation."

Boewe deals with "Hawthorne's customary way of using flowers in his fiction, his notions about biological propagation, the widespread opinions of his age about hybridization in plants and animals." This essay is an interesting examination of the famous story.

136. Cooke, Alice L. "Some Evidences of Hawthorne's Indebtedness to Swift," *University of Texas Studies in English*, XVIII (July 8, 1938), 140–162.

Miss Cooke traces Swift's influence in "Dr. Heiddeger's Experiment," "The New Adam and Eve," "Earth's Holocaust," "A Select Party," "The Hall of Fantasy," and "The Pygmies."

Hawthorne "understood Swift's dexterity in the use of satire, ridicule, and allegory. He appreciated the fantastic tricks of Swift's imagination. He responded to Swift's simplicity and directness. But he apparently considered that Swift's perspective was all wrong. He felt that humanity, for all its frailties, had something of spiritual nature which acted as a redeeming power."

137. Dauner, Louise. "The 'Case' of Tobias Pearson: Hawthorne and the Ambiguities," *American Literature*, XXI (January, 1950), 464–472.

Miss Dauner sees "The Gentle Boy" as a tale that is more concerned with the spiritual ambiguities of life than with any specific definition of Christianity. She draws interesting parallels between Hawthorne and Melville's work, particularly in regard to "The Gentle Boy" and *Pierre*.

Tobias Pearson of "The Gentle Boy" is a minor figure, "but for whatever it may be worth, the Melvillian ambiguity of his case is firmly drawn and firmly resolved: there is no final lightening of the dark colors, no adjustment for the possibility of alternate choices." Although Tobias, like Pierre, is a good man, he becomes so "enmeshed in a close-linked chain of causes and effects" that he "is a disillusioned, embittered, and defeated man." He acts according to the "simplest Christian ethic," like Pierre, "in an impulse of pure generosity and loving-kindness. And like Pierre, the very pillars of the Christian temple, ironically symbolized here by the persecuting Puritans, shatter about him and crush him in the ruins."

138. Dichmann, Mary E. "Hawthorne's 'Prophetic Pictures,'" *American Literature*, XXIII (May, 1951), 188–202.

Miss Dichmann suggests that an examination of "The Prophetic Pictures" should "illuminate a consideration of Hawthorne's aesthetic theory and of his conception of the artist's position in the social order." The tale contains the central paradox of Hawthorne's attitude toward art: the creative work is "man's most spiritual achievement" but it is also a "dark necessity" which "impels the artist by virtue of his very artistry toward the unpardonable sin, the violation of the human heart." In some fundamental sense Hawthorne could not resolve "the spiritual nature of artistic creation and the evil that may result from it."

139. Durr, Robert Allen. "Hawthorne's Ironic Mode," *The New England Quarterly*, XXX (December, 1957), 486–495.

Durr's essay serves as a modification on the general assumption that "since Hawthorne was 'serious' he could not also be comic and satiric." Durr demonstrates, quite convincingly, that "Hawthorne was most *effectively* serious precisely at those times when he was most deliberately ironic." He analyzes many of the lesser known tales: "P's Correspondence," "Mrs. Bullfrog," "The Ambitious Guest," "The Threefold Destiny," "Howe's Masquerade," "Peter Goldthwaite's Treasure," "The Hollow of the Three Hills," "Egotism; or the Bosom Serpent," and others.

140. Erlich, Gloria Chasson. "Deadly Innocence: Hawthorne's Dark Women," *The New England Quarterly*, XLI (June, 1968), 163–179.

Gloria Erlich believes that "Hawthorne's range and interest are indeed much narrower than is generally thought, that they are, in fact, obsessively narrow." Most of his work is concerned with the Fall of Man, and most of his characters represent Satan, Adam, Eve, and a figure who is generally an onlooker or a commentator. Hawthorne's central question, as illustrated most obviously in *The Scarlet Letter*, is whether it is "possible for a man and a woman to return to the Golden Age when innocent relations between the sexes were possible." Whatever ambiguity is present rests mostly with the style. Underlying Hawthorne's apparent ambiguity is the persistent paradox that woman, the traditional source of comfort, can also be the temptress. The answer to these beautiful and dangerous women—Hester, Zenobia, Miriam—who represent quite simply Eve, is the Virgin, represented by Priscilla and Hilda. The transition from temptress or Eve to Virgin or Mary is often very rapid.

141. Fisher, Marvin. "The Pattern of Conservatism in Johnson's *Rasselas* and Hawthorne's Tales," *Journal of the History of Ideas*, XIX (1958), 173–196.

Fisher considers Hawthorne's comments on Dr. Johnson in his tale *Our Old Home* and compares the two writers, especially in terms of their feeling that "traditional human values" must be preserved.

142. Gross, Seymour L. "Hawthorne's 'My Kinsman, Major Molineux'; History as Moral Adventure," *Nineteenth-Century Fiction*, XII (September, 1957), 97–109.

Gross believes that history gives this story its controlling aspect and provides the proper background for a tale of initiation in which discipline is seen as necessary for survival. He seeks to correct what he believes to be Mrs. Q. D. Leavis' misreading of the tale—she sees the story as almost exclusively an historical allegory—by emphasizing the "moral superstructure which rises out of the historical situation." The tale becomes, in his view, a development of Robin's thematic discovery.

———. "Hawthorne's Revision of 'The Gentle Boy,'" *American Literature*, XXVI (May, 1954), 196–208.

Gross discovers that the revisions tend to be in the direction of establishing a fair balance between the Puritans and the Quakers. In revising, Hawthorne tended to delete material and, when viewed in their totality, these deletions "exhibit how Hawthorne has managed to give his piece a firmer point of view . . . In short, he has clarified the terms of his tragedy." Gross is successful in his emphasis on Hawthorne's conscious artistry. He concludes that "For Hawthorne, more than for any of his contemporaries except for Melville, the existence of an Evil Principle was a reality;

and this tale, ultimately, contemplates the tragedy of an innocent child and a Christian adult caught up by his elemental condition of existence, of which the historical act of persecution is but a grim reflection."

————. "Hawthorne Versus Melville," *Bucknell Review*, XIV (December, 1966), 89–109.

Gross first traces the common problems which confronted Hawthorne and Melville: the lack of "a well-defined novel tradition" and of "a well-defined cultural community"; their tendency to write romances rather than novels because of the influence of Transcendentalism; the difficulties of publishing in nineteenth-century America. In spite of these and other similarities, Hawthorne and Melville ought to be distinguished.

Gross analyzes the differences between *Redburn* and "My Kinsman, Major Molineux," citing Melville's novel as an exercise in "objective horror" and Hawthorne's story "an exploration of the tragic but salutary aspects of experience." He also compares "Young Goodman Brown" and "Benito Cereno," attempting to prove that Hawthorne and Melville have "essentially different casts of mind." Hawthorne accepted the tragic condition whereas Melville constantly questioned it; Hawthorne accepted the order of things whereas Melville "had to know why life should be the way it is."

This essay is an intelligent, traditional examination of the differences between the two writers.

143. Gwynn, Frederick L. "Hawthorne's 'Rappaccini's Daughter,'" *Nineteenth-Century Fiction*, VII (December, 1952), 217–219.

Gwynn reads the tale "as Hawthorne wrote it—from his and Giovanni's point of view." He feels that "the key to the tale is the last agonized sentence spoken by the dying Beatrice to Giovanni: 'Oh, was there not, from the first, more poison in thy nature than in mine?' The answer to this question lies in Hawthorne's own running comments on Giovanni, the very supports of the fable's careful structure." Gwynn believes that "Giovanni Guasconti is a weak male character who fails to resolve Hawthorne's dualism of Head vs. Heart. Dimmesdale and Giovanni have heart, but they do not have enough of it to be mature, admirable men."

144. Heilman, R. B. "Hawthorne's 'The Birthmark,' Science as Religion," *The South Atlantic Quarterly*, XLVIII (October, 1949), 575–583.

Aylmer's attempt to make science into religion causes his own moral confusion and his subsequent breakdown. "The images and the drama together define the spiritual shortcomings of this new revelation." Aylmer is more the tragic hero than the villain: there is a disinterested aspiration in him as well as pride and detachment from reality. Georgianna is "less the innocent victim than the fascinated sharer in magic who conspires in her own doom."

145. Joseph, Brother. "Art and Event in 'Ethan Brand,'" *Nineteenth-Century Fiction*, XV (December, 1960), 249–257.

Brother Joseph relates the tale to its source in *The American Notebooks* (3), providing an "insight into Hawthorne's creative method" and a sound interpretation of the story. "Biographically the characters and incidents of 'Ethan Brand are scattered pieces of valuable metal unsuspectingly capable of forming a beautiful design. Introducing into their midst a magnetic idea—that of the unpardonable sin—Hawthorne attracted these scattered pieces one to another so as to form them into a harmonious whole."

146. Lesser, Simon O. "The Image of the Father: A Reading of 'My Kinsman, Major Molineux' and 'I Want to Know Why,'" *Partisan Review*, XXII (Summer, 1955), 372–380. This essay is included in the author's *Fiction and the Unconscious*. Boston: Beacon Press, 1957.

Lesser offers a psychoanalytical interpretation of the tale, which is provocative; but his reaction against moralistic criticism—literature, he maintains, is not "centrally concerned with moral problems"—is unnecessarily extreme. Lesser concludes that Robin "is destroying an image of paternal authority so that, freed from its restraining influence, he can begin life as an adult."

For a refutation of this position see Roy Harvey Pearce, "Robin Molineux on the Analyst's Couch: A Note on the Limits of Psychoanalytic Criticism," *Criticism*, I (1959), 83–90.

147. Levin, David. "Shadows of Doubt: Specter Evidence in Hawthorne's 'Young Goodman Brown,'" *American Literature*, XXXIV (November, 1962), 344–352.

Levin analyzes the idea of "specter" and shows its relationship to the tale. He insists upon Hawthorne's historical knowledge in creating "Young Goodman Brown": "We must not underestimate his use of historical materials even when he is writing allegory; nor should we let an interest in patterns of image and symbol or an awareness that he repeatedly uses the same types of character obscure the clear literal significance of individual stories."

In his analysis of "Young Goodman Brown," Levin insists upon a literal interpretation of the story. Thus Hawthorne is presenting "a perfectly clear, consistent portrayal of a spectral adventure into evil." The Devil presents evidence to a prospective convert "who is only too willing to be convinced. . . . The story is not about the evil of other people but about Brown's doubt, his discovery of the *possibility* of universal evil."

148. McKeithan, D. M. "Hawthorne's 'Young Goodman Brown': An Interpretation," *Modern Language Notes*, LXVII (February, 1952), 93–96.

McKeithan argues that Goodman Brown's difficulties arise from his faulty judgment. He feels that Brown is not representative of all mankind and that his vision of the world is warped. "This is not the story of the disillusionment that comes to a person when he discovers that many supposedly religious and virtuous people are really sinful: it is, rather, a story of a man whose sin led him to consider all other people sinful. . . . He did not judge them accurately: he misjudged them."

See Paul Miller, "Hawthorne's 'Young Goodman Brown': Cynicism or Meliorism," (151) for a modification of this point of view.

149. McMullen, Joseph T. and Guilds, John C. "The Unpardonable Sin in Hawthorne: A Re-Examination," *Nineteenth-Century Fiction*, XV (December, 1960), 221–237.

The authors attempt a more exact definition of this important theme in Hawthorne's fiction. In Christian theology, the unpardonable sin is generally limited to the sin against the Holy Ghost. Despair is actually the unpardonable sin—despair without penitence; but the individual can return from sin through faith and penitence.

McMullen and Guilds analyze "Ethan Brand," "The Man of Adamant," and *The Scarlet Letter*, concluding that too few scholars "have observed that in his [Hawthorne's] fiction salvation depends upon spiritual achievement rather than any 'semblance of an unspotted life.'"

150. Melville, Herman. "Hawthorne and His Mosses," *The Literary World*, August 17, August 24, 1850. See also *The Works of Herman Melville*, ed. Raymond W. Weaver, Vol. XIII. London: Constable & Co., Ltd., 1924, 123–143. A copy of this essay can be found in *The Shock of Recognition, The Development of Literature in the United States Recorded by the Men Who Made It*, ed. Edmund Wilson. New York: Farrar, Straus and Cudahy, 1943, pp. 187–204.

Melville calls for a national literature in this article and cites Hawthorne as a leading figure in that movement, urging Americans to recognize this genius: "For genius, all over the world, stands hand in hand, and one shock of recognition runs the whole circle round." He praises Hawthorne for the humor displayed in many of his sketches, but he responds deeply to "this great power of blackness" in Hawthorne that "derives its force from its appeal to that Calvinistic sense of Innate Depravity and Original Sin, from whose visitations, in some shape or other, no deeply thinking mind is always and wholly free."

151. Miller, Paul W. "Hawthorne's 'Young Goodman Brown': Cynicism or Meliorism," *Nineteenth-Century Fiction*, XIV (December, 1959), 255–264.

Miller is concerned with the question of whether Young Goodman Brown is meant to typify all of mankind or only one segment of it. He suggests that Hawthorne meant Goodman Brown to represent only a part of mankind. The figures Brown sees in the forest are real witches or pharisees and their pharisaism led them to hypocrisy. Miller believes that in "Young Goodman Brown," Hawthorne "is pleading that what survives of Puritan rigorism in society be sloughed off, and replaced by a striving for virtue starting from the confession of common human weakness."

152. Orians, G. Harrison. "Hawthorne and 'The Maypole of Merry Mount,'" *Modern Language Notes*, LIII (March, 1938), 159–167.

Orians indicates that there are a number of sources for the tale, including *Massachusetts Historical Collections* and Baylies's *Memoir of New Plymouth* (Boston, 1830).

————. "The Source of Hawthorne's 'Roger Malvin's Burial,'" *American Literature*, X (November, 1938), 313–318.

The chief source of the tale was probably The Reverend Thomas Symmen's *Historical Memoirs of the Late Fight at Piggwacket* (1725), which was reproduced in Farmer and Moore's *Collections, Typographical, Historical and Bibliographical* (1822–1824), and available in the Salem Athenaeum before 1828.

————. "The Sources and Themes of Hawthorne's 'The Gentle Boy,'" *The New England Quarterly*, XIV (December, 1941), 664–678.

The chief source was William Sewell's *History of the Quakers*, which Hawthorne had taken from the Salem Athenaeum. Other sources were Hutchinson's *History of Massachusetts* (1764), William Hubbard's *General History of New England* (1815), Neal's *History of New England* (1720), Morton's *New England Memorial* (1669), Morse and Parish's *Compendious History of New England* (1804), and Felt's *Annals of Salem* (1827).

In "The Gentle Boy," Hawthorne is basically concerned with the themes of isolation, prejudice, and bitterness.

153. Poe, Edgar Allan. "Tale Writing: Nathaniel Hawthorne," *Godey's Lady's Book* (November, 1847). See also *Complete Works of Edgar Allan Poe*, ed. James A. Harrison. New York, 1902, 17 volumes, XIII, 141–155. This famous review-essay has been reprinted often. It may be found in *The Shock of Recognition, The Development of Literature in the United States by the Men Who Made It*, ed. Edmund Wilson. New York: Farrar, Straus and Cudahy, 1943, pp. 154–169.

Poe believes that Hawthorne "is not original in any sense" and that he took his tone and subject matter from the German author, Tieck. Poe has the highest regard for Hawthorne, but his attitude toward the New Englander has altered since his earlier essay, published in *Graham's Magazine* in 1842; then he had considered Hawthorne original. In "Tale Writing: Nathaniel Hawthorne," Poe revises his judgment and characterizes Hawthorne as "peculiar." Moreover, Poe disapproves of Hawthorne's tendency toward allegory: "One thing is clear, that if allegory ever establishes a fact, it is by dint of overturning a fiction. . . . Under the best circumstances, it must always interfere with that unity of effect which, to the artist, is worth all the allegory in the world. Its vital injury, however, is rendered to the most vitally important point in fiction—that of earnestness or verisimilitude."

Poe formulates his notion of what a short story ought to be—"in the whole composition there should be no word written, of which the tendency, direct or indirect, is not to the one pre-established design"—and he praises Hawthorne's *Tales* as belonging "to the highest region of Art—an Art subservient to genius of a very lofty order." Nevertheless he warns Hawthorne that "he is too infinitely fond of allegory," and advises him to "mend his pen, get a bottle of visible ink, come out from the Old Manse, cut Mr. Alcott, hang (if possible) the editor of the *Dial*, and throw out of the window to the pigs all his odd numbers of the *North American Review*." Poe's suggestion that Hawthorne break with the transcendentalists was mistaken; Hawthorne, was of course, one of their sharpest critics. His essay, however, is of great importance, particularly in terms of the technique of the short story.

154. Shroeder, John W. "Hawthorne's 'Egotism: or, The Bosom Serpent' and Its Source," *American Literature*, XXI (May, 1959), 150–162.

Shroeder makes interesting parallels between the narrative of Spenser's first book in *The Faerie Queene*, "The Legend of the Knight of the Red Crosse, or of Holinesse," and Hawthorne's "Egotism: or, the Bosom Serpent."

Not only did Hawthorne borrow the image of bosom serpent itself from Spenser; he patterned the whole of Roderick Elliston's tale on Spenser's legend of The Red Crosse Knight. Plot and characters correspond exactly; Roderick Elliston is Spenser's Red Crosse Knight; Rosina parallels Una; George Herkimer, the sculptor, is the equivalent of Prince Arthur; Scipio, Elliston's Negro servant, parallels the dwarf. The theme is also the same: the hero's spiritual progress from jealousy to pride and eventually, after suffering, repentance, and forgiveness, to redemption and the conquest of the field." In working out the many parallels between the two pieces, Shroeder uses five parts: Estrangements, the Deadly Sins, Incarceration, Release, and Reunion. He concludes that "the Spenserian plot, characters, details, and allegorical method of "Egotism" seem to have been altogether private, in fact, and intended for the author's edification alone."

155. Stein, William Bysshe. "The Parable of the Antichrist in 'The Minister's Black Veil,'" *American Literature*, XXVII (November, 1955), 386–392.

The point of the story, Stein argues, is the betrayal of Hooper, a minister who has become an antichrist. He makes a comparison between Paul's second epistle to the Corinthians and the tale, pointing out that the two men assume that "the closeness of the laity to God resides in the nature of the relationship between the people and the minister. But whereas Paul vehemently protests the shortcomings of personal ministration, Hawthorne is noncommittal." Once Hooper puts on the veil, the people are alienated from him and from the word of God he preaches. The veil, Hawthorne strongly suggests, is to be associated with the black veil of the devil.

156. Stibetz, E. "Ironic Unity in Hawthorne's 'The Minister's Black Veil,'" *American Literature*, XXXIV (May, 1962), 182–190.

Stibetz believes that Hooper must be considered wrong, although his sin is conveyed ironically. The overt sin is consciously preached through the veil parable and the sermon and the second sin is unconsciously embodied in the minister's egotistic assumptions and actions. Hooper's monomania forces him to be spiritually alone at the moment of his death.

By relating the tale to the entire body of Hawthorne's work, Stibetz offers an interesting reading of "The Minister's Black Veil." On one level Hawthorne presents "his fundamental belief in man's proneness to hide or rationalize his most private thoughts or guilt . . . On another level, Hawthorne reaffirms his equally constant belief that man is often guilty of pridefully and harmfully exalting one idea, frequently a valid truth in itself, to the state of the absolute."

157. Walsh, Thomas F. Jr. "The Bedeviling of Young Goodman Brown," *Modern Language Quarterly*, XIX (December, 1958), 331–336.

Walsh feels that "the only solution to the problem" of what occurs in the forest "lies in the tale's complex symbolic patterns" and he calls attention to three sets of symbols: "first, Faith, Brown's wife, represents religious faith and faith in mankind; second, Brown's journey into the forest represents an inward journey into the black, despair depths of his soul; third, the devil represents Brown's darker, doubting side, which eventually believes that evil is the nature of mankind." What actually happened in the forest must remain a question; but in the complex symbolic pattern of the tale, Hawthorne creates his vivid meaning.

The Scarlet Letter:

158. Abel, Darrel. "The Devil in Boston," *Philological Quarterly*, XXXII (October, 1953), 366–381.

Abel considers the role of Chillingworth in *The Scarlet Letter* and views him as "a Miltonic Satan" who is similar to "the villain of an historical romance." Chillingworth "embodies concepts of human nature and its moral possibilities which more resemble the Calvinist humanism of the seventeenth century in England than the transcendentalist optimism of nineteenth-century New England." Chillingworth did not fail in the way the modern humanist views failure but "in the sense of the Puritan humanist, to whom human failure is a lapsing from excellence or from the possibility of excellence." Hawthorne did not intend us to view Chillingworth as badness incarnate but rather as goodness perverted. Abel concludes his essay with a suggestive discussion of fate and free will and what he calls *karma*, "the conception that a human being defines his own character continuously and progressively through the tendency of his choices." He feels that this *karma* concept "is most thoroughly illustrated in the character of Chillingworth, who gradually debased his own character by deliberate persistence in a wrong course."

————. "Hawthorne's Dimmesdale: Fugitive from Wrath," *Nineteenth-Century Fiction*, XI (September, 1956), 81–105.

Abel treats moral degeneration and regeneration in Dimmesdale's character as "the main tragic problem" of the novel. The plot of the novel "consists of the struggle between God and the devil for the soul of Arthur Dimmesdale. Through Dimmesdale's character Hawthorne develops his concepts of "sinfulness and regeneration." Abel distinguishes four parts in *The Scarlet Letter*: "(1) that in which organized society is the 'activating agent'; (2) that in which Roger Chillingworth is the activating agent; (3) that in which Hester Prynne is the activating agent; and (4) that in which God is the activating agent and is revealed to have been the ultimate activator in the three earlier parts which had other ostensible agents. In all stages of the action, Arthur Dimmesdale is the character mainly acted upon."

————. "Hawthorne's Hester," *College English*, XIII (March, 1952), 303–309.

Hawthorne is sympathetic toward Hester, but still he maintains the distance necessary for criticism. There is no question that Hester is meant to be a sinner, but critics are misguided when they claim that she is a heroine who elicits Hawthorne's admiration.

————. "The Theme of Isolation in Hawthorne," *Personalist*, XXXII (January, April, 1951), 42–58, 182–190.

In Hawthorne's view, "a person's moral existence depends upon his maintaining a delicate balance between the real and the ideal, self and society."

159. Bonham, Sister Hilda. "Hawthorne's Symbols *Sotto Voce*," *College English*, XX (January, 1959), 184–186.

Sister Bonham examines the relevance of the needlework symbolism in *The Scarlet Letter*. Each reference to Hester's skill at needlework "adds another deft stroke to [Hawthorne's[portrait of a strong-willed, passionate, sensitive, speculative, large-hearted woman, at the same time indicating the severe limits placed on her contacts with the community."

160. Carpenter, Frederic I. "Scarlet A Minus," *College English*, V (January, 1944), 173–180.

Carpenter treats Hester Prynne independently and finds that the imperfection of the novel arises from "Hawthorne's own confusion between his heroine's transcendental morality and mere immorality. Explicitly, he condemned Hester Prynne as immoral; but implicitly, he glorified her as courageously idealistic."

Carpenter writes of the three general views of *The Scarlet Letter*—that of the traditional moralist, the romantic enthusiast, and the transcendental idealist. Carpenter agrees with the latter group, believing that Hester "envisions the transcendental ideal of positive freedom, instead of the romantic ideal of mere escape." His interpretation is limited, however, because he considers Hester alone and thus distorts her role in the romance.

161. Cowley, Malcolm. "Five Acts of *The Scarlet Letter*," in *Twelve Original Essays on Great American Novels*. Edited by Charles Shapiro. Detroit: Wayne State University Press, 1958, pp. 23–44.

The Scarlet Letter is closer in form to stage drama than it is to ordinary novels. In spite of Poe's feeling that a unity of effect cannot be achieved in a novel, Hawthorne succeeds in creating that effect in *The Scarlet Letter*; furthermore, he disregards another standard (held by those critics who admired Shakespeare) by not having any comic relief in his novel. The book has the "unity of effect and the strict economy of means of a perfect tale."

Cowley notes some of the key notebook entries that were later incorporated into the novel and then turns to those technical problems which are not reflected in Hawthorne's journals but which Hawthorne solved brilliantly. They include the social background, which he handled by inventing a few additional characters (Governor Bellingham, the Reverend John Wilson, and Mistress Hibbens) who represent the society in its essential aspects; the presentation of his novel as a moral essay or allegorical picture rather than a chronicle of events—Hawthorne approached his material like a playwright and viewed his characters "almost as if they were appearing on a stage. . . . The fact is that *The Scarlet Letter* can be read, and gains a new dimension from being read, as a Racinian drama of dark necessity."

Cowley divides the book into five acts: Act I, Scene 1 (Chapters I to III) takes place in the marketplace of Boston; Scene 2 (Chapter IV) is in a room in the prison Act II, Scene 1 (Chapters VII and VIII) is in the governor's hall; Scene 2 (Chapter X) is in Chillingworth's laboratory. Act III (Chapter XII) takes place on the scaffold of the pillory. Act IV, Scene 1 (Chapters XIV and XV) is on the seashore, "where Chillingworth is gathering herbs to concoct his medicines"; Scene 2 (Chapters XVI through XIX) is laid in the forest. Act V (Chapters XXI–XXIII) is in the marketplace.

In addition to his kinship with Racine, Hawthorne has "recaptured, for his New England, the essence of Greek tragedy."

162. Doubleday, Neal. "Hawthorne's Hester and Feminism," *PMLA*, LIV (September, 1939), 825–828.

Doubleday sees *The Scarlet Letter* as a novel that is critical of feminism for having obscured the real nature of woman. The portrait of Hester is sympathetic, not satirical. She learns, finally, "that a woman estranged from normal experience in whatever way cannot see her own problems in perspective." Hawthorne felt that here was no abstract solution for a problem complicated by human nature; yet through his picture of Hester, he criticizes the movement of feminism so popular in his time.

163. Eisinger, Chester E. "Pearl and the Puritan Heritage," *College English*, XII (March, 1951), 323–329.

Pearl symbolizes the difference between the law of nature and that of the state: "She is the hypostatization, in miniature, of the Puritan conception of nature and the nature of the state." In this sense she comes to symbolize the natural realm, beyond the possibility of grace. Hawthorne's intention in the novel is "to reclaim Pearl from nature and to restore her to the jurisdiction of God and man. . . . It is through Dimmesdale's expiation that Pearl becomes a human being."

164. Garlitz, Barbara. "Pearl: 1850–1955," *PMLA*, LXXII (September, 1957), 689–699.

Miss Garlitz discusses the various interpretations of Pearl in the criticism of *The Scarlet Letter*. The child has been considered a relief to the gloom in the novel and the relief of innocence; she has been called a "curious elf-child"; she has been characterized as a wild innocent of nature, like Wordsworth's Lucy children. Most contemporary critics consider Pearl amoral, but Miss Garlitz suggests that the girl is the reflection of Hester's passion: "a microcosm of Hester's moral chaos . . . Pearl is a mixture of Hawthorne's sober observation of childhood and of his continuing belief in the sinless child."

165. Gerber, John. "Form and Content in *The Scarlet Letter*," *The New England Quarterly*, XVII (March, 1944), 25–55.

Gerber divides the novel into four parts and points out that the community, Chillingworth, Hester, and Dimmesdale, respectively dominate each other. Form and content are completely integrated in a state of interdependence. Hawthorne has so adjusted form and content "that in the first three parts of the book the activating character serves to multiply sin, intensify isolation, and diminish the hope of reunion. Only in the fourth does he allow the chief character, Dimmesdale, to reverse the process."

See G. Thomas Tanselle, "A Note on the Structure of *The Scarlet Letter*," *Nineteenth-Century Fiction*, XVII (December, 1962), 283–285, for a revision of Gerber's structural approach.

166. Gleckner, Robert. "James's *Madame de Mauves* and Hawthorne's *The Scarlet Letter*," *Modern Language Notes*, LXXIII (December, 1958), 580–586.

Gleckner compares the two books, especially in terms of their similar treatment of the forest: "in both novels the renunciation, the sacrifice is a necessary condition to the preservation of good, of reality, of truthfulness, of the dignity and inviolability of the human soul." In studying the two novels, the reader can discover James's implicit criticism of Hawthorne's allegorical method.

167. Hart, J. E. "*The Scarlet Letter:* One Hundred Years After," *The New England Quarterly,* XXIII (September, 1950), 381–395.

Hart makes numerous comparisons between Hawthorne's character and that of the figures in the novel. Hester's past, for example, functions for her as Hawthorne's did for him. Her scarlet letter had the same therapeutic value that Hawthorne's solitude had for him. "To relate the pattern of Hawthorne's life to the attitude and actions of the characters in the novel is to discover that they represent different sides of his own personality. Through them he explores the necessity of Art as a way of expiating his feeling of guilt towards his Past, as well as the relationship of the isolated individual to the outside world."

Hart's ideas are too tentatively stated to be persuasive.

168. Hoeltje, H. H. "The Writing of *The Scarlet Letter,*" *The New England Quarterly,* XXVII (September, 1954), 326–346.

Hoeltje measures the effect of Hawthorne's dismissal from the Salem Custom House on the novel. Hoeltje tends to sentimentalize Hawthorne's reactions; in spite of his difficulties, "Hawthorne consoled himself with the assurance that everything was for the best." Hawthorne shared his wife's conviction that "Man's accidents are God's purposes."

169. MacLean, Hugh N. "Hawthorne's *Scarlet Letter:* The Dark Problem of This Life," *American Literature,* XXVII (March, 1955), 12–24.

MacLean maintains that "Hawthorne was determined to set forth, not only his 'sense of his own age,' but his interpretation of the ageless 'dark problem of this life'"; and he calls attention to various motifs that run through the book: "death and life, darkness and light, ugliness and beauty." The theme of the book is the contrast between man's weakness and God's power, and it is revealed in Dimmesdale's search for salvation, Chillingworth's manipulation of Dimmesdale, and Pearl's desire to discover a heavenly father.

170. MacShane, Frank. "The House of the Dead: Hawthorne's Custom House and *The Scarlet Letter,*" *The New England Quarterly,* XXXV (March, 1962), 93–101.

MacShane sees many of the same ideas and characters appearing in the novel and the introduction. "The major themes of isolation, guilt, decadence and the sinister power that one person or institution can exercise over another all appear" in "The Custom House." MacShane also makes connections between Hawthorne as a surveyor and Arthur Dimmesdale as a minister. Hawthorne felt that his position involved personal hypocrisy in a manner similar to that of Dimmesdale. From still another point of view, Hawthorne resembled Hester. "As Hester is given the opportunity to reconcile herself with God and to embark on a period of spiritual renewal because Society has judged her a sinner, so Hawthorne is 'saved' by being dismissed from The Custom House. Both Hawthorne and Hester were to make this discovery in isolation when they were thrown on their own resources and no longer dependent on either the strong arm of the Republic or the Puritan Church."

171. O'Donnell, Charles R. "Hawthorne and Dimmesdale: The Search for the Realm of Quiet," *Nineteenth-Century Fiction*, XIV (March, 1960), 317–332.

Hawthorne is concerned in *The Scarlet Letter* with the problem of the artistic consciousness in society, especially as reflected in the characters of Hester and Dimmesdale. The central conflict for Hawthorne is the need "to be a part of the human brotherhood and his inability to participate on the level of common humanity." The tension of *The Scarlet Letter* lies in Hester and Dimmesdale's moral illusion of being torn between isolation and integration." This tension is suggested symbolically by the civilization and wilderness dichotomy in the book.

172. Roper, Gordon. "The Originality of Hawthorne's *The Scarlet Letter*," *Dalhousie Review*, XXX (April, 1950), 62–79.

Roper sees Hawthorne's major novel as an "examination and acceptance of the darker ambiguities of life." Hawthorne was "concerned fundamentally not with the idiosyncrasies of human behavior in any immediate locality at any one time, but with abstractions, the general truths about human behavior." *The Scarlet Letter* is Hawthorne's mature interpretation of sin and its consequences. The three central figures are not meant to be heroine, hero, and villain. They are personifications: "Hester stands for the Heart, Chillingworth The Head, and Dimmesdale the Spirit." Roper ends his essay by underscoring Hawthorne's use of organic form.

In general, this essay is sound; but it assumes too readily that Hawthorne was not dealing with real people in real situations.

173. Sandeen, Ernest. "*The Scarlet Letter* as a Love Story," *PMLA*, LXXVII (September, 1962), 425–435.

Sandeen modifies the usual interpretation of *The Scarlet Letter* "as a story of sins and sinners." He concludes that Hawthorne "has directed the bias of our sympathy toward Hester and Arthur—especially toward Hester, for if Arthur is the fulcrum of the dramatic conflict, Hester is the emphatic center. Of course, our sympathy takes in Arthur too, for Hester's sake if not entirely for his own, and we like him most when he is most the lover."

Sandeen's interpretation is interesting, but, as Leslie Fielder has pointed out in *Love and Death in the American Novel* (70), it is rather difficult to conceive of Dimmesdale as a lover.

174. Sewall, Richard B. "*The Scarlet Letter*," in *The Vision of Tragedy*. New Haven: Yale University Press, 1959, pp. 86–91.

Hawthorne wrote in the true vein of tragedy and "dealt not with doctrinaire injunctions but with actions in their entirety, with special regard . . . for their consequences." The consequences, in Hawthorne's view, are never clear and they involve man "not only externally as a social being but internally, to his very depths."

Sewall juxtaposes Hawthorne with Emerson, to Hawthorne's advantage. Hawthorne possessed, as Henry James once remarked, "'a cat-like faculty of seeing in the dark'; but he never saw through the dark to radiant light. What light his vision reveals is like the fitful sunshine of Hester's and Dimmesdale's meeting in the forest—the tragic opposite of Emerson's triumphant gleaming sun that 'shines also today.'"

175. Walcutt, Charles C. "*The Scarlet Letter* and Its Modern Critics," *Nineteenth-Century Fiction*, VII (March, 1953), 251–264.

This essay lists the various interpretations of *The Scarlet Letter* and estimates their value. Walcutt has discovered five different readings of the novel: 1. The "orthodox Christian" or orthodox Puritan reading which is based on the "idea that sin is permanently warping." 2. The "Fortunate Fall," an interpretation which amplifies upon that of the "orthodox Christian" and which views Dimmesdale and Hester as redeemed. 3. The "romantic reading," which insists that "society is guilty of punishing individuals who have responded to a natural urge." 4. The "transcendental" reading, which is a variant of the "romantic" reading and which maintains that Hester and Dimmesdale, in lacking genuine self-reliance, were "not true to themselves." 5. The "relativist readings" which "concentrate upon the psychological implications of the sense of guilt." Walcutt concludes that "the ultimate source of ambiguity in *The Scarlet Letter* lies in the fact that although Hawthorne firmly believes sin to be permanently warping, he does not in his heart love the Providence which ordains it thus."

176. Ziff, Larzer. "The Ethical Dimensions of 'The Custom House,'" *Modern Language Notes*, LXXIII (May, 1958), 338–344.

Ziff relates Hawthorne's theory of the romance, as stated in "The Custom House" Introduction, and Hawthorne's theory of the good life. Hawthorne felt that he had not achieved enough of a balance between the "actual and the imaginary," that he had dealt with the past too exclusively. Ziff suggests that this is the reason why Hawthorne turned to the immediate world around him.

The House of the Seven Gables:

177. Abel, Darrel. "Hawthorne's House of Tradition," *The South Atlantic Quarterly*, LII (October, 1953), 561–578.

Abel sees the structure of the work in five parts as the development of Hawthorne's attitudes toward tradition. He emphasizes the fact that *The House of the Seven Gables* is a romance rather than a novel, that "it is an allegory of love versus self-love, of human tradition versus personal ambition." The first movement of the book is concerned with the description of the house itself and announces the theme; the second deals with the building of the house; the third focuses upon the House in apparent prosperity, but actually in incipient decay; the fourth movement traces the dilapidation of tradition; and the fifth is the climactic continuation of the fourth. Hawthorne's point in *The House of the Seven Gables* is that "though the individual tries to make life firmly his own, it is not a part of him; he is a part of it."

178. Beebe, Maurice. "The Fall of the House of Pyncheon," *Nineteenth-Century Fiction*, XI (June, 1956), 1–17.

As the title implies, this essay is a comparative study of *The House of the Seven Gables* and Poe's "The Fall of the House of Usher." Beebe suggests that Hawthorne's novel has the organic shape of a spiral curve and that an understanding of Poe's story will clarify Hawthorne's romance—"the romance is unified not only as a static picture, but also as a dramatic narrative." The organic quality of the book is represented by the House itself, which is the central character, the various people representing parts of the whole house. "*The House of the Seven Gables* is a novel in which plot, characters, symbols, theme, setting and even the past–present–future time sequence are fused together in such a way that each element overlaps or is included within the others."

179. Dillingham, William B. "Structure and Theme in *The House of the Seven Gables*," *Nineteenth-Century Fiction*, XIV (June, 1959), 59–70.

Dillingham divides the novel into "a series of antitheses with three particular contrasts dominating the book"—in the first six chapters Hawthorne stresses "the desirability of a democratic way of life over an aristocratic one"; from chapter 7 through chapter 14, he emphasizes "psychological isolation"; and in the last seven chapters he reflects "the main theme by pointing up the dichotomy between appearance and reality." The theme of the book is man's dependence on his fellow man, "the necessity of man's close communion with his fellow beings."

180. Griffith, Clark. "Substance or Shadow: Language and Meaning in *The House of the Seven Gables*," *Modern Philology*, LI (February, 1953), 187–195.

Griffiths concentrates on the chapter dealing with Governor Pyncheon's death and indicates its thematic relevance to the novel. He is particularly interesting in his interpretation of the various symbols—the house and the portrait—that recur throughout the book.

181. Levy, Alfred J. "*The House of the Seven Gables;* The Religion of Love," *Nineteenth-Century Fiction*, XVI (December, 1961), 189–203.

Levy's treatment of *The House of the Seven Gables* is an extension of Maurice Beebe's essay. He contends that "the characters themselves, especially Phoebe, provide the vital structural backbone and account as well for thematic unity." Levy analyzes the characters at some length and suggests that they are the organizing principles of the novel. Since *The House of the Seven Gables* produces no tragic struggle, it has no catharsis; the curse is man-made and can be "successfully purged by enlightened man's efforts." He concludes that *The House of the Seven Gables* "is a book with faith in young people; it is, fundamentally, optimistic."

182. Marks, Alfred H. "Who Killed Judge Pyncheon? The Role of the Imagination in *The House of the Seven Gables*," *PMLA*, LXXI (June, 1956), 355–369.

Judge Pyncheon is a materialist and a Philistine in the book. Marks concentrates on Pyncheon's death and then compares him with Clifford, Hepzibah, Phoebe, and Holgrave, characters of imagination; "in the death of Judge Pyncheon [Hawthorne] seems to bring about the victory of the imagination on its own terms." Hawthorne is struggling, in this novel, with "the impossible problem of saying yes in a negative way." Judge Pyncheon, who is anti-spiritual and opportunistic, is defeated; Clifford Hepzibah, Phoebe, and Holgrave—spiritual, imaginative, and religious—are victorious.

183. Orel, Harold. "The Double Symbol," *American Literature*, XXIII (March, 1951), 1–6.

Orel considers chapter XVIII of *The House of the Seven Gables*, in which Judge Pyncheon sits in a chair as "his two relatives, Hepzibah and Clifford, are wildly fleeing from the house." The double symbol is Hawthorne's use of "light and time," and Orel feels that it "may well provide a clue to Hawthorne's art, insofar as it indicates the general direction pursued by the art . . . Darkness and light co-exist in the medium of time, measurable by mechanical clocks. We may present to others an aspect of light, but if our souls be dark, eventually we are driven in upon ourselves; if not in this world, then in the next . . ."

The Blithedale Romance:

184. Beatty, Lillian. "Typee and Blithedale: Rejected Ideal Communities," *Personalist*, XXXVII (October, 1956), 367–378.

Both Hawthorne and Melville could not fully share a sympathy with any idealized state of society. The reasons for rejecting the "ideal" communities of Typee and Blithedale are threefold: man must not alienate himself from society to achieve the ideal; distrust of any scheme for improvement; and intellect should not be glorified at the expense of the heart. Creatively, both Hawthorne and Melville were able to reject utopianism by treating it satirically.

185. Crews, Frederick C. "A New Reading of *The Blithedale Romance*," *American Literature*, XXIX (May, 1957), 147–170.

This essay offers a provocative interpretation of a novel that, as Irving Howe points out, always seems to be "a better book than it actually is, for its themes would appear so close to our current preoccupations that they need merely be stated in order to arouse interest."

Crews sees Coverdale, the narrator of the novel, as a man torn between the actual and the ideal type of truth. "The point of departure from previous criticism is that whereas Coverdale's limitations as a story teller have hitherto been ascribed to Hawthorne, I ascribe them only to Coverdale. The 'story' that he tells is not in itself the center of attention; it is the act of telling that is important. . . . *Blithedale* belongs to a tradition that includes *Gulliver's Travels* and *Ulysses*—books whose greatness lies in the author's ability to express his deepest judgments through a narrator who is himself a subject of judgment."

Crews points out that Hawthorne's definitions of the Unpardonable Sin is "the separation of the intellect from the heart" and forms the meaning of the book as well as its formal structure. "The Blithedale colony and Coverdale's Blithedale romance are both representative of the ideal," Crews suggests, the former of moral and the latter of aesthetic perfection, both of which demand transcendence in the mundane world.

186. Davidson, Frank. "Towards a Re-evaluation of *The Blithedale Romance*," *New England Quarterly*, XXV (September, 1952), 374–383.

After indicating the various interpretations of the novel, Davidson examines the uses of veil imagery and discovers that the veil symbolizes the theme of *The Blithedale Romance*. Almost everything in the romance "is partially hidden or totally obscured by a veiling medium or mask." The veil appears in many forms: as the Veiled Lady; in the name of Zenobia, which is called "a sort of mask"; and as Coverdale's hermitage. It also is used in other ways: Coverdale tells his story in retrospect; Zenobia has a manner that is like a mask; the members of the Blithedale experiment estrange themselves from the real world; Zenobia promises Coverdale that she will assume "a black in comparison to a silvery sheen prominent throughout the story."

187. Hedges, William L. "Hawthorne's *Blithedale:* The Function of the Narrator," *Nineteenth-Century Fiction*, XIV (March, 1960), 303–316.

This essay is a refutation of Crews's article (185). "Coverdale, Crews contends, is so unreliable that we must suspect him of fabricating whole episodes, like the chapter on Zenobia's legend. And if we are to understand the book we must be prepared to second-guess him at nearly every point. But the key to the mystery apparently exists only in Crews's mind. He provides no clear criteria to enable the reader to determine when he is seeing things clearly and when he is being misled by the narrator." Hedges feels that Coverdale becomes aware of evil in Blithedale and does not find the love that he originally sought.

188. Murray, Peter B. "Mythopoesis in *The Blithedale Romance,*" *PMLA,* LXXV (December, 1960), 591–596.

The point of view of *The Blithedale Romance* is particularly important. Coverdale tells his story imaginatively, using the same perceptions about life as one finds in the Greek season myths. The seasons in the novel are "organically related to the destinies of the characters and their relationships to one another." Murray emphasizes the mythopoetic power of the novel: Westervelt "suggests the demonic and death-bearing aspect of deity"; Hollingsworth represents the Messianic and creative as well as the god of the forge (Vulcan or Hephaestos) "who creates living works of art, artificial human beings whom he enslaves." Coverdale is the figure who shapes these various mythopoetic qualities; he "lifts the veil of man, Nature, and deity, and finds a duality of personality and will in men and gods, and great irony in the manner of Nature's control over humans, who are symbolized both as mortal creatures of earth and, simultaneously, even through the same symbols, as gods."

189. Stanton, Robert. "The Trial of Nature: An Analysis of *The Blithedale Romance,*" *PMLA,* LXXVI (December, 1961), 528–538.

Stanton establishes Hawthorne's use of correspondence between Nature and the human spirit in the romance. In the novel, Hollingsworth makes a disastrous choice between Nature and the spirit; Coverdale, Hollingsworth's countertype, fails to make this choice; Zenobia and Priscilla symbolize Nature and spirit. "*Blithedale* ends with an affirmation—but its affirmation rests upon negation, and its hope rests upon despair."

The Marble Faun:

190. Abel, Darrel. "A Masque of Love and Death," *University of Toronto Quarterly,* XXIII (October, 1953), 9–25.

This is an illuminating examination of *The Marble Faun* in which Abel suggests the theatrical techniques of the book. Abel claims that Hawthorne entertains four answers to the question of evil: aesthetic, naturalistic, fatalistic, Puritan. His conclusion is to be content "in the stoic view that contemplative detachment from the world's vicissitudes is the nearest approach man can make to a moral vision of life."

There are three types of characters in *The Marble Faun:* persons, who represent individual humanity; types, who represent categories of humanity; and symbols, who represent "simplified and intensified embodiments of distinct human traits or complexes of traits." Abel sees Hawthorne's characters as people in a "medieval morality play, each being not primarily a complex, unique, and 'real' person, but an embodiment of a possible human trait." Hawthorne endows his characters "with enough distinctness and accidentality to make them appear possible and actual human beings."

191. Brodtkorb, Paul, Jr. "Art Allegory in *The Marble Faun*," *PMLA*, LXXVII (June, 1962), 254–267.

Brodtkorb explores some of the implications of *The Marble Faun's* "persistent concern with art" and the "gothic plotting of the final chapters in terms of a governing allegory of the life of art." He argues that Hilda maintains her artistic ideals and her chastity, and thus saves the great painters of the past from the decadence of modern Europe. He criticizes the ending of the novel for not developing any one of the possibilities that were logically implicit in the premises of the book.

192. Brown, Merle E. "The Structure of *The Marble Faun*," *American Literature*, XXVIII (November, 1956), 302–313.

Brown suggests that the title of the British publication, *Transformation*, indicates the structure of *The Marble Faun*. Each character moves from a state of innocence to a knowledge of evil and ultimately to some form of reconciliation. Innocence, experience, isolation, pilgrimage, and return define the movement of Miriam, Donatello, Hilda, and Kenyon, and establish the structure of the book.

193. Liebman, Sheldon W. "The Design of *The Marble Faun*," *The New England Quarterly*, XL (March, 1967), 61–78.

Liebman believes that "Hawthorne's design or structure . . . must be delineated before Hawthorne's ethics and metaphysics can be defined and his artistic accomplishment appreciated." He suggests some of the mistakes previous critics have made: their tendency to assume that Hawthorne is speaking through any one character or even through himself and their concentration on a single aspect of the novel. Liebman attempts a broader perspective and examines the book in terms of character, scene, allusion, and metaphor.

Liebman's reading of the novel is sensible. He notes that "the most obvious motif of Hawthorne's *The Marble Faun* is the Fall myth and that within that myth Miriam represents Eve, Donatello Adam. Liebman is aware, however, that the Adamic myth will not wholly define the novel, particularly in regard to Hilda and Kenyon who are set in opposition to Miriam and Donatello. Rejecting Merle Brown's notion (192) that the structure of *The Marble Faun* is based on either a myth motif or an explicit thematic motif, Liebman views the novel in terms of "oppositions between images, idea, and time, and place."

194. Pearce, Roy Harvey. "Hawthorne and the Twilight of Romance," *The Yale Review*, XXXVII (Spring, 1948), 487–506.

Pearce discusses the difficulties Hawthorne underwent in the writing of *The Marble Faun* and the change in his critical theory as he became increasingly interested in the setting of his fiction. The fact that he had substituted a foreign background for the familiar Puritan setting explains the deficiencies of *The Marble Faun*; in Pearce's view, Hawthorne lacked a genuine understanding of his experiences in Italy. In

Hawthorne's best stories "general operative truth [is] located immediately in the symbol, in a character's symbolic situation, growing out of a kind of *milieu* in which the symbol would have real existence."

195. Waples, Dorothy. "Suggestions for Interpreting *The Marble Faun*," *American Literature*, XIII (November, 1941), 224–239.

"Hawthorne is investigating for himself the nature of good and evil." Mrs. Waples makes comparisons with Freud and Thomas Mann (especially his use of "timelessness" and repetition-compulsion). The novel, she concludes, "is at its best, that is to say, most acceptable as to its moral content, where it is most modern; where faun and sceptre are clear in their symbolic opposition, and where in a mysterious timelessness reality the instinct for life and the instinct for death repeat the ancient story of the Fall."

The Later, Unfinished Fiction:

196. Abel, Darrel. "Immortality or Mortality—*Septimius Felton:* Some Possible Sources," *American Literature*, XXVII (January, 1956), 566–570.

Abel studies the influences on *Septimius Felton* in order to "throw light upon the settled preoccupations of Hawthorne and confirm other evidences of what were persistent literary influences upon his work." Abel does not pretend that tracing sources of this novel is of great significance in itself, but he wishes to illustrate those "persistent influences" which operated upon Hawthorne's imagination. In Septimius Felton's "plans for his earthly immortality," Abel finds a parallel with Gulliver in Swift's *Gulliver's Travels*. Septimius Felton's career also parallels that of Saint Simon at a number of points, particularly in regard to social reform. In his meditation on death, Septimius Felton resembles some of the characters of Shakespeare who are also prone to a style that alternates "from self-question to thoughts on the general fate of mankind."

VI. Bibliographical Index

The number in parentheses, at the end of each item, refers to the annotated entry of the same number.

Editions, Other Primary Materials, and Bibliographies:

Blair, Walter. "Hawthorne," *Eight American Authors: A Review of Research and Criticism.* Edited by Floyd Stovall. New York Modern Language Association of America, 1956. **(7)**

Hawthorne, Nathaniel. *The American Notebooks by Nathaniel Hawthorne.* Edited by Randall Stewart. New Haven: Yale University Press, 1932. **(3)**

————. *The Centenary Edition of the Works of Nathaniel Hawthorne.* Edited by William Charvat, Roy Harvey Pearce, and Claude Simpson. Textual editors: Fredson Bowers and Matthew Bruccoli. Columbus: Ohio State University Press, 1962– . **(2)**

————. *The Complete Works of Nathaniel Hawthorne.* With Introductory Notes. 12 volumes. Edited by G. P. Lathrop. Boston: Houghton Mifflin, 1883. **(1)**

————. *The English Notebooks by Nathaniel Hawthorne.* Edited by Randall Stewart. New York: Modern Language Association of America, 1941. **(5)**

————. *Hawthorne as Editor:* Selections from His *Writings in The American Magazine of Useful and Entertaining Knowledge.* Edited by Arlin Turner. Baton Rouge: Louisiana State University Press, 1941. **(6)**

————. *Hawthorne's Dr. Grimshawe's Secret.* Edited by Edward H. Davidson. Cambridge: Harvard University Press, 1954. **(4)**

Jones, Buford. *A Check List of Hawthorne Criticism, 1951–1966,* with a Detailed Index. Hartford: Transcendental Books, 1967. **(7)**

Leary, Lewis, ed. *Articles on American Literature, 1900–1950.* Durham: Duke University Press, 1954. **(8)**

Spiller, Robert E. *et al. The Literary History of the United States.* Bibliography, Volume III, prepared by T. H. Johnson. New York: Macmillan, 1948. Supplement, ed. Richard M. Ludwig. New York: Macmillan, 1959, pp. 61–76. **(9)**

Woodress, James, ed. *American Literary Scholarship*, an annual. Durham: Duke University Press, 1963– . **(7)**

Biographies and Critical Biographies:

Arvin, Newton. *Hawthorne*. Boston: Little, Brown, 1929. **(10)**

————. ed. *The Heart of Hawthorne's Journals*. Boston and New York: Houghton Mifflin Co., 1929. **(10)**

Cantwell, Robert, *Nathaniel Hawthorne: The American Years*. New York: Rinehart & Company, Inc., 1948. **(11)**

Conway, Moncure D. *Life of Nathaniel Hawthorne*. New York: Scribner and Welford, 1890. **(12)**

Hawthorne, Julian. *Hawthorne and His Circle*. New York: Harper & Bros., 1903. **(13)**

————. *Hawthorne and His Wife*. 2 Volumes. Boston: J. R. Osgood, 1884. **(13)**

Hoeltje, Hubert H. *Inward Sky, The Mind and Heart of Hawthorne*. Durham: Duke University Press, 1962. **(14)**

[Jackson], Edward Mather. *Nathaniel Hawthorne, A Modest Man*. New York: Thomas Y. Crowell Company, 1940. **(15)**

James, Henry. *Hawthorne*. London: Macmillan, English Men of Letters, 1879. **(16)**

Lathrop, George Parsons. *A Study of Hawthorne*. Boston: James R. Osgood, 1876. **(17)**

Loggins, Vernon. *The Hawthornes, The Story of Seven Generations of an American Family*. New York: Columbia University Press, 1951. **(18)**

Martin, Terence. *Nathaniel Hawthorne*. New York: Twayne Publishers, Inc., 1965. **(19)**

Morris, Lloyd. *The Rebellious Puritan: Portrait of Mr. Hawthorne*. New York: Harcourt, Brace and Company, 1927. **(20)**

Page, H. A. [pseudonym for Alexander Japp]. *Memoir of Nathaniel Hawthorne*. London: Henry S. King & Co., 1872. **(21)**

Stewart, Randall. "Hawthorne and the Civil War," *Studies in Philology*, XXXIV (January 1947), 91–106. **(22)**

————. "Hawthorne and Politics," *The New England Quarterly*, V (April, 1932). 237–263. **(22)**

————. "Hawthorne in England: The Patriotic Motive in the Notebooks," *The New England Qurtearly*, VIII (March, 1935), 3–13. **(22)**

————. "Hawthorne's Speeches at Civil Banquets," *American Literature*, VII (January, 1936), 415–423. **(22)**

————. *Nathaniel Hawthorne, A Biography*. New Haven: Yale University Press, 1948. **(22)**

————. "Recollections of Hawthorne by his Sister Elizabeth," *American Literature*, XVI (January, 1945), 316–331. **(22)**

Turner, Arlin. "Hawthorne's Literary Borrowings," *PMLA*, LI (June, 1936), 543–562. **(23)**

————. "Hawthorne and Reform," *The New England Quarterly*, XV (September, 1942), 700–714. **(23)**

————. "Hawthorne as Self-Critic," *South Atlantic Quarterly*, XXXVII (April, 1938), 132–138. **(23)**

————. *Nathaniel Hawthorne, An Introduction and Interpretation*. New York: Barnes & Noble, Inc., 1961. **(23)**

Van Doren, Mark. *Nathaniel Hawthorne*. New York: William Sloane, American Men of Letters, 1949. **(24)**

Wagenknecht, Edward. *Nathaniel Hawthorne: Man and Writer*. New York: Oxford University Press, 1961. **(25)**

Whicher, Stephen. "Review of *Nathaniel Hawthorne*, A Biography," *American Literature*, XXI (November, 1949), 354–357. **(22)**

Woodberry, George E. *Nathaniel Hawthorne*. Boston: Houghton Mifflin, American Men of Letters Series, 1902. **(26)**

Criticism:

Abel, Darrel. "The Devil in Boston," *Philological Quarterly*, XXXII (October, 1953), 366–381. **(158)**

————. "Hawthorne's Dimmesdale: Fugitive from Wrath," *Nineteenth-Century Fiction*, XI (September, 1956), 81–105. **(159)**

————. "Hawthorne's Hester," *College English*, XIII (March, 1952), 303–309. **(158)**

————. "Hawthorne's House of Tradition," *The South Atlantic Quarterly*, LII (October, 1953), 561–578. **(177)**

————. "Immortality vs. Mortality—Septimius Felton: Some Possible Sources," *American Literature*, XXVII (January, 1956), 566–570. **(196)**

————. "A Masque of Love and Death," *University of Toronto Quarterly*, XXIII (October, 1953), 9–25. **(190)**

————. "The Theme of Isolation in Hawthorne." *Personalist*, XXXII (January, April, 1951), 42–58, 182–190. **(158)**

Adams, Richard P. "Hawthorne: The Old Manse Period," *Tulane Studies in English*, VIII (1958), 115–151. **(132)**

————. "Hawthorne's Provincial Tales," *The New England Quarterly*, XXX (March, 1957), 39–57. **(125)**

Anderson, D. K., Jr. "Hawthorne's Crowds," *Nineteenth Century-Fiction*, VII (June, 1952), 39–50. **(48)**

Askew, Melvin W. "Hawthorne, the Fall and the Psychology of Maturity," *American Literature*, XXXIV (November, 1962), 335–343. **(133)**

Astrov, Vladmir, "Hawthorne and Dostoevski as Explorers of the Human Conscience," *The New England Quarterly*, XV (June, 1942), 296–319. **(49)**

Baxter, Annette. "Independence or Isolation: Hawthorne and James on the Problem of the Artist," *Nineteenth-Century Fiction*, X (December, 1955), 225–231. **(50)**

Beatty, Lillian. "Typee and Blithedale: Rejected Ideal Communities," *Personalist*, XXXVII (1956), 367–378. **(184)**

Beebe, Maurice. "The Fall of the House of Pyncheon," *Nineteenth-Century Fiction*, XI (June, 1956), 1–17. **(178)**

Bell, Millicent. "Hawthorne's 'Fire-Worship': Interpretation and Source," *American Literature*, XXIV (March, 1952), 31–39. **(134)**

————. *Hawthorne's View of the Artist*. New York: State University of New York, 1962. **(27)**

Bewley, Marius. *The Complex Fate: Hawthorne, Henry James and Some Other American Writers*. London: Chatto and Windus, 1952. **(51)**

————. *The Eccentric Design: Form in the Classic American Novel*. New York: Columbia University Press, 1959. **(51)**

Bier, Jesse. "Hawthorne on the Romance: His Prefaces Related and Examined," *Modern Philology*, LIII (August, 1955), 17–24. **(52)**

Blair, Walter. "Color, Light, and Shadow in Hawthorne's Fiction," *The New England Quarterly*, XV (March, 1942), 74–94. **(53)**

Bode, Carl. "Hawthorne's *Fanshawe*: The Promise of Greatness," *The New England Quarterly*, XXIII (June, 1950), 235–242. **(128)**

Boewe, Charles. "Rappaccini's Garden," *American Literature*, XXX (March, 1958), 37–49. **(135)**

Bonham, Sister Hilda. "Hawthorne's Symbols Sotto Voce," *College English*, XX (January, 1959), 184–186. **(159)**

Bridge, Horatio. *Personal Recollections of Nathaniel Hawthorne*. New York: Harper, & Brothers 1893. **(28)**

Brodtkorb, Paul, Jr. "Art Allegory in *The Marble Faun*," *PMLA*, LXXVII (June, 1962), 254–267. **(191)**

Brown, Merle E. "The Structure of *The Marble Faun*," *American Literature*, XXVIII (November, 1956), 302–313. **(192)**

Brownell, W. C. "Hawthorne," *American Prose Masters*. New York: Scribner's, 1909, pp. 63–130. **(54)**

Buitenhuis, Peter. "Henry James on Hawthorne," *The New England Quarterly*, XXXII (June, 1959), 207–225. **(55)**

Carpenter, Frederic I. "Puritans Preferred Blondes: The Heroines of Melville and Hawthorne," *The New England Quarterly*, IX (June, 1936), 253–272. **(56)**

————. "Scarlet A Minus," *College English*, V (January, 1944), 173–180. **(160)**

Chandler, Elizabeth L. "A Study of the Sources of the Tales and Romances Written by Nathaniel Hawthorne Before 1853," *Smith College Studies in Modern Languages*, VII, No. 4 (1926), 1–64. **(57)**

Charney, Maurice. "Hawthorne and the Gothic Style," *The New England Quarterly*, XXXIV (March, 1961), 36–49. **(58)**

Chase, Richard. *The American Novel and Its Tradition*. Garden City, New York: Doubleday & Co., 1957. **(59)**

Clark, Harry Hayden. "Hawthorne: Tradition *versus* Innovation," in *Patterns of Commitment in American Literature*, ed. Marston LaFrance. Toronto: University of Toronto Press, 1967, 19–37. **(60)**

Cooke, Alice L. "Some Evidence of Hawthorne's Indebtedness to Swift," *University of Texas Studies in English*, XVIII (July, 8, 1938), 140–162. **(136)**

Cowley, Malcolm. "Five Acts of *The Scarlet Letter*," *Twelve Original Essays on Great American Novels*, Edited by Charles Shapiro. Detroit: Wayne State University Press, 1958. **(161)**

————. "Hawthorne in the Looking Glass," *Sewanee Review*, LVI (Autumn, 1948), 545–563. **(61)**

————, ed. *The Portable Hawthorne*. New York: The Viking Press, 1948. **(61)**

Crews, Frederick. "A New Reading of *The Blithedale Romance*," *American Literature*, XXIX (May, 1957), 147–170. **(185)**

————. *The Sins of the Fathers: Hawthorne's Psychological Themes*. New York: Oxford University Press, 1966. **(29)**

Cronin, Morton. "Hawthorne on Romantic Love and the Status of Woman," *PMLA*, LXIX (March, 1954), 89–98. **(62)**

Dauner, Louise. "The 'Case' of Tobias Pearson: Hawthorne and the Ambiguities," *American Literature*, XXI (January, 1950), 464–472. **(137)**

Davidson, Edward. *Hawthorne's Last Phase*. New Haven: Yale University Press, 1949. **(30)**

Davidson, Frank. "Hawthorne's Hive of Honey: a Few Specific Influences of Shakespeare and Milton," *Modern Language Notes*, LXI (January, 1946), 14–21. **(63)**

————. "Thoreau's Contribution to Hawthorne's Mosses," *The New England Quarterly*, XX (December, 1947), 535–542. **(63)**

————. "Toward a Re-evaluation of The Blithedale Romance," *The New England Quarterly*, XXV (September, 1952), 374–383. **(186)**

Dichmann, Mary E. "Hawthorne's 'Prophetic Pictures,'" *American Literature*, XXIII (May, 1951), 188–202. **(138)**

Dillingham, William B. "Structure and Theme in *The House of the Seven Gables*," *Nineteenth Century Fiction*, XIV (June, 1959), 59–70. **(179)**

Donohue, Agnes McNeill. *A Casebook on the Hawthorne Question*. New York: Thomas Y. Crowell Company, 1963. **(64)**

Doubleday, Neal. "Hawthorne's Criticism of New England Life," *College English*, II (April, 1941), 639–653. **(65)**

————. "Hawthorne's Hester and Feminism," *PMLA*, LIV (September, 1939), 825–828. **(162)**

————. "Hawthorne's Inferno," *College English*, I (May, 1940), 658–670. **(65)**

————. "Hawthorne and Literary Nationalism," *American Literature*, XII (January, 1941), 447–453. **(65)**

————. "Hawthorne's Satirical Allegory," *College English*, III (January, 1942), 325–337. **(65)**

Durr, Robert Allen. "Hawthorne's Ironic Mode," *The New England Quarterly*, XXX (December, 1957), 486–495. **(139)**

Erlich, Gloria Chasson. "Deadly Innocence: Hawthorne's Dark Women," *The New England Quarterly*, XLI (June, 1968), 163–179. **(140)**

Eisinger, Chester E. "Hawthorne as Champion of the Middle Way," *The New England Quarterly*, XXVII (March, 1954), 27–52. **(66)**

————. "Pearl and the Puritan Heritage, " *College English*, XII (March, 1951), 323–329. **(165)**

Erskine, John. "Hawthorne," *Cambridge History of American Literature*. Edited by William P. Trent, John Erskine, Stuart P. Sherman, and Carl Van Doren. New York: G. P. Putnam's Sons, II, 16–31. **(67)**

————. "Nathaniel Hawthorne," *Leading American Novelists*. New York: Henry Holt & Company, 1910, 179–275. **(67)**

Fairbanks, Henry G. "Hawthorne Amid the Alien Corn," *College English*, XVII (February, 1956), 263–268. **(31)**

————. "Hawthorne and Confession," *Catholic Historical Review*, XLVII (April, 1957), 38–45. **(31)**

————. *The Lasting Loneliness of Nathaniel Hawthorne, A Study of the Sources of Alienation in Modern Man*. Albany, New York: Maji Books, Inc., 1960. **(31)**

————. "Sin, Free Will, and 'Pessimism' in Hawthorne," *PMLA*, LXXI (December, 1956), 975–989. **(31)**

Faust, Bertha. *Hawthorne's Contemporaneous Reputation: A Study of Literary Opinion in America and England, 1828–1864*. Philadelphia: University of Pennsylvania Press, 1939. **(68)**

Feidelson, Charles, Jr. *Symbolism and American Literature*. Chicago: The University of Chicago Press, 1953. **(69)**

Fick, Leonard. *The Light Beyond: A Study of Hawthorne's Theology*. Westminister, Md.: Newman Press, 1955. **(32)**

Fiedler, Leslie. *Love and Death in the American Novel*. New York: Criterion Books, 1960. **(70)**

Fields, James T. "Hawthorne," *Yesterdays with Authors*. Boston: J. R. Osgood, 1871, pp. 41–124. **(71)**

Fisher, Marvin. "The Pattern of Conservatism in Johnson's *Rasselas* and Hawthorne's Tales," *Journal of the History of Ideas*, XIX (1958), 173–196. **(141)**

Flint, Allen. "Hawthorne and the Slavery Crisis," *The New England Quarterly*, XLI (September, 1968), 393–408. **(72)**

Fogle, Richard Harter. *Hawthorne's Fiction: the Light and the Dark*. Norman: University of Oklahoma Press, 1952. **(33)**

Folsom, James K. *Man's Accidents and God's Purposes: Multiplicity in Hawthorne's Fiction*. New Haven: College and University Press, 1963. **(34)**

Foster, C. H. "Hawthorne's Literary Theory," *PMLA*, LVII (March, 1942), 241–254. **(73)**

Fussell, Edwin. "Hawthorne, James and 'The Common Doom,'" *American Quarterly*, X (Winter, 1958), 438–453. **(74)**

Garlitz, Barbara. "Pearl: 1850–1955," *PMLA*, LXXII (September, 1957), 689–699. **(164)**

Gerber, John. "Form and Content in *The Scarlet Letter*," *The New Engand Quarterly*, XVII (March, 1944), 25–55. **(165)**

Gleckner, Robert. "James's *Madame de Mauves* and Hawthorne's *The Scarlet Letter*," *Modern Language Notes*, LXXIII (December, 1958), 580–586. **(166)**

Goldstein, J. S. "The Literary Source of Hawthorne's *Fanshawe*," *Modern Language Notes*, LX (January, 1945), 1–8. **(129)**

Gorman, Herbert. *Hawthorne, A Study in Solitude*. New York: George H. Doran, Company, 1927. **(35)**

Green, Martin. "The Hawthorne Myth: a protest," *Re-Appraisals: Some Commonsense Readings in American Literature*. New York: W. W. Norton and Co., 61–85. **(75)**

Griffith, Clark. "Substance or Shadow: Language and Meaning in *The House of the Seven Gables*," *Modern Philology*, LI (February, 1953), 187–195. **(180)**

Gross, Robert Eugene. "Hawthorne's First Novel: The Future of a Style," *PMLA*, LXXVIII (March, 1963), 60–68. **(139)**

Gross, Seymour. "Hawthorne's 'My Kinsman, Major Molineux': History as Moral Adventure," *Nineteenth-Century Fiction*, XII (September, 1957), 97–109. **(142)**

—————. "Hawthorne's Revision of 'The Gentle Boy,'" *American Literature*, XXVI (May, 1954), 196–208. **(142)**

—————. "Hawthorne versus Melville," *Bucknell Review*, XIV (December, 1966), 89–109. **(142)**

Gross, Theodore L. "Nathaniel Hawthorne: The Absurdity of Heroism," *The Yale Review*, CVII (Winter, 1968), 182–195. **(76)**

Gwynn, Frederick L. "Hawthorne's 'Rappaccini's Daughter,'" *Nineteenth-Century Fiction*, VII (December, 1952), 217–219. **(143)**

Hall, Lawrence Sargent. *Hawthorne: Critic of Society*. New Haven: Yale University Press, 1944. **(36)**

Hart, J. E. "*The Scarlet Letter:* One Hundred Years Later," *The New England Quarterly*, XXIII (September, 1950), 381–395. **(167)**

Hawthorne, Manning. "Hawthorne and Utopian Socialism," *The New England Quarterly*, XII (December, 1939), 726–730. **(77)**

—————. "Nathaniel Hawthorne at Bowdoin," *The New England Quarterly*, XIII (June, 1940), 246–279. **(77)**

—————. "Parental and Family Influences on Hawthorne," *Essex Institute Historical Collection*, LXXVI (January, 1940), 1–13. **(77)**

Hayford, Harrison. "Hawthorne, Melville, and the Sea," *The New England Quarterly*, XIX (December, 1946), 435–452. **(78)**

Hedges, William L. "Hawthorne's Blithedale: The Function of the Narrator," *Nineteenth-Century Fiction*, XIV (March, 1960), 303–316. **(187)**

Heilman, R. B. "Hawthorne's 'The Birthmark': Science as Religion," *The South Atlantic Quarterly*, XLVIII (October, 1949), 575–583. **(44)**

Hicks, Granville. *The Great Tradition, An Interpretation of American Literature Since the Civil War*. New York: The Macmillan Company, 1933. **(79)**

Hoeltje, H. H. "The Writing of *The Scarlet Letter*," *The New England Quarterly*, XXVII (September, 1954), 326–346. **(168)**

Hoffman, Daniel. *Form and Fable in American Fiction*. New York: Oxford University Press, 1961. **(80)**

Honig, Edwin. *Dark Conceit: The Making of Allegory*. Evanston: Northwestern University Press, 1959. **(81)**

Howard, Leon. "Hawthorne's Fiction," *Nineteenth-Century Fiction*, VII (March, 1953), 237–250. **(33)**

————. *Literature and the American Tradition*. New York: Doubleday & Co., 1960, 114–128. **(82)**

Howe, Irving. "Hawthorne and American Fiction," *American Mercury*, LXVIII (March, 1949), 367–374. **(83)**

————. *Politics and the Novel*. New York: Horizon Press, Inc., 1957, 162–175. **(83)**

Jacobson, Richard J. *Hawthorne's Conception of the Creative Process*. Cambridge: Harvard University Press, 1965. **(37)**

Joseph, Brother. "Art and Event in 'Ethan Brand,'" *Nineteenth-Century Fiction*, XV (December, 1960), 249–257. **(145)**

Kariel, Henry. "Man Limited: Nathaniel Hawthorne's Classicism," *The South Atlantic Quarterly*, LII (October, 1953), 528–542. **(84)**

Kaul, A. N., ed. *Hawthorne, A Collection of Critical Essays*. Englewood Cliffs, N. J.: Prentice Hall, Inc., 1966. **(85)**

————. "Nathaniel Hawthorne: Heir and Critic of the Puritan Tradition," *The American Vision, Actual and Ideal Society in Nineteenth-Century Fiction*. New Haven and London: Yale University Press, 1963, 139–213. **(85)**

Kesselring, M. L. *Hawthorne's Reading, 1828–1850*. New York: Bulletin, New York Public Library, 1949. **(86)**

Kimbrough, Robert. "'The Actual and the Imaginary': Hawthorne's Concept of Art in Theory and Practice," *Transactions of the Wisconsin Academy of Sciences, Arts, and Letters*, L (1961), 277–293. **(87)**

Lang, H. J. "How Ambiguous is Hawthorne?" *Geister Einer Freien Gesellschaft*. Heidelberg: Queele and Meyer, 1962. **(88)**

Laser, Marvin. "'Head,' 'Heart,' and 'Will' in Hawthorne's Psychology," *Nineteenth-Century Fiction*, X (September, 1955), 130–140. **(89)**

Lawrence, D. H. *Studies in Classic American Literature*. New York: T. Seltzer, 1923. **(90)**

Leavis, Q. D. "Hawthorne as a Poet," *Sewanee Review*, LIX (April, June, 1951), 179–205 and LIX (July, September, 1951), 426–458. **(91)**

Leibowitz, Herbert A. "Hawthorne and Spenser: Two Sources," *American Literature*, XXX (January, 1959), 459–466. **(92)**

Lesser, Simon O. "The Image of the Father: A Reading of 'My Kinsman, Major Molineux' and 'I Want to Know Why,'" *Partisan Review*, XXII (Summer, 1955), 372–380. **(146)**

Levin, David. "Shadows of Doubt: Specter Evidence in Hawthorne's 'Young Goodman Brown,'" *American Literature*, XXXIV (November, 1962), 344–352. **(147)**

Levin, Harry. *The Power of Blackness*. New York: Alfred A. Knopf, Inc., 1958. **(93)**

Levy, Alfred J. "*The House of the Seven Gables*: The Religion of Love," *Nineteenth-Century Fiction*, XVI (December, 1961), 189–203. **(181)**

Lewis, R. W. B. "The Return into Time: Hawthorne," *The American Adam: Innocence, Tragedy, and Tradition in the Nineteenth Century*. Chicago: University of Chicago Press, 1955. **(94)**

Liebman, Sheldon, W. "The Design of *The Marble Faun*," *The New England Quarterly*, XL (March, 1967), 61–78. **(193)**

Lohmann, Christoph. "The Burden of the Past in Hawthorne's American Romances," *The South Atlantic Quarterly*, LXVI (Winter, 1967), 92–104. **(92)**

Lueders, E. G. "The Melville-Hawthorne Relationship in *Pierre* and *The Blithedale Romance*," *Western Humanities Review*, IV (August, 1950), 323–334. **(93)**

Lundblad, Jane. *Nathaniel Hawthorne and the European Literary Tradition* (Essays and Studies on American Language and Literature), No. 6; Upsala and Cambridge: Harvard University Press, 1947. **(38)**

————. *Nathaniel Hawthorne and the Tradition of Gothic Romance* (Essays and Studies on American Language and Literature, No. 4; Upsala and Cambridge: Harvard University Press, 1946. **(38)**

McKeithan, D. M. "Hawthorne's 'Young Goodman Brown': An Interpretation," *Modern Language Notes*, LXVII (February, 1952), 93–96. **(148)**

MacLean, Hugh N. "Hawthorne's *Scarlet Letter*: The Dark Problem of This Life," *American Literature*, XXVII (March, 1955), 12–24. **(169)**

McMullen, Joseph T. and Guilds, John C. "The Unpardonable Sin in Hawthorne: A Re-examination," *Nineteenth-Century Fiction*, XV (December, 1960), 221–237. **(149)**

MacShane, Frank. "The House of the Dead: Hawthorne's Custom House and *The Scarlet Letter*," *The New England Quarterly*, XXXV (March, 1962), 93–101. **(170)**

Male, Roy R. "The Dual Aspects of Evil in 'Rappaccini's Daughter,'" *PMLA*, LXIX (March, 1954), 99–109. **(39)**

————. "'From the Innermost Germ,': The Organic Principle in Hawthorne's Fiction," *Journal of English Literary History*, XX (September, 1953), 218–226. **(39)**

————. "Hawthorne and the Concept of Sympathy," *PMLA*, LXVIII (March, 1953), 138–149. **(39)**

————. *Hawthorne's Tragic Vision*, Austin: University of Texas Press, 1957. **(39)**

Marks, Alfred H. "Who Killed Judge Pyncheon? The Role of the Imagination in *The House of the Seven Gables*," *PMLA*, LXXI (June, 1956), 355–369.　　**(182)**

Marx, Leo. *The Machine in the Garden*, Technology and the Pastoral Ideal in America. New York: Oxford University Press, 1964, 1–33, 265–281.　　**(97)**

Matthiessen, F. O. *American Renaissance: Art and Expression in the Age of Emerson and Whitman*. New York: Oxford University Press, 1941, 179–368.　　**(98)**

Maxwell, Desmond E. S. "The Tragic Phase: Melville and Hawthorne," *American Fiction: The Intellectual Background*. New York: Columbia University Press, 1963, 151–191. **(99)**

Melville, Herman. "Hawthorne and His Mosses," *The Literary World*, 1850.　　**(150)**

Miller, James E. "Hawthorne and Melville; The Unpardonable Sin," *PMLA*, LXX (March, 1955), 91–114.　　**(100)**

Miller, Paul W. "Hawthorne's 'Young Goodman Brown': Cynicism or Meliorism," *Nineteenth-Century Fiction*, XIV (December, 1959), 255–264.　　**(151)**

Mills, Barriss. "Hawthorne and Puritanism," *The New England Quarterly*, XXI (March, 1948), 78–102.　　**(101)**

Murray, Peter B. "Mythopoesis in *The Blithedale Romance*," *PMLA*, LXXV (December, 1960), 591–596.　　**(188)**

O'Connor, William Van. "Hawthorne and Faulkner: Some Common Ground," *Virginia Quarterly Review*, XXXIII (Winter, 1957), 105–123.　　**(102)**

O'Donnell, Charles R. "Hawthorne and Dimmesdale: The Search for the Realm of Quiet," *Nineteenth-Century Fiction*, XIV (March, 1960), 317–332.　　**(171)**

Orel, Harold. "The Double Symbol," *American Literature*, XXIII (March, 1951), 1–6. **(183)**

Orians, G. Harrison. "Hawthorne and 'The Maypole of Merry Mount,'" *Modern Language Notes*, LIII (March, 1938), 159–167.　　**(152)**

――――――. "Hawthorne and Puritan Punishments," *College English*, XIII (May, 1952), 424–432.　　**(103)**

――――――. "Scott and Hawthorne's *Fanshawe*," *The New England Quarterly*, XI (June, 1938), 388–394.　　**(131)**

――――――. "The Source of Hawthorne's 'Roger Malvin's Burial,'" *American Literature*, X (November, 1938), 313–318.　　**(152)**

――――――. "The Sources and Themes of Hawthorne's 'The Gentle Boy,'" *The New England Quarterly*, XIV (December, 1941), 664–678.　　**(152)**

Parkes, H. B. "Poe, Hawthorne, Melville: An Essay in Sociological Criticism," *Partisan Review*, 2 (February, 1949), 157–165.　　**(104)**

Parrington, Vernon L. "Nathaniel Hawthorne, Skeptic," *Main Currents in American Thought*. New York: Harcourt, Brace, and Company, 1927.　　**(105)**

Pearce, Roy Harvey, "Hawthorne and the Sense of the Past, or, the Immortality of Major Molineux," *Journal of English Literary History*, XXI (December, 1954), 327–349. **(184)**

Pearce, Roy Harvey, ed. *Hawthorne's Centenary Essays*. Columbus: Ohio State University Press, 1964.　　**(40)**

————. "Hawthorne and the Twilight of Romance," *The Yale Review*, XXXVII (Spring, 1948), 487–506. **(194)**

Pochmann, Henry A. "Nathaniel Hawthorne," *German Culture in America*, Philosophical and Literary Influences. Madison: The University of Wisconsin Press, 1957, pp. 381–389. **(106)**

Poirier, Richard. "Visionary to Voyeur: Hawthorne and James," *A World Elsewhere*, The Place of Style in American Literature. New York: Oxford University Press, 1966, pp. 93–143. **(107)**

Poe, Edgar Allan. "Tale Writing: Nathaniel Hawthorne," *Godey's Lady Book* (November, 1847). **(153)**

Ragan, James. "Hawthorne's Bulky Puritans," *PMLA*, LXXV (September, 1960), 420–423. **(108)**

Rahv, Philip. "The Dark Lady of Salem," *Partisan Review*, VIII (September-October, 1941), 362–381. **(109)**

Randel, William. "Hawthorne, Channing, and Margaret Fuller," *American Literature*, X (January, 1939), 472–476. **(110)**

Reid, Alfred. *The Yellow Ruff and The Scarlet Letter*, A Source of Hawthorne's Novel. Gainesville: University of Florida Press, 1955. **(41)**

Ringe, Donald L. "Hawthorne's Psychology of the Head and Heart," *PMLA*, LXV (March, 1950), 120–132. **(111)**

Rohenberger, Mary. *Hawthorne and the Modern Short Story*. The Hague and Paris: Mouton and Co., 1966. **(112)**

Roper, Gordon. "The Originality of Hawthorne's *The Scarlet Letter*," *Dalhousie Review*, XXX (April, 1950), 62–79. **(172)**

Rourke, Constance. *American Humor: A Study of the National Character*. New York: Harcourt, Brace, and Company, Inc., 1931. **(113)**

Ryskamp, Charles. "The New England Sources of *The Scarlet Letter*," *American Literature*, XXXI (November, 1959), 257–272. **(41)**

Sandeen, Ernest. "*The Scarlet Letter* as a Love Story," *PMLA*, LXXVII (September, 1962), 425–435. **(173)**

Schneider, H. W. *The Puritan Mind*. New York: Henry Holt and Co., 1958, 256–264. **(114)**

Schubert, Leland. *Hawthorne, the Artist: Fine-Art Devices in Fiction*. Chapel Hill: The University of North Carolina Press, 1944. **(42)**

Schwartz, Joseph. "Three Aspects of Hawthorne's Puritanism." *The New England Quarterly*, XXXVI (June, 1963), 192–208. **(115)**

Sewall, Richard B. "*The Scarlet Letter*," in *The Vision of Tragedy*. New Haven: Yale University Press, 1959, pp. 86–91. **(174)**

Shroeder, John W. "Hawthorne's 'Egotism: or, The Bosom Serpent' and Its Source," *American Literature*, XXI (May, 1959), 150–162. **(154)**

————. "'That Inward Sphere': Notes on Hawthorne's Heart Imagery and Symbolism," *PMLA*, LXV (March, 1950), 106–119. **(110)**

Spiller, Robert E. "The Artist in America: Poe, Hawthorne," *The Cycle of American Literature*. New York: The New American Library of World Literature, 1957, pp. 61–76.   **(117)**

Stanton, Robert. "Dramatic Irony in Hawthorne's Romances," *Modern Language Notes*, LXXI (June, 1956), 420–426.   **(118)**

—————. "Hawthorne, Bunyan, and the American Romances," *PMLA*, LXXVI (March, 1956), 155–165.   **(118)**

—————. "The Trial of Nature: An Analysis of *The Blithedale Romance*," *PMLA*, LXXVI (December, 1961), 528–539.   **(189)**

Stein, William Bysshe. *Hawthorne's Faust, A Study of the Devil Archetype*. Gainesville: University of Florida Press, 1953.   **(43)**

—————. "The Parable of the Antichrist in 'The Minister's Black Veil,'" *American Literature*, XXVII (November, 1955), 386–392.   **(155)**

Stibetz, E. "Ironic Unity in Hawthorne's 'The Minister's Black Veil,'" *American Literature*, XXXIV (May, 1962), 182–190.   **(156)**

Stewart, Randall. *American Literature and Christian Doctrine*. Baton Rouge: Louisiana State University Press, 1958, 73–89.   **(119)**

Taylor, J. Golden. *Hawthorne's Ambivalence Toward Puritanism*. Logan, Utah: Utah State University Press, 1965.   **(44)**

Tharpe, Joe. *Nathaniel Hawthorne: Identity and Knowledge*. Carbondale: Southern Illinois Press, 1967.   **(45)**

Trilling, Lionel. "Reality in America," *The Liberal Imagination*. New York: The Macmillan Company, 1948.   **(100)**

Trollope, Anthony. "The Genius of Nathaniel Hawthorne," *North American Review*, CXXIX (September, 1879), 203–222.   **(120)**

Von Abele, Rudolph. *The Death of the Artist: A Study of Hawthorne's Disintegration*, The Hague: Martinus Nijhoff, 1955.   **(46)**

Waggoner, Hyatt. *Hawthorne, a Critical Study*. Cambridge: Harvard University Press, 1955.   **(47)**

—————. *Nathaniel Hawthorne*. Minneapolis: University of Minnesota Press, 1962 (University of Minnesota Pamphlets on America Writers, No. 23).   **(47)**

Walcutt, Charles C. "*The Scarlet Letter* and Its Modern Critics," *Nineteenth-Century Fiction*, VII (March, 1953), 251–264.   **(175)**

Walsh, Thomas F., Jr. "The Bedeviling of Young Goodman Brown," *Modern Language Quarterly*, XIX (December, 1958), 331–336.   **(157)**

Waples, Dorothy. "Suggestions for Interpreting *The Marble Faun*," *American Literature*, XIII (November, 1941), 224–239.   **(188)**

Warren, Austin. *Rage for Order*. Chicago: University of Chicago Press, 1948, pp. 84–103.   **(121)**

Wegelin, Christof. "Europe in Hawthorne's Fiction," *Journal of English Literary History*, XIV (September, 1947), 219–245.   **(122)**

Whicher, Stephen. "Review of *Nathaniel Hawthorne: A Biography*," *American Literature*, XXI (November, 1949), 354–357. **(22)**

Whipple, Edwin P. "Hawthorne," *Character and Characteristic Men*. Boston: Houghton Mifflin, 1866, pp. 218–242. **(123)**

Williams, Stanley. "Nathaniel Hawthorne," *The Literary History of the United States*. Volume 1. New York: The Macmillan Co., 1948. **(124)**

Winters, Yvor. *Maule's Curse: Seven Studies in the History of American Obscurantism*. Norfolk, Conn.: New Directions, 1938. **(125)**

Wright, Nathalia. "The Language of Art: Hawthorne," *American Novelists in Italy*. Philadelphia: University of Pennsylvania Press, 1965, pp. 138–167. **(126)**

Yates, Norris. "Ritual and Reality: Mask and Dance Motifs in Hawthorne's Fiction," *Philological Quarterly*, XXXIV (October, 1955), 56–70. **(127)**

Young, Philip. "Hawthorne and 100 Years: A Report from the Academy," *Kenyon Review*, XXVII (Spring, 1965), 215–232. **(40)**

Ziff, Larzer. "The Ethical Dimensions of 'The Custom House,'" *Modern Language Notes*, LXXIII (May, 1958), 338–344. **(176)**

Herman
Melville

by Theodore L. Gross

CONTENTS •• *Herman Melville*

I.   Introduction

THE ECLIPSE OF Herman Melville's reputation constitutes, in Newton Arvin's words, "the heaviest count in our literary annals against the American mind." Although Melville was recognized during his lifetime, he was generally known as the author of *Typee* and *Omoo*; his later, more complex work— *Mardi*, *Moby-Dick*, *Pierre*, and *The Confidence Man*—was not well-received and, as a consequence, he ceased to write for a public audience. Melville's failure to attract sympathetic and sophisticated readers, his growing resentment that his best work was unappreciated, and his retirement from professional authorship are a dramatic indictment of literary values in nineteenth-century America. The growth of his recognition in the twentieth century has been a well-deserved example of cultural compensation and mirrors, in turn, the major direction of modern scholarship and criticism.

In 1921 Raymond Weaver published *Herman Melville: Mariner and Mystic*, the first full-length biography of Melville. Weaver had been encouraged by Carl Van Doren to write a centennial essay on Melville for the *Nation*, and in the process of doing research Weaver discovered that there were "no 'official' biographies at all." He also learned that "Melville had started off well enough, but went wrong somehow—living to an incredible forty years of sedulous obscurity."[1] Weaver investigated Melville's manuscripts, correspondence, and business papers, and published a biography that contained important source material for subsequent scholars. As a pioneering biography, Weaver's study naturally suffered from certain limitations. It concentrated on Melville's early life and work and devoted only a small section to the years from 1857–1891; it did not include or reflect the important correspondence between Melville and the editor Evert Duyckinck; and it made the biographical fallacy of assuming that much of Melville's fiction was autobiographical. Despite Weaver's rather romanticized version of Melville's life

---

[1] An explanatory note to Carl Van Doren's letter, July 1, 1919. Hershel Parker, in his edition of *The Recognition of Herman Melville: Selected Criticism Since 1846* (36) observes that "published accounts have not revealed the extent to which Van Doren himself was responsible for the [Melville] revival."

and literature, _Herman Melville: Mariner and Mystic_ established Melville as a major American author and attracted the interest of many scholars and critics. In 1924 Weaver performed an equally important service by editing all of Melville's known works, including the first published version of _Billy Budd,_ for Constable and Company of London. Although incomplete, this is still the only collected edition of Melville's work.[2]

Melville's recognition in the 1920's was based almost exclusively on the renewed interest in _Moby-Dick._ Two other biographies—by John Freeman in 1926 and Lewis Mumford in 1929—reproduced Weaver's factual errors and continued to neglect Melville's later career. Whereas Weaver had drawn two chapters of "history" from _Redburn,_ Freeman now assumed that "Wellingborough [Redburn] is Herman Melville" and that the novel is the story of Melville's sea journey to Liverpool in 1837. Mumford described Melville's youth as though it were a novel, concluding that _Redburn_ is "autobiography, with only the faintest disguises"; nevertheless he succeeded in making Melville more available to readers, and he began to consider works other than _Moby-Dick._

Melville's reputation did not substantially change in the early 1930's, although many critics analyzed his work from a popular and superficial point of view. Ludwig Lewisohn felt that "the recent reestimate of Melville" was exaggerated, and he expressed the Freudian notion that Melville's escape to the sea at the age of seventeen was a flight from a "cold and handsome mother" on whom he had an "overpowering fixation"; other critics felt that the Melville renaissance was only ephemeral, and they relegated him to a position as a minor American writer. Almost no new information appeared, and Melville's life and work, whenever they were represented in anthologies, were distorted. In 1938, however, Willard Thorp published his seminal _Herman Melville: Representative Selections,_ and in 1939 Charles Anderson brought out _Melville in the South Seas;_ these two works, more than any others, established the beginning of the genuine Melville revival.

Thorp wrote a long introduction to his anthology in which he traced, with the scrupulousness of modern scholarship, the basic experiences of Melville's life and the major aspects of his thought. The Melville who emerges is a more balanced figure than the brooding and tormented author of previous critics, a major nineteenth-century American writer whose entire literary achievement is significant. One year later Charles Anderson's _Melville in the South Seas_ distinguishes between the autobiographical elements and the purely imaginative adventures in Melville's novels of the South Seas. By making this distinction, Anderson showed how self-conscious Melville was in the use of his experiences and how imaginative he proved to be as an artist. Other scholars followed Anderson's direction: William Gilman, in _Melville's Early Life and Redburn_ (1951) separated fact from fiction in Melville's life from 1819 to 1841; Howard P. Vincent, in _The Trying Out of Moby Dick_ (1949)

---

[2] See entries 2 and 3 for information about more recent editions.

and Merrell R. Davis, in *Mardi: A Chartless Voyage* (1952) treated *Moby-Dick* and *Mardi* in a similar fashion, indicating the degree to which Melville struggled to create meaningful works of art.

During the period from 1940 to 1970 scholars concerned themselves with all phases of Melville's work: his sources; his mythology; his political and social views; his linguistic techniques; and his tragic vision. In addition to the recognition accorded his early writing and *Moby-Dick*, individual critics have made high estimates of *Pierre, The Piazza Tales,* and *The Confidence Man.* Melville's use of myth and symbolism, of satire and irony, of fantasy and dream, have appealed to the modern imagination; his relentless uncertainty about eschatalogical problems commands our ambiguous and doubting mind; his response to natural and primitive forces, his sympathy for human limitations, his scorn of cant and hypocrisy, his recognition of and attempt to understand the sources of evil in an age when philosophical thinkers shun the problem—all these attitudes, as expressed by a genuinely honest and open intelligence, have persuaded us that Melville's vision of the world is essentially ours. Of all the nineteenth-century American authors, Melville has seemed most pertinent to the age of analysis in which modern man lives. A penetrating critic of his time, Melville spans the century and reminds the contemporary American of those deep and persistent conflicts at the source of his being. "I love people who *dive*," Melville wrote in admiration of Emerson; and in this complex and compelling author, who insisted that he stood for the heart, we discover a writer who had the courage and the talent to explore, as he wrote in *Moby-Dick*, "the horrors of the half-known life," the many ambiguities of our common and often unseen human nature.

II. Chronology

Herman Melville's maternal ancestors, the Gansevoorts, settled in Albany, New York, in the seventeenth century. They were master-brewers and soon established themselves as landed gentry. Melville's grandfather was General Peter Gansevoort, a hero of the American Revolution and a model for the grandfather in *Pierre*; his mother, Maria, married Allan Melville several years before the novelist's birth. Allan Melville's ancestry was almost as impressive as his wife's, for the relatives had been important merchants in Boston. But by the time of Melville's birth, his father, who had been an affluent importer, was experiencing severe financial strain because of the depression that followed the war of 1812.

1819　Herman Melville was born on August 1 in New York City, the third child of Allan and Maria Gansevoort Melville.

1826–1830　Melville attended New York Male High School.

1830　After his importing business failed, Allan Melville took his family of eight children to Albany, New York.

1832　Allan Melville died, and Herman was compelled to leave the Albany Academy which he had attended for two years. He worked in a bank and on his uncle's farm, and he helped in his brother Gansevoort's fur factory. When his brother's business failed, Herman taught in elementary school.

1838　The Melvilles moved to Lansingburgh, New York, and Herman studied surveying at the Lansingburgh Academy.

1839　"Fragments From a Writing Desk" appeared on May 4 and 18 in the *Democratic Press and Lansingburgh Advertiser*. Melville's uncle Gansevoort arranged his employment on the *St. Lawrence*, a cargo ship sailing for Liverpool. Herman shipped out on June 5 and returned on October 1. In the winter he taught school at Greenbush, New York.

1841　Melville sailed from New Bedford on the whaling ship *Acushnet* on January 3, and traveled around Cape Horn, to the Galapagos Islands, the Marquesas, and other islands. On July 9, 1842, he jumped ship with Richard T. Greene at Nuka Hiva in the Marquesas Islands. He spent a month in the Taipi valley and on August 9 joined the Australian whaling ship, the *Lucy Ann*. He was kept in confinement in Tahiti for a short time and then went on a brief whaling trip with the *Charles and Henry*, arriving in Honolulu. On August 17, 1844, he sailed aboard the frigate *United States* and came home in October. On October 14, he was mustered out of the Navy.

1846   *Typee*, which was based on his experiences in the Marquesas, appeared. His brother Gansevoort died on May 12.

1847   *Omoo*, which used his adventures in Tahiti, was published. Melville married Elizabeth Shaw, daughter of the Chief Justice of Massachusetts, on August 4, and settled in at 103 Fourth Avenue in New York.

1849   Melville's son Malcolm was born on February 16. *Mardi* and *Redburn* published. Melville wrote *White Jacket* during the summer, and on October 11, he traveled to Europe to secure better terms for the novel.

1850   *White Jacket* published. Melville moved to "Arrowhead," a home near Pittsfield, Massachusetts, and became friendly with Hawthorne, who lived in Lenox. His review of *Mosses from an Old Manse* appeared in the *Literary World*.

1851   *Moby-Dick* published in London on October 18, 1851, and in New York four weeks later. Melville's son Stanwix born on October 22.

1852   *Pierre; or, the Ambiguities* published. The novel was a commercial failure, and his family encouraged him to change his occupation. Melville, however, became even more of a professional author and began to write the short stories—"Bartleby, the Scrivener," "Cock-a-Doodle-Doo!," and others—which were eventually included in *The Piazza Tales*.

1853   Melville's daughter Elizabeth born on May 22. His books were destroyed in the Harper and Brothers fire of December 10.

1855   *Israel Potter*, the historical novel he had planned in 1849, was published serially in *Putnam's* magazine and in book form in the spring. Melville's daughter Frances was born on March 2.

1856   *The Piazza Tales* appeared. Melville wrote *The Confidence Man* in the winter of 1855–56. His health declined, and after finishing *The Confidence Man*, his father-in-law financed a trip to the Holy Land. Melville left on October 11 and returned on May 20, 1857. He then lectured in various cities.

1857   *The Confidence Man* published.

1863   Melville sold his property in Pittsfield and moved to New York City. He wrote poems about the Civil War, which were eventually collected and published as *Battle-Pieces and Aspects of the War*.

1866   *Battle-Pieces and Aspects of the War* published. Melville became a district inspector of Customs in New York on December 6 and held the position for almost twenty years. During this period he wrote only poetry.

1867   Melville's son Malcolm was killed accidentally by his own gun on September 11.

1876   Melville published *Clarel: A Poem and Pilgrimage in the Holy Land*, a long narrative poem whose publication was subsidized by his uncle, Peter Gansevoort.

1886   Melville's son Stanwix died.

1888   Melville published *John Marr and Other Sailors* privately in twenty-five copies. From 1888 until April, 1891, he worked on Billy Budd, Foretopman.

1891   *Timoleon* published privately. Melville died at New York on September 28.

1924   *Billy Budd, Foretopman* first published.

III. Editions, Other Primary Materials, and Bibliographies

Editions:

1. *Complete Works of Herman Melville.* Howard P. Vincent, general editor. Chicago and New York: Hendricks House, 1947– .

The individual volumes that have thus far been published, varying in quality, include *Collected Poems* (edited by Howard P. Vincent, 1947), *Piazza Tales* (edited by Egbert S. Oliver, 1948), *Pierre, or, the Ambiguities* (edited by Henry A. Murray, 1949), *Moby-Dick, or, the Whale* (edited by Luther S. Mansfield and Howard P. Vincent, 1952), *The Confidence Man* (edited by Elizabeth S. Foster), and *Clarel* (edited by Walter E. Bezanson, 1960). These volumes have been brought out in trade, textbook, and subscription editions, the latter fully annotated.

    The Collected Poems is marred by errors; *Piazza Tales* is an accurate text of Melville's stories; *Pierre, or the Ambiguities* contains a ninety-page introduction from the psychoanalytic point of view; *Moby-Dick* is a reliable text, although it will be superseded by the edition being prepared by Harrison Hayford and Hershel Parker (4); *The Confidence Man* contains an introduction which is the best single treatment of the novel.

2. *The Works of Herman Melville.* Standard Edition. 16 volumes. London: Constable and Company, 1922–1924.

This is the only edition of Melville's work. The last four volumes were published as supplements in 1924: XIII, *Billy Budd and Other Prose Pieces*; XIV, XV, *Clarel*; XVI. *Poems* (*Battle-Pieces, John Marr and Other Sailors, Timoleon, and Miscellaneous Poems*).

3. *The Writings of Herman Melville, The Northwestern-Newberry Edition.* Evanston, Illinois: Northwestern University Press. Edited by Harrison Hayford, Hershel Parker, and G. Thomas Tanselle, 1968– .

This will be the definitive edition of Melville's works. The following volumes have been published: I. *Typee: A Peep at Polynesian Life*, with an Historical Note by

Leon Howard, 1968; II. *Omoo*, A Narrative of Adventures in the South Seas, with an Historical Note by Gordon Roper, 1968; IV. *Redburn*, with an Historical Note by Hershel Parker, 1968.

These are three of fifteen volumes planned. *Mardi* (Volume III) is due to appear in 1970. The editorial matter has been placed at the end of the text.

4. *Moby-Dick*. Edited by Harrison Hayford and Hershel Parker. New York: W. W. Norton and Co., Inc., 1967.

This volume, although designed as a textbook, is the best edition of *Moby-Dick* available and will form the basis for the edition in *The Writings of Herman Melville* (3).

The editors take into account the fact that Melville must have corrected the American proofs from which the English edition was printed; therefore, some readings in the English edition have authority. The annotation of the volume is not excessive. Maps, a glossary of nautical terms, a pictorial account of "whaling and whalecraft" by John B. Putnam, and eight contemporary engravings are included. Letters, reviews, and relevant criticism are added in a supplement of 200 pages.

Other Primary Materials:

5. *Journal of a Visit to London and the Continent by Herman Melville, 1849–1850.* Edited by Eleanor Melville Metcalf. Cambridge: Harvard University Press, 1948, 189 pp.

"The complete text of Melville's *Journal of 1849* appears here for the first time. The Journal was a private record that was never intended for publication, but what its author never purposed, its humanity claims for it now."

Mrs. Metcalf, Melville's granddaughter, states that "the immediate purpose of this trip was to find a publisher for *White Jacket*, perhaps necessary since the comparative unpopularity of *Mardi*, and the death of his brother, Gansevoort, who had marketed *Typee* for him in London."

The text, which is reliable, has little more than 20,000 words but is amplified by Mrs. Metcalf's full and illuminating notes.

6. *Melville's Journal of a Visit to Europe and the Levant*, October 11, 1856–May 6, 1857. Edited by Howard C. Horsford. Princeton: Princeton University Press, 1955, 299 pp.

Horsford's volume is a revised version of Raymond Weaver's edition of Herman Melville's *Journal Up the Straits* (1935). It is the authoritative and standard work and reveals what Melville confided in his private notebooks on his journey to Europe and the Levant in 1856–1857. There is an informative introduction with biographical background and commentary on Melville's state of mind, the travel logs as literary notebooks, and the manuscripts themselves.

See William Gilman's informative review of the edition in *American Literature*, XXVIII (March, 1956), 82–93, Horsford's rebuttal, and Gilman's rejoinder in *American Literature*, XXVIII (January, 1957), 520–523.

7. *The Letters of Herman Melville.* Edited by Merrell R. Davis and William H. Gilman. New Haven: Yale University Press, 1960, 398 pp.

This volume contains 271 letters, 15 of which are fragments and two others reconstructions of fragmentary drafts. The editors have arranged their material so that they present "only the characteristics within Melville's intention that seem important to the reading and understanding of the letters, reserving all the particular idiosyncrasies . . . for the textual notes."

Fifty-five letters are published here in full for the first time, 42 of which were previously unpublished, but few of them are of importance. The remaining 174 letters were published elsewhere.

8. *Melville's Billy Budd.* Edited by F. Barron Freeman. Cambridge: Harvard University Press, 1948, 381 pp.

Freeman gives the history of the *Billy Budd* manuscripts and adds to *Billy Budd, Foretopman, Billy Budd, Sailor,* a 12,000-word tale. In his 126-page introduction, Freeman illuminates the latter part of Melville's intellectual life and denies "the conscious of unconscious sexual symbolism" of the book.

This was the first attempt to establish a "definitive" text. It contains many errors, however, and Harvard University Press engaged an editor, Miss Elizabeth Treeman, to correct the manuscript. The book was reissued in June, 1953, with Miss Treeman's *Corrigenda.*

9. *Billy Budd, Sailor,* by Herman Melville: Reading Text and Genetic Text. Edited by Harrison Hayford and Merton M. Sealts, Jr., Chicago: The University of Chicago Press, 1962. 431 pp.

This is the definitive edition of *Billy Budd.* In the "Introduction," the authors concern themselves with "Growth of the Manuscript," "History of the Text," and "Perspectives for Criticism." The manuscript, they suggest, was incomplete when Melville died. The novel began with a short prose note to the ballad "Billy in the Darbies" and not with the *Somers* affair, as many scholars have assumed; indeed, the *Somers* incident is only a "cogent analogue" to the book. The editors present chronologies of the various drafts of the novel; indicate that the *Indomitable* should be called the *Bellipotent*; and exclude the Preface from the volume.

The changes in the reading text do not involve any major changes. The genetic text is entirely valuable, however, for it demonstrates Melville's craftsmanship in developing his story.

Bibliographies:

> **10.** Leary, Lewis, ed. *Articles on American Literature, 1900–1950*. Durham: Duke University Press, 1954. 337 pp.

This volume, not annotated, offers a listing of all important articles published between 1900–1950.

> **11.** Spiller, Robert E. et al. *The Literary History of the United States*. Bibliography, Volume III, prepared by T. H. Johnson. New York: The Macmillan Co., 1948, pp. 647–654. Supplement, ed. Richard M. Ludwig. New York: The Macmillan Co., 1959.

These bibliographies offer a good survey of the important studies on Melville.

> **12.** Williams, Stanley T. "Melville," *Eight American Authors: A Review of Research and Criticism*. Edited by Floyd Stovall. New York: The Modern Language Association of America, 1956, pp. 206–270. Reprinted by W. W. Norton, 1963, with a Bibliographical supplement by J. Chesley Mathews, pp. 438–445.

This essay is a thorough estimate of Melville scholarship, leavened by Williams' wit and common sense.

This valuable bibliography, briefly annotated, should be supplemented by the annual bibliographies which appear in *Publications of the Modern Language Association of America* and in *American Literary Scholarship*, an annual, edited by James Woodress. Durham: Duke University Press, 1963– . The student should also consult the *Annual Melville Bibliography*, compiled by S. C. Sherman, J. H. Birss, and Gordon Roper, 1951– .

IV. Biographies and Critical Biographies

13. Anderson, Charles Roberts. *Melville in the South Seas.* New York: Columbia University Press, 1939. 522 pp.

This seminal work was the first full account of Melville's travels between 1841–1844. In distinguishing between the autobiographical facts of Melville's fiction and those which were of Melville's own invention, *Melville in the South Seas* is an important corrective to the biographies by Weaver (45), Freeman (24), and Mumford (35). Weaver tends to treat Melville's experiences on the sea too superficially and Mumford presents them too romantically. Anderson's work is the definitive study of Melville's use of his experiences in the South Seas.

"*Typee, Omoo, White-Jacket,* and *Moby-Dick* (as a romance of the sea rather than as a 'hideous and intolerable allegory') have been all along his most popular books; and, as literature, they are beyond question his best. It is with these, and with *Mardi* and *The Piazza Tales* insofar as they relate to the South Seas, that the present study is concerned—an analysis of the books and a record of the experiences out of which they were drawn.... his four-year residence in the South Seas is the most significant part of his life for the literary biographer, for it furnished the experiences which make up the great body of his published work."

Anderson's portrait of the early Melville is that of a balanced and buoyant man who shipped out on the *Acushnet* because of an adventurous desire to see exotic lands. "The figure of Herman Melville that emerges from the ensuing pages is a simpler and more convincing one than the conventional dramatization. His South Sea experiences, stripped of their romantic trappings, are still bright with high-hearted adventure. The books that embody them are here set forth less as masterpieces of creative imagination than as deliberately manufactured travel records—on the whole joyous—partly borrowed from the writings of other voyagers, partly fictionized autobiography, embellished and printed for the sake of propaganda. And the romantic young character who thus discovered the South Seas for literature apparently found authorship a delightful, stimulating, and reasonably profitable career, at least during the first few years. Such was Herman Melville at the height of his early popularity. The portrait contains slight touch of foreboding gloom or impending tragedy, small hint of the "mystic" or the philosopher, no trace of the beard which later muffled the lamentations of America's mid-Victorian Jeremiah."

See also Anderson's "Contemporary American Opinions of *Typee* and *Omoo*," *American Literature*, XI (March, 1939), 23–38. Anderson notes that the contemporary reception of *Typee* and *Omoo* was more favorable in England than in the United States, "only one out of fifteen [reviews] being actually unfavorable. . . . America was proud of Herman Melville; England enjoyed him."

14. Arvin, Newton. *Herman Melville*. New York: William Sloane Associates, Inc., 1950; reprinted New York: Viking Compass Books, 1957, 312 pp.

This study, which won the National Book Award as the most distinguished non-fiction book of 1950, is one of the best introductions to Melville's work. As in his examination of Hawthorne, Arvin explores the psychological behavior of Melville's family and its effect on the developing novelist. From the Melvilles the author inherited wildness; from the Gansevoorts stolidity. The boy idolized his merchant father, Allan, and when his father's business failed in 1830, Melville's security—as well as that of his family—was destroyed: "The wonderful security, material, social, emotional, of his infancy and childhood had collapsed abruptly, and what was now in store for him, as for his family, was a chronic insecurity: anxiety, renewed hopes, humiliation, the beginnings of restoration, and then repeated disasters and repeated falls."

Arvin traces Melville's growing dislike of his mother, his increasing ambivalence about religion, and his resistance to all forms of authority. The latter attitude was formed early in his life and was intensified by his travels to Liverpool and the South Sea islands. "Melville was already, at the age of twenty-four, a deeply neurotic person in one of the most creative meanings of the word, and . . . his hatred of discipline and authority, of the paternal principle in that sense, reasonable though much of it was, was a hatred that had its source in a malady." This distaste for discipline and authority informs *Typee*, *Omoo*, *Redburn*, *White-Jacket* and *Moby-Dick*. After *Moby-Dick*, Melville lost his popularity and suffered from what Arvin calls psychoneurotic fatigue. The eclipse of Melville's reputation and the consequent decline of his career as well as of his personal affairs is "the heaviest count in our literary annals against the American mind. In the last years of his life Melville concluded that if he could not have fame on his own exacting terms, he would not have it on any terms: what he would have was its contrary, obscurity; and the cultivation of obscurity, the giving it a positive personal value, became one of the leading motives of his later life."

Interwoven in this moving account of Melville's life is Arvin's acute analysis of the individual works. *Typee* and *Omoo* "tell the story of a quest or pilgrimage—a pilgrimage not, certainly 'from this world to that which is to come,' but from the world of enlightened rationality, technical progress, and cultural complexity backward and downward and, so to say, inward to the primordial world . . ."

Redburn is concerned with "the initiation of innocence into evil"; *Mardi* is full of skepticism and doubt, in themselves not the themes for a great work. In these books as well as in *White-Jacket*, Melville was searching for the right symbolic method, which he discovered in *Moby-Dick*.

Arvin considers *Moby-Dick* not as a tragedy but as an "heroic poem, an epic. The kind of life Melville was raising to the fictive level in this book was not the kind that has ever furnished, or could furnish, the stuff for plays or novels; it was a life in some of its aspects reminiscent of that led by the Achaen peoples in the days of their folk-wanderings or by the German peoples in the days of theirs." Arvin traces the "epiclike pattern" of the book, calling attention to the imagery of lances, harpoons, cutting spades, all of which are similar to Homer's depiction of armor. He defines *Moby-Dick* as a "symbolist prose romance."

Some of Arvin's judgments seem unnecessarily arbitrary. He views *Pierre* as "four-fifths claptrap" and "Benito Cereno" as "unduly celebrated"; in general he dismisses Melville's prose after the writing of *Moby-Dick*. A more serious reservation is Arvin's tendency to underscore and thus distort the sexual implications of Melville's work. This seems particularly true in his treatment of *Moby-Dick*, where he terms the novel as "an 'oneric' projection of unconscious wishes that stem from a conflict between comradeship and romantic love." His analysis is illuminating—as it is everywhere in this valuable book—but it is, we must remember, a rather special angle of vision.

15. Bernstein, John. *Pacificism and Rebellion in the Writings of Herman Melville.* Studies in American Literature, Volume I. The Hague: Mouton & Company, 1964. 232 pp.

This volume, a 1961 Pennsylvania dissertation, treats Melville's fiction and poetry in terms of two broadly defined themes or attitudes: 1. Melville's religious values—his rejection of physical violence as the way to solve differences. 2. Melville's "resistance against or defiance of any authority or control," either sacred or secular.

Bernstein is more successful in presenting Melville's rebel heroes than in treating passive resisters like Bartleby and the Handsome Sailor. In his analysis of *Moby-Dick*, he points out that the conflict between Ahab and Starbuck "is at least as philosophically significant as is the old man's pursuit of the Whale."

16. Berthoff, Warner. *The Example of Melville.* Princeton: Princeton University Press, 1962. 218 pp.

This important study makes a strong case for Melville as a literary artist. The concern of the book, in Berthoff's words, "is with the example Melville presents as a writer, as it still lies before us in his work." After demonstrating Melville's growth from 1846–1956, Berthoff devotes separate chapters to the setting, characters, story-telling, words, sentences, paragraphs, and chapters of Melville's fiction. He emphasizes the period after 1852 and shows that Melville's prose was more disciplined and grew more controlled artistically. Berthoff's interpretation of *Billy Budd* is particularly convincing; he suggests that the allegorical interpretations prove "nothing in themselves about either" Melville's "intentions or his achievement."

"Melville was neither an ideologue nor a converter nor an analyst. A Melville, on the other hand, a mere writer devoting himself without restraint (whatever else he has in mind) to the forming of his work and to a corresponding mastery of letters causes as much to happen as they do; he only outlives them. And that is the great virtue of his example, morally speaking. That is his unique and irreplaceable contribution—to have made so brave a show of renewing the lost opportunities of that life which, however often it defeats us and however finally, is the one life we are given, and which still (by a reciprocal charity it would take a life's work even to learn the extent of) remains somehow to be made."

17. Bowen, Merlin. *The Long Encounter: Self and Experience in the Writings of Herman Melville.* Chicago: University of Chicago Press, 1960. 282 pp.

"This study calls attention . . . to the part played by the concept of selfhood in the writings of Herman Melville and attempts to show, in an examination of particular works, how this persistent concern helped to determine his subject matter, his imagery, his view of character, the shape of his narratives, and his at times equivocal attitude toward his material."

Bowen divides his study into two major sections: "In Part I an attempt is made to draw together from all of Melville's writings the materials for an account of the two actors, protagonist and antagonist, of this drama. . . . With Part II, 'The Meeting', we move from the problem of perception and judgment to the problem of action, and consider the characterizing responses to life made by those characters who are presented as having to some significant extent taken the dimensions of reality's dark side."

The common denominator in Melville, from *Mardi* to *Billy Budd*, is concern with the problem of self-discovery, self-realization. Melville's characters, Bowen maintains, may be classified into three groups, according to the way they make their confrontations: the defiant ones (Prometheans or Enceladans); the submissive ones (the way of weakness); and the armed neutralists.

Although this study is worth examining, it suffers from excessively rigid categorization and from a lack of attention to the growth of Melville's mind and art.

18. Braswell, William. *Melville's Religious Thought*, An Essay in Interpretation. Durham, North Carolina: Duke University Press, 1943. 154 pp.

Braswell traces Melville's growing doubt, his movement from an early belief to a later disbelief. "Melville counseled resignation to the inscrutable laws of the universe. Deeply as man may be grieved by the rigid and sometimes merciless working of these laws, his duty is to accept them and to lay about him doing the best he can. There is no attempt to justify the ways of God to man."

In the first section of his book, Braswell offers a good account of Melville's religious background; the influences of his family and friends on his character; and the effect of his vast reading on his artistic sensibility. In Chapter 2, entitled "Voyager into the 'World of Mind,'" Braswell explores Melville's thought through a close analysis of *Mardi* and notes that the questions which most concerned Melville were the problem of evil in the universe; the nature of the divinity of man; man's hope for immortality; the dogma of innate depravity; and original sin. Braswell's chapter on *Moby-Dick*—"Accuser of the Deity"—suggests that Melville undertook deliberately to write a wicked book in which he accuses (through Ahab) the Deity of permitting evil in the universe. The limitation of this section lies in Braswell's tendency to see Melville as Ahab—the blasphemer—too much. Similarly, when he treats *Pierre* he tends to assume too easily that the Plinlimmon pamphlet would have helped Pierre in escaping his plight. Finally he stresses too heavily Melville's use of Richard Burton's notion of the four souls within man (the vegetal, sensible, rational, and spiritual). His consideration of Hawthorne's famous description of Melville on his way to the Holy Land, however, is sensible. Hawthorne had noted that Melville "had pretty much made up his mind to be annihilated"; and Braswell stresses Melville's growing skepticism.

The last chapter of this interesting study, "The Long Search for Place," is valuable in its discussion of *Clarel*, *Timoleon*, and *Billy Budd*. Braswell concludes that Melville rejected science because it made him more conscious of his ignorance about spiritual matters.

19. Chase, Richard. *Herman Melville: A Critical Study*. New York: The Macmillan Company, 1949. 305 pp.

This volume, whose central ideas were first suggested in "An Approach to Melville" (*Partisan Review*, May–June, 1947, pp. 285–295), is a stimulating and highly original interpretation of Melville's work, but it must be used with great care by the uninitiated reader. Emphasizing politics, myth, Freudian psychology, and folklore, Chase's study is less well-balanced than his later work on Whitman, Emily Dickinson, and the American novel; but despite its exaggerated statements and arbitrary judgments, it explores aspects of Melville's art that cannot be ignored.

Chase claims to have a twofold purpose in writing *Herman Melville: A Critical Study*. "My first purpose in writing this book is to set the works of Herman Melville before the reader in something like their full imperfect glory. My second purpose is to contribute a book on Melville to a movement which may be described (once again) as the new liberalism—that newly invigorated secular thought at the dark center of the twentieth century which, whatever our cultural wreckage and disappointment, now begins to ransom liberalism from the ruinous sellouts, failures, and defeats of the thirties." In Chase's view, Melville "stood opposed to the social pieties of transcendentalism very much as we must now oppose the progressive liberalism which was born fifteen or twenty years ago. . . . In sloughing off a facile idea of progress, Melville accepted what that sloughing-off implied: a tragic view of life.

"I do not wish to present Melville as primarily a political thinker. I am interested in his views of personality, culture, art, and morals."

Chase's interpretation, especially in terms of the short stories, is always interesting but is unduly strained. One should read Alfred Kazin's cogent review of this book, "On Melville as Scripture," *Partisan Review*, XVII (January, 1950), 67–75. Kazin considers Chase mistaken in making "Melville a scripture for the New Liberalism."

The second approach of Chase's study—that of myth—was prefigured by the author's *Quest for Myth* (1948). "In Melville's writing," Chase maintains, "there are two basic kinds of heroes, both akin, in their several variations, to the central figure of Prometheus. The first kind of hero is the false Prometheus, who in one way or another violates the deep-running, natural, and psychic rhythms of life which are necessary for all creative enterprise. The second kind of hero is the Handsome Sailor: the true hero in whom Prometheus tends to put on the full tragic manhood of Oedipus. This second kind of hero is briefly sketched or symbolized as Marnoo, Jack Chase, Bulkington, and Ethan Allen. In each case, he is a full-statured man, great in body, heart, and intellect, a man with great pain of experience behind him, a young man, but still so fully created a man that, in the case of Jack Chase, Ishmael is moved to call him 'sire.'"

The third and fourth aspects of this critical biography are the Freudian point of view that Chase brings to his interpretation of Melville's life and the influence of folklore on Melville's work. Chase's Freudian bias seems too often gratuitous; but the sections on folklore are invaluable and provide the best portions of the study. Chase traces the degree to which American life of the 1830's and 1840's influenced *Moby-Dick*. For a full elaboration of this approach and one that is in part dependent on Chase's pioneering work see Daniel Hoffman's *Form and Fable in American Literature* (60).

For a negative review of Chase's study, see Malcolm Cowley, "Mythology and Melville," *New Republic*, LXXIII (October, 30 1950), 125, in which Cowley maintains that "symbols are not equivalents or identities of the values symbolized; they are real persons or objects that suggest those values among others. . . . To say that Isabel in Pierre is 'Darkness or Babylon' is like saying that she's "'no *more than*' either, and hence *is not* a human being . . . or even truly a character in a novel."

20. Curl, Vega. *Pasteboard Masks*, Fact as Spiritual Symbol in the Novels of Hawthorne and Melville. Cambridge: Harvard University Press, 1931, 45 pp.

This is an early work on a subject that was later developed more fully by F. O. Matthiessen (71). Curl deals with Hawthorne and Melville's views on Transcendentalism, convinced that the spirit of the 1840's shows itself most clearly in "the material that they treat." They are not concerned with the appearance of the fact, for these "are but the masks through which the real significance of life may be dimly apprehended. Different as the two men are in temper and outlook, however, they yet have much in common. For in both there is found an interest in the intangible and the spiritual, in the less often proved regions of man's experience. Neither of them is writing, as previous American authors had been writing, of the world of society or of ordinary adventure. Hawthorne is concerned with the psychological and moral, Melville with the Metaphysical; both are writing, for almost the first time in American literature, of something apart from the physical and the common-place."

21. Dryden, Edgar A. *Melville's Thematics of Form:* The Great Art of Telling the Truth. Baltimore: Johns Hopkins, 1968. 226 pp.

Dryden seeks "to describe the internal morphology of Melville's fictional world and to trace the implications of the form of his vision of things as it gradually develops throughout the span of his career as a writer." Dryden's subtitle comes from Melville's definition of fiction in "Hawthorne and His Mosses": fiction is "the great Art of Telling the Truth."

Melville's attraction to the modern reader, in Dryden's view, stems from his involvement with a "tension between the realm of romance and that of reality." Like so many other nineteenth-century authors, Melville did not obey a strict Jamesian sense of form; he was more concerned with penetrating below the surface of things. In an elaborate first chapter, "Metaphysics, the Art of the Novel," during which he analyzes Melville's essay on Hawthorne closely, Dryden points out that "Melville's Truth is a positive threat to sanity and life. To face it directly, in one's 'own proper character,' is to be driven mad." All of Melville's narrators are in pursuit of Truth and all of them are, in some way, portraits of the artist at work.

Dryden goes on to examine the early novels in terms of the narrators: "Because of his double-role of author-hero the Melvilleian narrator is both creature and creator, man and artist. Dryden reads *Typee, Omoo, Redburn,* and *White-Jacket* with this view in mind. In the creation of *Moby-Dick,* Melville was far more self-conscious than critics have suggested. The narrator takes on a pseudonym and calls himself Ishmael; he is responsible not only for plot, character, and dialogue but for the construction of the drama. He is also an actor in the book and his achievement is "the result of a victory of art over life." In *Pierre* and *Israel Potter,* the Author-Hero fails; in *The Confidence Man* the novelist is an "impostor," as Melville abandons form. "In *Pierre* and *The Confidence Man* Melville dramatizes a theory of history which sees human progress as the successive swallowing up of one fiction by a new and more artificial one."

26. Finkelstein, Dorothee Metlitsky. *Melville's Orienda.* New Haven: Yale University Press, 1961. 317 pp.

This is a helpful study of Melville's reading and his use of sources relating to the Middle East and Far East. "My purpose has been to show the depth and extent of Melville's concern with western Asia and to indicate how it affected his work.

"By isolating the evidence of this interest in the Near East, it is possible to establish two components in Melville's idea of the Orient. On the one hand there is the existential unique, and personal experience of the East, which is analyzed by James Baird in *Ishmael* (90), Baltimore, 1956. On the other hand there is a conscious, historical awareness, which was a general trend of Melville's age. It is this latter side that I intend to explore."

The investigation of this book is in two directions: "Part I shows that Melville shared in the general preoccupation with the Near East manifest on the American literary scene during the years when he became an author (Chapter 1), as shown by the books he is known to have read, or may be assumed to have read on internal and circumstantial evidence (Chapter 2). The influence of the material examined in this part is chronologically traced in his writings.

"In Part II, conversely, I have attempted to project the historical background of Melville's sources from his own writings. Chapters 4 and 5 are grouped around historical figures, central to a given area of the Near East, which consistently recur in Melville's works and were equally important to other writers of his age in Europe and America. Chapter 6 moves from the historical explorers, prophets, and conquerors of the Near East and their image in Melville to the characters, images, and symbols of Melville's own creation that suggest Near Eastern origin."

Although Dorothee Finkelstein offers extensive new material, especially in her examination of *Mardi*, she does not analyze this material very provocatively. Her book is valuable in focusing attention on Melville's interest in the Near East, Egyptology, Ottoman—politics, and the Dead Sea Scrolls.

23. Franklin H. Bruce. *The Wake of the Gods: Melville's Mythology.* Stanford: Stanford University Press, 1963. 236 pp.

"This study, rather than tracing Melville's knowledge of mythology, tries to show how Melville consciously used myths, mythologies, comparative mythology, and mythological theories in his major works—*Mardi, Moby Dick, Pierre, Bartleby, Benito Cereno, The Confidence Man,* and *Billy Budd.* My central thesis is that Melville's mythology determines and defines large parts of the structure and meaning of these works."

Franklin's book is a valuable examination of Melville's myth-making powers. He indicates the comparative mythology practiced by writers in Melville's time and analyzes closely *Mardi, Moby-Dick, Pierre,* "Bartleby," "Benito Cereno," *The Confidence-Man,* and *Billy Budd.*

"In the first three major works, the characters create their gods: *Mardi* is a book almost entirely about mythmaking; the central struggle of *Moby-Dick* derives from a myth created by Ahab and the whale-men's imagination; *Pierre,* after his hereditary persuasions are destroyed, constructs from the pieces a god to imitate.

But with Bartleby a figure appears who is perhaps a god, and *The Confidence-Man* depends for its central joke in the Confidence man's being in fact a god. The joke is that the Fidèle's passengers are being fleeced by a real god, a god not only created by them but totally unrecognized by them. Only the readers of *The Confidence-Man* know that a god prowls the Fidèle's decks; they alone recognize him, and they alone define him. . . . *Billy Budd* returns to the central theme of mythmaking, but the mythic God created by Vere and his sailors is as much a god as the Confidence Man. Billy Budd shows step by step the creation of a myth, complete with the rituals and ethics of a particular primitive mythology. Melville's mythology has thus come full circle."

The chapters on *Mardi* and *Moby-Dick* are more enlightening than that on *Pierre*, where the material of the novel is less congenial to Franklin's thesis.

24. Freeman, John. *Herman Melville*. London: Macmillan and Co., English Men of Letters Series, 1926. 200 pp.

Freeman's critical biography is based on the materials discovered by Raymond Weaver (45), although it does offer some original commentary and criticism. Freeman's general view is that "during the first half of his life Melville invested himself with illusions and found them to be but illusions; during the second half he was trying to make terms with the bareness that remained, and trying to avoid an exhausting, cynical conclusion." Although he tends to see Melville rather simply—"Melville was a normal healthy child living a normal commonplace life"—Freeman is aware of the inner conflicts in Melville's life. He defines these conflicts largely in relation to isolation. "Isolation, the friendliness of man, the failure to see God, the growing sense, too, that contact with men was an embarrassment more than refreshment—by these he was driven inwards and fingered in silence the problems that beset him."

25. Geist, Stanley. *Herman Melville, The Tragic Vision and the Heroic Ideal*. Cambridge: Harvard University Press, 1939. 76 pp.

This brief study, an Honors Thesis at Harvard University, is an interesting, yet overwritten and distorted, interpretation of Melville's work from a single piont of view. Geist maintains that "Of all the demands which he made upon life, the most unremitting was the demand that it be heroic . . . Thus his mature considerations of democracy centered about the subject of heroism. It was his ardent wish that in democratic America, where the new continually corroded the old, where conventions of thought had not become frozen patterns, where no aristocracy of 'bastards' blood thwarted the rise of genuine merit, a new race of giants would arise, counterparts of the great giants who had walked abroad in former times. . . . It has been said that he dreamed of a brotherhood of men: but his dream was, in fact, of a brotherhood of supermen."

Geist resorts to rather extravagant statements which do not always clarify the works under consideration. A more serious reservation is that he does not take into account Melville's later period when he wrote works like *The Encantadas* and *The Confidence-Man* and expressed a deep fear and distrust of the heroic ideal. One should also be careful in relying upon the factual information in this essay, for it is marred by errors.

For a modified view of Geist's thesis, see Theodore L. Gross, "Herman Melville: The Nature of Authority" (56).

26. Hetherington, Hugh W. *Melville's Reviewers, British and American, 1846–1891.* Chapel Hill: University of North Carolina Press, 1961. 304 pp.

This is a thorough study of the critical reception of Melville's works during his lifetime. The contents include Reviewers, British and American; *Typee*; *Omoo*; *Mardi*; *Redburn*; *White-Jacket*; *Moby-Dick*; After *Moby-Dick*; and "Dead Letters." Hetherington points out that Melville initially published his first six books in London, "thus committing his reputation, far more than has in recent years been realized, to the mercies of the professional book-tasters of Edinburgh, Dublin, and London."

Hetherington's book is particularly useful in suggesting why specific novels were better received in one country than in another.

27. Hillway, Tyrus. *Herman Melville.* New York: Twayne Publishers, 1963. 176 pp.

Hillway has written a sensible guide to Melville's works. Because his book is part of a series and thus restricted in length and scope, Hillway does not probe the individual works very deeply; but his individual analyses of the novels and his account of Melville's life are thoroughly reliable.

Hillway's aims are clearly stated in his introduction: "What the book [*Herman Melville*] does attempt is to introduce to its readers authenticated information about Melville's life and works, a brief review of recent research, and a summary of the author's personal critical judgments. In effect, it offers a fresh appraisal of Melville in the light of the best current scholarship. . . .

"The first chapter presents a brief discussion of Melville's 'accidental' discovery of his vocation as writer and of his literary methods and style. . . .

"Chapters II, III, and IV deal with details of Melville's life and the events that surrounded the writing and publication of his books. . . .

"Chapters V through VIII examine Melville's works one by one, beginning with *Typee* (1846). . . . Chapter IX discusses the Melville Revival of the twentieth century."

Hillway is particularly interesting in his sensitive account of Melville's pertinence to the modern reader: "For Melville to rise to his present prominence as a writer has required an analytical age . . . In a milieu in which readers urgently strive to know life as it really is, there has developed a very natural respect not only for Melville's acute powers of observation but also for his intellectual honesty. In many ways, his principal ethical and social ideas, though couched in the language of his own time, fit remarkably well into the intellectual currents of the twentieth century."

Hillway concludes that "Melville's ultimate state may be described as a tentatively optimistic skepticism. He saw that man is capable of envisioning an ideal without achieving its realization. . . . Every man's life constitutes a record of compromise between absolute good and worldly necessity."

This critical study takes full account of the most recent research and, because it offers so balanced a treatment of Melville's life and literature, is one of the best brief accounts of this complex author.

28. Howard, Leon. *Herman Melville: A Biography*. Berkeley: University of California Press, 1951; reprinted, 1958. 365 pp.

This biography is "a co-operative venture" with Jay Leyda's *Melville Log* (31). Howard has written the formal narrative biography while Leyda provides the source material for the biography. As Howard states in his introduction, "even when I used more complete documents than could be printed in the *Log*, I have tried to make my own text circumstantially allusive to it in a way which would enable an interested student of Melville to locate my basic sources of information. . . . The major aim of my own researches has been to place the basic facts of Melville's life in their proper physical, historical, intellectual, and literary context and to draw from them the inferences necessary for a coherent and human narrative."

Howard is opposed to the "new criticism" and to what he considers the excessive psychologizing of literary figures. He wishes simply to restore "the human element" in Melville's books and to present "the observable evidence" of Melville's life. His book, he states, was written with no other intent "than to understand the author of *Moby Dick* and other books as a human being living in nineteenth-century America."

One can sympathize with Howard's aim; one can understand his impatience with some of the more extreme hypotheses of Melville's "inner life" that appeared before his own work. Howard himself has produced a substantial biography that gives the reader reliable information concerning all of Melville's experiences; but what is lacking in this book is precisely that sense of Melville's "inner life," the understanding of the intellectual tensions that resulted in Melville's greatest works. Howard's view that "the strange gaiety in the chapters of *Pierre* . . . was originally, perhaps, nothing more than the awkward geniality of casual writing" is highly questionable. His conclusion that in *The Confidence-Man* Melville did not know whether "he was writing ironically or enthusiastically" also does not seem sound. In general, the interpretative sections of this are weaker than the strictly biographical. As an authoritative account of Melville's life, however, Howard's book is indispensable.

See Howard's brief discussion of Melville's life and work in *Herman Melville*. Minneapolis: University of Minnesota, 1961. 48 pp. Howard concludes that "Herman Melville's strongest claim to greatness is that his imaginative development kept abreast of the times—despite neglect and adversity and more than one failure, the acuteness and depth of his sensitivity never failed."

29. Humphreys, A. R. *Herman Melville*. Edinburgh: Oliver and Boyd, Ltd., 1962. Reprinted by Grove Press, Inc., 1962, 120 pp.

This is an intelligent survey of Melville's life and works. Because of space limitations, Humphreys does not examine the poems. Like other American authors best known to the world, Melville stands in the tradition of antimaterialism and nonconformity. After brief and rather traditional interpretations of Melville's first five novels, Humphreys offers a 42-page examination of *Moby-Dick*.

Hawthorne precipitated Melville's sense of the tragic, and Melville's reading of Carlyle and Emerson affected his style and method. Humphreys notes Ahab's demoniac qualities but adds that "enough of intermittent humanity diversifies Ahab's monomania to make him genuinely a tragic figure, a great man in ruin." The figures who counterbalance Ahab are Starbuck, the representative of human decency; Captain Boomer of the *Samuel Enderby*, who represents "the central vigour of the profession [of whaling] and stands for a responsible attitude"; and especially Ishmael, who is the "book's consciousness" and provides tone of feeling to relieve Ahab's blackness.

Humphreys concludes his brief study with sections on *Pierre, Israel Potter, The Piazza Tales*, and *Billy Budd*.

30. James, C. L. R. *Mariners, Renegades, and Castaways*, The Story of Herman Melville and the World We Live in. New York: C. L. R. James, 1953.

James launches his book with a strange premise: "the book has been written in such a way that a reader can read it from beginning to end and understand it without having read a single page of Melville's books. I believe that this is the spirit of what Melville had to say." What follows is a romantic recapitulation of *Moby-Dick*, with concentration on Ahab and his relationship to the rise of totalitarianism in Nazi Germany. James runs through the plot, quoting extensively from the novel in a way that seems calculated to engage young readers. After his extensive treatment of *Moby-Dick*, James then offers some biographical information, a lengthy account of *Pierre*, and some observations on the stories. The last chapter is a private reminiscence and has little to do with Melville.

31. Leyda, Jay. *The Melville Log: A Documentary Life of Herman Melville*, 1819–1891, 2 Volumes. New York: Harcourt, Brace and Co., 1951. 899 pp.

"In the making of this book I have tried to hold to one main aim: to give each reader the opportunity to be his own biographer of Herman Melville, by providing him with the largest possible quantity of materials to build his own approach to this complex figure. The only way I knew to do this was to put together everything that could be known about his life, to bring the reader close to Melville's progress through as many of his days as could be restored, so that the reader may watch him as he works, sees, reacts, worries—to make those seventy-two years, from 1819 to 1891, and a portion of the America they were lived in, in Henry James's words, *visitable*. This approach forbade an emphasis on any part of his life to the exclusion of any other part, and forbade the neglect of material that seemed, in itself, of small importance. I trust the reader will find enjoyment in traveling alongside Melville— through good days and bad days, through great aims and trivial duties—as his body and mind grow and change—in a constant *present*, accumulating past experiences, but without knowing a future."

Leyda's book, which provides the basic material for Leon Howard's biography (28), is an invaluable source book. The author has brought together the many facts of Melville's life and the pertinent documents which relate to his background. He has used letters, diaries, ships' logs, journals, reviews, real-estate advertisements, royalty statements, newspapers, and books; and he has arranged all of this information in chronological order so as to reveal the Melville who actually existed in the nineteenth-century rather than the Melville who has been "created" by so many critics and readers.

32. Mason, Ronald. *The Spirit Above the Dust*. London: John Lehmann, 1951. 269 pp.

Mason discusses Melville's work and philosophy rather than his life. He is interested primarily in presenting Melville to an English audience.

After a brief account of Melville's life, Mason devotes chapters to *Typee* (a "statement of innocence"), *Omoo*, and *Mardi* ("the transition and the power of the symbol"). "Embodied in *Mardi* is not only [Melville's] fullest statement yet of the theme of the conflict between Innocence and Experience, that topic common to all his past and future writing, but what is more important than this, the emergence of the tragic vision." Mason considers *Redburn* an "assault upon Innocence" and *White-Jacket* "an abandonment of isolation." He devotes a valuable chapter to the influence of Hawthorne on Melville and then three chapters to *Moby-Dick*: the Prelude, the Symbol, and the Myth. *Moby-Dick* has continued to be enjoyed "as epic and encyclopedia, tract and tragedy, handbook and heroic romance, and it proclaims unmistakably Melville's spiritual desolation. The deepest tragedy of Ahab is not his own violent destruction but the survival and the loneliness of Ishmael." Mason's other chapters consider *Pierre* ("the defeat of innocence"), *The Piazza Tales* ("Tartarus of a Traveller"), *The Confidence-Man* ("the embittered masquerade"), the Poems, and *Clarel* ("the spirit above the dust").

Mason's most important single chapter contains a close analysis of *Clarel*. The accent in the poem is "upon the compensating element; the honey in the wilderness, the spirit above the dust." The poem points to "a potential but untried faith"; it is *Billy Budd* that becomes Melville's "calm and authoritative revelation."

33. Metcalf, Eleanor Melville. *Herman Melville: Cycle and Epicycle.* Cambridge: Harvard University Press, 1953. 311 pp.

In this biography of the Melville family—of the Gansevoorts, the Lansings, and the Shaws—Mrs. Metcalf quotes extensively from diaries, journals, and reminiscences, and includes 100 letters of Melville, most of them published before. She provides a running narrative which occupies one fifth of the book. Her aim is to "re-create the intimate social scene in which a man of genius lived and moved, but failed to find his being." One third of the volume is devoted to the six years between *Typee* and *Pierre* and includes literary correspondence with Dana, Duyckinck, Hawthorne and the English publisher Bentley. Mrs. Metcalf traces Melville's conflict between his pride of being part of a distinguished family and his not being understood (artistically) by that family.

This study is generally objective and free of sentimentality. Mrs. Metcalf includes documents which reveal her grandfather's brooding quality. She notes, for example, that when Melville went to Palestine in 1856, he was so depressed that the family "had begun to suffer not only from insufficient funds for daily needs, but far more from bursts of nervous anger and attacks of morose conscience."

Herman Melville: Cycle and Epicycle is particularly revealing in its picture of Melville's difficult relations with his family, their pride in his early success, and their increasing concern over his morbid reaction to the public failure of his work.

34. Miller, James E., Jr. *A Reader's Guide to Herman Melville.* New York: Farrar, Straus, and Cudahy, 1962. 266 pp.

To one familiar with James E. Miller's work on Whitman and F. Scott Fitzgerald, this critical study is a disappointment. In formal terms—in its style and structure—it seems hastily conceived. In its function as a "guide" it is incomplete, for it omits a discussion of Melville's poetry and some of the short stories.

Miller's general consideration of Melville's work, however, is sensible. "From the beginning to the end, in the total design of his work, we may trace the intricate pattern as it reiterates the basic truths he discovered and dramatized: the impossibility and catastrophe of the assumption of innocence; the necessity of connecting with the chain of human sympathies in an acceptance of the universal burden of guilt. Though Melville shifted his form, changed his settings, varied his characters, we shall find that this basic view persisted. He must have come to realize (as we have come to know) that this singular vision nourished his creative imagination and at the same time gave it form and shape."

Melville's work constitutes a coherent whole whose basic pattern involves three groups of characters: those who refuse to acknowledge that evil is omnipresent in the universe and wear a "mask" (Taji, Ahab, Pierre, Benito Cereno, Bartleby,

The Confidence Man, Billy Budd, and Claggart); those who accept the fact of evil and are "maskless" (Babbalanja, Jack Chase, Bulkington, Plinlimmon, and Israel Potter); and young "wanderers" or "seekers" who have not decided which of these two attitudes to take (Tommo, Omoo, Redburn, White Jacket, Ishmael, and Clarel).

35. Mumford, Lewis. *Herman Melville: A Study of His Life and Vision.* New York: Harcourt, Brace & Co., 1929. 256 pp. Revised edition, 1962.

Mumford analyzes Melville's mind with perception and sensitivity, especially when one considers how early his book was written in the history of Melville scholarship; but he errs by accepting much of Melville's writing as autobiographical. His chief contribution to the development of early Melville criticism was to contradict previous views of Melville as a misanthropic man and to present the author as more "normal" and well balanced. The interpretative sections of this study are still illuminating; the biographical information has been rendered obsolete by Anderson (13), Gilman (84), Davis (86), Leyda (31), Howard (28), and other subsequent scholars. Mumford acknowledges his early errors—especially his misinterpretation of Ethan Brand as a figure modeled upon Melville—and corrects most of them in his revised edition, published in 1962.

See Michael P. Zimmerman, "Herman Melville in the 1920's," *Bulletin of Bibliography*, XXIV, 117–120, 139–144. Zimmerman claims that Mumford's biography "was meant to be an exemplar for those Americans in 1929 who, as Mumford saw them, had given over their lives to the meaningless accumulation of material goods and the single-minded pursuit of a successful career."

36. Parker, Hershel, ed. *The Recognition of Herman Melville, Selected Criticism Since 1846.* Ann Arbor: The University of Michigan Press, 1967. 364 pp.

Parker collects most of the important American and British reviews and essays on Melville's work since the appearance of *Typee* (1846). By presenting the criticism chronologically, the editor is able to present "Melville's gradual recognition." He divides his book into four sections: 1. Reviews and Early Appraisals: 1846–1876; 2. Academic Neglect and Prophecies of Renown: 1884–1912; 3. The Melville Revival: 1917–1932; 4. Academic Recognition: 1938–1967.

The first three sections are especially interesting, for they include reviews and brief essays that are rarely reprinted and that reveal the temper of nineteenth- and early twentieth-century criticism. The last section is necessarily selective, although it does include essays by the most significant critics responsible for the full flowering of Melville scholarship: Willard Thorp's essay on *Mardi*, *Moby-Dick*, and *Pierre* from *Herman Melville: Representative Selections* (1938); F. O. Matthiessen's treatment of Melville's language in *American Renaissance* (1941); and William Gilman's analysis of *Redburn* from his *Melville's Early Life and Redburn* (1951). The last two essays—Walker Cowen's study of Melville's marginalia and John D. Sellye's examination of Melville's irony—indicate recent trends in Melville scholarship.

✗ **37.** Pommer, Henry Francis. *Milton and Melville*. Pittsburgh: University of Pittsburgh Press, 1950. 172 pp.

Pommer cites the many influences in Milton's poetry on Melville's work but neglects Miltonic prose works like *Areopagitica*. Milton was a popular author among Americans in the first half of the nineteenth century and was particularly honored in the Melville household. Melville read, to a great extent, for confirmation of his own ideas, and Milton served to confirm many of his doubts. The two authors shared much in common: both attacked priestcraft but not religion; both had a creed of individualism and of toleration; both were deeply influenced by the Bible; both were concerned with the nature of evil; and both denied aristocratic trappings.

Pommer first traces Milton's influence on Melville's minor works, citing specific lines from Milton's various works and concluding that "Melville's knowledge of Milton provided one method by which he could shift from a less richly to a more richly connotative style, increasing the flow of concepts in his readers' minds." He then turns to Milton's influence on Melville's vocabulary and sentence structure and the poetic and epic influences of *Paradise Lost*. Both Milton and Melville use alliteration, rhythm, similes, soliloquies, and pathos; both create heroes with characteristics. Pommer concludes this informative study with the influence of Satan on the creation of Jackson (in *Redburn*), Claggart (in *Billy Budd*), and Ahab (in *Moby-Dick*).

38. Rosenberry, Edward H. *Melville and the Comic Spirit*. Cambridge: Harvard University Press, 1955. 211 pp.

"It was as a comic writer that [Melville] won his early fame," Rosenberry points out, and he insists that all of Melville's works until 1856 are basically comic. Melville's ideal is a marriage of the comic and the tragic visions, "not by chance, but by a continuous, creative act of will . . . At the source of Melville's literary comedy was a warm and robust personality."

Rosenberry detects "all four theoretical and somewhat arbitrary phases" in Melville's comic artistry: 1. The jocular-hedonic "is instantly translatable into the simple idea of fun" (*Typee, Omoo, Redburn*, and *White-Jacket*). 2. The imaginative-critical is "more literary in its origins, more sophisticated in its tone, more ulterior in its motives" (*Mardi*). 3. The *philosophical-psychological* is concerned with "the ambiguous nature of values themselves" (*Moby-Dick* and *Pierre*). 4. The *dramatic-structural* phase "fuses the desperate elements of comedy and tragedy into a balanced work of art" (short stories like "Bartleby, the Scrivener").

Although *Moby-Dick* is an example of the "philosophical-psychological," it also exemplifies "all four modes of comic art." After the creation of *Moby-Dick*, Melville's comic vision declined. *The Confidence Man* is "darkness and silence . . . an echo"; and after 1856 Melville ceased to write humorously altogether.

This book is valuable in reminding the reader of an important aspect of Melville's work, but Rosenberry's assertion that everything Melville wrote through

1856 is comic becomes unduly exaggerated and distorts the overall pattern of Melville's fiction.

39. Sealts, Merton M. *Melville as Lecturer*. Cambridge: Harvard University Press, 1957. 202 pp.

Sealts has gathered from fifty-four extant newspaper reviews and summaries "composite texts." Through these texts he has studied Melville's thought from 1857 to 1859, modifying present biography and criticism. In a 123 page essay, Sealts relates Melville to the entire Lyceum movement. He also connects the themes of the lectures to the prose of the 1850's and the later poetry, concluding that Melville, an alien to the late 1850's in America, felt more at home in the past, among the ancients or among his own memories. After tracing Melville's career as a lecturer, Sealts offers his "texts of lectures with commentary" and an appendix of Melville's "Notebooks of Lecture Engagements" and "Melville's Memoranda of Travel Expenses, 1857–58."

Sealts' study is particularly useful in illuminating Melville's state of mind toward the middle of his life. Melville, Sealts points out, preferred the past to the late 1850's in which he lived.

See also Sealts' *Melville's Reading, A Check-List of Books Owned and Borrowed*. Madison: University of Wisconsin Press, 1966, 134 pp. Sealts includes the record of Melville's reading: books owned and borrowed; and an analytical index to the check-list.

40. Sedgwick, William Ellery. *Herman Melville: The Tragedy of Mind*. Cambridge: Harvard University Press, 1944; reprinted, New York: Russell & Russell, Inc., 1962. 255 pp.

This study traces the unfolding of Melville's tragic sensibility, without taking recourse to Melville's private life and referring to those difficulties he had in his family life. Sedgwick maintains that Melville searched in vain for truth in tragic terms. "This drama of human growth is much more to the fore and directly before us in Melville's books from first to last than in Shakespeare's plays. It begins with *Typee* and closes with *Billy Budd*, written in the last year of Melville's life, and which stands to *Moby-Dick* and *Pierre* in much the same relation in which *The Tempest*, say, stands to Shakespeare's greatest tragedies. . . . To Melville, as to the angels, the ultimate truth presented itself in the form of the age-old questions of Christian theology. Like them, too, he 'found no end in wand'ring mazes lost.'"

Sedgwick has chapters on *Typee, Mardi, Redburn, White-Jacket, Moby-Dick, Pierre, After Pierre, Clarel*, and *Billy Budd*. In general the author makes more references to Shakespeare than are justified—he tends to exaggerate the influence of Shakespeare and neglect the importance of Melville's contemporaries.

He also maintains, in his analysis of *Clarel*, that Roman Catholicism was attractive to Melville; but this has not been supported by subsequent research into

Melville's life. Sedgwick's book is often ingenious and sometimes brilliant, but much of his work has been superseded by later studies.

41. Stern, Milton R. *The Fine Hammered Steel of Herman Melville*. Urbana: University of Illinois Press, 1957. 297 pp.

Stern treats *Typee, Mardi, Pierre*, and *Billy Budd* but not *Moby-Dick*. Melville's basic theme, he suggests, is a cosmic and anti-idealistic "naturalism." "Melville became the historically and socially orientated, rather than cosmically and socially oriented, empirical idealist. . . . Whatever its foundations, whatever its excuse, human conduct finally must be historically responsible and communal. There must be not 'cleavage' but juncture of 'spirit,' mind, and 'brute,' for any one alone is the murderousness of one-self rather than the generation of man-self. Thus many years before literary naturalism became ill-defined in the narrow channels of literary Naturalism, Melville the classical democrat, the ethical relativist, the devout empiricist, demonstrated that naturalistic perception in the years of the modern could and must take from woe not only materialism, but also the humanism and the deep morality of social idealism, which are the true beginnings of wisdom."

Thus Melville's work functions as a warning of the dangers and inadequacies of idealism. By always suggesting to the reader the concrete fact as opposed to the idealistic system, Melville creates a literature of relativism and credibility.

Stern's major thesis makes sense, but it seems overbearing, burdensome, and excessively extended in its treatment; furthermore, one can seriously question his assumption that Melville was a monist. The philosophical direction of Melville's mind points, it would seem, toward dualism. This dualistic view of the world is most elaborately dramatized, of course, in *Moby-Dick*. For a brief discussion of Melville's dualism, see Charles Cook's essay, "Ahab's 'Intolerable Allegory'" (92).

Stern has published individual essays which are, more or less, extensions of his critical study. See, for example, "Some Techniques of Melville's Perception," *PMLA*, LXXIII (June, 1958), 251–259 (reprinted in *Discussions of Moby-Dick*, edited by Milton Stern) and "Melville's Tragic Imagination: The Hero Without a Home," *Patterns of Commitment in American Literature*, edited by Marston LaFrance. Toronto: University of Toronto Press, 1967, pp. 39–52. In the latter essay, Stern states that "It has been fashionable to call Melville's imagination tragic, but to do so demands a certain precision of terms. I think that Melville's vision is not tragic in a classic sense. . . . Modern as it is, Melville's vision tends toward the naturalistic and the existential in its sense of death, or the consciousness, thereof, as a basis of value."

42. Stone, Geoffrey. *Melville*. New York: Sheed and Ward, 1949. 336 pp.

This study is written from a Roman Catholic bias, but it does not impose any doctrine upon the writings of Melville. Stone, who states that his "book is addressed to the general reader," brings an acute intelligence to bear upon Melville's Calvinism.

Melville, in Stone's view, "had not, indeed, ever departed very far from the Calvinist attitude, whose incipient Manichaenism had colored what doctrines he had held as well as his revolt against other doctrines. A large measure of his anguish had been caused by his demand that all those things which he discretely observed and experienced in the universe be correlated in some rationally coherent scheme; but the basic irrationality with which he gave primacy to his own will made that scheme impossible. The deepest experience, his books insisted, showed some inscrutable malice sinewing the universe."

The best section of this valuable book is devoted to an analysis of *Billy Budd.* Stone does not accept the novel as a "testament of acceptance," for Melville insisted on the validity of the two types of justice. "As in *Pierre* the two orders of time, chronometrical and horological, followed from the ambiguity at the heart of creation, so in Billy Budd followed the two orders of justice, earthly and heavenly."

43. Sundermann, K. H. *Herman Melville's Gedankegut: Eine Kritische Untersuchung Seiner Weltanschaulicher Grundieen.* Berlin: Verlag Arthur Collignon, 1937. 227 pp.

This was the first important book on Melville in a foreign language. Sundermann maintains that Melville was no systematic philosopher but rather a thinker like Sir Thomas Browne, Goethe, Carlyle, and Emerson. He divides his study into three parts: 1. The religious element in Melville's work. In this section, Sundermann finds Melville rebellious, gloomy, and contemptuous of science. 2. The philosophical element. The author traces the discrepancy between Melville's idealism and actuality. 3. The historical element. Sundermann relates Melville to New England transcendentalism and concludes that Melville was not so independent in theorizing about history as he was about religion and art because of his democratic influences.

Sundermann's book is worth reading—if one can read German with ease—but it tends to be too cursory on too many topics, and it neglects the symbolism in Melville's work. The finest single portion of the book is the author's extended analysis of *Clarel.*

44. Thompson, Lawrance. *Melville's Quarrel With God.* Princeton: Princeton University Press, 1952. 474 pp.

Thompson attempts to come to terms with the complexity of Melville's religious attitudes. He states his case quite clearly:

"Disillusionment with one's inherited (and therefore second-hand) religious beliefs is such a familiar phase of human growth that one might suppose Melville could have worked out his own religious readjustments without carrying into later life any ineffaceable scars; that his own personal and firsthand religious experience might have modified his inherited beliefs until he could have arrived at some concept of God more acceptable and congenial to his temperament. By contrast, one might fear that Melville's concept of the Calvinistic God might gradually have become so repulsive that he might have moved through doubt and skepticism to a denial of the existence of God. This final step he never took. . . .

"Increasingly embittered by a conjunction of unfortunate experiences, immediately, during and after the writing of *Mardi*, Melville arrived at a highly ironic conclusion: believing more firmly than ever in the God of John Calvin, he began to resent and hate the attributes of God, particularly the seemingly tyrannous harshness and cruelty and malice of God. Thus, instead of losing faith in his Calvinistic God, Melville made a scapegoat of him, and blamed God for having caused so many human beings to rebel."

Thompson is "interested in Melville's spiritual idiom primarily because it controlled and determined his artistic idiom." He believes that Melville worked out his spiritual problems by pretending "to praise and honor the orthodox Christian viewpoint despite his personal doubts . . . the pretense gave the illusion of proceeding in a direction exactly opposite from the anti-Christian direction of the story itself, the plot itself."

In his treatment of *Moby-Dick*, Thompson suggests that Ishmael's overt meanings reflect "a sympathy with the Christian doctrine of obedience and acceptance"; but "the underlying and insinuated meaning [hints] at a deliberate and sly ridicule of concepts sacred to Christian doctrine." Melville hated God, Thompson believes, for introducing God into man's life.

Thompson's treatment indicates the danger of pursuing a thesis tenaciously. He does not take account of the important biographical information provided by Jay Leyda in *The Melville Log* (31) and by Leon Howard in his biography (28) of Melville. Because he is so intent on proving his thesis, Thompson writes in a forced and argumentative fashion, italicizing phrases from Melville's work that tend to support his thesis. Thompson's insistent notion that Melville was not an ambivalent author, that he knew God was evil, and that his books prove this assertion is a simplification of a highly complex author.

See Marius Bewley, "A Truce of God for Melville," *Sewanee Review*, LXI (Autumn, 1953), 682–700 for an objection to Thompson's interpretation.

45. Weaver, Raymond. *Herman Melville, Mariner and Mystic*. New York: George H. Doran Company, 1921. 399 pp.

Weaver's book is the first full-length biography of Melville. Weaver had access to Melville's manuscripts, correspondence, and business papers, and published for the first time source material that has been used by later critics. He did not take advantage of the Melville correspondence in the Duyckinck Collection of the New York Public Library, and he made the biographical fallacy of assuming that much of Melville's work was autobiographical—he drew two full chapters of "history," for example, from *Redburn*. Finally, he neglected Melville's later period; only one tenth of his biography is devoted to the period from 1857–1891. Weaver's image of Melville was that of the unappreciated genius who had tendencies toward mysticism and fought vainly against the low literary criteria of his day. This picture of Melville as the brooding, misanthropic writer has been altered by subsequent scholars, but there is still a good deal of truth in Weaver's characterization. All Melville scholars owe him a great debt.

See Michael P. Zimmerman, "Herman Melville in the 1920's," *Bulletin of Bibliography*, XXIV, 117–120, 139–144. Zimmerman suggests that Weaver's biography was "a dark melodrama in which a doomed American writer wars with his puritanical and conformist age."

46. Wright, Nathalia. *Melville's Use of the Bible*. Durham: Duke University Press, 1949. 203 pp.

Although critics had long been aware of Melville's interest in the Bible, no one formulated his complete debt until Nathalia Wright published *Melville's Use of the Bible*. She indicates that the Bible was one of Melville's chief sources for symbols, language, and ideas. Her individual chapters deal with Imagery; Characters and Types; Themes and Plots; and Style. Melville had particular fondness for the antique and the exotic, Mrs. Wright suggests, and his feeling for movement was the keenest aspect of his sensibility. In her chapter, "Themes and Plots," the author notes "four major Scriptural themes" in Melville's work: "the theme of prophecy in *Moby-Dick*; the theme of wisdom literature cursorily from *Mardi* to *Billy Budd*; the theme of the Gospel ethics in *Mardi*, *Pierre*, and *The Confidence Man*; and the theme of the crucifixion in *Billy Budd*."

See Mrs. Wright's earlier essay, "Biblical Allusion in Melville's Prose," *American Literature*, XII (May, 1940), 185–199, which is a preliminary examination of this phase of Melville's work. "In the thirteen volumes of prose there are approximately 650 references to Biblical characters, places, events, and books."

V. Criticism

General Essays:

47. Bewley, Marius. *The Eccentric Design*. New York: Columbia University Press, 1959, pp. 187–219.
The doubts that tormented Melville were due to his inability to keep the terms of good and evil distinct from each other; and this inability was caused by the democrat's "close identification between God and democratic society." Melville became deeply disillusioned with the American mind, as one can see in his work of the 1850's but especially in *The Confidence Man*. In *Moby-Dick*, Melville tried to introduce order into his moral universe, and he succeeded in establishing a polarity between good and evil; "but in *Pierre* and *The Confidence Man* the distinction he had made in his great masterpiece could not be sustained, and a pursuit of the knowledge of good and evil was replaced by a suffocating sense of the ambiguity which he formally and cynically seemed to formulate and preach as the ultimate knowable moral truth."

Bewley takes issue with Lawrance Thompson's assertion (44) that in *Moby-Dick* Melville is attacking God; on the contrary, "he is attempting to rescue the idea of the good, to push back from his darkening consciousness that instinctive reaction of the disillusioned American: hatred of creation itself . . . Ahab's attitude is the antithesis of life because it represents a rejection of creation." In the later novels, Bewley concludes, a formlessness appeared because Melville felt that a moral action was not possible.

Bewley's analysis of Melville's loss of belief in democracy and its effect on his fiction is provocative, but it suffers from its tendency to emphasize the "abstract, intellectualizing . . . American tradition."

48. Brooks, Van Wyck. *The Times of Melville and Whitman*. New York: E. P. Dutton, 1947, pp. 142–175.
Brooks believes that despite Melville's loss of confidence, "this faith [in America] superabounded him in the great productive years that reached their highest point in

Moby-Dick, when he shared the general Mazzinian belief that nations have their missions and Whitman's special belief in the mission of his own." Melville took "to theorizing" too much, in Brooks's view, and he "lacked the developing sense of a craft." His remarks about Melville's relation with Hawthorne are interesting.

Brooks's sympathetic treatment of Melville is worth noting, although it is highly impressionistic and often does not focus precisely on Melville. As Robert Spiller points out, in his review (*American Literature*, X, January, 1949, 45–61), "the book would almost better have been called *The Times of Horace Greeley*, for the events of the era are seen from the offices of the New York *Tribune*, and Greeley rather than Melville, or even Whitman, provides the angle of vision."

49. Canby, H. S. "Hawthorne and Melville," *Classic Americans: Eminent American Writers from Irving to Whitman*. New York: Harcourt, Brace & Co., 1931, pp. 226–262.

Canby sees Hawthorne and Melville as "skeptics at a turning point of civilization." *Moby-Dick* "is Melville's answer to Transcendentalism and his wildly imaginative comment on the intellectual pride of the nineteenth-century." If Melville "went wild after 'Moby Dick' and merely puzzled his readers, it was because he was both too late and too early to get the full effects of his genius."

50. Charvat, William, "Melville's Income," *American Literature*, XV (November, 1943), 251–261.

Charvat investigates Melville's income after 1851. From 1846–1851 Melville was a financially successful author. From 1851–1861 his income from books was an average of $228 a year. Although he had a total of $63,370 in legacies during his life, Melville was a poor manager and was always in debt.

51. Chase, Richard, ed. *Melville: A Collection of Critical Essays*. Englewood Cliffs: Prentice Hall, 1962.

In addition to his introduction, Chase includes the following essays: D. H. Lawrence, "Herman Melville's *Typee* and *Omoo*," from *Studies in Classic American Literature* (64); Newton Arvin, "*Mardi, Redburn, White-Jacket*," from *Herman Melville* (14); Alfred Kazin, "'Introduction' to *Moby Dick*," from Riverside Edition of *Moby Dick*, 1950 (110); Richard Chase, "Melville and Moby Dick," from *The American Novel and Its Tradition* (51); Henry A. Murray, "*In Nomine Diaboli*," *The New England Quarterly*, XXIV (December, 1951), 435–452 (112); R. P. Blackmur, "The Craft of Herman Melville: A Putative Statement," from *The Lion and the Honeycomb* (94); Marius Bewley, "Melville and the Democratic Exprience," from *The Eccentric Design: Form in the Classic American Novel* (48); Richard Harter Fogle, *Melville's Shorter Tales* (138); Daniel G. Hoffman, "The Confidence-Man: His Masquerade," from *Form and Fable in American Fiction* (61); Robert Penn Warren, "Melville the

Poet," from *Selected Essays of Robert Penn Warren* (168); F. O. Matthiessen, "Billy Budd, Foretopman," from *American Renaissance* (71).

See the individual entries for commentary on these essays.

————. *The American Novel and Its Tradition.* New York: Doubleday & Co., 1957, pp. 89–115.

In *Moby-Dick*, Melville dramatizes the central truth of his fiction: "that man lives in an insolubly dualistic world, that his profoundest awareness does not transcend the perception of his paradoxical situation, caught as he is between eternal and autonomous opposites such as good and evil, heaven and hell, God and Satan, head and heart, spirit and matter."

Chase traces the creative growth of *Moby-Dick* and generally subscribes to George Stewart's theory that there were "two Moby-Dicks" (81). He then calls attention to the influence of *King Lear* and *Macbeth* as well as that of Hawthorne on the novel. Melville viewed a work of art as an imperfect form which should be left only potentially complete, and in this sense he is closer to Whitman than to Hawthorne. *Moby-Dick* is an epic romance, with elements of melodrama, comedy, and folklore.

Chase includes a note on *Billy Budd* in which he suggests that the novel "dramatizes the conservative idea that society must follow a middle way of expediency and compromise."

For a refutation of Chase's essay see Martin Green's "Melville and the American Romance," *Re-Appraisals: Some commonsense readings in American Literature.* New York: W. W. Norton & Company, Inc., 1965, pp. 87–112. Green maintains that *Moby-Dick* is successful insofar as it is epic and not romance—the practical features of the book carry most its meaning. There is no unity "between the epic and the romance parts of *Moby-Dick*"; furthermore, the romantic elements generally fail because we cannot believe in their imaginative possibility. "Melville does not *know* why Ahab does the things he does. Because he has not fully imagined him."

————, ed. *Selected Tales and Poems by Herman Melville.* New York: Rinehart & Co., 1950, 417 pp.

This anthology contains Melville's most important short stories: "Benito Cereno," "Bartleby the Scrivener," "Jimmy Rose," "The Fiddler," "The Lightning-Rod Man," "I and My Chimney," "The Bell-Tower," "The Paradise of Bachelors and the Tartarus of Maids," "The Encantadas," and "Billy Budd." There is also a rich selection of Melville's Civil War poems as well as his poetry on other subjects.

Chase's introduction echoes his remarks in his critical study (19).

52. Cowie, Alexander, "Herman Melville," *The Rise of the American Novel.* New York: American Book Company, 1951, pp. 362–411.

This is a sensible survey of Melville's life and work. It is highly sympathetic, devoting sections to Life and Works; *Moby-Dick;* Later Works; and Mariner, Mystic,

Thinker, Critic, and Artist. Cowie views Melville as a "skeptic but not by any means an atheist." His individual analyses are intelligent and reliable, although he stands perhaps in too much awe of Melville. As for Melville's text, "it invites analysis for biographical and historical purposes, but the real secret of its power and magic must remain, like the sea, forever inscrutable."

53. Feidelson, C. N. *Symbolism and American Literature.* Chicago: The University of Chicago Press, 1953. 355 pp.

Feidelson sees Emerson and Melville as the polar figures of the American symbolist movement. Emerson "represented the upsurge of a new capacity, Melville the relapse into doubt. Emerson was the theorist and advocate, Melville the practising poet. Emerson embodied the monistic phase of symbolism, the sweeping sense of poetic fusion; Melville lived in a universe of paradox and knew the struggle to implement the claims of symbolic imagination. Yet neither was really an independent agent: their methods were reciprocal, and each entailed the other. Though Melville speaks to us today as Emerson does not, they stand on common ground, which is also common ground with our own sensibility. Melville assumed the ambient idea that Emerson made explicit, and if we feel Melville as one of ours, we must take Emerson into the bargain, whether we like it or not."

After discussing Emerson's theories about symbolism and art, Feidelson seeks to understand the reasons for Melville's modern appeal. "The Melville cult," he feels, "is consciously at least a response not to an artist but to a man, a personality. Melville has been considered a troubled, ironic, demonic writer and this figure appeals to us." Feidelson finds Melville's symbolism most clearly presented in *Pierre* and he offers an illuminating and extended comparison with Andrew Gide's *Les Faux-Monnayeurs.* "As in Gide's novel, every character [of *Pierre*], including the author, is a counterfeiter; man's life is a construct; the artist is the archetypal man."

Feidelson's estimate of *The Confidence Man* is that it is "inconclusive"; *Billy Budd* "marks the indecisive end of a campaign which could neither be wholly lost nor wholly won."

54. Forster, E. M. *Aspects of the Novel.* New York: Harcourt Brace and Company, 1927, 138–143. Reprinted as a Harvest Book, 1954.

"The essential *Moby-Dick*, its prophetic song, flows athwart the motion and the surface morality like an undercurrent. It lies outside words. . . . Nothing can be stated about *Moby Dick* except that it is a contest. The rest is song."

Forster focuses upon the sermon about Jonah and upon Ishmael's friendship with Queequeg. He also has a short appreciative passage about *Billy Budd.*

55. Foster, Elizabeth S. "Melville and Geology," *American Literature,* XVII (March, 1945), 50–65.

"Geology added a little to Melville's literary resources: it gave him opportunities for humor in *Mardi*, and in *Moby Dick* it supplied some of [the] characteristic imagery." Miss Foster suggests that Melville's knowledge of geology disturbed his theological orientation.

See also Miss Foster's "Another Note on Melville and Geology," *American Literature*, XXII (January, 1951), 479–487, which is a reply to Tyrus Hillway's "Melville Geological Knowledge," *American Literature*, XXI (May, 1949), 232–237.

56. Gross, Theodore L. "Herman Melville: The Nature of Authority," *The Colorado Quarterly*, XVI (Spring, 1968), 397–412.

This essay is concerned with Melville's "criticism of Emersonian self-reliance, his deep skepticism about the nature of confidence and optimism—and authority." In Melville's early work—*Typee* and *Omoo*, *Redburn* and *White-Jacket*—the conflict between idealism and authority is clearly drawn. In *Moby-Dick* Melville creates his "most brilliant expression of the abusive effects of power and manipulation"; in "Benito Cereno," "Bartleby, the Scrivener," and *The Confidence Man* one witnesses the breakdown of the will as Melville becomes increasingly misanthropic. Although in *Billy Budd* Melville recognizes the necessity of authority and still expresses "his faith in the human spirit," Captain Vere is really "the ideal" rather than "the actual" authoritarian. Melville's best work—*Moby-Dick*; "Benito Cereno"; "Bartleby, the Scrivener"; and *The Confidence Man*—expresses an ever-increasing distrust of power and speaks of the authority that actually exists. "We remember Melville as a profound critic of misused self-reliance in its various forms—the apocalyptic dominance of Ahab, the quiet tyranny of Bartleby, the naked aggression of Babo, the tyrannous cunning and duplicity of the Confidence Man—and as we become more aware of the dangers of the singular will, of ruthless power and authority, we find the image of ourselves reflected in the mirror of Melville's fiction and seek to escape that image."

57. Guetti, James, *The Limits of Metaphor: A Study of Melville, Conrad, and Faulkner.* Ithaca: Cornell University Press, 1967.

Guetti is concerned with a new major tradition in the novel which "reveals more and more clearly a fundamental imaginative instability, reveals a failure to compose experience in any way or to create coherent metaphorical structures of any sort." One of the most significant aspects of the formal disintegration in the novel is actual verbal phenomena. Guetti's treatment of Melville is contained in a chapter entitled "The Language of Moby-Dick."

There are three basic forms of language in *Moby-Dick:* sustained special vocabularies, like those used when Melville describes whales and whaling; reports on what others have said about whales and Moby Dick, in the form of an allusion or a Greek myth, which creates a large body of figurative language; and "the use of figurative language that within itself is both complex and unresolved, language that is significant as an explicit admission by the narrator that he cannot know or say what is most important." The chapter on Cetology illustrates Melville's narrative technique throughout *Moby-Dick:* "the exploration of special and artificial kinds of language that serve to draw our attention to the limitations of such language."

Guetti notes Ishmael's habit of making indefinite statements and its effectiveness in the narration of *Moby-Dick.* A reader "encounters Ishmael's many linguistic approaches to the story, all of which are indirect, all of which are possible, and none exclusive of other possibilities. In the creation of *Moby-Dick,* Melville "discovered more than even he, at the time, was aware. For this novel may be considered the prototype of those works of prose fiction that are concerned with the problem of imaginative failure and the uses of language that . . . the 'failure' entails."

58. Hayman, Allen, "The Real and the Original: Herman Melville's Theory of Prose Fiction," *Modern Fiction Studies,* VIII (Autumn, 1962), 211–233.

Melville believed that "the surface verisimilitude of the realistic novelist was less important than the 'vital truth.'" In order to formulate Melville's theory of prose fiction, Hayman has turned to the fictions themselves, letters, journals, and a few of Melville's reviews. Hayman discusses Melville's review of Hawthorne's *Mosses from an Old Manse,* in which he expresses admiration for Hawthorne's "power of blackness," and then turns to Chapter XXXIII of *The Confidence Man,* a pertinent text for Melville's meaning of reality in fiction—the actualities of the everyday world are less important than the reality and it is reality with which Melville is concerned. In the famous "Agatha" letter, which Melville wrote to Hawthorne and suggested that the story of Agatha was more suited to the older writer's temperament, Melville is concerned primarily with the truth of the story and the symbolic value of the material. In all of his views of fiction, Melville was different from the critics of his day: he wrote neither the historical romance nor the sentimental domestic novel, and as he developed himself, he became less concerned with the "surface verisimilitude" of the realist.

59. Hoeltje, Hubert H. "Hawthorne, Melville, and 'Blackness,'" *American Literature,* XXXVII (March, 1965), 41–51.

Hoeltje examines Melville's essay on Hawthorne's *Mosses* in some detail. He denies Randall Stewart's remark that "'Hawthorne and His Mosses' is one of the great critical essays of the nineteenth century." Melville's essay "lacks a necessary ingredient of greatness—namely Truth."

The tendency on the part of critics has been to agree too quickly with Melville that Hawthorne's fiction is characterized by "blackness." Hawthorne valued, far more than Melville notes, an essay by Henry T. Tuckerman (which was published in *The Southern Literary Messenger* and reprinted in Littell's *Living Age* on July 11, 1864). Hoeltje feels that Tuckerman's piece is more balanced and judicial than Melville's. Hoeltje's reservations about those critics who accept Melville's remarks without question may be justified; but he measures Melville too much as a "formal" critic who should have written a more harmonious essay rather than as a creative writer who saw into the essence of Hawthorne's work. The essay is also marred by Hoeltje's bias in favor of Hawthorne.

60. Hoffman, Daniel F. *Form and Fable in American Fiction.* New York: Oxford University Press, 1961, pp. 221–313.

Hoffman explores the reliance of Melville "upon allegory, Gothicism, didacticism, religion and travel writings, and traditions of folklore, popular culture, and mythology."

Moby-Dick is, first of all, "the greatest hunting story in American literature." Hoffman explores the inner meaning of the novel in terms of "myth, magic, and metaphor." He notes the combination of folk humor and fear of the supernatural in the novel; the use of the tall tale; and the relationship of the biblical Jonah story to the book. He offers an interesting analysis of *The Confidence Man* in terms of its many masks, and notes the influence of Thomas Bangs Thorpe on Melville. Melville's "progress from blithe good humor through the extremities of romantic egoism to the despairing ironies of *The Confidence Man* marked both a personal tragedy and the experience of his culture."

61. Honig, Edwin. *Dark Conceit, The Making of Allegory.* Evanston: Northwestern University Press, 1959. 210 pp.

Melville's fiction was a reaction against the social and sentimental novel so popular in England and America. He used the sea as a setting in which he could go beyond "pasteboard characterization and historicism. . . . Melville's problem, like Hawthorne's, was to find a method whereby a vigorous moral and esthetic authority could be recreated in fiction. For him, as for his predecessors, the challenge was to map out the relation of the unknown country of allegory to the known countries and conditions of contemporary actuality." In *Moby-Dick*, Melville succeeded in creating a "literal dimension for his allegorical narrative." The undistorted facts about whaling support the allegorical elements in the novel.

62. Howard, Leon. "Melville's Struggle with the Angel," *Modern Language Quarterly*, I (June, 1940), 195–206.

Melville's struggle is with the Angel of Art. Howard maintains that Melville had less formal skill as a writer than most of his critics claim. He borrowed most of his technical devices. Ahab is based on Coleridge's view of the Shakespearean tragic hero; the "quest" plot is taken from Hawthorne. Melville relied mostly on suspense and allusiveness.

63. Kaul, A. N. "Herman Melville: The New World Voyageur," *The American Vision: Actual and Ideal Society in Nineteenth-Century Fiction.* New Haven: Yale University Press, 1963, pp. 214–279.

For Kaul's general intentions in this study, see the entry under his name in the Hawthorne bibliography (85).

In his treatment of Melville, Kaul stresses the relationship between the heroes and the societies they confront. In *Typee*, savage societies are viewed as superior to civilized ones; the theme of *Redburn* is the initiation of a friendless boy into a corrupt society; *White-Jacket* is concerned with "the war within a nation rather than the war of nations"; in *Moby-Dick*, Melville attempts to reconcile the "material drives behind the colonization of the new continent with the moral-metaphysical vision that accompanied it." Ahab despises the fact that he must depend upon others for the realization of his revenge and because of his "desolation of solitude," he succumbs to his overmastering perversity. Contrasted with Ahab's isolation is the communal brotherhood of Ishmael and Queequeg.

"Even in the fresh and youthful *Typee* Melville's dream of the ideal possibilities of life is not naive. It does not fail to take into account the grimmer realities of man's nature and the nature of the world he lives in. Likewise in his later work, when blackness has moved into the center of the universe, he acknowledges the brightness that is the other side of life. The acknowledgment is by no means equally explicit in all cases. More often the ideal finds an inverted expression in the very intensity of its denial in the actual. . . . For all his relevance to our time, he was the poet of a more hopeful age."

64. Lawrence, D. H. *Studies in Classic American Literature.* New York: T. Seltzer, 1923. Reprinted by Doubleday Anchor Books, 1953, pp. 142–174, and by Edmund Wilson, ed., *The Shock of Recognition, The Development of Literature in the United States by the Men Who Made It.* New York: Farrar, Straus and Cudahy, 1943, pp. 1031–1061.

For a statement of Lawrence's general intentions in this volume see the entry in the Hawthorne bibliography (90).

For Lawrence, Melville is "the greatest seer and poet of the sea . . . a modern Viking." Lawrence devotes two chapters to Melville, one on *Typee* and *Omoo* and another on *Moby-Dick*. Melville returned to the Pacific Ocean, the oldest of oceans, largely because he hated human life and hated the world. In *Typee* he found the paradise he was looking for, although he wasn't happy there and pined for "Home and Mother." Like other westerners, Melville could not return to primitivism, however sympathetic toward it he may have been. Still Melville believed that Paradise existed; as a consequence he was always in Purgatory. "*Omoo* is a fascinating book: picaresque, rascally, roving. Melville as a bit of a beachcomber. The crazy ship *Julia* sails to Tahiti, and the mutinous crew are put ashore. Put in the Tahitian prison. It is good reading."

In *Moby-Dick*, "The artist was so *much* greater than the man. The man is rather a tiresome New Englander of the ethical mystical-transcendentalist sort: Emerson, Longfellow, Hawthorne, etc. So unrelieved, the solemn ass even in humour. . . . But he was a deep, great artist, even if he was rather a sententious man. He was a real American in that he always felt his audience in front of him. But when he ceases to be American, when he forgets all audience, and gives us his sheer apprehension of the world, then he is wonderful, his book commands a stillness in the soul, an awe." Lawrence analyzes *Moby-Dick* in detail, quoting extensively and concluding that it "is a great book, a very great book, the greatest book of the sea ever written. It moves awe in the soul. . . . Melville knew. He knew his race was doomed. His white soul, doomed. His great white epoch, doomed. Himself, doomed. The idealist, doomed. The spirit, doomed . . . [*Moby-Dick*] is hunted, hunted, hunted by the maniacal fanaticism of our white mental consciousness. We want to hunt him down. To subject him to our will. And in this maniacal conscious hunt of ourselves we get dark races and pale to help us, red, yellow, and black, east and west, Quaker and fire-worshipper, we get them all to help us in this ghastly maniacal hunt which is our doom and our suicide."

65. Levin, Harry. *The Power of Blackness: Hawthorne, Poe, Melville.* New York: Alfred A. Knopf, 263 pp., reprinted as a Vintage Book, 1960.

For a fuller description of Levin's general intentions see the entry in the Hawthorne bibliography (93). Levin believes that "Symbolism has been the intrinsic mode of American writing" and he applies it to Melville. His treatment of Melville is divided into two chapters: "The Avenging Dream" and "The Jonah Complex." In "The Avenging Dream, Levin traces the thread of blackness that runs through the five books which lead up to *Moby-Dick*. The starting point is a "*roman vécu* of earthly paradise." Levin emphasizes the pastoral qualities of *Typee* and *Omoo* and then traces Melville's growing sensitivity to blackness, especially in *Redburn*. In *Moby-Dick* Melville fused "his practical observation with his speculative imagination. Blackness was counterbalanced there by whiteness in such dazzling radiance that its successor was bound to be an anticlimax." Blackness reaches one of its richest expressions in "Benito Cereno."

"The Jonah Complex" is primarily devoted to *Moby-Dick*. Melville moves, in this novel, from the known to the unknown, from light toward dark, and creates a "glorified whaleman" who is "a culture-hero, a dragon-slayer and therefore a liberator, a crusader under the patronage of Saint George, a demi-god claiming descent from Perseus."

66. Lewis, R. W. B. "Melville: The Apotheosis of Adam," in *The American Adam: Innocence, Tragedy, and Tradition in the Nineteenth Century.* Chicago: The University of Chicago Press, 1955; reprinted as a Phoenix paperback edition, 1958, pp. 127–155.

Lewis views Melville as the one American artist who made the Adamic myth "manifest." "In this chapter we consider how the one novelist in nineteenth-century America gifted with a genuine myth-making imagination was able to elevate the anecdote to the status of myth, and so give it a permanent place among the resources of our literature . . . For Melville took the loss of innocence and the world's betrayal of hope as the supreme challenge to understanding and art."

Lewis analyses "The Tryworks"—chapter 96 in *Moby-Dick*—"as a summary of Melville's attitude to innocence and evil and as an example of Melville's way with the material (attitudes, tropes, language) available to him." He then examines *Typee* and *Redburn* as novels concerned with the initiation into evil. *Moby-Dick*, in Lewis's treatment, "is an elaborate pattern of countercommentaries, the supreme instance of the dialectical novel—a novel of tension without resolution." In *Billy Budd*, "Melville's own cycle of experience and commitment, which began with the hopeful dawn and 'the glorious, glad, golden sun,' returns again to the dawn—but a dawn transfigured, 'seen in mystical vision.' Melville salvaged the legend of hope for life and for literature: by repudiating it in order to restore it in an apotheosis of its hero."

67. Lewisohn, Ludwig. *Expression in America.* New York: Harper & Brothers, 1932, pp. 188–189, 193.

Lewisohn expressed a reaction against the renewed interest in Melville's work. "A younger generation, in search of that 'usable' American past which Van Wyck Brooks so earnestly and sagaciously demanded long ago, has fastened its flag to his [Melville's] mast. Has not that generation been both deceived and self-deceived? Has it not substituted its desire and ideal for the reality? Melville was not a strong man defying the cruel order of the world; he was a weak man fleeing from his own soul and from life, a querulous man, a fretful man. . . . No, Melville is not even a minor master. His works constitute rather one of the important curiosities of literature."

68. Lucid. Robert F. "The Influence of *Two Years Before the Mast* on Herman Melville," *American Literature*, XXXI (November, 1959), 243–256.

"Melville can be said to be working from, if not in, a tradition which Dana established. . . . Melville was influenced by Dana's personal suggestions, by a factual voyage narrative that Dana almost surely recommended, and finally by a whole genre which Dana was influential in popularizing."

Lucid points out that Dana and Melville discussed literary problems and that Dana felt free to make suggestions to Melville about his work.

69. MacShane, Frank. "Conrad on Melville," *American Literature*, XXIX (January, 1958), 463–464.

MacShane reproduces a letter to Humphrey Milford, who requested a preface to an edition of *Moby-Dick* which Oxford wanted to publish. Conrad declined and wrote: "Years ago I looked at *Typee* and *Omoo*, but as I didn't find there what I am looking for when I open a book I did not go further. Lately I had in my hand *Moby Dick*. It struck me as a rather strained rhapsody with whaling for a subject and not a single sincere line in the three volumes of it."

70. Marx, Leo. *The Machine in the Garden,* Technology and the Pastoral Ideal in America. New York: Oxford University Press, 1964.

Ishmael is "an alienated American seafarer aboard a whaling ship, which is an extension of Western civilization." Ishmael avoids the trap of "sentimental pastoralism," for he discovers that in a whaling world "man's primary relation to nature is technological. . . . Throughout *Moby-Dick* Melville uses machine imagery to relate the undisguised killing and butchery of whaling to the concealed violence of 'civilized' Western society."

71. Matthiessen, F. O. *American Renaissance: Art and Expression in the Age of Emerson and Whitman.* New York: Oxford University Press, 1941, pp. 179–191, 317–516.

This seminal work was the first to explore deeply Melville's artistic accomplishment in terms of tragedy. In a chapter entitled "The Vision of Evil," Matthiessen offers a cogent definition of tragedy: "The creation of tragedy demands of its author a mature understanding of the relation of the individual to society, and, more especially, of the nature of good and evil. . . . Tragedy does not pose the situation of a faultless individual (or class) overwhelmed by an evil world, for it is built on the experienced realization that man is radically imperfect. Confronting this fact, tragedy must likewise contain a recognition that man, pitiful as he may be in his finite weakness, is still capable of apprehending perfection, and of becoming transfigured by that vision."

Matthiessen then compares Melville with Hawthorne, noting the debt of the younger writer, and comments upon Melville's criticism of Emerson and the transcendentalists. He offers excellent close analyses of *Redburn, Mardi,* and *White-Jacket* and traces Melville's developing ability to merge external and internal experience; his explication of the fall from the yard-arm in *White-Jacket* (in the chapter, "The Last of the Jacket") is particularly fruitful. Matthiessen also emphasizes the great influence of Shakespeare on the writing of *Moby-Dick;* the structure and language of the novel; the connections between Melville and Hawthorne in *Pierre;* and the "affirmation of the heart" in *Billy Budd.*

Melville confronts the dualism in life more directly than either Emerson or Hawthorne but emerges, in Matthiessen's view, as an "American Hamlet," unable, like Hawthorne, to resolve his conflict.

72. Maxwell, Desmond E. S. "The Tragic Phase: Melville and Hawthorne," *American Fiction, The Intellectual Background.* New York: Columbia University Press, 1963, pp. 141–191.

The object of Melville's work was to illuminate the correspondence between "the seen and the unseen that stirs, half-recognised, within it." Maxwell examines *White-Jacket* closely, and considers it a novel of "unconditional antagonisms: the despotic laws of man against the compassion of Christ; death against life; evil, in all its forms, against a transcendent good, visible in man; democratic reform against reactionary *laissez-faire*." In *Moby-Dick* these contradictions are expressed more fully, although as a work of tragedy "it does not show us a tragic hero not only enduring a tragic fate but recognising in what the tragedy consists." Maxwell has high praise for *The Confidence Man*, a novel which "portrays a society where both the desire and the ability to appreciate good and evil were, not dead, but distempered; where epiphanies went unrecognised though, like the merchant's still granted. It is not, therefore, a society without God."

73. Miller, James E. "Melville's Search for Form," *Bucknell Review*, VIII (December, 1959), 260–276.

Melville is considered a classic author, but he is often criticized for his faulty craftsmanship. Miller takes issue with R. P. Blackmur's reservations about Melville as an artist (94). If we consider Melville as a writer in the tradition of the novel, then his limitations are apparent; but if we consider him as an author who is creating a unique form inherent in any great classic, these very faults becomes virtues. Melville was "an author of an amalgam of allegory, epic, satire, philosophy." In *Typee* and *Omoo* he wrote travel literature; in *Mardi* he created allegory, satire, and romance, in *Redburn* and *White-Jacket* he wrote sea stories; in *Moby-Dick* he developed a tragedy and an epic; in *Pierre* he composed the novel itself and in *The Confidence Man* legend and folklore, allegory and comedy. Melville's quest for form was really a search for order, a desire for faith and belief. He was not "content to accept without question the dominant form of his day—the novel. . . . There is hardly a kind of literature he did not sample or assimilate: travel book, sea yarn, sociological study, philosophical tract, allegory, epic, domestic or historical romance, tragedy or comedy."

74. Miller, Perry. *The Raven and the Whale: The War of Words and Wits in the Era of Poe and Melville.* New York: Harcourt, Brace and Company, 1956, 370 pp.

This study is valuable for its presentation of the actual literary world in which Melville functioned. Miller traces the literary wars that occurred in the years from 1840 through 1855 between Lewis Gaylord Clark, who was an antiromantic editor of the *Knickerbocker* magazine, and Evert A. Duyckinck, an editor for Wiley and Putnam and the sponsor of Poe, Melville, and "the young America."

Miller indicates that most of the reviews of Melville's books were biased. Duyckinck was one of the few writers who commended Melville's work to the public. He praised *Typee* and *Omoo* as "truthful and as works of genius"; he had good words for *White-Jacket* and *Moby-Dick;* and he defended *Mardi* to a hostile public. Ultimately Melville declaimed his independence from "Young America." The chapter in *Pierre* called "Young America in Literature" is his private letter to

Duyckinck, in which he curses the editor for bringing him into the world of Young America. Nevertheless, Melville's *Israel Potter* (1855) was the last stand of Young America, a bitter attack on Benjamin Franklin and the average citizen.

————. "Melville and Transcendentalism," *Moby-Dick Centennial Essays.* Edited with an Introduction by Tyrus Hillway and Luther S. Mansfield. Dallas: Southern Methodist University Press, 1953, pp. 123–152.

Melville was thoroughly schooled in the conventions of the romantic novelists Scott and Cooper, and like them he emphasized the moral supremacy of nature over the city. As he developed from 1846 to 1852, "he progressively utilized the conventions of his romance to destroy the romantic thesis." Melville turned to metaphysical brooding, the "German disease" of many contemporary Americans; this tendency harmed his fiction.

Miller traces Melville's growing disenchantment with Emerson's brand of transcendentalism and points out that even though Melville grew increasingly impatient with Emerson, many of his ideas stemmed from transcendental ideas. "*Moby-Dick* and *Pierre* are not Christian works. There is compassion in them, but no intercession and no forgiveness, because their terms are not those of God and man, but resolutely of man in nature. They are, in the common use of the word, tragic; but they do not despair. They remain, to the end, implacably, defiantly, and unrepentantly Transcendental."

75. *Modern Fiction Studies*, Herman Melville Number, VIII (Autumn, 1962).

This number contains seven essays and an excellent checklist of works about Melville.

The essays are Allen Hayman, "The Real and the Original: Herman Melville's Theory of Prose Fiction" (58); Howard C. Horsford, "The Design of the Argument in *Moby-Dick*" (109); Sister Mary Ellen, "Duplicate Imagery in *Moby-Dick*"; John T. Frederick, "Symbol and Theme in Melville's *Israel Potter*"; Kingley Widmer, "The Negative Affirmation: Melville's 'Bartleby'"; Jesse D. Green, "Diabolism, and Democracy: Notes on Melville and Conrad"; William T. Stafford, "The New *Billy Budd* and the Novelistic Fallacy: An Essay-Review."

Maurice Beebe, Harrison Hayford, and Gordon Roper prepared the "Criticism of Herman Melville: A Second Checklist."

76. Monson, S. E. ed. "Melville's 'Agatha' Letter to Hawthorne," *The New England Quarterly*, II (April, 1929), 296–307.

Melville gave Hawthorne memoranda of a true story of bigamy presented to him by a New Bedford lawyer. In the accompanying letter he suggested to Hawthorne how the story ought to be worked up into fiction. Melville's letter provides a good understanding of his literary methods.

77. Parrington, Vernon L. *Main Currents in American Thought*. Volume Two. New York: Harcourt, Brace and Company, 1930. 258–267.

Parrington regards Melville as an eccentric figure when compared with Whitman, Emerson, and William Cullen Bryant, and calls him a "pessimist." He then characterizes him as "an arch romantic who vainly sought to erect his romantic dreams as a defense against reality, and suffered disaster."

Melville "was in love with the ideal" and Parrington compares him with James Branch Cabell. Like other early critics, Parrington believed that Melville was an escapist who was unable to face life. Parrington's weakness in belletristic criticism has been thoroughly analyzed by Lionel Trilling in his essay, "Reality in America," *The Liberal Imagination*. New York: The Macmillan Co., 1951, pp. 1–19.

78. Pochmann, Henry A. "Herman Melville," *German Culture in America*. Madison: The University of Wisconsin Press, 1957, pp. 436–440.

Pochmann relates Kant to Melville and shows that Kant "furnished Melville with the backbone upon which to build his anatomy of despair." Of the German authors, Melville knew most about Kant. "Melville was attracted to German thought in much the same way that Emerson was drawn to it—by the hope that it would help him in the problem of squaring his heart by his head."

79. Rourke, Constance. *American Humor: A Study of the National Character*. New York: Harcourt, Brace and Company, Inc., 1931. Reprinted by Doubleday Anchor Books, 1953, pp. 154–160.

Melville was a legend-maker and in *Moby-Dick* he drew upon whaling lore from many sources. "Passages of comic fantasy are strewn through the narrative," beginning with the encounter of Ishmael and Queequeg. The ship itself contains representatives of all the American comic types: Negro, Indian, mountaineer, Shaker prophet, and others. Miss Rourke concludes her brief essay by saying that "with the writing of his one great book Melville's work was finished"; but she neglects the rich comedy and satire in many of the stories and especially in the novels, *Israel Potter* and *The Confidence Man*.

80. Short, R. W. "Melville as Symbolist," *The University of Kansas Review*, XV (Autumn, 1948), 38–46. Reprinted in *Interpretations of American Literature*. Edited by Charles Feidelson, Jr. and Paul Brodtkorb. New York: Oxford University Press, 1959, pp. 102–113.

Short considers the contention on the part of many critics that Melville's work, especially *Moby-Dick*, is allegoric. He believes that the letter that Melville wrote to Mrs. Hawthorne, in which he speaks of *Moby-Dick* as a book "susceptible of an allegoric construction," has misled critics. What Melville did intend, "he lacked critical vocabulary to define, for the critics of the mid-nineteenth century wrote intelligibly of allegory and realism, but falteringly if at all of varieties of symbolism or use of myth, the language of Melville's artistic strategy." Short compares Melville with Shakespeare, pointing out that both authors "were concerned with elements of experience behind the immediate fog of physical reality. Like other writers with this concern, they need a myth-world. . . . Melville's method, then, allows his symbols to accumulate meanings in the course of their use, as they knock about in his myth-world, and so a single meaning attached to them often has at least a partial validity. Allegorical interpretation of a medieval or puritanic sort, however, defeats the larger aspect of the work, for Melville's view of reality is a more oriental view, based upon a sense of the ultimate interdependence, rather than the isolation, of experiential units."

This essay is an extremely sensible interpretation of the technique of *Moby-Dick*, and an important corrective to those analyses that tend to impose a rigid framework on the novel.

81. Stewart, Randall. *American Literature and Christian Doctrine*. Baton Rouge: Louisiana State University Press, 1958, pp. 89–102. This essay may also be found in "The Vision of Evil in Hawthorne and Melville," *The Tragic Vision and the Christian Faith*. Edited by Nathan A. Scott, Jr. New York: Associated Press, 1957, pp. 257–262.

Stewart offers a fourteen-page reading of *Moby-Dick* and *Billy Budd*. Ahab's character deteriorates in the course of the novel as he stifles "his humanities." In creating Ahab, Melville may have been influenced by Hawthorne's character of Ethan Brand—both are fire-worshippers; both have made a Faustian pact; both are suicides. "*Moby-Dick* is the greatest classic, in America, of man's defiance. Man is prone to defiance: it is another manifestation, and a chief one, of Original Sin."

In *Billy Budd* there is a residue of goodness in the memory of Billy. "*Billy Budd* certainly is a brilliant and moving statement of the ultimate Christian lesson of resignation to God's overruling Providence, and it is pleasant, as well as reasonable, to think that Melville in his last years felt the truth of this view."

The student will discover nothing new in this criticism, but he will encounter a sensible interpretation of Melville's two greatest works.

————. "Melville and Hawthorne," *South Atlantic Quarterly*, LI (July, 1952), 436–446. Reprinted in *Moby-Dick Centennial Essays*. Edited by Tyrus Hillway and Luther S. Mansfield. Dallas: Southern Methodist University Press, pp. 153–164.

This essay concentrates on the friendship between Melville and Hawthorne, particularly in terms of the influence that Hawthorne had on his younger friend. Stewart refutes Lewis Mumford's notion that Melville was the model for Hawthorne's Ethan Brand and that this unflattering portrait was the reason for their diminishing friendship; "Ethan Brand" was published before Melville met Hawthorne. Stewart suggests that geographical separation was the chief cause for the loss of close friendship that had flowered in the Berkshires from August, 1850, until November, 1851.

Stewart states that "A good deal in fact has been done with the influence of Shakespeare's works, and almost nothing, so far as I know, with Hawthorne's. I have no intention of attempting to make good this deficiency in the present paper." It is regrettable that Stewart does not offer at least the tentative outlines for such a study, rather than write a fairly obvious essay on the relationship between the two authors and only suggest that Hawthorne's two major influences on Melville were allegory and his sense of "blackness." He concludes by expressing doubt that "Hawthorne's influence was 'germinous'"; it was primarily "fostering and stimulating." The two writers were deeply American in their cultural attitudes.

82. Thorp, Willard, "Herman Melville," *The Literary History of the United States*, Volume 1. New York: The Macmillan Company, 1948. 3 volumes. pp. 440–471.

Thorp considers the connections between Hawthorne and Melville and then attempts an answer to why Melville was even less popular, after the writing of his early novels, than Thoreau and Whitman: "In an age which increasingly believed in the rightness of material success and was content with the compromise of agnosticism, this spectacle of a once popular novelist who permitted his mind to 'run riot amid remote analogies' was, to say the least, bewildering." Thorp has interesting, though necessarily brief, comments to make about the individual novels: the "I" of *Typee* "is not merely a reporter, but an enterprising young man, full of spirit and curiosity, and also somewhat shrewd and sly"; *Omoo* is episodic, a novel whose tone is "irresponsible gaiety"; *Mardi* is the beginning of Melville's "long quest for the ultimate truth"; *Moby-Dick* is concerned with one of the great episodes of national life, whaling; *Pierre* is a novel which deals with the ambiguities of life—it is, Melville's "second novel" in that it stems from his imagination rather than from his experiences. "The stories written after *Pierre* deal almost exclusively with human relationships, not with metaphysical considerations."

83. Van Doren, Carl. *Cambridge History of American Literature*. Volume 1. New York: The Macmillan Co., 1917, 322–323.

Van Doren was one of the first critics to recognize the importance and originality of *Moby-Dick*. "Too irregular, too bizarre, perhaps, ever to win the widest suffrage, the immense originality of *Moby-Dick* must warrant the claim of its admirers that it belongs with the greatest sea romances in the whole literature of the world."

84. Winters, Yvor. "Herman Melville, and the Problems of Moral Navigation," *Maule's Curse, Seven Studies in the History of American Obscurantism*. Norfolk, Conn.: New Directions, 1938, pp. 53–89.

Winters provides an extensive analysis of the symbolism of *Moby-Dick*, which he views as an "antithesis of the sea and the land: the land represents the known, the mastered, inhuman experience; the sea the half-known, the obscure region of instinct, uncritical feeling, danger, and terror."

Winters berates critics for saying that *Moby-Dick* is "careless, redundant, or in any sense romantic. . . . The book is less a novel than an epic poem." It is, particularly, an American epic. Winters finds the prose of *Moby-Dick* closer to the poetry of *Paradise Lost* than to the prose of a novelist like Edith Wharton. Ahab is another Coriolanus, "but in dimensions epical, in the quality of his mind and of his sin metaphysical, and in his motivating ideas Calvinistical."

Winters also admires *Benito Cereno*, *The Encantadas*, and *Billy Budd*. He finds *The Confidence Man* "unsatisfactory philosophy" and "repetitious as narrative."

Winters' essay is unnecessarily contentious in its manner, although it is worth the student's attention; his interpretation is, after all, rather traditional.

Typee:

85. Firebaugh, Joseph J. "Humorist as Rebel: The Melville of *Typee*," *Nineteenth-Century Fiction*, IX (September, 1954), 108–120.

Melville's "richly tolerant humor is the palliative of his rebellion." Too many contemporary critics concentrate upon Melville's gloom and skepticism; in fact, Melville possessed a strong comic strain and in *Typee* we can see, at first glance, "a salty, sailorly humor—a commonplace humor—a rather unsubtle humor." Melville was capable of laughing at "the primitive while admiring it": what he did was to make "the primitive a basis for satire on civilization."

Redburn:

86. Gilman, W. H. *Melville's Early Life and* Redburn. New York: New York University Press, 1951. 378 pp.

This study is the definitive work on Melville's life from 1819 to 1841. Gilman poses the central problem that his book seeks to resolve: "The known facts of Melville's life, though meager, corresponded to the events in his books. His books must therefore be his own story in his own words. Such assumptions underlie an important body of modern criticism and biography that focus upon the man in Melville at the expense of the artist. At the same time, laborious scholarship has proved that some of Melville's books are not the outright personal revelation for which they had been mistaken. To date no such study has been made of the relation between Melville's early life and *Redburn*, the book which seems to picture his boyhood and youth. What is the true nature of this book? Is it the confessions and reminiscences of a writer limited to the depiction of literal truth? Or is it shaped by an artist with a fertile imagination and a vigorous creative power?"

Gilman separates fact from fiction. He substantially challenges, for example, "the truth of the flight to London" and he proves that Melville's description of five hundred immigrants on board the Highlander was purely fictional. Gilman's evaluation of the novel as a work of art is generally sound, although excessively high: "it is superior to anything in its genre, and many single chapters are superior to things outside the genre."

The appendices in this study are valuable, especially "The Reputation of *Redburn*" (pp. 274–287).

Gilman's study is especially suggestive in its new picture of Melville's parents. He indicates that they were not so religious as had been suspected and that Maria Melville was not the oppressive mother one reads of in previous studies.

87. Schweter, James. "*Redburn* and the Failure of Mythic Criticism," *American Literature*, XXXIX (November, 1967), 279–297.

Most critics view *Redburn* as a gloomy book and have interpreted it from two points of view: the biographical, represented by the work of Weaver (45), Freeman (24), Mumford (35), and Gilman (86), and the mythic, represented by Arvin (14), Mason (32), and Lewis (65). The mythic approach to the novel and of Melville's work in general flourished in the 1950's when myth criticism was particularly popular. Schweter maintains that, like the biographical method, the mythic method "does not hold up—that it is contradicted repeatedly by some of the most important tonal and structural features of the novel."

Melville employs an ironically comic tone which is employed in the putative sense that R. P. Blackmur first noted (94). Redburn is not "a guileless spirit" like Billy Budd and Donatello (of Hawthorne's *Marble Faun*); and his transition from "Son-of-a-Gentleman" to "Sailor Boy" is not a "fall." In Redburn's rejection of Harry Bolton and Jackson and Melville's own rejection of the genteel and "Jacksonian" viewpoints, Melville strove for balance and independence.

Mardi:

88. Davis, Merrell R. *Melville's Mardi, A Chartless Voyage*. New Haven: Yale University Press, 1952. 240 pp.

Together with Charles Anderson's *Melville and the South Seas* (13) and William H. Gilman's *Melville's Early Life and* Redburn (86), Davis's study separates fact from fiction in Melville's life and work and serves as a corrective to the biographies of Weaver (45), Freeman (24), and Mumford (35).

There are three parts to Davis's book: 1. Melville's return from the South

Pacific in 1844 and his excitement about writing a book. 2. The history of *Mardi* during two years from 1847–1848. 3. An analysis of the published book.

"This study is concerned with the literary and biographical background, the genesis, writing, and meaning of Herman Melville's *Mardi: and a Voyage Thither*. I have tried to assemble for the first time all the available material for a study of the inception and growth of the book and for a detailed analysis of it as an independent literary production. I have done so in the belief that *Mardi*, despite its flaws, is peculiarly fitted to illustrate Melville at work and is an important focal point in his early literary career."

Davis believes that *Mardi* moves from a "narrative beginning"—pictorial and suspenseful, humorous and whimsical—to a philosophical quest. "If a meaning for the quest is to be stated it might better be described in the general terms which one finds represented in the poet's moral in Emerson's 'Sphinx.'"

This work is invaluable not only for its analysis of *Mardi* but for its depiction of the way Melville shaped a work during a crucial period in his life. Davis concludes that "Since the Narrator's quest through *Mardi* is a literary device to bind together the book's varied and disparate ingredients and at the same time to give coherence of meaning to the narrative, the attempt to find a perfectly consistent allegory in the book is fruitless."

Moby-Dick:

89. Auden, W. H. *The Enchafèd Flood or The Romantic Iconography of the Sea.* New York: Random House, 1950. 154 pp.

Auden's book is "an attempt to understand the nature of Romanticism through an examination of its treatment of a single theme, the sea." Auden divides his study into three parts: "The Sea and the Desert"; "The Stone and the Shell"; and "Ishmael—Don Quixote." His first two sections deal with the general attraction of the subject of the sea to Romantic writers; his last section concentrates more specifically on *Moby-Dick*.

Auden discusses *Moby-Dick* in terms of various types of heroic authority—Aesthetic, Ethical, and Religious—and he relates the novel to other great works concerned with heroism. Ishmael is similar to Don Quixote, although there is a "crucial difference between them . . . Ishmael is self-conscious and Don Quixote is completely self-forgetful." Auden offers perceptive analyses of the individual chapters in the book: Starbuck "keeps to his belief but at the cost of refusing to experience. . . . Starbuck fears God; Stubb fears suffering. Starbuck knows what he fears; Stubb doesn't. . . . [Flask] has developed the underdog's Philistinism; he trivialises everything . . . [Pip] is bound to Ahab because they have both suffered a catastrophe, Ahab through his own deliberate original attack on the whale, Pip through the thoughtless action of the decent fellow Stubb . . . [Ahab's] whole life, in fact, is one of taking up defiantly a cross he is not required to take up."

Auden also analyzes *Billy Budd*, viewing the young sailor as the Religious Hero and Claggart as the Devil or the negative Religious Hero.

This study is valuable, particularly as it considers *Moby-Dick* in a wide cultural context.

90. Baird, James. *Ishmael*. Baltimore: The Johns Hopkins Press, 1956. 455 pp.

Baird is primarily concerned with Melville's psychological use of Oceania, and his study is influenced by the work of Suzanne Langer, Paul Tillich, and especially Jung. In interpreting *Moby-Dick*, Baird uses "autotypes" and "archetypal emblems." The autotype, he explains, is "a die impressing material potentially sympathetic or susceptible to religious symbolism." Writers need new symbols because the old (that is, the Protestant) symbols have died. Most Western artists have sought illumination or resuscitation from the Orient and from Oceania. Melville, on the other hand, is a genuine primitive: he rejected Western culture and, deeply aware of the collapse of Protestantism, he went to the East to construct an "autotype."

Baird's concentration on the primitivism and symbolism in *Moby-Dick* is illuminating, but his expression tends to be too private and murky, too pretentious. Ultimately the book promises more than it offers. As Perry Miller notes in a perceptive review of the book (*American Literature*, XXVIII, January, 1957, 535–537), "Melville is a noble, an angry, an exasperated man—but, good heavens! We do him no justice when we turn him into so egregious an exception to his time and place that we must invent an esoteric vocabulary to obfuscate the real issues of his life and of his art."

91. Battenfeld, David H. "The Source for the Hymn in *Moby-Dick*," *American Literature*, XXVII (November, 1955), 393–396.

This essay examines the hymn that Father Mapple leads his congregation in before he delivers his sermon. Battenfeld claims that the source is the "rhymed version of the first part of Psalm 18, as found in the psalms and hymns of the Reformed Protestant Dutch Church, the Church in which Melville was brought up." He juxtaposes the original with Melville's version and discovers that Melville's changes and revisions are of two kinds. Melville applies the general theme of the Psalm to the story of Jonah and makes stylistic revisions, all of which, in Battenfeld's opinion, are improvements.

92. Belgion, Montgomery. "Heterodoxy on *Moby-Dick*?" *Sewanee Review*, LV (Winter, 1947), 108–125.

Belgion maintains that *Moby-Dick* has "no concealed meaning. . . . Unquestionably this theory . . . that in reality *Moby-Dick* has a cosmic theme cannot hold. It is a hindrance, not a help, to the fullest enjoyment of the book." Belgion takes issue with Sedgwick's interpretation of *Moby Dick* (40). The story is not necessarily symbolical.

It is a tale of pursuit, a whaling adventure whose power is "magnified and made far-reaching in suggestions thanks to being given a fabulous dimension." Belgion calls attention to the American character of *Moby-Dick* and Melville's affinities with Emerson, Thoreau, Hawthorne, Whitman, and Poe in his tendency to philosophize in the midst of narrative. The derivations of Melville's greatest work are European: the Bible, Sir Thomas Browne, and Shakespeare.

93. Bezanson, Walter E. "*Moby-Dick:* Work of Art," *Moby-Dick Centennial Essays*, with an Introduction by Tyrus Hillway and Luther S. Mansfield. Dallas: Southern Methodist University Press, 1953, pp. 30–58.

Bezanson protests that *Moby-Dick* has been treated from almost every point of view, but it has not been deeply considered as a work of art. In approaching the novel aesthetically, Bezanson discusses the subject matter—whaling—and points out that Melville made great use of "logbooks, histories, and personal narratives while composing *Moby-Dick* in 1850–1851." This inert matter has been converted aesthetically by Melville through what Bezanson calls a dynamic and a structure.

By the term "dynamic" he means "the action of forces or bodies at rest." Various elements in the book dramatize the whaling matter: the characters of Ahab and Moby Dick but especially that of Ishmael, who is "the real center of meaning and the defining force of the novel." There are fundamentally two Ishmaels in *Moby-Dick:* the narrator, who is an older person, and the character in the book itself, who is a younger man. Ishmael, the narrator, has a complex character that is defined by his healthy sense of laughter; his passion for faraway places; his love of action; his "instinct for the morally and psychologically intricate"; and his "inexhaustible sense of wonder." Of greatest interest to the reader is "the narrator's unfolding sensibility."

In discussing the structure of *Moby-Dick*, Bezanson considers Ishmael's "unfolding sensibility" in terms of rhetoric, symbolism, dreams, dramatic form, sermons, and chapter sequences. The rhetoric of the novel is straight-forward exposition, poetic, idiomatic, and also composite (a blending of the expository, the poetic, and the idiomatic). In *Moby-Dick* "the persistent tendency . . . is for facts, events, and images to become symbols." The tendency toward symbolism suggests another aspect of structure—that of dreams (Ishmael and Stubb among others have important dreams). Bezanson writes of structure also in terms of chapter construction, which "grows out of the sermon form," and the narrative line of the book, which is directed by the whale pursuits and killings and, most important, the series of ship meetings.

This is a thoughtful essay in which the author offers many ways of reading *Moby-Dick* for aesthetic pleasure without insisting on "an overreaching formal pattern" to the novel. *Moby-Dick*, he concludes, is not "classical" but romantic; nevertheless, it has the kind of organized development associated with the romantic novel.

94. Blackmur, R. P. "The Craft of Herman Melville: A Putative Statement," *The Lion and the Honeycomb*. New York: Harcourt, Brace and World, Inc., 1955, pp. 124–144. Reprinted in *Melville: A Collection of Critical Essays*, ed. Richard Chase. Englewood Cliffs, New Jersey: Prentice Hall, 1962, pp. 75–90.

Blackmur focuses on *Moby-Dick* and *Pierre* and offers a suggestive interpretation of the sources of power in both novels. He considers "the tools of craft" which Melville used "under two heads: dramatic form with its inspiring conventions, and the treatment of language itself as a medium." Melville did not make any original contribution to the novel form, and his decline after *Pierre* was due to the difficulties of an American novelist functioning at that time and to the fact that Melville saw that he was essentially a "poet rather than a novelist."

The clue to Melville's special quality as an artist rests in his work saying "what it was doing or going to do, and then, as a rule" stopping short. In *Moby-Dick* Melville attempted to use allegory as a form, but it "broke down again and again and with each resumption got more and more verbal, and more and more at the mercy of the encroaching event it was meant to transcend. It was an element in the putative mode in which, lofty as it was, Melville himself could not long deeply believe." *Moby-Dick* and *Pierre* are examples of the putative form: neither plot works out; dramatic motive is weak; the dialogue is "limp and stiff and flowery in one book as the other"; characters are wooden. Because Melville expressed himself putatively, "because he was unable to master a technique—that of the novel—radically foreign to his sensibility," he could not write fiction in the last part of his life.

95. Bloom, Edward. "The Allegorical Principle," *English Literary History*, XVIII (1951), 163–190.

Bloom calls attention to the passage in Chapter XLV of *Moby-Dick* in which Melville says that unwitting landsmen "might scout at Moby Dick as a monstrous fable, or still worse and more detestable, a hideous and intolerable allegory." Bloom uses this passage to insist that the book should not be interpreted allegorically. But it seems inappropriate to assume that Melville did not want his book viewed, at least in part, as an allegory.

For a modification of this interpretation, see Charles Cook's "Ahab's 'Intolerable Allegory'" (97).

96. Brodtkorb, Paul, Jr. *Ishmael's White World, A Phenomenological Reading of Moby Dick*. New Haven: Yale University Press, 1965, 170 pp.

This book, which bears a similarity and an apparent debt to Charles Feidelson's *Symbolism in American Literature* (53), views Melville's epistemology in correspondence with "phenomenology." *Moby-Dick* is completely Ishmael's white world, in Brodtkorb's view. "If we are to understand the total existence called 'Ishmael,' we must re-experience the limits of his world, that world at which his dubious ironies point. We must again become aware that because his language evokes phenomena which can, after all, be apprehended in many ways (a 'whale' may be seen with equal validity as Flask's 'magnified mouse' or Job's Leviathan), *how* Ishmael perceives phenomenon at any given moment is a kind of prereflective 'choice.'"

Brodtkorb believes "Ishmael's book is founded in his own boredom, dread, and despair. These moods are the unity of his consciousness, and of his book. They are the correlatives of his book's 'objects,' and as moods that are neither frivolous nor fleeting . . . Ishmael goes to sea in endless repetition to create meaning out of emptiness. For him, there is no Bible to reveal Truth. The only experienced truth is human truth, and that is dependent on each man living out his own vision. Ishmael is a mental traveler who accepts with minimal illusions and defenses his human condition in that world of experience to which like the lone figure floating on a coffin at the end, humanity seems abandoned."

97. Cook, Charles H., Jr. "Ahab's 'Intolerable Allegory,'" *Boston University Studies in English*, I (1955–56), 45–52. Reprinted in *Discussions of Moby-Dick*, ed. Milton R. Stern. Boston: D. C. Heath and Company, 1960, pp. 60–65.

The whale "holds one kind of meaning for Melville and Ishmael and a different and more specific meaning for Ahab." For Melville, and thus the reader, it holds a multiplicity of meanings—the whale is finally dualistic. Man, however, has a monistic nature, and Ahab's monistic view of the whale turns into monomania. Ishmael, speaking for Melville, realizes that "the whale's face is a *tabula rasa* or a white screen"; Ahab "converts this facelessness into an intolerable allegory" and thus "commits the tragic error which Ishmael avoids."

98. Cook, Reginald L. "Big Medicine in *Moby Dick*," *Accent*, VIII (Winter, 1948), 102–109. Reprinted in *Discussions of Moby Dick*, ed. Milton R. Stern. Boston: D. C. Heath and Company, 1960, pp. 19–24.

Cook concentrates on the "magic" in *Moby-Dick*. He cites the "natural magic" of the book: the physical aspects of the whale ("with its immense head and comparatively small eye, its incredible power and remarkable propulsion") and Moby Dick's ability to dive two thousand feet below the surface of the water. But his chief concern is with Ahab, whose humanity makes the book credible and who "is bent upon supernatural revenge." "Ahab rejects the Christian way and turns by reversion to the forms of magic—'big medicine.'" Examples of Ahab's reversion to magic are his communal drinking of a liquor "hot as Satan's foot"; his forging of his lance (and his cry that "*Ego non baptizo te in nomine patris, sed in nomine diaboli!*"); the "ceremonial rituals, the divinations of the Parsee and Ahab's dream, demonological connotations, harpoon cults, the masked god of the White Whale, the fetishistic death-lance, chant-like exclamations." Cook suggests that "In seventeenth-century New England Ahab would be accused of wizardry and condemned as a sorcerer."

Big medicine in *Moby-Dick* is also "indirectly associated with Captain Ahab. The tattooed Queequeg worships a little hunchback glistening black ivory god called Yojo with gutteral pagan psalmody. The Manx-man is popularly invested with powers of discernment. The impromptu ritual enacted when the Christian Ishmael 'marries' the pagan Queequeg—together smoking the tomahawk pipe, pressing foreheads in embrace, dividing personal wealth and offering burnt biscuit to Yojo with salaams, are certain evidences of 'medicine.' So, too in the appearance of Fedallah: the tall, swart, black-jacketed, white-turbaned, protuberant Parsee who raises the Spirit Spout and prophesies Ahab's fate. Nor can we exclude the tattooed body of Queequeg, a perfect marvel of totemism." Cook concludes that Ahab's equivocal defeat is "the failure of magic as an effective force in the manipulation of natural forces."

This essay is a sensible analysis of an important aspect of *Moby-Dick*, one that gives the book an uncanny, Gothic and supernatural quality.

99. Cowan, J. A. "In Praise of Self-Reliance: The Role of Bulkington in *Moby-Dick*," *American Literature*, XXXVIII (January, 1967), 547–556.

Cowan disputes the tendency of critics (Stern, Chase, Rosenberry, and others) to claim that Melville satirizes Transcendentalism in *Moby-Dick*.

Ahab represents a negative form of self-reliance, but Bulkington, who appears only twice in *Moby-Dick*, is positively self-reliant. He possesses a "quiet alienation" and seeeks truth in a way that makes him a conscious parallel of Emerson's "great man."

100. Dahl, Curtis. "Moby Dick's Cousin Behemoth," *American Literature*, XXXI (March, 1959), 21–29.

Dahl traces the "striking parallels between" Cornelius Matthews' *Behemoth: A Legend of the Mound-Builders* (1839) and *Moby-Dick*. Matthews' novel "concerns the struggle by an ancient American race to slay a gigantic mastodon surviving from past geologic ages, The ravaging Behemoth is finally hunted down and slain, after several disastrous attempts, by a doughty Mound-Builder hero named Bokulla. . . . Behemoth is certainly Moby Dick's cousin; Bokulla is a distant relation of Ahab."

Dahl's parallel is interesting and sensible, particularly in his recognition that, despite similarities between the two books, there are also basic differences.

101. Damon, S. F. "Why Ishmael Went to Sea," *American Literature*, II (November, 1937), 281–283.

Melville had failed as a clerk in the New York State Bank and as a clerk in his brother's shop; he turned to haying on his uncle's farm and finally to teaching for one term. He was not successful in any of these pursuits and this sense of failure, rather than his reading of *Two Years Before the Mast*, may have determined his going to sea.

For a more persuasive account of Melville's attraction to the sea, see Anderson (13).

102. Fiedler, Leslie. *Love and Death in the American Novel*. New York: Criterion Books, 1960; reprinted New York: Meridian Books, 1962, 523–552.

Fiedler underscores the themes of love and death in *Moby-Dick*. Ishmael and Quee-queg represent love whereas Ahab and Fedallah signify death; in both cases, two males—one white, one colored—are bound together in a relationship of innocent homosexuality. These four characters represent two polar aspects of the id—the beneficient (Ishmael and Queequeg) and the destructive (Ahab and Fedallah). Fedallah (who symbolizes fire) and Queequeg (who symbolizes water) matter only thematically and express the central struggle of love and death. Because Queequeg, around whom the Western or sentimental story functions, triumphs over Fedallah, who is suggestive of the Faustian or Gothic elements in the book, Eros triumphs over Thanatos.

Fiedler's case is more convincing in its interpretation of the relationship between Ishmael and Queequeg than between Ahab and Fedallah. He suggests that Ishmael views his relation with Queequeg as marital and thinks of himself in the feminine role. When Ahab begins to dominate the novel this relationship fades, but we are reminded of it again at the end of the novel as Ishmael uses Queequeg's coffin for a lifebuoy. Ahab's relationship with Fedallah can be seen, as Fiedler suggests, as one between Faust and the devil; and clearly Fedallah is a destructive force in the novel. But in drawing contrasts between Ishmael-Queequeg and Ahab-Fedallah, Fiedler makes the reader feel that the book is more neatly structured than it is; the contrasts are more convincing in Fiedler's essay than in the novel itself. Nevertheless, Fiedler analyzes *Moby-Dick* more provocatively than most critics, and his interpretation is valuable. Incidental observations compel the reader to re-evaluate the novel. Fiedler suggests, for example, some of the various themes in the book,: the initiation into manhood; the dream of a return into an unremembered womb and a rebirth; inversion of the psyche in a world below the level of ego and its consequent re-constitution; flirtation with madness so as to see otherwise unseeable things; and a dying into immortality. He also notes the many paradoxes of death in the book: Queequeg's coffin as a lifebuoy; Ahab's calling himself immortal but dying; Ishmael's considering himself already dead but living on and being reborn. These and other perceptions attempt to take the reader below the surface of the novel to discover the secret motto of *Moby-Dick*: "I baptize you not in the name of the father, the son, and the holy ghost, but in the name of the devil."

103. Gleim, William S. *The Meaning of Moby Dick*. New York: The Buck Row Book Shop, 1938, 149 pp.; reprinted by Russell and Russell, 1962.

Gleim's book is an expansion of his essay, "A Theory of *Moby Dick*," which appeared in *The New England Quarterly*, II (July, 1929), 402–419. "*Moby Dick*," he writes, "is really two stories: an ostensible story that treats of material things; and another story, hidden in parables, allegories, and symbolism, which treats of abstract things. And these two stories are parallel and analogous to each other.

"Indeed, without casting the least doubt upon Melville's sincerity, the book may be regarded as gigantic hoax, in which he satirized all man-made religions, and challenged the perspicacity of his contemporaries."

The Meaning of Moby Dick is too homiletic, too overwritten and hyperbolic. In Gleim's view, everything in *Moby Dick* is allegorical: "But inasmuch as Melville admitted that 'the whale book was susceptible of an allegorical construction,' there is nothing gratuitous in assuming any episode in it to be allegorical, if it is susceptible of an interpretation which is consistent with the general subject matter." As a consequence, Gleim strains to discover allegory on numerous levels. The three harpooners, Queequeg, Tashtego, and Daggoo represent religion, sin, and ignorance; Ishmael symbolizes "spiritual and rational man." Much of the power and primary meaning of the novel is lost in this elaborate allegorical framework with which the author has burdened *Moby-Dick*.

104. Heflin, Wilson L. "Melville and Nantucket," *Moby-Dick Centennial Essays*, Edited by Tyrus Hillway and Luther S. Mansfield. Dallas: Southern Methodist University Press, 1953, pp. 165–179.

This essay traces Melville's familiarity with Nantucket and his use of the island in *Moby-Dick*. Nantucket symbolized to Melville and his contemporaries (as it does to us today) the ancient traditions of whaling—the romance, the excitement, the dangerous life of mariners who went to sea in search of leviathan." Heflin uses logbooks to present new information about the voyage of the *Acushnet*, Melville's whaler, and Melville's own career as a whale-hunter.

105. Hetherington, Hugh W. "Early Reviews of *Moby-Dick*," *Moby-Dick Centennial Essays*. Edited by Tyrus Hillway and Luther S. Mansfield. Dallas: Southern Methodist University Press, 1953, pp. 89–122.

Hetherington examines the important reviews of *Moby-Dick* in British and American magazines in the period immediately following publication of the book. His conclusion is that "the notion of the book's rejection—first expressed by Lewis Mumford and more or less accepted by F. O. Matthiessen, Alexander Cowie, and Howard P. Vincent—is not true." Reviewers noted the book, although there were conflicting opinions as to its meaning. Later estimates were mostly negative and attacked the book for its "immoral" qualities and its failure "to conform to the accepted canons of the novel."

106. Hicks, Granville. "A Re-Reading of *Moby-Dick*," *Twelve Great American Novels*. Edited by Charles Shapiro. Detroit: Wayne State University Press, 1958, pp. 44–69.

Hicks calls attention to the farcical quality in the first 25 chapters of the novel and then suggests that *Moby-Dick* is certainly a realistic book, but it has aspects that reach far beyond mere realism: a facetious tone, poetic power, tragic grandeur, metaphysical considerations, and dramatic force. Hicks discusses the last chapters in some detail and concludes that Ahab's "natural endowments make him a king among men, as truly a king as any found in Greek tragedy; his life is absolutely consecrated to an end that only a 'deep' man could conceive of. To seek to strike a final blow against the evil in the universe, this is a madness to which only great minds are liable."

This essay is a general tribute to the novel, with passing perceptions that are engaging but not particularly profound, or original.

107. Hillway, Tyrus. *Melville and the Whale*. Stonington, Connecticut: Stonington Publishing Co., 1950. 11 pp.

This book offers a full account of Melville's knowledge of cetology and his uses of sources pertaining to cetology.

————. "A Preface to *Moby-Dick*," *Moby-Dick Centennial Essays*. Edited by Tyrus Hillway and Luther S. Mansfield. Dallas: Southern Methodist University Press, 1953, pp. 22–29.

Moby-Dick is a study of human character confronting his destiny. Hillway studies Ahab's humanity and suggests that Ahab "voices implied protest of all humanity." By isolating himself from mankind, Ahab goes mad, for he has withdrawn "from the common level of mankind into an egocentric stratosphere between the world of man and the heaven of God." Pip stirs Ahab's heart, Starbuck his mind. Hillway concludes that the meaning of the book is that "To rebel against one's destiny, to defy God, leads only, it is clear, to tragedy."

108. Hillway, Tyrus and Mansfield, Luther S., editors. *Moby-Dick: Centennial Essays*. Dallas: Southern Methodist University Press, 1953, 182 pp.

This volume includes five critical essays—Henry Murray, "In Nomine Diaboli" (111); Tyrus Hillway, "A Preface to *Moby-Dick*" (107); Walter Bezanson, "*Moby Dick*: Work of Art" (92); Henry Nash Smith, "The Image of Society in *Moby Dick*" (120); and Ernest E. Leisy, "Fatalism in *Moby Dick*" (111)—and four historical essays: Hugh Hetherington, "Early Reviewers of *Moby-Dick*" (105); Perry Miller, "Melville and Transcendentalism" (74); Randall Stewart, "Melville and Hawthorne" (81); and Wilson Heflin, "Melville and Nantucket!" (104).

109. Horsford, Howard C. "The Design and Argument in *Moby-Dick*," *Modern Fiction Studies*, VIII (Autumn, 1962), 233–251.

Moby-Dick is concerned with the intellectual disintegration of faith. Ahab conceives of creation as a place of suffering, indifferent injustice, ruthless energy and merciless, predatory nature. These qualities the captain also ascribes to the Creator. Melville adapts the idea of David Hume, the Scottish philosopher, and suggests in *Moby-Dick* that "all we can know, finally, of all the baffling phenomena presented by some possibly objective world is sheer illusion, a symbolic construct of only our own minds. . . . Beyond the veil, behind the mask, beneath the inscrutable whiteness may be—nothing. Ahab's power lies in his self-reliant attempt to define himself against both society and nature. The power of the novel is in the encompassing vision transcending this." The unresolved tension of *Moby-Dick* is the desire to discover meaning in experience and an experienced meaninglessness. "If there is to be a moral order at all in this world, man—weak, flawed, fallible as he is—must somehow forge it himself out of his own human experience."

110. Kazin, Alfred. " 'Introduction' to *Moby-Dick*," From the Riverside Edition of *Moby-Dick*. Boston: Houghton Mifflin Company, 1950, Riverside A9.

Kazin emphasizes the poetic power of *Moby-Dick*, its large and primitive force. *Moby-Dick* "is written with a personal force of style, a passionate learning, a steady insight into our forgotten connections with the primitive. It sweeps everything before it; it gives us the happiness that only great vigor inspires." Kazin sees *Moby-Dick* as "an epic, a long poem on an heroic theme, rather than the kind of realistic fiction that we know today"; and he concentrates on the point of view in the book. "The book grows out of a single word, 'I', . . . Ishmael, then, was to put man's distinctly modern feeling of 'exile,' of abandonment, directly at the center of his stage." Kazin then turns to Ahab whom he sees as a tragic hero—"someone noble by nature, not by birth, who would have 'not the dignity of kings and robes,' but that abounding dignity which has no robed investiture. . . . The greatest single metaphor in the book is that of bigness."

111. Leisy, Ernest E. "Fatalism in *Moby-Dick*," *Moby-Dick Centennial Essays*. Edited by Tyrus Hillway and Luther S. Mansfield. Dallas: Southern Methodist University Press, 1953, pp. 76–88.

Leisy views *Moby-Dick* as Melville's symbolic struggle to discover why God created evil. "In this epic struggle Melville ignores the common feud of man with man and passes on to the deeper, universal feud of man with Fate and Infinity." There is a predominant tone of doom throughout the book as Ahab insanely pursues Moby-Dick, the symbol of his own fate, and consequently suffers isolation from other men. "Life is evil, further, because there is no freedom of the will"; and it is "evil because the growth of knowledge presents no solution." Melville thus acknowledges the "futility of human effort" and in Ahab's determinism, his "vestigial Puritanism had its fling." In *Pierre*, the novel that followed *Moby-Dick*, Melville abjured all philosophy; it was not until *Billy Budd* that he was able to find "a stoical balance between earthly truth and heavenly."

112. Murray, H. A. *"In Nomine Diaboli,"* *The New England Quarterly,* XXIV (December, 1951), 435–452. Reprinted in *Discussions of Moby Dick,* ed. Milton Stern, 25–34, and *Melville: A Collection of Critical Essays,* ed. Richard Chase, 62–74.

This is an important psychoanalytical interpretation of *Moby-Dick.* After a general tribute to Melville and specifically to *Moby-Dick,* Murray asserts that "all interpretations which fail to show that *Moby-Dick* is, in some sense, wicked, have missed the author's avowed intention. . . . Captain Ahab is an embodiment of that fallen angel or demi-god who in Christendom was variously named Lucifer, Devil, Adversary, Satan. The Church Fathers would have called Captain Ahab 'Antichrist' because he was not Satan himself, but a human creature possessed of all Satan's pride and energy."

Murray sees Ahab as the captain of the repressed nature of man, or the Id. The white whale represents the Superego, the internal institution responsible for these repressions. Moby-Dick is the Calvinistic God of nineteenth-century American society; and Ahab considers the whale as the New England conscience, as that "wall, shoved near to me," and also as the God of the Old Testament, the God who brought Jeremiah into darkness. The tension of the novel is consequently between an insurgent Id in conflict with an oppressive cultural Superego. Starbuck represents the rational, realistic Ego overcome by the Id.

Murray asks the question, Why should Melville aggress against Western orthodoxy? Why should he have written a "wicked book"? Freud states that one finds deep-seated aggression in one who is frustrated by Eros. Melville had spent a year in Polynesia and returned to marry a Puritan girl, the daughter of the Chief Justice of Massachusetts. His target in *Moby-Dick* becomes "the upper-middle class culture of his time". In the novel itself, Ahab's self-inflated egotism and unleashed wrath attacked the whale, who represented the Calvinistic strictures, because it blocked the advance of evolutionary love. "It's a good book, then, and Melville felt as spotless as a lamb."

This essay is a model of the psychiatric, archetypal approach to fiction. Although one may question the many connections Murray makes between Melville's life and the novel—at the same time as one realizes that these connections have great cogency in Murray's deft treatment of them—one can see the clear Freudian implications in *Moby-Dick* itself.

113. Olson, Charles. *Call Me Ishmael: A Study of Melville.* New York: Reynal & Hitchcock, 1947. 119 pp.

Olson emphasizes the great impact of Shakespeare on Melville's sensibility, particularly in the period before and during the writing of *Moby-Dick.* The specific elements in Shakespeare's drama that influenced Melville were madness, villainy, and evil, and the play that held the greatest importance to Melville was *King Lear.* Olson makes many comparisons between the characters of *King Lear* and *Moby-Dick.*

Melville was moved by the stricken goodness of Lear, Gloucester, and Edgar, and puts Ahab through humbling experiences that are parallel to those of Lear. Ahab's relation to Pip is similar to Lear's relationship with the Fool and Edgar; like Lear, Ahab learns from Pip, especially after the boy's drowning.

Olson touches upon other interesting aspects of Melville's craft as he analyzes *Moby-Dick* in detail: the significance of the whaling industry; the presence of black magic (in this sense *Moby-Dick*, especially in the chapter on the Doubloon, is closer to the world of *Macbeth* than *Lear*); the Faust legend; the use of dramatic techniques that are especially Elizabethan (stage directions, soliloquies, supernatural effects, and properties like the doubloon).

114. Parke, John. "Seven Moby-Dicks," *The New England Quarterly*, XXVIII (September, 1955), 319–338. Reprinted in *Discussions of Moby-Dick*, ed. Milton R. Stern. Boston: D. C. Heath and Company, 1960, 66–76.

The novel has seven layers of meaning: "The physical adventure, the spiritual exaltation of hazardous voyaging, the interaction of husbandment, are there as fresh and valid as ever. The pride and retribution thesis still stands, and the nemesis of self-mutilation through the exalting of will at the expense of instinct. On the metaphysical level, however, chaos, even if thought of only as externally cosmic, is an old, old image of man's, the adversary of all enshrined deities; its confrontation by man is fit matter for grand tragedy. But as an internal moral and emotional predicament the chaos of evil and idealism and madness the individual is certainly the most compelling phase of the archetype, and the one which evokes more and deeper echoes than any other. . . . Ahab's tragedy . . . is, then, his inability to locate and objectify evil in himself, or to accept it and deal with it prudently as part of the entire created world, and so *grow* despite it and because of it."

In *Moby-Dick*, Melville's major point is that man cannot avoid the question of evil. In this sense he anticipated the modern attempt to deny the concept of evil.

115. Paul, Sherman. "Melville's 'The Town-Ho's Story,'" *American Literature*, XXI (May, 1949), 212–222. Reprinted in *Discussions of Moby-Dick*, ed. Milton Stern, 87–92.

Although "The *Town-Ho* Story," chapter LIV of *Moby-Dick*, "can stand alone artistically and was actually printed separately in *Harper's* in 1851," it is "integrally necessary to the deepest meaning of the significance of the white whale . . . 'The Town-Ho's Story' contains Melville's germ of tragedy and his portrayal of the retributive justice of the whale." Paul emphasizes the democratic theme of the story. In the conflict between Steelkilt and Radney on Town-Ho, Melville prepares the reader for the greater tragedy to come. "The central meaning of the story is the reaffirmation of the heart."

For another version of the meaning of "The *Town-Ho* Story," see Don Geiger, "Melville's Black God: Contrary Evidence in 'The *Town Ho's* Story,'" *American Literature*, XXV (January, 1954), 464–471. Reprinted in *Discussion of Moby Dick*, ed. Milton Stern, 93–97.

Geiger feels that the Town Ho's story presents impressive evidence that Melville "rejected important features of the Calvinistic version of God." He disagrees with Paul's belief that "Ahab's tragedy comes to mean the same thing as Radney's" and that Lawrance Thompson's feeling that the "episode is an epitome of the total book's portrait of a wicked God." The story "records the divine punishment of injustice. . . . The God of the *Town-Ho* episode is, in fact, a barely distorted caricature of the orthodox Calvinist God. . . . This is Melville's ultimate image of the Calvinist God of the Puritan. However just He may occasionally be, He is without love or mercy, or even common fairness. It is no wonder that the book's epilogue shows the sole survivor of the disaster, Ishmael, floating on a coffin lifebuoy like an 'orphan': the features of the God are not the features of a human Father ('He' has become 'It'), and lonely Ishmael floats like a man already dead in an inhumane universe."

116. Pavese, Cesare. "The Literary Whaler," *Sewanee Review*, LXVIII (Summer, 1960), 407–418.

Pavese deplores the tendency of modern man to see any escape as a form of primitivism. Melville's ideal "is Ishmael, a sailor who can row half a day behind a whale with his illiterate companions, and then retire to a masthead to meditate on Plato." Pavese regards the balance of Melville's robustness and artistic sensitivity (dramatized by Ishmael) with great sympathy. He views Melville as a genuine skeptic and comments upon *Moby-Dick*, *Pierre*, *Mardi*, and *The Confidence-Man*; except for *Moby-Dick*, *The Encantadas*, and *Benito Cereno*, the works fail because "the rational element might be said to kill the transcendental." In *Moby-Dick*, Melville explores the demonism of the universe, "the conscious power which underlies natural destructive forces, the invisible world of which the visible is but a picture. . . ."

117. Percival, M. O. *A Reading of Moby Dick*. Chicago: University of Chicago Press, 1950, 135 pp.

This study is particularly useful to the student who is bewildered by the complexities of *Moby-Dick*. It offers a well-balanced and cogent analysis of the major themes of the novel and ought to be read before one approaches the more specialized interpretations of other critics.

Percival views the purpose of Ishmael's journey as a search for peace of mind; the pursuit of the whale becomes, as for Ahab, a study of good and evil. The reader senses that the characters are on a fated journey, from which they will not return— one can see these portents in the sections that deal with the Spouter Inn in New Bedford, which resembles the Leviathan and which is the heart of darkness itself.

The theme of the book is expressed in Father Mapple's sermon, taken from the text of Jonah: the rule of right is the obedience to the will of God, self-surrender and not self-affirmation. Ahab (like King Ahab in the biblical Book of Kings) forsakes the commandment of the Lord and discovers evil in *Moby-Dick*. The novel is concerned with the paradox of good and evil. To avoid this paradox is to go the way of Starbuck; the mate has too much faith and thus cannot see the paradox of good and evil clearly enough to understand Ahab. To see the paradox eye to eye and yet withhold a vengeful hand is to go Ishmael's way.

Percival quotes the Hasidic maxim, "There is no room for God in him who is full of himself," and he suggests that this is Ahab's problem. Ahab had a secular faith in God. He thought he could depend on God for fair play, but the loss of his leg in the battle with Moby Dick was foul play and now he seeks an eye for an eye, a tooth for a tooth. He broods over the thought that he has been "elected" to be the spirit and jest of some malevolent deity, and his despair ultimately becomes madness.

Percival is particularly helpful in defining the importance of the individual ships that the *Pequod* passes on its way to Moby Dick. He also examines closely the final scenes in which Ahab becomes what he believes, informing Moby Dick with evil because he has become evil himself.

The danger of this book is that Percival has a tendency to view *Moby-Dick* in too internalized and metaphysical a manner. He uses the language of Blake, Boehme, St. Augustine, and Kierkegaard, and creates a philosophical tension in the novel that is compelling but that neglects the external action of the book. In this sense Percival sees Moby Dick as evil; Ahab as doubt and demonic defiance; Starbuck and Stubb as submission; Pip as love; Ishmael as faith. But these characters are human beings on an important primary level that must be emphasized. Despite these reservations, however, Percival's book will be immensely helpful to students first approaching the novel.

118. Sewall, Richard B. "Moby-Dick," in *The Vision of Tragedy*. New Haven: Yale University Press, 1959, pp. 92–105.

Ishmael leaves for his journey in a generally optimistic mood, unaware of any dark idea. "The rest of his story shows how shallow his optimism" is, as he moves steadily toward tragic truth. Ishmael is far more than simply the chorus to Ahab as tragic hero; "he is a constant link to the known and familiar." He does not deny the horror of the universe but wants to be "social with it." Ishmael's view of life is fundamentally stoic not tragic. "Ishmael recedes as Ahab occupies the foreground," largely because the sailor cannot control the dramatic intensity of Ahab's fury. Ahab, in his first pose, "is more than man—and more than tragic man: he is a self-appointed God." In his second pose, "he is less than man, a mere agent of destiny." Melville does not justify nor condemn Ahab, nor does he describe him as good or evil; "but by carrying him through his fatal action in all its tensions, paradoxes, and ambiguities, the book, like a true tragedy, goes deeply into the mysteries of all moral judgments."

119. Slochower, Harry. "*Moby Dick:* The Myth of Democratic Expectancy," *American Quarterly*, II (Fall, 1950), 259–269.

Although American history has been brief, the country has its own myth—that of a "new, open, expanding world in which 'the sky is the limit,' and where one can hit it rich, where anybody, regardless of his origins, can go 'from rags to riches.' ... Melville is among those who are beginning to question the ethic of expansionism and coordination. Ahab's Pacific journey objectifies this ambivalent attitude. It is an extension of the continental experience, a venture into the promising unknown."

Slochower relates Melville to Schopenhauer, Freud, Dante, the Renaissance, Myths, Hamlet, Sigfried, and modern existentialism; and he makes connections between Ahab and the figures of myth, particularly the Fisher King of the Holy Grail legend and Job in the Bible. "Melville's *Moby Dick* is the first major American literary myth sounding the central motifs of creation and quest. Its distinctive American quality lies in its uncertain attitude toward creation."

Slochower's treatment of *Moby-Dick* is interesting but too sweeping in its unsubstantiated references.

120. Smith, Henry Nash. "The Image of Society in *Moby-Dick*," *Moby-Dick Centennial Essays*. Edited by Tyrus Hillway and Luther S. Mansfield. Dallas: Southern Methodist University Press, 1953, pp. 59–75.

The major theme of *Moby-Dick* is man's alienation from a society which has two aspects: a lower level of brutal competition, represented by the sharks, and an illusory level of freedom and peace. In *Moby-Dick*, Melville is concerned with criticizing the rapacity of political and economic institutions and emphasizing that this greed denies man's basic goodness and nobility. Smith points out, however, that "if society is evil, some human relationships are nevertheless good. These can be designated by the general name of brotherhood or community, and Ishmael's love for Queequeg is the most obvious example of a redeeming force brought to bear upon him in the course of action. . . . Men can be saved although society is damned. . . . And even though Melville is unable to provide us with a fully specified resolution of his problem, his book forces us to recognize that for him, at least, American society of the mid-nineteenth century represented not the benign present and hopeful future proclaimed by official spokesmen, but an environment threatening the individual with a disintegration of personality which he could avoid only by the half-miraculous achievement of a sense of community, of brotherhood, unattainable within the official culture—a sense of community to be found, in fact, only among 'meanest mariners, and renegades and castaways.'"

121. Stanonick, Janez. *Moby Dick, The Myth and the Symbol: A Study in Folklore and Literature*. Ljubljana: Ljubljana University Press, 1962. 215 pp.

This book relates the symbolism of *Moby-Dick* to the folklore of the white whale. The author rejects the theory that Melville relied on Jeremiah N. Reynolds' account of "Mocha Dick" and suggests that he depended on another version "published, perhaps even several times, during the second half of the 1830's." Stanonick believes that Melville originally intended to have Queequeg as the hero of the novel since "in popular tradition the man who kills the White Whale is always a negro." But Queequeg was too comic a character to serve as the hero and Melville, on the advice of Hawthorne, turned to Ahab.

Stanonick directs the reader's attention to the novels of Charles M. Newell, which center on the actions of the White Whale, and claims that they contain material "which was current in America before Melville published his novel." In the second part of his study, he gives a survey of popular beliefs about whales in general and analyzes Melville's use of folklore elements. "My main emphasis, however, is on the popular traditions which had in all probability been brought to America by settlers from Europe."

Stanonick's ideas are interesting, but they rely too heavily on internal evidence.

122. Stern, Milton R. Editor. *Discussions of Moby Dick*. Boston: D. C. Heath and Company, 1960, 134 pp.

Stern reprints the comments of leading critics on *Moby-Dick*. The table of contents reads as follows: I. Contemporary Reactions: Hugh D. Hetherington, "Early Reviews of *Moby-Dick*" (105) . II. Ritual, Myth, and Psychology: Reginald L. Cook, "Big Medicine in *Moby Dick*" (98); Henry A. Murray, "In Nomine Diaboli" (112); D. H. Lawrence, "Moby Dick, or the White Whale" (64); Harry Slochower, "*Moby Dick:* The Myth of Democratic Expectancy" (119); Alfred Kazin, "An Introduction to *Moby-Dick*" (110) . III. Ahab and Evil: Charles H. Cook, Jr., "Ahab's 'Intolerable Allegory'" (97); John Parke, "Seven *Moby-Dicks*" (114); R. E. Watters, "The Meanings of the White Whale" (128) . IV. The Games: Sherman Paul, "Melville's 'The *Town-Ho's* Story'" (115); Don Geiger, "Melville's Black God: Contrary Evidence in 'The *Town-Ho's* Story'" (115); James Dean Young, "The Nine Gams of the Pequod" (130)). V. General Considerations: R. E. Watters, "Melville's 'Isolatoes'" (128); Milton R. Stern, "Some Techniques of Melville's Perception"; Robert Penn Warren, "Melville the Poet." (168) .

See the individual entries for commentary.

123. Stewart, George R. "The Two *Moby-Dicks*," *American Literature*, XXV (January, 1954), 417–448.

Stewart investigates the implications suggested by the "sharp contrast between the opening of *Moby-Dick* and the rest of the novel." He sees the book as tripartite: Chapters I–XV, in which the original story is presented with only slight revision; 2. Chapters XVI–XXII, in which the original story is presented with important revisions; and 3. Chapters XXIII–Epilogue, in which we have the novel as Melville reconceived it.

124. Stoll, E. E. "Symbolism in *Moby-Dick*," *Journal of the History of Ideas*, XII (June, 1951), 440–446.

Stoll claims that *Moby-Dick*, like all good stories, is ambiguous, and all the attempts to analyze the novel are the result of "the prevalent taste for symbolism itself." *Moby-Dick* is a story of suspense, but "not one of really ecumenical or perennial importance." It is "the story of a man's lifelong revenge upon a whale for thwarting him in his money-making designs upon its blubber."

125. Vincent, Howard P. *The Trying-Out of Moby-Dick*. Boston: Houghton Mifflin, 1949; reprinted Carbondale: Southern Illinois Press, 1965.

Vincent traces the development of *Moby-Dick* and Melville's use of sources. He divides his study into five sections: "Loomings"; "The Breaching of Moby-Dick"; "The Narrative Beginnings"; "The Cetological Center"; and "The Narrative Conclusion." In "Loomings" he discusses the scholarly neglect of *Moby-Dick* and sets forth his own intentions: "*The Trying-Out of Moby-Dick* . . . combines a study of the whaling sources of *Moby-Dick* with an account of its composition, and suggestions concerning interpretation and meaning." "The Breaching of *Moby-Dick*" considers Melville's development before the writing of *Moby-Dick;* the first draft of *Moby-Dick*, which Vincent calls "a cetological handbook surrounded by adventure"; and the influence of Hawthorne on the second draft of the novel. In the section entitled "The Narrative Beginnings," Vincent analyzes the novel through Chapter 28, viewing Ishmael as "the metaphysical and spiritual norm of the novel" and tracing Ahab's development from "a typical whaling master into a tragic hero." The fourth part—"The Cetological Center"—is the most valuable section of the book, for it analyzes the chapters on whaling in detail; Vincent concludes by suggesting that "the cetological center of *Moby-Dick* is neither digressive nor diversive; it is not an intrusion." In his last section, "The Narrative Conclusion," Vincent returns to "the search for *Moby-Dick*," which "has never really been forgotten: it hovers over every expository chapter of the cetological center."

This study is valuable, especially as it indicates how Melville struggled to make his book concrete.

126. Walcutt, C. C. "The Fire Symbolism in *Moby-Dick*," *Modern Language Notes*, LIX (May, 1944), 304–310.

When Ahab cries, "Oh: thou clear spirit of clear fire . . ." (in Chapter CXIX) more than melodrama emerges. The statement is "the key which explains many paradoxical and confusing references to fire and enables us to relate the fire symbolism to the central meaning of the book." Ahab "realizes that evil (Emerson would say Fate) cannot be destroyed but that man rises to greatness in struggling with it."

————. "The Soundings of *Moby-Dick*," *Arizona Quarterly*, 24 (Summer, 1968), 101–117.

Walcutt concerns himself with the creation of *Moby-Dick*. He notes the influence of Hawthorne and Shakespeare. The thesis of *Moby-Dick* "cannot be simply or clearly stated. It has to be 'rendered,' to use Henry James's famous word, and the rendering involves indirections and ambiguities that carry the reader more and more deeply into the maze of Truth." Walcutt mentions six possible views that Melville takes of the universe: 1. The universe and God are all-good and essentially spiritual. This is the transcendental view. 2. An omnipotent God permits evil in man and nature. This is the position of Christian dualism. 3. God and evil are interdependent. This is the Zoroastrian or Manichean view. 4. The universe or God is evil. 5. "The universe is chaotic." 6. "The universe is orderly but godless, therefore indifferent."

127. Ward, J. A. "The Function of the Cetological Chapters in *Moby-Dick*," *American Literature*, XXVIII (May, 1956), 164–183.

The "sheer weight of facts keeps the metaphysical and spiritual meaning of *Moby-Dick* solidly anchored to matter-of-fact reality. . . . In every aspect of the novel, Melville's effort to balance the extraordinary with the ordinary is evident . . . the cetological chapters give the illusion of objectivity and the effect of a wide life. . . . As Melville reveals the inability of science to comprehend even the surface of the whale, he succeeds not only in establishing the superiority of the creature to man, but also in showing the insufficiencies of empirical knowledge."

128. Watters, R. E. "The Meanings of the White Whale," *University of Toronto Quarterly*, XX (January, 1951), 165–168. Reprinted in *Discussions of Moby Dick*. Edited the Milton R. Stern. *Discussions of Moby Dick*. Boston: D. C. Heath and Co., 1960, 77–86.

There are "innumerable meanings of the white whale." The ordinary sailors look upon the white whale as "dangerous and intelligent, and therefore perhaps 'evil' in the sense of harmful." Starbuck shares this view—he kills whales "for a living, not for adventure." To Stubb "whaling is simply glorious fun." Flask is "the complete materialist"—an "ignorant and destructive mediocrity." The three harpooners "do their duty" but "feel no responsibility to the owners." To Fedallah the white whale means death, "an instrument of a forseen fate." To Ahab, "Moby Dick was a composite entity—physical power, wilful intelligence, and malignant divinity—a trinity of body, mind, and spirit in opposition to Ahab. Which of the three a reader chooses to emphasize as *the* meaning for Ahab is, as Melville clearly implies, a reflection of the reader's own personal character." Ishmael is concerned with the whiteness of the whale; to him "the meaning of the whale . . . seems to be either the totality or essential of all meanings—in a word, attainable only by omniscience."

————. "Melville's 'Isolatoes,'" *PMLA*, LX (December, 1945), 1138–1148. Reprinted in *Discussions of Moby-Dick*, ed. Stern, 107–114.

This essay is concerned with the Hawthornian theme of isolation as it presents itself in *Moby-Dick*. The isolatoes are those people, who, "because of birth or achievement or character . . . were set apart from normal relationships." The isolated figures Watters discusses are the narrators of *Typee* and *Omoo*, who are set apart because of their education; Taji in *Mardi*, White Jacket, Redburn, Ishmael, Isabel in *Pierre*, Israel Potter, and John Marr. Ahab and Pierre are voluntary isolatoes." Pierre was "like Ahab in two ways: he was determined to eradicate something he believed to be evil, and he was proudly self-reliant." Watters concludes that "Throughout his works, then, Melville displayed his belief that happiness is not obtainable by the individual in isolation, but may be found in shared experiences—in community of thought and action and purpose. The man whose solitude is thrust upon him is to be deeply pitied. The man whose isolation is self-imposed through repudiation of his social ties creates sorrow for himself and pain for others."

See also Watters' "Melville's 'Sociality,'" *American Literature*, XVII (March, 1945), 33–49, in which he explores the doctrine of the racial and social community as an ideal to set opposite the isolated individual in Melville's work.

129. Wright, Nathalia. "*Moby Dick:* Jonah's or Job's Whale ?" *American Literature*, XXXVII (May, 1965), 190–195.

Moby-Dick is indeed "a Job's Whale rather than Jonah's. The sheer density of the cetological chapters is overwhelmingly persuasive. The unhuman universe in which Ishmael survives, floating on a calm sea past passive creatures of prey day and night before being rescued, is finally distinguished, moreover, by a profound peaceful-ness—at least as profound as that of the metaphysical universe in *Billy Budd* on the morning of Budd's execution, when sky and air have first a luminousness and then a clarity of supernatural quality."

Ahab shares Job's original sense of injustice, but unlike Job, Ahab does not change his attitude or point of view by any new insight into this world.

130. Young, James Dean. "The Nine Gams of the *Pequod*," *American Literature*, XXV (January, 1954), 449–463. Reprinted in *Discussions of Moby Dick*. Edited by Milton R. Stern, 98–106.

Young views the meeting of the Pequod and the other ships as an "integrated series" rather than as separate encounters.

"All nine gams of the Pequod are important relations to the world. Each gam deals to some degree with the problem of communication and the problem of alternative; each is a focal point in the action and part of the matrix for the narra-tive. . . . Through these meetings at sea, the Pequod experiences difficult relations to the world, communication is uncertain, and alternatives are inadequate."

Pierre:

131. Braswell, William. "The Satirical Temper of Melville's *Pierre*," *American Literature*, VII (January, 1936), 424–438.

Braswell tries to show "that a demoniac comic spirit within Melville was responsible for some of the curious features of the novel." He relates the strange style, characterization, and theme "to the unfortunate situation which [Melville] was in at the time of writing *Pierre*," and concludes that Melville, who "intended to shock readers of that day," succeeded in his attempt.

————. "The Early Love Scenes of Melville's *Pierre*," *American Literature*, XXII (November, 1950), 283–289.

Braswell maintains that Melville was being ironic in the early scenes which most critics find impossibly sentimental. Melville was putting the "tall style of *Moby-Dick* on stilts." Melville found a kind of perverse amusement in writing the early passages of *Pierre* and self-consciously used exaggeration, far-fetched conceits, and an elaborate satirical description of love.

    Braswell's analysis strains too much in defending Melville's art. It would seem that his approach to Pierre and Isabel at the outset of the book is far more confused in tone and attitude than Braswell is willing to admit.

132. Hillway, Tyrus. "Pierre, the Fool of Virtue," *American Literature*, XXI (May, 1949), 201–211.

Melville did not have any philosophical system. In his novels "the search for truth proves futile, the defiance of destiny wholly foolhardy, and the apparent distinction between virtue and vice horrifyingly ambiguous." Hillway notes that it is a mistake to take Plotinus Plinlimmon's philosophy as Melville's. He believes that Melville's own views are most nearly represented by Babbalanja in *Mardi* and that his "religious criticisms were directed against insincerity of institutionalized Christianity," as personified by The Reverend Mr. Falsgrave in *Pierre*. In the novel three of the basic spiritual questions present themselves: "How to reconcile the world and the aspirations of the soul? . . . If the voice of God is merely silence, what is truth? Finally, can man act as a free agent?" Melville answers none of these questions but offers us only a "cramping frustration."

133. Moorman, Charles. "Melville's *Pierre* and The Fortunate Fall," *American Literature*, XXV (March, 1953), 13–30.

Moorman relates *Pierre* to the felix culpa tradition by investigating the novel's imagery. Pierre leaves Saddle Meadows believing that his fall will be fortunate, for by embracing Isabel he will be "embracing a new life more wonderful than the sterility of Saddle Meadows." His life in the city, however, is filled with frustration and disappointment, and there does not seem to be anything fortunate about his fall.

Yet he is a superior person in the last half of the novel—wiser and more self-honest. Melville does not subscribe to the myth of the "fortunate" Fall; there is no grace in innocence and in *Pierre* no solution. Elsewhere in Melville's work—in *Moby-Dick* and *Billy Budd*—he concludes that "man must accept both earth and sky, both horological and chronometrical, both land and sea. While there can be no compromise of 'virtuous expediency,' there can be an acceptance of both laws, heavenly and earthly."

See James Kissane, "Imagery, Myth, and Melville's *Pierre*," *American Literature*, XXVI (January, 1955), 564–572 for a rebuttal. Kissane believes that "Mr. Moorman has . . . described a lumbering, grotesque, but powerful novel by catching hold of one of its auxiliary appendages." He examines Moorman's essay and attempts to show some of the limitations inherent in "the tendency to approach fiction through imagery and myth."

————. "Melville's Pierre in the City," *American Literature*, XXVII (January, 1956), 571–577.

This is an extension of Moorman's first article. He wishes to do two things:

"1. To defend briefly the applicability of the myth approach to *Pierre*, and 2. To correct what Mr. Kissane believes to be the main fault in my argument, my 'inability to account for the conclusion of *Pierre*'. . . ."

Once again, Moorman insists that *Pierre* is "a considered and deliberate reworking of the 'fortunate fall' tradition of sin and redemption. . . ."

134. Murray, Henry A. "Introduction," *Pierre, or the Ambiguities*, in *Complete Works of Herman Melville*. Howard P. Vincent, General Editor. Chicago and New York: Hendricks House, 1954, pp. 504.

Pierre, in Murray's view, is the burning out of the *Moby-Dick* volcano. Murray first offers a psychoanalytical analysis of Melville's condition at the time of composition. His spiritual state included both a moral conflict and an underlying will to annihilate himself—the stages are clear from *Mardi* to *Billy Budd*. In *Pierre* he has an ambivalent or ambiguous attitude. Every significant object both attracts and repels Pierre; there is a radical defect in every person who has appealed to him, and he begins hating what he has loved, although, unconsciously, he continues loving the object of his hate. No wholehearted embracement of anyone is possible. In addition, Pierre's heart is divided and thus every chosen course is flawed in one way or another; no one decision is proper to him, and he arrives at a state of paralysis in which all is meaningless and worthless. The moral of the book is, therefore, that there is no moral; man cannot reconcile this world with his own soul.

In *Pierre* Melville was writing the biography of his self-image, and his perception does not go much further than Pierre's. Murray identifies each of the characters as members of Melville's own family, and then defines the book in terms of three long acts. Act I is devoted to the paradise at Saddle Meadows, in which Pierre's deep attachment to his mother is seemingly perfect—the Oedipus Complex is very pronounced as the mother is represented as Queen Mother, Pierre as a Romeo figure, Lucy Tartan as an image of selfless love (the Juliet figure). Pierre, as the "American Fallen and Crucified Angel," sees the Fall from grace and is consequently haunted. Act II is concerned with the Fall from grace, particularly in terms of Pierre's realization that his father was a seducer and that Isabel is his half-sister, a forlorn orphan. From this point, Pierre sees only images of corruption, and he pledges himself to Isabel. Isabel, as the rational woman, and Lucy, as the natural woman, are contrasted throughout the book. If Pierre can resurrect Isabel, who is the personification of his unconscious, he himself will be reborn.

If Act I has its analogue in *Romeo and Juliet*, Act II can be seen in terms of *Hamlet*. Pierre acts differently from Hamlet; he fears that if he does not do something immediately, he will become unable to act at all. Act III deals with an attempted resolution to Pierre's problems. That resolution is presented through Plotinus Plinlimmon's pamphlet, "Chronometricals and Horologicals," which Pierre reads in the coach coming from Saddle Meadows to the city. Chronometers give absolute time (the New Testament or Christ) and Horologes give local time (our own moral code). Man must set his moral aspirations to realizable levels and thus be able to attain them. God does not expect us to live as Christ did; he demands no more than a virtuous prudence from man. Since man cannot attain the Christian ideal he turns either to hypocrisy or atheism. Plinlimmon is opposed to self-dedication, benevolence, and reform; Melville agrees with him in part, but ultimately he sides with Pierre, who can not live alone and needs Isabel. In the end, however, he yields to self-pity and condemns her; Isabel has presented the death-wish to Pierre, and she attracts Pierre to her. The end of the novel is almost exclusively devoted to Pierre's regression and deterioration.

As one can see from this brief description, Murray's analysis is remarkably suggestive, particularly in regard to a novel so obviously characterized by personal torment as *Pierre*.

135. Wright, Nathalia. "*Pierre*: Herman Melville's *Inferno*," *American Literature*, XXXII (May, 1960), 167–181.

Nathalia Wright compares the structure and some of the scenes in *Pierre* and the *Inferno*. Both works are divided into two parts. Although Saddle Meadows in *Pierre* seems a paradise, it is in fact close to Dante's *Inferno*: "pride and hypocrisy abound, adultery is committed, and incestuous and murderous impulses are harbored." When Pierre goes to the city, he is said to have crossed a river (like the poet and guide of the *Inferno*, as they are ferried over the Styx). The last part of *Pierre* is similar to the last three circles of Dante's Hell. So pervasive was Dante's influence on Melville when he wrote *Pierre*, that the novel is virtually "an anatomy of sin."

This is an intelligent essay, particularly because Mrs. Wright does not force her comparisons: "Certain differences between it and the *Inferno*—notably the absence of characters corresponding to Beatrice, Virgil, and the angel who opens the gates of the City of Dis—are at least as important as the similarities."

Israel Potter:

136. Frederick, John T. "Symbol and Theme in Melville's *Israel Potter,*" *Modern Fiction Studies,* VIII (Autumn, 1962), 265–275.

The first chapter of *Israel Potter* is Melville's own; the next 90 pages follow substantially the narrative of *The Life and Remarkable Adventures,* Melville's source for the novel. Afterwards, Melville inserts a good deal of original material—Chapter 26 is the height of Melville's creative achievement in *Israel Potter.* Frederick asks for a revaluation.

137. McCutcheon, Roger P. "The Technique of Melville's *Israel Potter,*" *South Atlantic Quarterly,* XXVII (April, 1928), 161–174.

McCutcheon compares Melville's text with its source, *The Life and Remarkable Adventures,* and notes that Melville's was mostly original and that about "two-thirds of the book" are made up of Melville's additions. The portraits of Benjamin Franklin, John Paul Jones, and Ethan Allan are essentially original.

General:

138. Fogle, R. H. *Melville's Shorter Tales.* Norman, Oklahoma: University of Oklahoma Press, 1960, 150 pp.

In this study, Fogle analyzes closely fifteen of Melville's tales and sketches. Most valuable and thorough are his interpretations of "Bartleby, the Scrivener," "Cock-a-Doodle-Doo!," "The Lightning-Rod Man," "The Bell-Tower," "I and My Chimney," "The Apple-Tree Table," "The Piazza," "The Encantadas," and "Benito Cereno."

Fogle summarizes his position by stating that "the purpose of the tales as of all Melville's fiction is to penetrate as deeply as possible into its metaphysical, theological moral, psychological, and social truths. . . . In these tales he wishes to conceal, however, his direct purposes, for artistic, personal, financial, and sometimes humorous reasons. Further, his state of mind at the time of writing is morbid, his sensibility heightened to the point of disease, and it must go veiled in public in sheer self-preservation. These concealments cause an interesting situation, in conflict with his other purposes of being free, uncommitted, impartially able to record the visible truth. . . .

"The tales have either the pattern of the quest, in which a seeker actively pursues truth, as in 'The Piazza' or 'Cock-a-Doodle-Doo,' or the naturally converse situation of a man's being thrust into circumstances which dismay and baffle but conclude by educating him, as for instance the lawyer-narrator of 'Bartleby.'

The quest and its object are represented primarily in visual terms, and thus the problem arises of point of view, alike mental and physical."

139. Slater, Judith. "The Domestic Adventurer in Melville's Tales," *American Literature*, XXXVII (November, 1965), 267–279.

"Cock-a-Doodle-Doo!," "The Lightning-Rod Man," "I and My Chimney," "Jimmy Rose," "The Apple-Tree Table," and "The Piazza" all treat what Miss Slater calls the "Ishmael" theme. This theme might be stated as follows: "how can such an individual [as Ishmael] without sacrificing his complexity of vision adjust himself, as he must, to 'home'? Melville answers that question indirectly in these particular tales by creating a series of domestic adventurers, widely different in personality, each of whom stands in a more or less mature relationship to his environment." Each of these narrators, like Ishmael, possesses a "doubleness of vision."

"Bartleby, the Scrivener":

140. Marx, Leo. "Melville's Parable of the Walls," *Sewanee Review*, LXI (Autumn, 1953), 602–627.

"Bartleby, the Scrivener" is a parable of Melville's fate as a writer in 1852. The story is "about a writer who forsakes conventional modes because of an irresistible preoccupation with the most philosophical questions." In this sense the story is "the most explicit and mercilessly self-critical statement of his own dilemma that Melville has left us." The walls in the story are the controlling symbols and represent enclosures "which hem in the meditative artist and for that matter every man." The entire story is "a compassionate rebuke to the self-absorption of the artist, and so a plea that he devote himself to keeping strong his bonds with the rest of mankind."

141. *Melville Annual 1965*, A Symposium: *Bartleby, the Scrivener*. Edited by Howard P. Vincent. Kent, Ohio: Kent State University Press, 1966, 199 pp.

This symposium was drawn from the proceedings of a conference of the Melville Society. There is a facsimile of "Bartleby" as originally published November and December, 1853, in *Putnam's Monthly Magazine*.

Henry A. Murray's "Bartleby and I" considers the story from different points of view but especially from the psychological. Melville created the "Bartleby complex." Four essays consider "Bartleby, the Scrivener" as it has been adapted in opera and film. There are also traditional essays by Maurice Friedman, who sees the story as one of alienation; A. W. Plumstead, who considers the art of the story; Marjorie Dew, who focuses on the words "preferences" and "assumptions"; William Bysshe Stein, who emphasizes Christian allusions and references; and Mario L. D'Avanzo, who stresses the influence of *Sartor Resartus* on the story. Howard P. Vincent offers an intelligent preface and Donald M. Fiene adds an instructive "Bibliography of Criticism."

"Benito Cereno":

142. Bernstein, John Albert. "'Benito Cereno' and the Spanish Inquisition," *Nineteenth-Century Fiction*, XVI (March, 1962), 345–350.

Bernstein suggests that Melville complicates his tale by making parallels with the Spanish Inquisition. What we witness on the *San Dominick* is a modern Inquisition, "an Inquisition which the colored races of the world are holding for the white race, an Inquisition which is brought about as a direct result of the white man's mal-treatment of the darker races."

This interpretation seems a rather elaborate extrapolation of the facts in the story.

143. Canady, Nicholas, Jr. "A New Reading of Melville's *Benito Cereno*," *Studies in American Literature*. Edited by Waldo McNeir and Leo. B. Levy. Baton Rouge: Louisiana State University Press, 1960, 49–57.

This essay considers Captain Delano in terms of the question of authority. Because Delano, has achieved a firm position of authority on his own ship, he automatically assumes that Benito Cereno is in complete charge of the *San Dominick*. "In the lengthy extracts from the testimony of Benito Cereno . . . Melville clearly distin-guishes between authority and power," The Negroes on the ship have used power, not authority. "Don Benito's authority is based upon legal right; the Negroes' power is based upon force. . . . It became the task of the courts to restore authority." In this story, Melville demonstrates the results of Benito Cereno's loss of power and the "misuse of power by usurping Negroes."

This essay is generally sound, but it excuses too easily Captain Delano's obtuse-ness, his inability to see the mutiny that is clearly occurring aboard the *San Dominick*. Because Captain Delano possesses authority does not mean that he would not perceive a captain who has failed to retain his command.

144. Cardwell, Guy. "Melville's Gray Story: Symbols and Meaning in *Benito Cereno*," *Bucknell Review*, VIII (May, 1959), 154–167.

Cardwell seeks to establish the fact that Amasa Delano is neither "the epitome of moral blindness nor an amiable but mechanical figure" but rather the "perceiving center" who has the innocent perceptiveness of Jack Chase and Billy Budd. The short novel is not a simple Manichean drama of good and evil but a mixture of the two—gray is the thematic color of the story, symbolizing Melville's subtle point of view. "Read for the second time *Benito Cereno* is, like a Greek tragedy, an exercise in dramatic irony. On first reading the irony is retrospective: the revelation of the entire ironic situation breaks upon the reader after the action of the story is completed. Consequently, the fundamental, weighty ironies of the story have little to do with maintaining interest and integrating the story structurally for first readers. But these ironies do lend unifying strength to the structure when viewed retrospectively."

145. D'Azevedo, Warren. "Revolt on the San Dominick," *Phylon*, XVII (June, 1956), 129–140.

D'Azevedo views the story as an expression of Melville's "hatred of human oppression. . . . Nowhere in the story can the reader detect any condescension toward the Negro characters, except in the thoughts of Captain Delano, whose personality and background are clearly defined for us by Melville. . . . Babo stands out as one of the great Negro figures created by white authors in American fiction." In the creation of this Negro character, Melville destroyed the stereotype so prevalent in the literature of other writers during this period. D'Azevedo emphasizes Babo's intelligence and heroism, and his noble motives of freeing himself and his companions from slavery. As a "story of the relationship between Negroes and whites," *Benito Cereno* "is far in advance of its time."

This essay simplifies Melville's attitude by imposing his moral view of Negroes upon his aesthetic use of color in the story. D'Azevedo struggles to redeem Melville from any prejudice, but his point is not borne out in the story itself.

For a conclusion similar to that of D'Azevedo, see Sterling Brown, *Negro Character in American Fiction* (Washington, D.C., 1937), pp. 12–13, whom D'Azevedo quotes with approval: "Although opposed to slavery Melville does not make *Cereno* into an abolitionist tract; he is more concerned with a thrilling narrative and character portrayal. But although the mutineers are bloodthirsty and cruel, Melville does not make them into villains; they revolt as mankind has always revolted. Because Melville was unwilling to look upon men as 'Isolatoes,' wishing instead to discover the 'common continent of man,' he came nearer to the truth in his scattered pictures of a few unusual Negroes than do the other authors of the period."

146. Dew, Marjorie. "*Benito Cereno*: Melville's Vision and Re-Vision," *A Benito Cereno Handbook*. Edited by Seymour L. Gross. Belmont, California: Wadsworth Publishing Company, Inc., 1965, pp. 178–184.

Melville "does three things to his source story: he enlarges Amasa Delano, he creates Babo, and he transforms Benito Cereno."

Miss Dew defends Melville's use of the deposition at the end of the novel from an aesthetic point of view. Things in the book have seemed chaotic but the deposition is Melville's way of saying that ordinary men can tidy up. Finally, "The opposition in Melville's *Benito Cereno* is not between good and evil but rather between average sensibilities and uncommon sensibilities. The question of the book is—can an ordinary man see? The suspense lies in—When will Delano see? Will he see? Can he see?"

147. Glicksberg, Charles I. "Melville and the Negro Problem," *Phylon*, XI (Autumn, 1950), 207–215.

Glicksberg defends Melville in his treatment of the Negroes in "Benito Cereno." Far from expressing overt contempt for the blacks aboard the *San Dominick*,

Melville expresses the typical prejudices of New Englanders through Captain Delano, who is intended as a dramatic device. "From the tone of the tale, from the cumulative internal evidence, the inference must be drawn that Melville did not attempt to blacken the blacks and whitewash the whites. Far from arousing feelings of hatred against the Negro, the incarnate image of evil, he presents a complex, artistically balanced story, which arouses mixed emotion. Though we sympathise with the plight of Don Benito, we admire the steadfast courage and indomitable spirit of Babo, a born leader, just as we admire the capacity for self-rule and the heroic resolution of the Negroes on board. If they went to extremes of butchery in their desperate bid for freedom, who shall presume to pass final judgment upon them? But the important consideration is that Melville is thoroughly consistent and honest in his limning of the race problem."

Glicksberg struggles too much to protect Melville from accusations of prejudice. It would appear that Melville has used the Negroes as symbols of evil in "Benito Cereno."

148. Green, Jesse D. "Diabolism, Pessimism, and Democracy: Notes on Melville and Conrad," *Modern Fiction Studies*, VIII (Autumn, 1962), 287–305.

Green acknowledges the many similarities between "Benito Cereno" and Conrad's work—especially *Heart of Darkness*; but he concentrates on the differences between the two authors. Melville preferred ambiguity, whereas Conrad employed a kind of "controlled skepticism."

For Conrad's direct view of Melville's work, see (68).

149. Guttman, Allen. "The Enduring Innocence of Captain Amasa Delano," *Boston University Studies in English*, V (Spring, 1961), 35–45.

Benito Cereno is unheroic and not intended as the hero of the story. "Babo, for all his ruthlessness and savagery, is the one person in the story to struggle against a moral . . . He was right to rebel."

Although Guttman disavows that this reading is dependent on other works by Melville, he does make references to *Moby-Dick*, claiming that his interpretation is true "to the spirit of the man who wrote admiringly to Hawthorne, 'There is the grand truth about Nathaniel Hawthorne. He says No! in thunder; but the Devil himself cannot make him say *yes*. For all men who say *yes* lie.'"

150. Haber, Tom Burns. "A Note on Melville's 'Benito Cereno,'" *Nineteenth-Century Fiction*, VI (September, 1951), 146–147.

Haber tries to prove that Cereno cut Babo on the cheek, after the scene in which he is shaved, and jeopardized his and Delano's life. The fact that Babo permitted Cereno to live indicates that he was capable of self-control.

For an opposing view, see Ward Pafford and Floyd Watkins, "'Benito Cereno': A Note in Rebuttal," *Nineteenth-Century Fiction*, VII (June, 1952), 68–71. These authors insist that the wound is self-inflicted; psychologically, Benito Cereno is incapable of this kind of action.

151. Hagopian, John V., et al. *Insight I: Analysis of American Literature* (Frankfurt Am Main, 1962), pp. 150–155.

The Negroes are not symbols of evil in the story. They are simply seeking revenge for evil that has been done to them. Their failure proves that "evil in the universe cannot be overcome, and it is inextricably linked with Christianity."

152. Jackson, Margaret Y. "Melville's Use of a Real Slave Mutiny in 'Benito Cereno,'" *CLA Journal*, IV (December, 1960), 79–93.

Miss Jackson criticizes Melville for even permitting a racist interpretation to be made of his story. Nevertheless, she stresses that his chief concern "is not with the slavery question per se, but rather with the problem of good and evil." Melville used the Negro as symbol of that "formidable force against which good could offer no substantial resistance."

153. Kaplan, Sidney. "Herman Melville and the American National Sin," *Journal of Negro History*, XLI (October, 1956), 311–338, XLII (January, 1957), 11–37. Reprinted in *The Image of the Negro in American Literature*, Edited by Seymour Gross and John Edward Hardy. Chicago: The Chicago University Press, 135–162.

Kaplan stresses the fact that we must not accept the events which recur in "Benito Cereno" as those which Melville sanctions. He takes issue with Schiffman (157) and Glicksberg (147), realizing that Melville's intention must be determined mainly by what he did with his plot, how he veined and fleshed it, and in part how he manipulated his source." It seems clear that Melville was thinking within the cultural concerns of his time. The inspiration for the mutiny may have come from the incident aboard the Spanish blackbird *Armistid* and the *Creole*, which were widely reported in the newspapers. It would seem that "Benito Cereno" certainly deals with slavery and rebellion and specifically with the character of the Negro as slave and rebel.

    In terms of the story itself, Kaplan views Delano as a good-natured fool who considers Negroes "jolly primitives" and whose conception of Negroes is regulated by their actions in the story. Benito Cereno is rendered far less cruel than he was in the earlier version of the story; he now is pathetic and beaten. Babo has motives which are clearly malign, closely related to "the baboon, ringleader of the Negroes who are primitives, beasts." Kaplan indicates that Melville's description of the Negroes is taken from the bestiary. Blackness in the story is unambiguously presented—it represents "malign evil." Instead of being a story which expresses Melville's anti-slaveryism, as some critics maintained, "Benito Cereno" seems "an 'artistic sublimation' . . . of notions of black primitivism dear to the hearts of slavery's apologists, a sublimation in fact of all that was sleazy, patronizing, backward and fearful in the works that preceded it.''

This essay is an intelligent and perceptive reading of "Benito Cereno," one that studies the tale organically rather than making judgments that are based on Melville's views in his own works.

154. Magowan, Robin. "Masque and Symbol in Melville's *Benito Cereno*," *College English*, XXIII (February, 1962), 346–351.

"To be brief, then, I feel that Melville's great achievement in *Benito Cereno* lies in the total atmosphere that he evokes and, in particular, in his creation of the world of the slave-ship, or floating coffin as it was then known. For in the *San Dominick* there is portrayed a world mortally corroded by the use to which it has been put, a shame world in which decay has taken on the allure of life and an intriguing counterfeit beauty which is like art.''

In this fact we may perceive Melville's condemnation of the evil of slavery. When Captain Delano comes aboard the *San Dominick* he witnesses a "black masque" in which Don Benito is the lord of misrule. Magowan traces the three main strands of symbolism in "Benito Cereno"—color, religion, and animal imagery.

155. Phillips, Barry. "'The Good Captain': A Reading of *Benito Cereno*," *Texas Studies in Literature and Language*, IV (Summer, 1962), 188–197.

Phillips stresses the idealism of Captain Delano, claiming that critics have misinterpreted the story because they view the problems of the story in terms of concepts whereas the primary problem is one of perception. The main object of perception is the *San Dominick* itself, which is "the most persistent symbol in the story," the emblem of "life's mysterious and ambiguous character." The *San Dominick* is a world where meanings are relative, inverted, multiplied, and hidden: Babo symbolizes the natural unknown; Delano—like all of Melville's idealists, as Milton Stern has shown (41)—is "exclusively a fool." The natural world of the *San Dominick* "is a stranger to the American idealist"—he emerges as a buffoon and Melville has nothing but contempt for him.

Although Phillips overemphasizes Captain Delano's absurd qualities and Melville's contempt of them, his interpretation is generally sound and perceptive.

156. Putzel, Max. "The Source and the Symbols of Melville's *Benito Cereno*," *American Literature*, XXXIV (May, 1962), 191–206.

Putzel compares Melville's story with the plays of Shakespeare and Sophocles in that the three writers see a universe "where seeming and being interreflect in an endless series, where suggestive ambiguities are as close as man can come to truth." The three basic characters see reality in different ways. Delano is the good-natured, optimistic commander, a man of property and order; Benito Cereno "is the victim of illness, disorder, disillusionment, and malign force"; Babo "is a sinister and primitive conundrum." The narrator is alien to all three characters. Putzel sees Delano as representative of the "American dream of philanthropic idealism," a man whose courage outruns his perception; Benito Cereno is "the Poe-esque exemplar of the decadent son of a decayed noble family, the sensitive, the congenitally weakened and diseased heir of empty and horrific grandeur." The author traces the differences between Melville's source and the tale he finally wrote. The source is Amasol Delano, *A Narrative of Voyages and Travels . . . Comprising Three Voyages Round the World: Together with a Voyage of Survey and Discovery* (Boston, 1817).

This essay continues the work of Harold H. Scudder, "Melville's *Benito Cereno* and Captain Delano's Voyages," *PMLA*, XLIII (June, 1928), 502.

157. Schiffman, Joseph. "Critical Problems in Melville's *Benito Cereno*." *Modern Language Quarterly*, XI (September, 1950), 317–324.

Schiffman disagrees with Stanley Williams (158) that Babo is evil, a creature of "motiveless malignity." Babo, in Schiffman's view, "was leading a rebellion of slaves in their fight for freedom, and all his acts of cruelty were dictated by this purpose." He also takes to task Rosalie Feltenstein (158) for not considering Melville's general attitudes toward slavery in interpreting the story. Schiffman cites Melville's depiction of Negroes in *Mardi*, *Redburn*, and *Moby-Dick*, and concludes that "it is in keeping with Melville's philosophy that Babo as a human being would desire freedom. . . . It is true that for most people of the Western Hemisphere black symbolizes evil and white symbolizes good. But this does not hold for Melville. He was a rebel against his age and culture, such a deep-going rebel that even his symbolism became unorthodox. To Melville white was evil, harsh, ugly—the unknown." Delano shares "the mental block" of most white westerners.

This is a very contentious essay and not very convincing. One may question whether it is entirely valid to establish Melville's attitude toward Negroes by citing other texts and then using them to interpret "Benito Cereno." Schiffman, changed his own position in his note to "Benito Cereno" in *Three Shorter Novels of Herman Melville*. New York: Harper & Brothers, pp. 230–235, in which he contrasts "Delano's obtuseness" and "Cereno's sensitivity," and concludes that "Writing in the violent decade just before the Civil War, when panic over slave insurrections was mounting, Melville, with characteristic ambivalence, treated slavery and the rebellion against it as a sign of evil in the universe. In high-lighting the savagery of the rebellion, Melville sullied his tale with racism—an element which detracts from the stature of *Benito Cereno*."

158. Williams, Stanley. "'Follow Your Leader': Melville's 'Benito Cereno,'" *Virginia Quarterly Review*, XXII (Winter, 1947), 61–76.

Williams concentrates on the religious imagery and events of the story, claiming that they reveal Melville's belief "concerning one of man's oldest institutions, the

Catholic Church." He considers the "themes of the fading glories of the Church and Spain" and finds the cloister a valid answer for "Benito Cereno." Cereno himself represents the deliquescence of the church in the Old World; Babo symbolizes primitivism; Delano represents the new emerging civilization, which is still philosophically naive.

For contradictory views, see H. Bruce Franklin, *The Wake of the Gods* (23), pp. 136–150; Rosalie Feltenstein, "Melville's 'Benito Cereno,'" *American Literature*, XIX (November, 1947), 245–255—Miss Feltenstein feels that the Inquisition is equally important to the meaning of the story as the peaceful cloister; Thomas E. Connoly's "A Note on Name-Symbolism in Melville," *American Literature*, XXV (January, 1954), 489–490 and Joan Bernstein's "*Benito Cereno* and the Spanish Inquisition," *Nineteenth-Century Fiction*, XVI (March, 1962), 345–349, both reactions to Miss Feltenstein's article.

"The Encantadas":

159. Newberry, I. "'*The Encantadas*': Melville's Inferno," *American Literature*, XXXVIII (March, 1966), 44–69.

Newberry claims that the tales have "a unified vision." "So far the issues discussed [in the treatment of 'The Encantadas'] seem to fall into two groups, the question of Melville's sources and the question of the unity of the cycle. This article discusses both these issues, especially the latter; the sources are examined mainly for the purpose of deriving evidence concerning structural unity and artistic intention . . . the first and last sections deal with two types of evil—evil as primal as well as a human force—while the central section offers a glimpse into the possibilities of 'escape.'"

Newberry believes that Melville felt the "world was created evil," and has remained basically unchanged. The central theme of the tale is "the effect of evil on life," a theme which binds the tales together and connects them with the other Piazza tales. After a thorough analysis of each of the sections of "The Encantadas," Newberry concludes that "the notes of hope in this over-all dark vision are scanty indeed."

"I and My Chimney":

160. Sealts, Merton M. "Herman Melville's 'I and My Chimney,'" *American Literature*, XIII (May, 1941), 142–154.

This story, written near the end of 1855, "is more than a mere descriptive sketch: it is Melville's subtle comment on a major crisis of his life." Sealts considers the chimney as Melville's heart and soul; the secret closet as a symbol of his dread that he may have an inherited inclination toward insanity; the Scribe as a figure modeled on Oliver Wendell Holmes; and Dacres as Melville's own father.

The significance of the story is Melville's disguised account "of the examination of his mind made a few years before the story was written, at the instigation of his family."

The Confidence Man:

161. Cawelti, John G. "Some Notes on the Structure of *The Confidence Man*," *American Literature*, XXIX (November, 1957), 278–288.

"Little attention has been given to the book's structure . . . and in this article I shall develop a structural analysis that appears to illuminate some of the novel's important themes and the way in which the author relates them." Cawelti concludes that "*The Confidence Man* is not a random collection of episodes; it is not the bitter polemic of a despairing man; it is not a philosophical leg-pull, but a serious, carefully planned attempt to present one man's vision of reality. As the vision sees ambiguity at the heart of things, so the basic structural principle is one that leaves the reader alone with enigma. One cannot deny, I think, that Melville prepared for this result painstakingly and skilfully."

Melville may have prepared his book carefully—although there is no proof of that fact—but *The Confidence Man* does not hold together structurally as well as Cawelti suggests.

162. Dubler, Walter. "Theme and Structure in Melville's *The Confidence Man*," *American Literature*, XXXIII (November, 1961), 308–319.

Melville's theme in *The Confidence Man* is basically simple. "His method of presenting this text, however, is highly complicated." In *The Confidence Man* Melville "did not attempt to establish a national or even a personal philosophy. Rather, he attempted to create a dramatic framework by means of which he could survey and comment upon the American scene."

Melville's book is a criticism of American values—the easy optimism, "excessive and cetological faith in science, business, and nature, its distortion of the real meanings of charity and benevolence, and, above all, its smug complacency and overconfidence." This dramatic technique consists mainly of the three unities of time, place, and action; the narrator's insignificance; and the stage-like dialogues or, at times, dialect.

163. Foster, Elizabeth. "Introduction," *The Confidence Man*, in *Complete Works of Herman Melville*. Howard P. Vincent, General Editor. Chicago and New York: Hendricks House, 1954, 392 pp.

Miss Foster notes that the general consensus of opinion is that *The Confidence Man* is misanthropic and cynical. She views the novel as a modern *Candide*, a satire on optimism, and points out that the book uses the satirical techniques of pervasive irony; suggestion; understatement; talk rather than action. Like Voltaire, Melville concludes that this is not the best of all possible worlds. In this running satire, Melville presents the difference between men's profession of Christianity and their practise; the theme of the book is the failure of Christians to be Christians and every mask belies its wearer. Like Shakespeare of the tragedies and the later plays, Melville is interested in appearance and reality; like the author of the Biblical Job, he deals with unexplained evil. Tha human spectacle is "half-melancholy, half farcical"; pessimism in the book goes hand in hand with comedy.

Particularly useful in this excellent introduction is Miss Foster's identification of the various avatars of *The Confidence Man*. The Lamblike man differs from those who follow him in that he commits no wrong—his message is love. The Negro, with his list of Confidence Men, is also symbolic. The Man-in-mourning has a false sense of optimism—he is sentimental. The Man in the gray coat and white tie preaches charity but is egoistic. The man with the big book (the Bible) symbolizes faith and asks people to "trust God"; the herb doctor symbolizes hope and suggests that everyone "trust nature"; the man with the brass plate symbolizes charity and asks the people to "trust man." The virtues of these men are their mask, for each man is in reality his opposite. The Cosmopolitan is an avatar of charity and brotherly love, but the stories of Colonel Moredock, the Indian hater and China Aster refute his message. Emerson is satirized through Mark Winsome. Toward the end of the novel, the cosmopolitan visits the case-hardened barber, who refuses to take down his sign, "No trust"; and in the last scene in the gentleman's cabin, the one light is the light of the Old and New Testament—if this light goes out, the world is left in darkness.

As bitter as Melville is, he does not feel that the loss of Christianity would be a good thing. One cannot trust God or nature, but one must cling to some faith in man. Thus Melville is like the figure in Arnold's "The Grand Chartreuse": a man wandering between two worlds, one dead, the other powerless to be born.

Miss Foster's introduction is a helpful guide to a difficult and often confusing novel.

164. Hoffman, Daniel G. "Melville's 'Story of China Aster,'" *American Literature*, XXII (May, 1950), 137–149.

Hoffman agrees with Richard Chase that *The Confidence Man* is Melville's "second-best book," and he compares it with the satire of Swift. More than any other major American author of the nineteenth century, with the possible exception of Twain, Melville used native folk traditions dramatically. Hoffman focuses upon the story of China Aster, which appears toward the end of the novel. Although the story seems independent, it restates the principal theme of *The Confidence Man* and "throws out implications which make the final dénouement inevitable." The links of the fable are threefold: in narrative content, which involves "borrowing money through pretensions of friendship"; in its demonstration of Mark Winsome's philosophy; and, most importantly, in its exploration of the conflict between the two opposing forces which illuminate the book: the Promethean-creative-civilizing-impulse versus its opposite, the surrender of moral judgments and the perversion of the Promethean spirit to private ends at the expense of mankind.

Poetry:

165. Barret, Laurence. "The Differences in Melville's Poetry," *PMLA*, LXX (September, 1955), 606–623.

The violence in Melville's poetry is deliberate and purposeful. "All the differences in Melville's poetry rise . . . from the history of his symbols." Melville used a highly personal symbolism which developed from metaphor: fire, the mountain, the pyramid, the colors white and green, the shark, the sea and land are rooted to individuals in the most direct sense. The wrenchings and the violences of Melville's poetry help to create a masculine style and suggest Melville's search for a form which makes it possible for man to live with ambiguities.

166. *The Battle Pieces of Herman Melville.* Edited with Introduction and Notes by Hennig Cohen. New York: Thomas Yoseloff, 1963, 302 pp.

This volume is especially valuable as a presentation of *Battle Pieces* to the modern reader. Cohen has provided a perceptive introduction in which he points out the many elements of internal unity in Melville's poetry, and offers commentaries on each of the individual poems.

Cohen indicates that "the central theme of *Battle Pieces* is one of opposition and reconciliation." The sources of Melville's poetry are the Bible, especially the old Testament; Milton; Shakespeare; his knowledge of soldiers in the war; and his reading of military life in journals like *Harper's Weekly*. Allied to the basic themes of opposition and reconciliation are two other themes: death and the integrity of the law.

The notes that follow the poems are excellent illustrations of how Melville's poetry can be examined closely and yield fruitful results. Cohen sets each poem in its historical context, explains the background, and then provides an *explication de texte* that inevitably sends the reader back to the poem being examined.

See also Cohen's edition, *Selected Poems of Herman Melville.* Garden City: Doubleday and Co., Inc., 1964, 259 pp., which follows the same technique of having commentaries at the end of the volume.

167. Bezanson, Walter E. "Melville's Reading of Arnold's Poetry," *PMLA*, LXIX (June, 1954), 365–391.

Bezanson deals with Melville's marginalia and then traces Melville's close reading of Arnold's poetry. Melville remained "convinced that the great questions are unanswerable and that life is harsh." In Arnold's poetry Melville found "major elements of his own self-image," one of "emotional doubt and reasoned hope—with reservations."

168. Warren, Robert Penn. "Melville the Poet," *Selected Essays of Robert Penn Warren.* New York: Random House, Inc., 1958, pp. 184–197. Reprinted in *Discussions of Moby Dick*, pp. 127–134 (117) and *Melville: A Collection of Critical Essays*, ed. Richard Chase, pp. 144–168 (51).

Warren offers some remarks supplementary to those of Matthiessen in his edition, *Selected Poems of Herman Melville.* He speaks of Melville's style, and though he admits that Melville was "a poet of shred and patches," he shows that he was a better "technical poet than critics have admitted." He analyzes "In a Bye Canal" and concludes that "the confusions of temper in this poem are not merely the result of ineptitude but are the result of an attempt to create a poetry of some vibrancy, range of reference, and richness of tone." He also examines "The March into Virginia," "The Portent," "America," and "The Maldive Shark," "What I wish to emphasize is the fact that there is an astonishing continuity between the early poems, especially *Battle-Pieces*, and *Clarel.* Under the terms of nature and history, the religious attitude of *Clarel* and 'The Lake' is already being defined."

Billy Budd:

169. Anderson, Charles R. "The Genesis of *Billy Budd*," *American Literature*, XII (November, 1940), 329–346.

"*Billy Budd, Foretopman* was the child of [Melville's] old age, completed before his death." Melville, Anderson points out, was in a reminiscent mood. In this essay, he identifies the sources of the novel. The ship, the *Indefatigable*, was modeled on the *Somers*; Captain Vere was based on Sir William George Fairfax; the mutiny closely followed the Great Mutiny of April and May, 1797 and the mutiny aboard the *Somers* in 1842. This latter story was reviewed in June, 1888, in an article, "The Mutiny on the *Somers*," printed in *The American Magazine*. In less than six months— on November 16, 1888—Melville had begun the writing of *Billy Budd*.

Philip Spencer, who had been involved in the *Somers* mutiny, may have been the model for Billy Budd; the Master-at-arms aboard the *United States* in 1843-1844 may have suggested the figure of Claggart.

"In Billy Budd," Anderson concludes, "borrowing is reduced to a minimum, and imaginative invention counts for almost everything that makes it, as one critic declares, a masterpiece in miniature."

See Newton Arvin's essay, "A Note on the Background of *Billy Budd*," *American Literature*, XX (March, 1948), 51–55, for additional material. Arvin suggests that the *Autobiography of Thurlow Weed* casts additional light on Chapter XVIII of *Billy Budd* and that Captain Vere may in part have been influenced by Melville's own cousin, Guert Gansevoort.

170. Braswell, William. "Melville's *Billy Budd* as 'An Inside Narrative,'" *American Literature*, XXIX (May, 1957), 133–146.

Braswell sees *Billy Budd* as "an inside narrative about a tragedy in Melville's own spiritual life." The *Indomitable* represents a microcosm of Melville and "aspects of his being are dramatized in Captain Vere, Billy Budd, and Claggart." Billy symbolizes "the heart" and Claggart "the head." Braswell connects Ahab's and Pierre's relationship with Billy Budd in their commitment to the heart. The mounting crises of the earlier novels reach their culmination in *Billy Budd*, and "the action of Captain Vere in regard to Billy indicates symbolically how Melville, with his faculties threatening mutiny, resolved his own greatest personal crisis." The novel might well be called Melville's apologia rather than his "testament of acceptance"; Melville is "sympathetic toward not only the Christlike Billy but also the philosophical Vere." In this sense he "bore his own cross" while writing *Billy Budd*.

171. Duersken, Roland A. "*Caleb Williams, Political Justice,* and *Billy Budd*," *American Literature*, XXXVIII (November, 1966), 372–376.

"Without insisting on a direct line of influence, the serious reader may find enlightening a comparison of the two authors' [Godwin's and Melville's] treatments of innocence, justice, duty, and virtue."

Melville received a copy of *Caleb Williams* in 1849 when he was in London. Certain parallels between *Caleb Williams* and *Billy Budd* immediately become evident. The subtitles of the two works are similar: Godwin's "Things as They Are" and Melville's "An Inside Narrative." Squire Faulkland resembles first Billy Budd and then Captain Vere. Duersken also notes the philosophical questions raised by Godwin in *Political Justice* (especially in the chapter on "Duty," Book II, Chapter III). "Perhaps the important distinction between the respective criteria of Godwin and Melville is that the former, in his assertion of abstract (individualized) justice, is ready to disregard all institutions and their requirements, while the latter cannot throw off a deep concern about society as it is presently constituted."

172. Glick, Wendell. "Expediency and Absolute Morality in *Billy Budd*," *PMLA*, LXVIII (March, 1953), 103–110.

Glick concentrates upon Lord Nelson, whom Melville speaks of for several pages in *Billy Budd*, and his relationship to Billy; both men are heroic and illuminate each other's character. Glick maintains that the digression on Nelson reveals the meaning of the final scene of the novel. "Might the answer be that the hanging of Billy Budd is Melville's final commentary upon the theme of the impracticability of absolute standards in a world necessarily ruled by expediency? . . . But in a society composed of men, not angels—in a society in which even Claggarts are to be found—an inferior standard, that of expediency, is the only workable one."

This is cogent analysis of the novel, but as Phil Withim points out (185), "It seems natural to compare Nelson with Vere" rather than with Billy Budd: "both are captains of ships in time of war, both are asked to deal with mutiny."

173. Hayford, Harrison, ed. *The Somers Mutiny Affair.* Englewood Cliffs, N.J.: Prentice Hall, 1959, 224 pp.

Hayford gives the story of the mutiny and its effect on American public opinion. This story is important as a background for *Billy Budd*. The author has collected documentary materials about the *Somers* mutiny affair. "The *Somers* was a U.S. Naval brig sailing home late in 1842." Hayford divides his book into five parts—The News Breaks, The Court of Inquiry, The Court Martial, The Court of Opinion, and Into Memory—and includes, in the last section, "brief selections from literary works by Herman Melville which drew upon his knowledge and feeling about the *Somers* case."

174. Ives, C. B. "*Billy Budd* and the Articles of War," *American Literature*, XXXIV (March, 1962), 31–39.

Billy Budd has been interpreted in terms of Melville's philosophy about good and evil, but there are "realistic elements worth examining . . . one of these is Captain Vere's appeal to the Articles of War to justify his hanging Billy." Ives's basic point is that Vere, as a captain of a man-of-war, was godlike "and might exercise his disciplinary discretion or even his disciplinary whims freely with little expectation of reproof." He is confident that the Articles of War did not control him. In his decision to hang Billy, Vere is committing a sacrificial gesture and an act of self-punishment that is entirely consistent with his character. "All of his life Vere had devoted himself abnormally to this emphasis, killing repeatedly the affections that manifested themselves only in moments of dreaminess, moments that embarrassed and irritated him when they were discovered. Billy represented all of this nearly-destroyed side of him—the affectionate side, the heart, the feminine . . ."

175. Kilbourne, W. G., Jr. "Montaigne and Captain Vere," *American Literature*, XXXIII (January, 1962), 514–517.

Kilbourne notes that Melville states that Captain Vere "was 'an exceptional character' who read 'history, biography and unconventional writers, who, free from the cant and convention, like Montaigne, honestly, and in the spirit of common sense philosophize upon realities."

Kilbourne draws parallels between Montaigne's humanism and political pragmatism and that of Melville.

176. Miller, James E., Jr. "*Billy Budd:* The Catastrophe of Innocence," *Modern Language Notes*, LXXIII (March, 1958), 168–176.

Billy Budd is a culminating "Titanic Innocent"—like Taji, Ahab, Pierre, and Mortmain. In *Billy Budd*, Melville found a new form for an old, familiar theme. The theme was stated as early as *White-Jacket*, that though God was full of the wisdom of heaven, His gospel seems lacking in the practical wisdom of earth. Billy is Christlike but also Adam, a subtly masked man of innocence. Captain Vere is "the man of moderation with heart and intellect in ideal balance."

[handwritten margin note: } Billy Christ } Vere God]

177. Noone, John B., Jr. "*Billy Budd:* Two Concepts of Nature," *American Literature,* XXXIX (November, 1957), 149–162.

Noone links the novel with a "clash of ideas which gave such vitality to the eighteenth century. . . . Quickly summarizing the 'moral' of this book, it appears that, even though man as heir to evil must have his being within the limits of the repressive forms supplied by reason, still, a judicious combination of instinct and reason can meliorate the crueler aspects of formalism, eventually producing a new set of objective conditions which require less repressive forms for man's governance. If this is not utopian optimism, neither is it unrelieved despair."

178. Pearson, Norman Holmes, "Billy Budd: 'The King's Yarn,'" *American Quarterly,* III (Summer, 1951), 99–114.

Although Melville undoubtedly depends upon such sources as Milton's poetry and the Bible, he never permits Billy to lose "his identity as a sailor." The analogies often made between Melville's tale and stories of Adam, Christ, Abraham, and Isaac have their validity, but "these are simply shifting similitudes, which reenforce but do not tie down" the basic naturalistic truths of the book.

179. Rathbun, John W. "*Billy Budd* and the Limits of Perception," *Nineteenth-Century Fiction,* XX (June, 1965), 19–34.

Encouraged by the authoritative textual and genetic edition of *Billy Budd, Sailor* (*An Inside Narrative*), edited by Harrison Hayford and Merton M. Sealts, Jr. (8) Rathbun explores the novel as a whole. He disavows two assumptions often made about the novel: that it is a tragedy and that the focus of the story is on any one character. He believes that the novel resembles a saint's play and that "social forms and conventions radically narrow the range of individual perception and response." Social norms subordinate the individual, even when an extraordinary person like Billy Budd appears. "No one in the novel is finally able to ascertain who Billy really is. Billy's character remains enigmatic. The symbolic roles he plays as Adam, as Isaac, as Christ, become at last meaningless and futile. . . . What Melville seems to be saying is that as social creatures we fail to properly understand our saints."

[handwritten margin note: } Billy saves & Adam]

180. Reich, Charles A. "The Tragedy of Justice in *Billy Budd,*" *The Yale Review,* LVI (March, 1967), 368–389.

Billy Budd is different from Melville's other works in that the characters of Billy and Claggart are not developed; only Captain Vere—the civilized, intellectual man—is viewed with any kind of complexity.

"There are at least three basic issues in *Billy Budd*. First, how and by what standards should Billy, or Billy's act, be judged? Second, how does Vere, the man committed to society, perceive the problem and respond? And third, how adequate are the standards which society has adopted?"

Billy is innocent in what he is, not in what he does; and the conflict that centers about him is between society and Nature, both of which contain good and evil. "His inability to adapt to society is the inability of nature to be civilized. Billy is incapable of acquiring experience."

Captain Vere cannot compromise in his decision—he is "forced to confront the imperatives of law." His character develops from that of the pedantic captain to that of the humane man. He learns that "if the law is to be followed, other values must be sacrificed." Vere chooses the law, however inadequate it may be.

"Billy's execution is thus an image of society's failure to make its actions fit its understanding. Society's spiritual knowledge of man is far in advance of its law."

For the contemporary reader, *Billy Budd* "is a reminder of the indispensable importance of the artistic vision in the structuring of society—an expression of the need for society to accept the natural in man."

181. Sherwood, John C. "Vere as Collingwood: A Key to *Billy Budd*," *American Literature*, XXXV (January, 1964), 476–484.

Vere is modeled after Cuthbert, Baron Collingwood, a man associated with the American Revolution who became a lieutenant, commander, and captain. Vere and Collingwood are linked by common characteristics: superior seamanship; courage; submission to duty and authority; humanity; strictness; conservatism; love of "serious" reading; and lack of sociability.

182. Stafford, William T., ed. *Melville's Billy Budd and the Critics*. San Francisco: Wadsworth Publishing Company, 1961.

Stafford reprints *Billy Budd* from Freeman's corrected text and presents numerous critical comments. The book is divided into five sections: 1. Early notices written during the 1920's (by Raymond Weaver, John Middleton Murry, John Freeman, and Lewis Mumford). 2. First extensive analysis of tale (E. L. Grant Watson, "Melville's Testament of Acceptance," *New England Quarterly*, VI (June, 1933), 319–327) with an opposite point of view (Phil Withim, "Billy Budd: Testament of Resistance," *Modern Language Quarterly*, XX (June, 1959), 115–127). 3. Five different readings: (a) Biographical (William Braswell, "Melville's Billy Budd as 'An Inside Narrative,'" *American Literature*, XXIX (May, 1957), 133–146; (b) Social (Wendell Glick, "Expediency and Absolute Morality in *Billy Budd*," *PMLA*, LXXVIII (March, 1953), 103–110); (c) A Mythic-psychoanalytical reading (From Chase, *Herman Melville*, 269–277); (d) Two Esthetic readings (Ray B. West, "The Unity of *Billy Budd*," *Hudson Review*, V (Spring, 1952), 120–127; (e) William York Tindall, "The Form of *Billy Budd*," from "The Ceremony of Innocence," R. M.

McIver, ed. *Great Moral Dilemmas on Literature, Past and Present*. New York: Harper and Brothers, 1956, 73–81. 4. Christian Sources in work by Nathalia Wright, Newton Arvin, Lawrance Thompson, Henry F. Pommer, Norman Holmes Pearson, Richard Chase, Richard Harter Fogle, Herbert Weisinger, and Adrian J. Jaffe. 5. Special Problems: the characters (discussed by Milton R. Stern, Leonard Casper, W. W. H. Auden, Geoffrey Stone, James Baird), the digressions (Mary Foley, M. L. Rosenthal, and A. J. M. Smith), and the author (W. H. Auden).

183. Tindall, William York. "The Ceremony of Innocence," in *Great Dilemmas in Literature, Past and Present*. New York: Harper & Row, 1956, pp. 73–81.

Tindall considers the form of *Billy Budd*. Although a first version of the manuscript reveals more action and less discourse, it is not so effective as the first version "with all its weight of digression and analysis." Melville worked for three years on *Billy Budd*, and he was deeply conscious of the form of the book. Tindall notes Melville's use of words and symbolism in giving form to the novel; at the center of this form "is neither Vere nor Billy but rather the teller of the story or Melville himself. . . . The effect of this form is moral in the sense of enlarging our awareness of human conditions or relationships and of improving our sensitivity. In such a form Kierkegaard's esthetic, moral, and divine become a single thing."

184. Watson, E. L. Grant. "Melville's Testament of Acceptance," *The New England Quarterly*, VI (June, 1933), 319–327.

Billy Budd is written with less romantic flourish than *Moby-Dick* and *Pierre*, but its symbolism is equally rich; indeed the "symbolism becomes all the more effective for being presented in a dry and objective manner. The title of the novel is purposely humorous in its obvious and peculiar denotation; Melville has chosen a simple man as hero of his tragedy. In writing *Billy Budd*, Melville is no longer the rebel he was when he composed *Mardi*, *Moby-Dick*, and *Pierre*. Billy Budd and Captain Vere are no rebels; between the two there is the spiritual understanding of acceptance.

185. West, Ray B., Jr. "The Unity of *Billy Budd*," *Hudson Review*, V (Spring, 1952), 120–127.

Billy Budd is concerned with " 'the crisis of Christendom,' with Christendom standing not only for the formal aspects of religion, but for all of the philosophical, political, and moral concerns of Man," Billy Budd is Christian man as well as historic man. In the writing of *Billy Budd* Melville discovers that man and God are the same. "Billy is budding man, yet he is also the budding God. . . . *Billy Budd* is not in itself a tragedy, although it is an expression of belief in the tragic predicament of man. If we distinguish it by supplying a name, I would suggest that it be called satiric-allegory."

186. Withim, Phil. *"Billy Budd:* Testament of Resistance," *Modern Language Quarterly*, XX (June, 1959), 115–127.

Withim takes issue with the interpretations of Watson (184) and other critics that *Billy Budd* represents "Melville's testament of acceptance." He takes a step in the direction of Joseph Schiffman (157) and others and views the novel as basically ironic. Billy Budd and Claggart are explicitly symbolic of good and evil; Captain Vere, however, is more complicated and creates the irony in the novel. The captain is not Melville's spokesman and there is a distance maintained between author and captain throught the story: "Vere has no nobility and above all no trust in man." Certain contraditions, Withim feels, refute the "testament of acceptance" theory: Melville continues beyond Billy's death; Captain Vere, as a spokesman for reason, would not represent Melville's argument, which favors instinct over reason; Vere's name first suggests *veritas* "truth," but then suggests *veritus* "fear," and then *vir* "man"; Melville uses as symbols of evil flogging, impressment, and arbitrary hanging, "when these evils had been corrected by the time he wrote this story"; Billy Budd is so simple that it is unrealistic to believe that his cry, "God Bless Captain Vere," means "full understanding, instinctive or otherwise." Billy Budd's final cry "is the crowning irony and really the climax of the story, for he was hanged unjustly. . . . Melville reminds us that we must keep up the good fight; evil must not remain uncontested. And he does so not by a call to arms but by demonstrating the consequences of unresisting acquiescence."

VI. Bibliographical Index

The number in parentheses at the end of each item, refers to the annotated entry of the same number.

Editions, Other Primary Materials, and Bibliographies:

Leary Lewis, ed. *Articles on American Literature, 1900–1950:* Durham: Duke University Press, 1954. **(10)**

Melville, Herman. *Billy Budd, Sailor*, by Herman Melville: Reading Text and Genetic Text. Edited by Harrison Hayford and Merton M. Sealts, Jr. Chicago: The University of Chicago Press, 1962. **(9)**

—————. *Complete Works of Herman Melville*. Howard P. Vincent, general editor. Chicago and New York: Hendricks House, 1947– . **(1)**

—————. *Journal of a Visit to London and the Continent by* Herman Melville, 1849–1850. Edited by Eleanor Melville Metcalf. Cambridge: Harvard University Press, 1948. **(5)**

—————. *The Letters of Herman Melville*. Edited by Merrell R. Davis and William H. Gilman. New Haven: Yale University Press, 1960. **(7)**

—————. *Melville's Billy Budd*. Edited by Barron Freeman. Cambridge: Harvard University Press, 1948. **(8)**

—————. *Melville's Journal of a Visit to Europe and the Levant*, October 11, 1956–May 6, 1857. Edited by Howard C. Horsford. Princeton: Princeton University Press, 1955. **(6)**

—————. *Moby-Dick*. Edited by Harrison Hayford and Hershel Parker. New York: W. W. Norton and Co., Inc., 1967. **(4)**

—————. *The Works of Herman Melville*. Standard Edition. 16 volumes. London: Constable and Company, 1922–1924. **(2)**

—————. *The Writings of Herman Melville. The Northwestern-Newberry Edition.* Evanston, Illinois: Northwestern University Press. Edited by Harrison Hayford, Hershel Parker, and G. Thomas Tanselle, 1968– . **(3)**

Spiller, Robert E. et al. *The Literary History of the United States*. Bibliography, Volume III, prepared by T. H. Johnson. New York: The Macmillan Co., 1948. Supplement, ed. Richard M. Ludwig. New York: The Macmillan Co., 1959. **(11)**

Williams, Stanley T. "Melville," *Eight American Authors: A Review of Research and Criticism*. Edited by Floyd Stovall. New York: The Modern Language Association of America, 1956. **(12)**

Biographies and Critical Biographies:

Anderson, Charles Roberts. *Melville in the South Seas*. New York: Columbia University Press, 1939. **(13)**

Arvin, Newton. *Herman Melville*. New York: William Sloane Associates, Inc., 1950. **(14)**

Bernstein, John. *Pacificism and Rebellion in the Writings of Herman Melville*. Studies in American Literature, Volume I. The Hague: Mouton & Company, 1964. **(15)**

Berthoff, Warner. *The Example of Melville*. Princeton: Princeton University Press, 1962. **(16)**

Bowen, Merlin. *The Long Encounter: Self and Experience in the Writings of Herman Melville*. Chicago: University of Chicago Press, 1960. **(17)**

Braswell, William. *Melville's Religious Thought*, An Essay in Interpretation. Durham: Duke University Press, 1943. **(18)**

Chase, Richard. *Herman Melville: A Critical Study*. New York: The Macmillan Company, 1949. **(19)**

Curl, Vega. *Pasteboard Masks*, Fact as Spiritual Symbol in the Novels of Hawthorne and Melville. Cambridge: Harvard University Press, 1931. **(20)**

Dryden, Edgar A. *Melville's Thematics of Form:* The Great Art of Telling the Truth. Baltimore; Johns Hopkins, 1968. **(21)**

Finkelstein, Dorothee M. *Melville's Orienda*. New Haven: Yale University Press, 1961. **(22)**

Franklin, H. Bruce. *The Wake of the Gods: Melville's Mythology*. Stanford: Stanford University Press, 1963. **(23)**

Freeman, John. *Herman Melville*. London: Macmillan and Co., English Men of Letters Series, 1926. **(24)**

Geist, Stanley. *Herman Melville, The Tragic Vision and the Heroic Ideal*. Cambridge: Harvard University Press, 1939. **(25)**

Hetherington, Hugh W. *Melville's Reviewers, British and American*, 1846–1891. Chapel Hill: University of North Carolina Press, 1961. **(26)**

Hillway, Tyrus. *Herman Melville*. New York: Twayne Publishers, 1963. **(27)**

Howard, Leon. *Herman Melville: A Biography*. Berkeley: University of California Press, 1951. **(28)**

—————. *Herman Melville*. Minneapolis: University of Minnesota, 1961. **(28)**

Humphreys, A. R. *Herman Melville*. Edinburgh: Oliver and Boyd, Ltd., 1962. **(29)**

James, C. L. R. *Mariners, Renegades, and Castaways*, The Story of Herman Melville and the World We Live In. New York: C. L. R. James, 1953. **(30)**

Leyda, Jay, *The Melville Log: A Documentary Life of Herman Melville*, 1819–1891, 2 Volumes. New York: Harcourt, Brace and Co., 1951. **(31)**

Mason, Ronald. *The Spirit Above the Dust*. London: John Lehmann, 1951.　　　**(32)**

Metcalf, Eleanor Melville. *Herman Melville: Cycle and Epicycle*. Cambridge: Harvard University Press, 1953.　　　**(33)**

Miller, James E., Jr. *A Reader's Guide to Herman Melville*. New York: Farrar, Straus and Cudahy, 1962.　　　**(34)**

Mumford, Lewis. *Herman Melville: A Study of His Life and Vision*. New York: Harcourt, Brace & Co., 1929.　　　**(35)**

Parker, Hershel, ed. *The Recognition of Herman Melville, Selected Criticism Since 1846*. Ann Arbor: The University of Michigan Press, 1967.　　　**(36)**

Pommer, Henry Francis. *Milton and Melville*. Pittsburgh: University of Pittsburgh Press, 1950.　　　**(37)**

Rosenberry, Edward H. *Melville and the Comic Spirit*. Cambridge: Harvard University Press, 1955.　　　**(38)**

Sealts, Merton M. *Melville as Lecturer*. Cambridge: Harvard University Press, 1957.　　　**(39)**

――――――. *Melville's Reading, A Check-List of Books Owned and Borrowed*. Madison: University of Wisconsin Press, 1966.　　　**(39)**

Sedgwick, William Ellery. *Herman Melville: The Tragedy of Mind*. Cambridge: Harvard University Press, 1944.　　　**(40)**

Stern, Milton R. *The Fine Hammered Steel of Herman Melville*. Urbana: University of Illinois Press, 1957.　　　**(41)**

Stone, Geoffrey. *Melville*, New York: Sheed and Ward, 1949.　　　**(42)**

Sundermann, K. H. *Herman Melville's Gedankegut: Eine Kritische Untersuchung Seiner Weltanschaulicher Grundieen*. Berlin: Verlag Arthur Collignon, 1937.　　　**(43)**

Thompson, Lawrence. *Melville's Quarrel With God*. Princeton: Princeton University Press, 1952.　　　**(44)**

Weaver, Raymond. *Herman Melville, Mariner and Mystic*. New York: George H. Doran Company, 1921.　　　**(45)**

Wright, Nathalia. *Melville's Use of the Bible*. Durham: Duke University Press, 1949.　　　**(46)**

Criticism:

Anderson, Charles Roberts. "Contemporary American Opinions of *Typee* and *Omoo*," *American Literature*, IX (March, 1937), 1–25.　　　**(13)**

――――――. "The Genesis of Billy Budd," *American Literature*, XII (November, 1940), 329–346.　　　**(16)**

――――――. "Melville's English Debut," *American Literature*, XI (March, 1939), 23–38.　**(13)**

Arvin, Newton. "A Note on the Background of *Billy Budd*," *American Literature*, XX (March, 1948), 51–55.　　　**(169)**

Auden, W. H. *The Enchafèd Flood or The Romantic Iconography of the Sea*. New York: Random House, 1950.　　　**(89)**

Baird, James. *Ishmael*. Baltimore: The Johns Hopkins Press, 1956.　　　**(90)**

Barret, Laurence. "The Differences in Melville's Poetry," *PMLA*, LXX (September, 1955), 606–623. **(165)**

Battenfeld, David H. "The Source for the Hymn in *Moby-Dick*," *American Literature*, XXVII (November, 1955), 393–396. **(90)**

Belgion, Montgomery. "Heterodoxy on *Moby-Dick?*" *Sewanee Review*, LV (Winter, 1947), 108–125. **(92)**

Bernstein, John Albert. "'Benito Cereno' and the Spanish Inquisition," *Nineteenth-Century Fiction*, XVI (March, 1962), 345–350. **(142)**

Bewley, Marius. *The Eccentric Design.* New York: Columbia University Press, 1959, pp. 187–219. **(47)**

Bezanson, Walter E. "*Moby-Dick:* Work of Art," *Moby-Dick Centennial Essays*, with an Introduction by Tyrus Hillway and Luther S. Mansfield. Dallas: Southern Methodist University Press, 1953, pp. 30–58. **(93)**

—————. "Melville's Reading of Arnold's Porety," *PMLA*, LXIX (June, 1954), 365–391. **(167)**

Blackmur, R. P. "The Craft of Herman Melville: A Putative Statement," *The Lion and the Honeycomb.* New York: Harcourt, Brace and World, Inc., 1955, pp. 124–144. **(94)**

Bloom, Edward. "The Allegorical Principle," *English Literary History*, XVIII (1951), 163–190. **(95)**

Braswell, William. "Melville's *Billy Budd* as 'An Inside Narrative,'" *American Literature*, XXIX (May, 1957), 133–146. **(170)**

—————. "The Satirical Temper of Melville's *Pierre*," *American Literature*, VII (January, 1936), 424–438. **(131)**

—————. "The Early Love Scenes of Melville's *Pierre*," *American Literature*, XXII (November, 1950), 283–289. **(131)**

Brodtkorb, Paul Jr. *Ishmael's White World, A Phenomenological Reading of Moby Dick.* New Haven: Yale University Press, 1965. **(96)**

Brooks, Van Wyck. *The Times of Melville and Whitman.* New York: E. P. Dutton, 1947, pp. 142–175. **(48)**

Cawelti, John G. "Some Notes on the Structure of *The Confidence Man*," *American Literature*, XXIX (November, 1957), 278–288. **(161)**

Canady, Nicholas, Jr. "A New Reading of Melville's *Benito Cereno*," *Studies in American Literature*. Edited by Waldo McNeir and Leo B. Levy. Baton Rouge: Louisiana State University Press, 1960, 49–57. **(143)**

Canby, H. S. "Hawthorne and Melville," *Classic Americans: Eminent American Writers from Irving to Whitman.* New York: Harcourt, Brace & Co., 1931, pp. 226–262. **(49)**

Cardwell, Guy. "Melville's Gray Story" Symbols and Meaning in *Benito Cereno*," *Bucknell Review*, VIII (May, 1959), 154–167. **(144)**

Charvat, William. "Melville's Income," *American Literature*, XV (November, 1943), 251–261. **(50)**

Chase, Richard. "An Approach to Melville," *Partisan Review* (May, June, 1947), 285–295.
    (19)

————. ed., *Melville: A Collection of Critical Essays.* Englewood Cliffs: Prentice Hall, 1962.
    (51)

————. *The American Novel and Its Tradition.* New York: Doubleday & Co., 1957, pp. 89–115.
    (51)

————. ed. *Selected Tales and Poems by Herman Melville.* New York: Rinehart & Co., 1950.
    (51)

Cook, Charles H., Jr. "Ahab's 'Intolerable Allegory,'" *Boston University Studies in English*, I (1955–56), 45–52. Reprinted in *Discussions of Moby-Dick*, ed. Milton R. Stern. Boston: D. C. Heath and Company, 1960, pp. 60–65.
    (97)

Cook, Reginald L. "Big Medicine in *Moby Dick*," *Accent*, VIII (Winter, 1948), 102–109.
    (98)

Cowan, J. A. "In Praise of Self-Reliance: The Role of Bulkington in *Moby-Dick*," *American Literature*, XXXVIII (January, 1967), 547–556.
    (99)

Cowie, Alexander. "Herman Melville," *The Rise of the American Novel.* New York: American Book Company, 1951, pp. 362–411.
    (52)

Dahl, Curtis. "Moby Dick's Cousin Behemoth," *American Literature*, XXXI (March, 1959), 21–29.
    (100)

Damon, S. F. "Why Ishmael Went to Sea," *American Literature*, II (November, 1930), 281–283.
    (101)

Davis, Merrell R. *Melville's Mardi, A Chartless Voyage.* New Haven: Yale University Press, 1952.
    (88)

D'Azevedo, Warren. "Revolt on the San Dominick, *Phylon*, XVII (June, 1956), 129–140.
    (145)

Dew, Marjorie. "*Benito Cereno*: Melville's Vision and Re-Vision," *A Benito Cereno Handbook.* Edited by Seymour L. Gross. Belmont California: Wadsworth Publishing Company, Inc., 1965, 178–184.
    (146)

Dubler, Walter. "Theme and Structure in Melville's *The Confidence Man*," *American Literature*, XXXIII (November, 1961), 307–319.
    (162)

Duersken, Roland. "*Caleb Williams, Political Justice*, and *Billy Budd*," *American Literature*, XXXVIII (November, 1966), 372–376.
    (171)

Feidelson, C. N. *Symbolism and American Literature.* Chicago: The University of Chicago Press, 1953.
    (53)

Fiedler, Leslie. *Love and Death in the American Novel.* New York: Criterion Books, 1960.
    (102)

Firebaugh, Joseph J. "Humorist as Rebel: The Melville of *Typee*," *Nineteenth-Century Fiction*, IX (September, 1954), 108–120.
    (85)

Fogle, R. H. *Melville's Shorter Tales.* Norman, Oklahoma: University of Oklahoma Press, 1960.
    (138)

Forster, E. M. *Aspects of the Novel.* New York: Harcourt, Brace and Company, 1927.
    (55)

Foster, Elizabeth S. "Introduction," *The Confidence Man*, in *Complete Works of Herman Melville*. Howard P. Vincent, General Editor. Chicago and New York: Hendricks House, 1954. **(163)**

————. "Melville and Geology," *American Literature*, XVII (March, 1945), 50–65 **(55)**

Frederick, John T. "Symbol and Theme in Melville's *Israel Potter*," *Modern Fiction Studies*, VIII (Autumn, 1962), 265–275. **(136)**

Geiger, Don. "Melville's Black God: Contrary Evidence in 'The *Town-Ho's* Story,'" *American Literature*, XXV (January, 1954), 464–471. **(115)**

Gilman, W. H. *Melville's Early Life and* Redburn. New York: New York University Press, 1951. **(86)**

Gleim, William S. *The Meaning of Moby Dick*. New York: The Buck Row Book Shop, 1938. **(103)**

Glick, Wendell. "Expedience and Absolute Morality in *Billy Budd*," *PMLA*, LXVIII (March, 1953), 103–110. **(171)**

Glicksberg, Charles I. "Melville and the Negro Problem," *Phylon*, XI (Autumn, 1950), 207–215. **(147)**

Green, Jesse D. "Diabolism, Pessimism, and Democracy: Notes on Melville and Conrad," *Modern Fiction Studies*, VIII (Autumn, 1962), 287–305. **(148)**

Gross, Theodore L. "Herman Melville: The Nature of Authority," *The Colorado Quarterly*, XVI (Spring, 1968), 397–412. **(56)**

Guetti, James. *The Limits of Metaphor: A Study of Melville, Conrad, and Faulkner*. Ithaca: Cornell University Press, 1967. **(57)**

Guttmann, Allen. "The Enduring Innocence of Captain Amasa Delano," Boston University Studies in English, V (Spring, 1961), 35–45. **(149)**

Haber, Tom Burns. "A Note on Melville's 'Benito Cereno,'" *Nineteenth-Century Fiction*, VI (September, 1951), 146–147. **(150)**

Hagopian, John V. et al. *Insight I: Analyses of American Literature* (Frankfurt Am Main, 1962), pp. 150–155. **(151)**

Hayford, Harrison, ed. *The Somers Mutiny Affair*. Englewood Cliffs, N. J.: Prentice Hall, 1959. **(173)**

Hayman, Allen. "The Real and the Original: Herman Melville's Theory of Prose Fiction," *Modern Fiction Studies*, VIII (Autumn, 1962), 211–233. **(58)**

Heflin, Wilson L. "Melville and Nantucket," *Moby-Dick Centennial Essays*. Edited by Tyrus Hillway and Luther S. Mansfield. Dallas: Southern Methodist University Press, 1953, pp. 165–179. **(104)**

Hetherington, Hugh W. "Early Reviews of *Moby-Dick*," *Moby-Dick Centennial Essays*. Edited by Tyrus Hillway and Luther S. Mansfield. Dallas: Southern Methodist University Press, 1953, pp. 89–122. **(105)**

Hicks, Granville. "A Re-Reading of *Moby Dick*," *Twelve Great American Novels*. Edited by Charles Shapiro. Detroit: Wayne State University Press, 1958, pp. 44–69. **(106)**

Hillway, Tyrus. *Melville and the Whale*. Stonington, Connecticut: Stonington Publishing Co., 1950. **(107)**

————. "A Preface to *Moby-Dick*," *Moby-Dick Centennial Essays*. Edited by Tyrus Hillway and Luther S. Mansfield. Dallas: Southern Methodist University Press, 1953, pp. 22–29. **(107)**

Hillway, Tyrus. "Pierre, the Fool of Virtue," *American Literature*, XXI (May, 1949), 201–211. **(132)**

Hillway, Tyrus and Mansfield, Luther S., editors. *Moby Dick: Centennial Essays*. Dallas: Southern Methodist University Press, 1953. **(108)**

Hoeltje, Hubert H. "Hawthorne, Melville and 'Blackness,'" *American Literature*, XXXVII (March, 1965), 41–51. **(59)**

Horsford, Howard C. "The Design and Argument in *Moby-Dick*," *Modern Fiction Studies*, VIII (Autumn, 1962), 233–251. **(109)**

Hoffman, Daniel G. *Form and Fable in American Fiction*. New York: Oxford University Press, 1961, pp. 221–313. **(60)**

————. "Melville's 'Story of China Aster,'" *American Literature*, XXII (May, 1950), 137–149. **(164)**

Honig, Edwin. *Dark Conceit, The Making of Allegory*. Evanston: Northwestern University Press, 1959. **(61)**

Howard, Leon. "Melville's Struggle with the Angel," *Modern Language Quarterly*, I (June, 1940), 195–206. **(62)**

Ives, C. B. "Billy Budd and the Articles of War," *American Literature*, XXXIV (March, 1962), 31–39. **(174)**

Jackson, Margaret Y. "Melville's Use of a Real Slave Mutiny in 'Benito Cereno,'" *CLA Journal*, IV (December, 1960), 79–93. **(152)**

Kaplan, Sidney. "Herman Melville and the American National Sin," *Journal of Negro History*, XLI (October, 1956), 311–338, XLII (January, 1957), 11–37. **(153)**

Kaul, A. N. "Herman Melville: The New World Voyageur," *The American Vision: Actual and Ideal Society in Nineteenth-Century Fiction*. New Haven: Yale University Press (1963), pp. 214–279. **(63)**

Kazin, Alfred. "On Melville as Scripture," *Partisan Review*, XVII (January, 1950), 67–75. **(19)**

————. "'Introduction' to *Moby-Dick*" From the Riverside Edition of *Moby-Dick*. Boston: Houghton Mifflin Company, 1950, Riverside A9. **(110)**

Kilbourne, W. G., Jr. "Montaigne and Captain Vere," *American Literature*, XXXIII (January, 1962), 514–517. **(175)**

Lawrence, D. H. *Studies in Classic American Literature*. New York: T. Seltzer, 1923. **(64)**

Leisy, Ernest E. "Fatalism in *Moby-Dick*," *Moby-Dick Centennial Essays*. Edited by Tyrus Hillway and Luther S. Mansfield. Dallas: Southern Methodist University Press, 1953. **(111)**

Levin, Harry. *The Power of Blackness: Hawthorne, Poe, Melville*. New York: Alfred A. Knopf, 1960. **(65)**

Lewis, R. W. B. "Melville: The Apotheosis of Adam," in *The American Adam: Innocence, Tragedy, and Tradition in the Nineteenth Century*. Chicago: The University of Chicago Press, 1955. **(66)**

Lewisohn, Ludwig. *Expression in America*. New York: Harper & Brothers, 1932. **(67)**

Lucid, Robert F. "The Influence of *Two Years Before the Mast* on Herman Melville," *American Literature*, XXXI (November, 1959), 243–256. **(68)**

McCutcheon, Roger P. "The Technique of Melville's *Israel Potter*," *South Atlantic Quarterly*, XXVII (April, 1928), 161–174. **(137)**

MacShane, Frank. "Conrad on Melville," *American Literature*, XXIX (January, 1958), 463–464. **(69)**

Magowan, Robin. "Masque and Symbol in Melville's *Benito Cereno*," *College English*, XXIII (February, 1962), 346–351. **(154)**

Marx, Leo. *The Machine in the Garden*, Technology and the Pastoral Ideal in America. New York: Oxford University Press, 1964. **(70)**

———. "Melville's Parable of the Walls," *Sewanee Review*, LXI (Autumn, 1953), 602–627. **(140)**

Matthiessen, F. O. *American Renaissance: Art and Expression in the Age of Emerson and Whitman*. New York: Oxford University Press, 1941, pp. 179–191, 317–516. **(71)**

Maxwell, Desmond E. S. "The Tragic Phase: Melville and Hawthorne," *American Fiction, The Intellectual Background*. New York: Columbia University Press, 1963, pp. 141–191. **(72)**

Melville Annual, 1965, A Symposium: *Bartleby, the Scrivener*. Edited by Howard P. Vincent. Kent, Ohio: Kent State University Press, 1966. **(141)**

Melville, Herman. *The Battle Pieces of Herman Melville*. Edited with Introduction and Notes by Hennig Cohen. New York: Thomas Yoseloff, 1963. **(166)**

Miller, James Jr. "*Billy Budd*: The Catastrophe of Innocence," *Modern Language Notes*, LXXIII (March, 1958), 168–176. **(176)**

———. "Melville's Search for Form," *Bucknell Review*, VIII (December, 1959), 260–276. **(73)**

Miller, Perry. *The Raven and the Whale: the War of the Words and Wits in the Era of Poe and Melville*. New York: Harcourt, Brace and Company, 1956. **(74)**

———. "Melville and Transcendentalism," *Moby-Dick Centennial Essays*. Edited with an Introduction by Tyrus Hillway and Luther S. Mansfield. Dallas: Southern Methodist University Press, 1953, 123–152. **(74)**

Modern Fiction Studies, Herman Melville Number, VIII (Autumn, 1962). **(75)**

Monson, S. E., ed. "Melville's 'Agatha' Letter to Hawthorne," *The New England Quarterly*, II (April, 1929), 296–307. **(76)**

Moorman, Charles. "Melville's *Pierre* and The Fortunate Fall," *American Literature*, XXV (March, 1953), 13–30. **(133)**

————. "Melville's Pierre in the City," *American Literature*, XXVII (January, 1956), 51–77. **(132)**

Murray, H. A. "In Nomine Diaboli, "*The New England Quarterly*, XXIV (December, 1951), 435–452. **(112)**

————. "Introduction," *Pierre, or the Ambiguities*, in *Complete Works of Herman Melville*. Howard P. Vincent, General Editor. Chicago and New York: Hendricks House, 1954. **(134)**

Newberry, I. "'*The Encantadas*': Melville's Inferno," *American Literature*, XXXVIII (March, 1966), 49–69. **(159)**

Noone, John B., Jr. "*Billy Budd:* Two Concepts of Nature," *American Literature*, XXXIX (November, 1957), 149–162. **(177)**

Olson, Charles. *Call Me Ishmael: A Study of Melville*. New York: Reynal & Hitchcock, 1947. **(113)**

Parke, John. "Seven Moby-Dicks," *The New England Quarterly*, XXVIII (September, 1955), 319–338. **(114)**

Parrington, Vernon L. *Main Currents in American Thought*. Volume Two. New York: Harcourt, Brace and Company, 258–267. **(77)**

Paul, Sherman. "Melville's 'The Town-Ho's Story,'" *American Literature*, XXI (May, 1949), 212–222. **(115)**

Pavese, Cesare. "The Literary Whaler," *Sewanee Review*, LXVIII (Summer, 1960), 407–418. **(116)**

Pearson, Norman Holmes. "Billy Budd: 'The King's Yarn,'" *American Quarterly*, III (Summer, 1951), 99–114. **(178)**

Percival, M. O. *A Reading of Moby Dick*. Chicago: University of Chicago Press, 1950. **(117)**

Phillips, Barry. "'The Good Captain': A Reading of *Benito Cereno*," *Texas Studies in Literature and Language*, IV (Summer, 1962), 188–197. **(155)**

Pochmann, Henry A. "Herman Melville," *German Culture in America*. Madison: The University of Wisconsin Press, 1957. **(78)**

Putzel, Max. "The Source and the Symbols of Melville's *Benito Cereno*," *American Literature*, XXXIV (May, 1962), 191–206. **(156)**

Rathbun, John W. "*Billy Budd* and the Limits of Perception," *Nineteenth-Century Fiction*, XX (June, 1965), 19–34. **(179)**

Reich, Charles A. "The Tragedies of Justice in *Billy Budd*," *The Yale Review*, LVI (March, 1967), 368–389. **(180)**

Rourke, Constance. *American Humor: A Study of the National Character*. New York: Harcourt, Brace and Company, Inc., 1931. **(79)**

Schiffman, Joseph. "Critical Problems in Melville's *Benito Cereno*," *Modern Language Quarterly*, XI (September, 1950), 317–324. **(157)**

Schweter, James. "*Redburn* and the Failure of Mythic Criticism," *American Literature*, XXXIX (November, 1967), 279–297. **(87)**

Sealts, Merton M. "Herman Melville's 'I and My Chimney,'" *American Literature*, XIII (May, 1941), 142–154. **(160)**

Sewall, Richard B. "Moby-Dick," in *The Vision of Tragedy*. New Haven: Yale University Press, 1959, pp. 92–105. **(118)**

Sherwood, John C. "Vere as Collingwood: A Key to *Billy Budd*," *American Literature*, XXXV (January, 1964), 476–484. **(181)**

Short, R. W. "Melville as Symbolist," *The University of Kansas Review*, XV (Autumn, 1948), 38–46. **(80)**

Slater, Judith. "The Domestic Adventurer in Melville's Tales," *American Literature*, XXXVII (November, 1965), 267–279. **(139)**

Slochower, Harry. "Moby-Dick: The Myth of Democratic Expectancy," *American Quarterly*, II (Fall, 1950), 259–269. **(119)**

Smith, Henry Nash. "The Image of Society in *Moby-Dick*," *Moby-Dick Centennial Essays*. Edited by Tyrus Hillway and Luther S. Mansfield. Dallas: Southern Methodist University Press, 1953, pp. 59–75. **(120)**

Stafford, William T., ed. *Melville's Billy Budd and the Critics*. San Francisco: Wadsworth Publishing Company, 1961. **(182)**

Stanonick, Janez. *Moby Dick, The Myth and the Symbol: A Study in Folklore and Literature*. Ljubljana: Ljubljana University Press, 1962. **(121)**

Stern, Milton R. Editor. *Discussions of Moby-Dick*. Boston, D. C. Heath and Company, 1960. **(122)**

Stewart, George R. "The Two Moby-Dicks," *American Literature*, XXV (January, 1954), 417–448. **(123)**

Stewart, Randall. *American Literature and Christian Doctrine*. Baton Rouge: Louisiana State University Press, 1958, pp. 89–102. **(81)**

—————. "Melville and Hawthorne," *South Atlantic Quarterly*, LI (July, 1952), 436–446. **(81)**

Stoll, E. E. "Symbolism in *Moby-Dick*," *Journal of the History of Ideas*, XII (June, 1951), 440–446. **(124)**

Thorp, Willard. "Herman Melville," *The Literary History of the United States*. Volume 1. New York: The Macmillan Company, 1948. 3 volumes, pp. 440–471. **(82)**

Tindall, William York. "The Ceremony of Innocence," in *Great Dilemmas in Literature, Past and Present*. New York: Harper & Row, 1956. **(183)**

Van Doren, Carl. *Cambridge History of American Literature*. Volume 1. New York: The Macmillan Co., 1917, 322–323. **(83)**

Vincent, Howard P. *The Trying-Out of Moby-Dick*. Boston: Houghton Mifflin, 1949. **(125)**

Walcutt, C. C. "The Fire Symbolism in *Moby Dick*," *Modern Language Notes*, LIX (May, 1944), 304–310. **(126)**

————. "The Soundings of *Moby Dick*," *Arizona Quarterly*, 24 (Summer, 1968), 101–117. **(126)**

Ward, J. A. "The Function of the Cetological Chapters in *Moby Dick*," *American Literature*, XXVIII (May, 1956), 164–183. **(127)**

Warren, Robert Penn. "Melville the Poet," *Selected Essays of Robert Penn Warren*. New York: Random House, Inc., 1958. **(168)**

Watson, E. L. Grant. "Melville's Testament of Acceptance," *The New England Quarterly*, VI (June, 1933), 319–327. **(184)**

Watters, R. E. "The Meanings of the White Whale," *University of Toronto Quarterly*, XX (January, 1951), 165–168. **(127)**

————. "Melville's 'Isolatoes,'" *PMLA*, LX (December, 1945), 1138–1148. **(127)**

West, Ray B. Jr. "The Unity of *Billy Budd*," *Hudson Review*, V (Spring, 1952), 120–127. **(185)**

Williams, Stanley. "'Follow Your Leader': Melville's 'Benito Cereno,'" *Virginia Quarterly Review*, XXII (Winter, 1947), 61–76. **(158)**

Winters, Yvor, "Herman Melville, and the Problems of Moral Navigation," *Maule's Curse, Seven Studies in the History of American Obscurantism*. Norfolk, Conn.: New Directions, 1938. **(84)**

Withim, Phil. "*Billy Budd:* Testament of Resistance," *Modern Language Quarterly*, XX (June, 1959), 115–127. **(186)**

Wright, Nathalia. "Moby Dick: Jonah's or Job's Whale?" *American Literature*, XXXVII (May, 1965), 190–195. **(129)**

————. "*Pierre:* Herman Melville's *Inferno*." *American Literature*, XXXII (May, 1960), 167–181. **(135)**

Young, James Dean. "The Nine Gams of the Pequod," *American Literature*, XXV (January, 1954), 449–463. **(130)**

Stephen
••• Crane
by Stanley Wertheim

CONTENTS ❧ ❧ ❧ *Stephen Crane*

I. Introduction

THE UNTIMELY DEATH of Stephen Crane at Badenweiler in Germany's Black Forest in the twenty-ninth year of his furiously creative life made comparison with the tragic fate of Thomas Chatterton or Edgar Allan Poe almost inevitable. But despite the romantic legends that haunted his short career and were solemnized in his obituaries, Crane was not, as Amy Lowell would have it, "A boy, spiritually killed by neglect."[1] Within the less than five-year period between the book publication of *The Red Badge of Courage* in the autumn of 1895 and the end, Crane enjoyed a high measure of fame as well as notoriety. Yet, his contemporary reputation depended almost exclusively upon the war novel, and he felt that his talent had ultimately been misjudged. *Maggie* fell stillborn from the press, and *The Black Riders*, although well received by a number of American reviewers, was frequently the object of derision. The works of fiction published subsequent to *The Red Badge* were invariably compared to it and judged repetitious or inferior. In his letters Crane lamented the obsession of the critics with "the damned 'Red Badge'" and "the accursed 'Red Badge'" and hoped desperately that readers might "discover now that the high dramatic key of The Red Badge cannot be sustained."[2] But it was all to no avail. The core of praise remained focused upon his one great success, and whatever else he wrote seemed anticlimatic.

The Red Badge of Courage shared in the immediate decline in Crane's reputation which followed his death in 1900. For fifteen years articles about him and his work all but disappeared from periodicals in England and in his own country. The literary histories of the period usually omitted Crane from their consideration of contemporary American authors, while a few referred to him as a man of genius who had failed to live up to his early promise. Hamlin Garland who had been the first literary man to recognize Crane's merit during his lifetime was appropriately the first to rediscover him. Characteristically, Garland's memoir in the *Yale Review* of April,

---

[1] *The Work of Stephen Crane*, ed. Wilson Follett (New York, 1925–1927), VI, xxix.
[2] *Stephen Crane: Letters*, ed. R. W. Stallman and Lillian Gilkes (New York, 1960), pp. 65, 87, 106.

1914 was filled with inaccuracies, but it reaffirmed the vitality of Crane's poetry and fiction and deplored the fact that his books remained neglected. In the fall of 1915 an impressionistic but intelligent essay by Edith Wyatt in the *New Republic* reminded the reading public of Crane's lesser-known works. Miss Wyatt did not mention *The Red Badge* at all but discussed *Maggie, George's Mother, The Monster,* and the two books of poetry and found in them all an unusual directness of expression, the product of an authentic firsthand vision.

Attention was also redirected to Crane's writings through the new popularity achieved by *The Red Badge of Courage* as a result of America's entry into World War I in 1917. Vincent Starrett's summary of Crane's achievement in an article in the *Sewanee Review* during the summer of 1920 was reprinted the next year as an introduction to his edition of Crane's short stories and sketches, *Men, Women and Boats.* Starrett's selection was not judicious. With such minor masterpieces as "An Experiment in Misery," "An Episode of War," "The Open Boat," and "The Upturned Face," he included a number of sketches from Crane's apprenticeship writing and later hackwork. Nevertheless, this popular Modern Literary collection prepared the way for Thomas Beer's biography, *Stephen Crane: A Study in American Letters* (1923). Beer confused and sentimentalized the facts of Crane's life, and the sources for much of his information are obscure or unverifiable. But his book once again stimulated an interest in Crane's work which resulted in the publication of Knopf's twelve-volume edition of *The Work of Stephen Crane* (1925–1927). Because of the relatively lax editorial standards of the time the texts in this edition are often unreliable, but they have unfortunately been widely reprinted. Each volume in the *Work* was prefaced with an essay by a person who had been acquainted with Crane or by a prominent critic or writer such as Joseph Hergesheimer, William Lyon Phelps, Amy Lowell, H. L. Mencken, and Sherwood Anderson.

All this activity helped to establish Crane's reputation as an important American writer, but little criticism and almost no relevant scholarship resulted from it. The young postwar rebels who admired Crane were more interested in the myth of the man than in his work. An image of Crane emerged as an iconoclast—an enemy of sentimentalism, provincialism, "puritanism," and the other qualities that the followers of Mencken attributed to American life. In a rather limited sense Crane came into his own, but his reputation was confined to the initiated. As Robert Littel commented in the spring of 1928, "a handful of critics have passed his immortality around among each other, but this has not resulted in his being read widely by intelligent people."[3] In England Crane had been almost completely ignored since 1900. Joseph Conrad wrote a sympathetic, if somewhat patronizing, introduction to Beer's biography, and in the London *Bookman* (December, 1924) Edwin Pugh boasted of his former personal intimacy with Crane. For the main body of English critics and readers, however, Crane's fall into obscurity was as meteoric

[3] "Notes on Stephen Crane," *New Republic,*" LIV (May 16, 1928), 391.

as his rise to fame. "If you would amuse yourself at the expense of booksellers, both small and great," wrote H. E. Bates, "inquire for the works of Stephen Crane."[4]

In America during the sociologically minded 1930's attention was turned away from Crane's war stories and refocused upon the Bowery tales. If *The Red Badge of Courage* received consideration, it was often grouped with *Maggie* and *George's Mother* as a pioneer work of American literary naturalism. But Crane was gaining recognition in academic circles, and as the decade of the Great Depression merged into the forties critics took note of the complex excellence of stories such as "The Open Boat," "The Blue Hotel," and "The Bride Comes to Yellow Sky." With the advent of World War II came a new demand for *The Red Badge*. It was reprinted in Heritage Press and Modern Library editions and made into a Pocket Book. An Armed Service Edition was distributed throughout the armed forces. "In 1945," reports John W. Stevenson, "Crane's novel had a larger circulation than it had ever had before in its fifty years of existence."[5] But analytical criticism still languished. For the most part, literary historians continued to assert that *The Red Badge* was a brilliant dissection of the psychology of heroism, the most realistic war novel ever written, and that Crane was a disciple of Tolstoy and Zola.

The second and assuredly more enduring revival of scholarly and critical interest in Crane's work began in 1950 with the almost simultaneous publication of John Berryman's Freudian biography and William M. Gibson's influential collection, *Stephen Crane: Selected Prose and Poetry*. The reappearance of the holograph manuscripts of *The Red Badge of Courage* and the printing of the most relevant textual variants from both the unfinished and final drafts in R. W. Stallman's *Stephen Crane: An Omnibus* (1952) made serious multilevel analysis of the novel possible. Stallman's highly controversial introductory essay, "Notes Toward an Analysis of *The Red Badge of Courage*," remains the starting point for modern explications, although his interpretation of the book as an allegory of spiritual redemption has more or less been discredited. Generally speaking, Berryman's biography, the Gibson and Stallman anthologies, and Daniel Hoffman's fine study. *The Poetry of Stephen Crane* (1957), defined the very best of Crane's fiction and poetry, and it is doubtful that many more of his works will be admitted to that category in the future.

Since mid-century, Stephen Crane's significance as a major American writer has been increasingly acknowledged. His writings are the subject of a large and diverse body of criticism, as is evident in the yearly checklist of Crane studies in *Thoth*, edited by Robert Hudspeth and subsequently by Robert S. Fraser and others at Syracuse University and the quarterly checklist in Joseph Katz's informative *Stephen Crane Newsletter* (University of South Carolina). Katz has also compiled

[4] "Stephen Crane: A Neglected Genius," *Bookman* (London), LXXXI (October, 1931), 10.

[5] "The Literary Reputation of Stephen Crane," *South Atlantic Quarterly*, LI (April, 1952), 300.

The Merrill Checklist of Stephen Crane (1969). Crane's letters have been collected, and the bulk of his journalism has been reprinted by R. W. Stallman and E. R. Hagemann and by Olov W. Fryckstedt.

Under the sponsorship of the Center for Editions of American Authors of the Modern Language Association, a standard edition of *The Works of Stephen Crane* edited by Professor Fredson Bowers is in progress at the University of Virginia. This new edition will include every known piece of Crane's creative writing and journalism except his letters and memoranda and will establish texts according to the standards of modern scholarship.

R. W. Stallman's *Stephen Crane: A Biography* (1968) approaches the definitive as closely as possible in the present state of our knowledge, despite an annoying number of minor factual errors, almost inevitable since much about Crane's life, particularly the early years, remains in the shadows. Stallman's forthcoming comprehensive bibliography (University of Iowa Press, 1971) will replace that of Ames W. Williams and Vincent Starrett (1948). It will, hopefully, define the Crane canon and list more than 800 secondary items.

The selective bibliography of Crane editions, biographies, and scholarship and criticism in English presented in the following pages describes and evaluates the most relevant items from the great body of material now available. Emphasis is placed upon books and articles published since the beginning of the second major revival of interest in Crane in 1950, although important items appearing before that date are also included. An attempt has been made to achieve a balanced perspective so that scholarship and commentary about all significant aspects of Crane's literary career and major works receive proper attention. It will be observed that despite increasing interest in Crane's shorter fiction, much recent criticism is still engaged in unearthing the sources and scrutinizing the themes and imagery of *The Red Badge of Courage*, and the tone of the essays about the war novel remains polemical. The reprinting of Crane's journalism and publication of manuscripts which has been undertaken within the past few years is doubtlessly valuable to the scholar, but in the final analysis Crane's reputation must rest upon the strength of *The Red Badge*, five or ten short stories, and a handful of poems.

II. Chronology

1871 Stephen Crane born November 1 in Newark, New Jersey, fourteenth and last child of Jonathan Townley Crane, pastor of the Central Methodist Church, and Mary Helen (Peck) Crane, daughter of a clergyman and niece of Methodist Bishop Jesse T. Peck. Stephen's Revolutionary War namesake had been delegate from New Jersey to the Continental Congress but had not signed the Declaration of Independence as Jonathan Crane believed.

1874–1880 Jonathan Crane minister of Methodist churches in Bloomington and then Paterson, New Jersey. Becomes pastor of Drew Methodist Church of Port Jervis, New York in March, 1878 and serves until his death in February, 1880.

1883 Family moves to Asbury Park, a resort town on the New Jersey coast. Stephen's brother, Townley operates a summer news reporting agency for the New York *Tribune*.

1885–1887 Stephen attends Pennington Seminary (New Jersey) where his father had been principal from 1849–1858.

1888 In January Crane enrolls in Claverack College and Hudson River Institute, a semi-military, co-educational high school and junior college in lower New York State. Publishes his first sketch in the school's literary magazine, *Vidette*. In summer months he assists Townley in gathering shore news at Asbury Park.

1890 Leaves Claverack after completing only two and a half years of the four-year course and enters Lafayette College (Easton, Pennsylvania) as a mining-engineering student. Joins Delta Upsilon fraternity. Is asked to leave the college after one semester because of academic deficiencies.

1891 Transfers to Syracuse University in January. Plays catcher and shortstop on the varsity baseball team. Becomes Syracuse correspondent for the New York *Tribune* and sketches out a first draft of *Maggie*. First short story, "The

King's Favor," appears in Syracuse University *Herald* in May. Also publishes a literary hoax, "Great Bugs at Onondaga," in *Tribune* on June 1. Meets Hamlin Garland at Avon by the Sea in August. Fails to return to college in the fall.

1892   Most of *Sullivan County Tales and Sketches* appear in the *Tribune*. Also a New York City sketch, "The Broken-Down Van" (July 10) which anticipates *Maggie*. *Tribune* columns are closed to Crane shortly after the appearance of his article satirizing the parade of the Junior Order of United American Mechanics at Asbury Park.

1893   *Maggie: A Girl of the Streets* privately printed in March under pseudonym of Johnston Smith. Crane is introduced to William Dean Howells by Garland. Begins composition of *The Red Badge of Courage*, probably in April. Lives in poverty in various New York City tenements.

1894   Crane takes his poems and a manuscript of *The Red Badge* to Garland in the spring. Social studies such as "An Experiment in Misery" published in the New York *Press*. A truncated version of *The Red Badge* appears in the Philadelphia *Press*, the New York *Press*, and an undetermined number of other newspapers in December.

1895   Crane journeys to the West and Mexico as a feature writer for the Bacheller-Johnson syndicate. Meets Willa Cather in Lincoln, Nebraska. *The Black Riders* appears in May. Publication of *The Red Badge of Courage* in Autumn projects Crane into fame both in England and the United States.

1896   *George's Mother*, an expurgated revision of *Maggie*, and *The Little Regiment* are published and *The Third Violet* is serialized by McClure's Syndicate. Crane defends Dora Clark, a reputed prostitute, from police persecution in New York and is harassed into leaving the city. Arrives in Jacksonville, Florida in November on his way to Cuba to report the insurrection for the New York *Journal*. Meets Cora Taylor at her "nightclub," the Hotel de Dream.

1897   The *Commodore*, carrying munitions to the Cuban rebels, sinks off the Florida coast on the morning of January 2. Crane and three others spend twenty-five to thirty hours on the sea in a ten-foot dinghy. Incident is the source for "Stephen Crane's Own Story" (New York *Press*, January 7) and "The Open Boat." Crane covers the Greco-Turkish War for the New York *Journal* and the Westminster *Gazette*. Cora, who accompanies him, sends back dispatches under the pseudonym "Imogene Carter." Crane publishes *The Third Violet*. They settle in England at Ravensbrook, Surrey as Mr. and Mrs. Stephen Crane. Crane meets Joseph Conrad, Henry James, Ford Madox

Ford. Writes some of his best short stories: "The Monster," "Death and the Child," "The Blue Hotel," and "The Bride Comes to Yellow Sky."

1898 Crane is rejected by the United States Navy for Spanish-American War service. Goes to Cuba as correspondent for the New York *World* and later for the New York *Journal*. Participates in combat at San Juan Hill and in other battles. *The Open Boat and Other Tales of Adventure* appears.

1899 Crane returns to England in January and rejoins Cora at Brede Place (Sussex), a decaying baronial mansion rented from Moreton Frewen. Publishes *War is Kind, Active Service, The Monster, and Other Stories.* Forced into hackwork to repay enormous debts incurred largely through Cora's extravagance. Suffers tubercular hemorrhage at Christmas party.

1900 *Whilomville Stories* and *Wounds in the Rain* published. Crane works on *The O'Ruddy.* Dies of tuberculosis on June 5 in a sanatorium at Badenweiler, Germany.

1901 *Great Battles of the World* appears, researched and probably written in part by Kate Frederic.

1902 *Last Words* published. Book contains a number of Crane's early pieces and eight new stories and sketches, some of which were completed by Cora.

1903 *The O'Ruddy* appears after delays caused by the reluctance of several other writers to finish the novel, which was finally completed by Robert Barr.

III.   Editions and Other Primary Materials

1. *The Work of Stephen Crane*, ed. Wilson Follett. 12 vols. New York: Alfred
   A. Knopf, Inc., 1925–1927; Reissued in 6 vols. New York: Russell & Russell,
   Inc., 1963.

Originally limited to 750 numbered sets, this edition was virtually inaccessible until
its reissue. Although not complete, the *Work* contains the bulk of Crane's creative
writing, but its textual unreliability and recent manuscript discoveries and attribu-
tions by R. W. Stallman, Daniel Hoffman, and Thomas A. Gullason make a new
collection essential. An authoritative edition of Crane's creative writing and journalism under the general editorship of Fredson Bowers is now being published by the
University of Virginia Press. Two volumes, *Maggie and George's Mother* and
Whilomville Stories, appeared in 1969 and two others, *Tales of Adventure* and *Tales
of War* in 1970.

In the *Work* Crane's writings are presented through the technique of contrast
rather than chronologically, and thus the stylistic and thematic development of the
author is completely obscured. Volume I contains *The Red Badge of Courage* and
"The Veteran," showing Henry Fleming as a youth and as an old man. In Volume II,
Tales of Two Wars, early stories from *The Little Regiment* are juxtaposed with later
Cuban war sketches, while Volume IX, entitled *Wounds in the Rain*, actually includes
non-Cuban stories such as the "Spitzbergen Tales." *Maggie*, Crane's first book,
appears in Volume X, along with *George's Mother* and "The Blue Hotel."

Few of the introductory essays have any genuine critical value, but they attest
to the high esteem in which Crane was held by a literary generation which had
rediscovered him. Joseph Hergesheimer was one of the first to define *The Red Badge
of Courage* as an initiation story. He expressed his appreciation of the humor to be
found in the novel but apparently did not understand its essential irony. William
Lyon Phelps contributed to the Byronic aspect of the Crane legend by calling
attention to "the chronic difficulties and obstacles with which he had to struggle.
He was as careful of his art as he was careless of his health; being one who saved his
life by losing it" (V, x). Amy Lowell had reservations about the intrinsic merit of
many of Crane's poems but considered him "A marvellous boy, potentially a genius,

historically an important link in the chain of American poetry" (VI, xxix). H. L. Mencken declared that "He was, within his limits, one of the noblest artists that we have produced" (X, xiii), and Sherwood Anderson characterized him as "an explosion" (XI, xi).

Wilson Follett's edition of *The Collected Poems of Stephen Crane* (1930) adds three posthumous poems to Miss Lowell's reprint of *The Black Riders* and *War is Kind* in Volume VI of the *Work*. Both Follett and Miss Lowell include "The Blue Battalions" as the last poem in *War is Kind*, but this poem was not printed in a book during Crane's lifetime. For the standard edition of Crane's poetry, see Entry 4.

2. *The Complete Short Stories and Sketches of Stephen Crane*, ed. with an Introduction by Thomas A. Gullason, Garden City, New York: Doubleday & Co., 1963.

Although not "complete" as its title indicates, this is at present the largest collection of Crane's shorter fiction. It offers two stories previously unpublished, "Dan Emmonds" and "The Camel," and twenty-one other reprinted in a book for the first time. Gullason has excluded what are obviously newspaper features, war dispatches, or historical sketches.

In the twelve-volume *Work* (Entry 1) Crane's stories are awkwardly arranged by the method of thematic contrast. Gullason uses a chronological approach, often hazardous, since it is difficult to date stories which were completed long before publication or which may have appeared initially in magazines not yet located. Another disadvantage of the chronological arrangement is that much of Crane's hackwork is interspersed with his best fiction. On the other hand, stylistic or thematic developments immediately become apparent. Crane was a painstaking artist who made constant alterations in stories as they appeared successively in newspapers, magazines, and collections, but one cannot always distinguish Crane's revisions from those of editors. In most instances, Gullason accepts the last version published in Crane's lifetime. This is confusing, since the dates and bracketed places of publication following each piece usually identify the first printing and not the text presented in this volume. The actual sources of these texts are not always clear, and spot checking discloses occasional inaccuracies.

Gullason's introduction is a highly informed account of Crane's career as a short story writer. The conventional assumptions that Crane was ignorant of history and current events, wrote hastily without revising, could not construct a plot, and was unable to create convincing characters are authoritatively refuted. Crane's first sketches were satiric and humorous burlesques, but his experiences in the New York slums were responsible for the grim realism of the Bowery novelettes, *Maggie* and *George's Mother*, and social studies like "An Experiment in Misery" and "Men in the Storm." With the newspaper serialization of *The Red Badge of Courage* in December, 1894, Crane turned to war fiction. *The Little Regiment* was experimental, but the stories written after he had experienced battle are more objective and psychologically sophisticated. Gullason cites "Death and the Child," "The Price of the Harness," "An Episode of War," and "The Upturned Face" as Crane's best war stories. The outstanding Western tales are "The Blue Hotel," "The Bride Comes to Yellow Sky," and "One Dash—Horses." Most critics consider the *Whilomville Stories* trivial, but Gullason feels that they are significant in revealing Crane's artistic control in his last years. Crane's greatest short stories—"The Open Boat," "The Blue Hotel," "The Monster," and "Death and the Child"—are "Greek" in their resemblance to classical drama, fusing poetic, symbolic, impressionistic, and tragic techniques. Gullason convincingly affirms Crane's qualitative importance as a writer of short fiction, but he says little about the many inferior stories and sketches also collected in this volume.

3. *The Complete Novels of Stephen Crane*, ed. with an Introduction by Thomas A. Gullason. Garden City, New York: Doubleday & Co., 1967.

With its companion volume of short stories and sketches (Entry 2), this edition of Crane's novels makes virtually all his fiction available to the general reader. Texts are based upon the first American editions, collated with manuscripts when they are extant. The 1896 *Maggie* is reprinted with important variants from the 1893 version given in an appendix. Other appendixes present uncancelled passages from *The Red Badge of Courage* manuscript, although Gullason disagrees with R. W. Stallman (Entry 43) that these are relevant and feels that they were deleted for sound artistic reasons; major variants from the manuscript and from the Heinemann edition of *Active Service;* and a chronology and selected bibliography centered upon Crane the novelist. The newspaper version of *The Red Badge* from the Philadelphia *Press* (December 3–8, 1894) is reprinted here for the first time.

Gullason's excellent introduction, the length of a short book, surveys Crane's antecedents, career, and reputation as a novelist. The classical and military legacy of Crane's forebears determined the family environment from which his rebellion was never complete and played a commanding role in shaping the themes of his novels. Crane's ambiguous attitude toward this heritage and toward the "mauve decade" in which he came into prominence became the emotional wellspring of his fiction. Tolstoy, Zola, Kipling, and even Homer may to some extent have influenced him, but Gullason rightly concludes that Crane learned most from the American literary background and from his mentors, Hamlin Garland and William Dean Howells.

Gullason's critiques of Crane's novels are judicious, but he undervalues *Maggie*, which he considers too slight to realize the potentialities of its theme, and prefers *George's Mother* because of its more restrained style and effective imagery. *The Red Badge of Courage* is Crane's one truly great novel, "a rich blend of romance, reality, naturalism, symbol, tragedy, epic, and myth" (p. 76). As in his earlier study of Crane's last three novels (Entry 29), Gullason views these works as a loose "trilogy" in which Crane makes attempts to write the traditional novel of manners, but he is now more restrained in his appreciation of *The Third Violet* and of *Active Service*, Crane's worst novel and the clearest proof of his inability to cope with the structural problems of an extended work. Unlike most recent critics who prefer to ignore it, Gullason finds *The O'Ruddy*, at least the approximately sixty percent of the novel written by Crane, "a rollicking good satiric romance written by a man who was in complete possession of his creative powers" (p. 94).

4. *The Poems of Stephen Crane: A Critical Edition*, ed. Joseph Katz. New York: Cooper Square Publishers, 1966.

With the exception of a few monotonously anthologized epigrams, Crane's poetry has been less accessible and perhaps in consequence less appreciated than his fiction. This authoritative edition supersedes Wilson Follett's *Collected Poems* (1930). It incorporates all poems printed in the two volumes which appeared in Crane's lifetime, *The Black Riders* and *War is Kind*, as well as those in periodicals to which he contributed and those which survive in verifiable holographs or typescripts. Poems, near poems, and fragments appearing in Crane's prose writings are rejected on the grounds that their composition was not governed by poetic considerations. Texts have been thoroughly collated to establish the author's final intention and variants are identified in exhaustive bibliographical notes for each poem.

The general introduction is a graceful essay about the publication background and the reception of Crane's poetry and also offers some discerning critical commentary. Katz recognizes a coherent structure in *The Black Riders*, an "envelope" in which a persona develops an identifiable point of view. The parables expose the absurdity of life, while the lyrics imply that nevertheless "life is worthwhile, brightened by a love that is no less significant for the despair at the sham in which it must exist and which must crush it" (p. xxx). In contrast, *War is Kind* is diffusive, bearing evidence of the commercial qualities of its publication, but a number of lyrics introduce a "choric counterpoint" that "contrasts with the diffusion of what would otherwise be the major voice to develop the dominant attitude, and the result—in the more successful poems—is a subtlety that distinguishes *War Is Kind* from the early volume" (p. xlviii).

5. *Stephen Crane: Uncollected Writings*, ed. with an Introduction by Olov W. Fryckstedt. Uppsala, Sweden: Acta Universitatis Upsaliensis, 1963.

Not all of Crane's uncollected writings are reproduced in this volume, and no previously unpublished manuscript material is presented. Fryckstedt gathers 123 sketches and articles which appeared in Crane's lifetime or within a year of his death. All but a small number of these had not since been reprinted. The articles are organized chronologically under seven subheadings, each marking a significant phase and geographical location in Crane's career as a writer and newspaper reporter: Syracuse and Asbury Park (1891-1892); New York City (1894-1895); The West and Mexico (1895); New York and Florida (1896–1897); Greece (1897); Cuba (1898); London

(1899–1900). Fryckstedt's scholarly and informative introduction is divided into seven corresponding sections which provide useful background information and discuss Crane's personal involvement in the social, political, and military events which were the subjects of his journalism.

The greater part of this material consists of ephemeral newspaper writing which is of interest primarily to the Crane specialist, particularly the biographer. Among Crane's most effective pieces of reporting are two articles not previously reprinted in a collection: "In the Depths of a Coal Mine," based on Crane's visit to the Scranton, Pennsylvania mining area for the S.S. McClure syndicate in the spring of 1894, and "Nebraskan's Bitter Fight for Life," an intense Philadelphia *Press* sketch (February, 1895) in which Crane described the valiant struggle of the Western farmers against the crop-destroying drought and winds of the previous summer. Other interesting pieces are Crane's evaluations of Harold Frederic's novels and "Ouida's Masterpiece," two of Crane's rare ventures into literary criticism; some of the more effective New York *Press* sketches of 1894 such as "An Experiment in Luxury," and "When Every One is Panic Stricken"; Crane's Mexican impressions, especially "Ancient Capital of Montezuma," studies of New York City's Tenderloin district, two of which were newly discovered by Fryckstedt; and a small number of war dispatches from Cuba, although most of these are quite prosaic. Fryckstedt's texts are extremely reliable, and this book will long remain the standard edition of Crane's journalism.

6. *Stephen Crane: Sullivan County Tales and Sketches*, ed. with an Introduction by R. W. Stallman, Ames, Iowa: Iowa State University Press, 1968.

This attractive volume, appropriately illustrated with some forceful rustic pen-and-ink drawings by "W.W.," incorporates the ten Sullivan County pieces brought together in Melvin Schoberlin's earlier edition (Syracuse University Press, 1949) and nine other sketches. "How the Donkey Lifted the Hills" is included as a companion fable to "The Mesmeric Mountain," although it is not a Sullivan County piece. Whether or not "The Snake" belongs in this category is conjectural. New to the Crane canon are "The Last of the Mohicans" (reproduced by R. W. Stallman in "Stephen Crane and Cooper's Uncas," *American Literature*, XXXIX [November, 1967], 392–396) and five other hunting sketches drawn from historical legends of the region and reproduced here from Sunday supplements of the New York *Tribune* during 1892. These were first reprinted by Thomas A. Gullason in *Southern Humanities Review*, II (Winter, 1968), 1–37. They are often engaging, but most interesting are the stories based upon Crane's camping trips with Louis E. Carr, Jr., Frederic Laurence, and Louis Senger in the hills between Port Jervis and Hartwood at various times in 1891 and 1892.

Each of these tales describes a situation in which a "little man" (the first of Crane's autobiographical protagonists despite Carr's identification of him with Senger) is isolated from his companions and placed in a position of danger to which he reacts with terror and impotent rage. In "Four Men in a Cave" he is pushed forward and forced to play poker with a crazed recluse who points a knife at his throat. "The Octopus" finds the campers fishing for pickerel. They are abandoned upon four stumps in the middle of a pond by their guide who refuses to return them to land but leaves them shivering in the night wind, "separated from humanity by impassible gulfs." Both "Killing His Bear" and "A Tent in Agony" depict the little man facing alone the charge of a wild bear who advances upon him with dripping jaws. In "An Explosion of Seven Babies" he is attacked by an enraged giantess who pursues him after he has intruded into her potato patch. The tales are intended to be humorous, but the constant threats of destruction, the howls of fear and wrath, the emphasis upon human isolation, and the hyperbolic rhetoric often turn what are basically ludicrous situations into terrifying experiences.

7. *The War Dispatches of Stephen Crane*, ed. R. W. Stallman and E. R. Hagemann. New York: New York University Press, 1964.

In the preface to this volume the editors list a number of Crane's war dispatches and other articles which they maintain have never previously appeared within a book. The intention to be first in the field was, however, frustrated by the prior publication of Olov W. Fryckstedt's edition of the *Uncollected Writings* (Entry 5) where most of the pieces listed are to be found. One of them, "Regulars Get No Glory," was included in a collection edited by William M. Gibson (Entry 25) as early as 1956.

Concise and informative introductions precede each of the three major sub-divisions of the book: The Greco-Turkish War; The Spanish–American War; The South African and the Boer Wars. Not all of Crane's nonfiction writings about war appear here. Some Cuban dispatches and late essays involving the Boer War are missing. The articles about Crane by fellow journalists, particularly Richard Harding Davis' account of Crane in Puerto Rico are biographically significant, as are dispatches by Imogene Carter (Cora Crane). Parodies of Crane as a war correspondent by Frank Norris and others provide comic relief for an otherwise grim subject. Frequently reprinted war stories such as "Death and the Child" and "The Price of the Harness" are included presumably in order to illustrate how Crane transformed the raw materials of journalism into works of art.

The quality of Crane's war dispatches is very uneven, and few have any appreciable literary value. Among the best are "Marines Signaling under Fire at Guantanamo" and "Regulars Get No Glory," which should be read as a significant background piece for Crane's finest Cuban story, "The Price of the Harness." In these two articles and in a small number of others there are traces of the vivid style and the sharp pen portraits of individuals in crisis characteristic of Crane's important war fiction. Only a passion for completeness (the bane of modern scholarship), however, could justify the reprinting of most of these dispatches, and this volume is neither complete nor authoritative. Much of the editorial paraphernalia is pointless and intrusive. The numerous manuscript variants given are often irrelevant. Place names and geographical areas are identified in maddening detail, and each passing allusion to a warship calls forth a statistical breakdown of its type, tonnage, length, speed, and principal armament.

8. *The New York City Sketches of Stephen Crane and Related Pieces*, ed. R. W. Stallman and E. R. Hagemann. New York: New York University Press, 1966.

Almost all the tales and sketches in Section One of this book (roughly two thirds of the volume) were previously collected by Thomas A. Gullason and Olov W. Fryckstedt (Entries 2 and 5). Among the new additions from manuscript sources are "The Landlady's Daughter," an uncompleted Bowery tale centered around a rooming house, and two short descriptions of the old Art Students' League building on East Twenty Third Street where Crane roomed during the winter of 1893–1894. Section Two includes a collection of newspaper articles (only one or two of which were written by Crane) about the notorious Crane–Dora Clark–Charles Becker affair in the autumn of 1896; a few manuscript fragments by Crane alluding to the incident, and "An Eloquence of Grief" with its first draft. Section Three presents a selection of Crane's Asbury Park sketches, and Section Four reprints "In the Depths of a Coal Mine" and "The Devil's Acre," respectively based on Crane's visits to Scranton, Pennsylvania and to the Death House of the New York State Penitentiary at Ossining.

Obviously, the "Related Pieces" of the last two sections are only distantly related, but this is the most complete collection of Crane's writings about New York, and the editors have made an effort to establish authoritative texts. The editorial apparatus is kept to a minimum, and the annotations are generally informative. The most interesting feature of this edition is the collection of newspaper articles about the Crane–Clark–Becker affair, many reprinted for the first time and hitherto virtually unobtainable. Crane's testimony in defense of Dora Clark at the Becker-Conway departmental hearing before Police Commissioner Grant, his replies to cross-examination, and the assault upon his character by defense witnesses provide an illuminating commentary upon his Bohemian life in New York. A particularly amusing parody by James L. Ford of the slanderous allegations made against Crane follows a series of editorials from New York City newspapers lauding Crane's courage and protesting the outrageous conduct of police authorities at the Becker-Conway trial. The story of Dora Clark's arrest and the subsequent court hearings in which Crane participated is recounted by Olov W. Fryckstedt, "Stephen Crane in the Tenderloin," *Studia Neophilologica*, XXXIV (1962), 135–163.

9. *Stephen Crane: Letters*, ed. R. W. Stallman and Lillian Gilkes. New York: New York University Press, 1960.

This collection might more accurately have been entitled "Stephen Crane: Correspondence," for of the 371 letters, notes, and inscriptions chronologically arranged from Jonathan Crane's announcement of Stephen's birth to Cora Crane's notice of his death, only about 225 were written by Crane himself. The remainder are by Cora, Hamlin Garland, William Dean Howells, Joseph Conrad, and others. Among the 184 previously unpublished items in this volume, there are 56 new Crane letters and inscriptions and 50 new items by Cora Crane, the latter consisting for the most part of frantic attempts to secure cash advances from Crane's English agent, James B. Pinker. After Crane's return from Cuba in January, 1899, he was hampered by failing health and so immersed in the hack writing which he found necessary to extricate himself from debt that he relinquished the greater part of his correspondence to Cora. In an appendix the editors include letters and essays about Crane written by his literary friends—notably Garland, Wells, Howells, and Conrad. These, together with the other correspondence in this volume, are invaluable biographical materials. Other Crane letters discovered in recent years have been published by Joseph Katz in *Stephen Crane Newsletter*.

As Stallman acknowledges, Crane's letters are undistinguished despite their biographical importance. The larger number of them are routine descriptions of everyday affairs and business communications; the financial bickering with literary agents soon becomes tedious. The letters reveal many of the paradoxes in Crane's personality which have puzzled biographers. They show him to have been simultaneously egocentric and generous, conscientious and irresponsible, rebellious and overly concerned about his reputation. The love letters to Nellie Crouse (first published in an edition by Edwin H. Cady and Lester G. Wells, Syracuse University Press, 1954) with their stilted literary manifestos and their alternating boasting and self-deprecation reveal the pathetic attempts of the young author to gain understanding and sympathy from a vain and superficial beauty. The most interesting of the letters are those dealing with Crane's relationships with Garland, Howells, Conrad, and Harold Frederic or describing highpoints in his life such as the publication of *The Red Badge of Courage*, the sinking of the *Commodore*, and the performance of "The Ghost at Brede Place" during his last Christmas party.

IV. Biographies and Critical Biographies

10. Beer, Thomas. *Stephen Crane: A Study in American Letters*. New York: Alfred A. Knopf, 1923.

As an experimenter in impressionistic prose, a novelist, and a cultural historian of Crane's era, Thomas Beer had a fortunate empathy with the mind and temperament of his subject. His image of Crane as a tragic genius, a latter-day Chatterton reviled or ignored by Philistine literary critics and stuffy academicians, has endured with only minor modifications into the present. Beer had access to Crane's contemporaries, and this pioneer biography is based upon interviews or correspondence with Joseph Conrad, Hamlin Garland, Corwin K. Linson, Edward Garnett, Paul R. Reynolds, Irving Bacheller, John Northern Hilliard, and many other important figures in Crane's literary career. Max Herzberg and Willis Clark contributed letters and biographical information, and a memoir by Joseph Conrad introduces the volume. Beer's tone is entirely appreciative, and there is virtually no criticism of Crane's work.

Beer succeeds admirably in demolishing the legends that Crane was an alcoholic, a drug addict, and a frequenter of prostitutes, but his desire to defend Crane against calumny prevents him from mentioning Cora Taylor's career as the madam of a Jacksonville house of assignation (and after Crane's death, a brothel) and the fact that she and Crane were never legally married. A sympathetic but largely unverifiable portrait of the artist emerges from this biography. The book is undocumented, and a large number of highly significant letters quoted by Beer have not yet come to light. The sources of his information for incidents in Crane's life or for opinions expressed by the young writer about persons, events, or books are often obscure or unreliable. Dates and the sequence of events are not clearly established, and there are many lacunae. Although scholars have long been aware of Beer's deficiencies, his anecdotes are usually granted a degree of authority, particularly when they serve to illustrate a thesis for which other external evidence is scarce.

11. Berryman, John. *Stephen Crane* (American Men of Letters Series). New York: William Sloane Associates, 1950. Reprinted with an additional Preface. Cleveland, Ohio: Meridian Books, 1962.

Indisputable facts about Stephen Crane's life have proved difficult to ascertain. The young author died at the age of twenty eight, but there are obscurities surrounding his brief career which Thomas Beer's impressionistic biography (Entry 10) did little to dispel, despite its forthright attack upon the scandals which formed the Crane legend. Berryman had the advantage of an accretion of almost twenty years of scholarship in the academic journals, and he mentions three extensive and important sources which he is not permitted to cite: They are Crane's love letters to Nellie Crouse; Corwin Linson's memoir (Entry 13); and Cora Crane's voluminous collection of papers at Columbia University. Berryman made excellent use of the information available to him, and this book is as comprehensive and accurate as possible under the circumstances. Some aspects of Crane's life remain inaccessible to the biographer. Little is actually known about his childhood and adolescence or his experiences as a free-lance reporter in New York City from the autumn of 1891 until the winter of 1894–1895. "I cannot help vanishing and disappearing and dissolving," Crane wrote to Ripley Hitchcock early in 1896. "It is my foremost trait."

The critical analyses of Crane's writings in this biography and the summary of his achievement in the penultimate chapter are sensitive and thoughtful. Berryman's good taste is reflected in the stories and poems he singles out for particular praise. Less fortunate are the psychoanalytic speculations which interlace the volume and are fully developed in the final chapter, "The Color of This Soul." Berryman traces sexual imagery and situations in Crane's work and incidents in his life which seem to show recurrent patterns and identifies them with the neurotic fixation on mother surrogates described in Freud's essay "A Special Type of Choice of Object Made by Men" (*Complete Psychological Works*, XI, 165–175). But there is very little evidence to show that Crane had a compulsive desire to rescue older, sexually discredited women or that because of a curious Oedipal obsession these were the only women whom he could love. Nellie Crouse and Lily Brandon Munroe do not fit into this category. Crane did show kindness to prostitutes, and his rescue of Dora Clark from police brutality made him notorious. While he may have had liaisons with questionable women such as Doris Watts and Amy Leslie, he was not necessarily in love with them. Cora, of course, was the exception, but Crane's love for her was based upon highly individual factors and not part of a recognizable pattern.

12. Gilkes, Lillian. *Cora Crane: A Biography of Mrs. Stephen Crane*. Bloomington, Indiana: Indiana University Press, 1960.

Cora Howorth Murphy Stewart (alias Taylor) was 32 years old, the veteran of two unsuccessful marriages, and the madam of what Miss Gilkes euphemistically terms "a pleasure resort" when she and Crane met at her business establishment, the Hotel de Dream, in Jacksonville in November, 1896. The *Commodore* disaster caused Crane to abandon his plans to report the Cuban insurrection, and he went to Greece as a war correspondent for the New York *Journal* and the *Westminster Gazette*. Cora joined him in London and accompanied him to the battleground where she became the first woman war correspondent, sending dispatches to the *Journal* under the byline "Imogene Carter." In June, 1897 the couple settled in England at Ravensbrook Villa, Surrey as Mr. and Mrs. Stephen Crane, but since Cora had not as yet secured a divorce from Captain Donald Stewart it is unlikely that any marriage ceremony had been performed. Cora was improvident and luxury loving, and the couple entertained lavishly at Ravensbrook, soon exhausting their small and sporadic income. While Crane was in Cuba reporting the Spanish–American War, Cora leased Brede Place, an ancient ruined manor in Sussex near Hastings. Although the rental was low, the Crane's lived here in baronial style, sinking ever further into inextricable debt until Stephen's death in June, 1900. Afterwards, Cora returned to Jacksonville where she opened a new bordello, differing from the Hotel de Dream primarily in that the girls lived on the premises, and embarked on another series of bizarre adventures.

Making scholarly use of Cora's notebooks, diaries, letters, and other manuscripts in the Columbia University Crane Collection, Miss Gilkes has written a scrupulously researched and lively biography of the fascinating woman who called herself Mrs. Stephen Crane. The book provides some new, although incidental, facts about Crane's personal and literary relationships in England. Even more entertaining is the vivid recreation of people and places "along the line" in Jacksonville during the twilight years of the Gilded Age. A pardonable bias toward her subject causes Miss Gilkes to understate the detrimental effects of Cora's prodigality upon Crane's later career. Cora apparently had no idea that his creative energies could be exhausted. "The beautiful thoughts in Stephen's mind are simply endless!" she wrote to Edward Garnett (*Letters*, Entry 9, p. 203), but to James B. Pinker, Crane's English agent, she sent desperate appeals for money, at times in payment for stories and sketches which were merely projected. Perhaps Crane was also extravagant, but it is difficult to avoid the impression that Cora's predilection for expensive households and her disorderly finances made it necessary for him to produce a great deal of inferior hackwork such as the posthumous *Great Battles of the World*. This material could readily be sold and paid twice as much as the best stories of his last years—"The Bride Comes to Yellow Sky," "The Open Boat," "The Blue Hotel," and "The Monster." For the economic basis of Crane's financial difficulties in England, see James B. Stronks, "Stephen Crane's English Years: The Legend Corrected," *Papers of the Bibliographical Society of America*, LVII (1963), 340–349.

13. Linson, Corwin K. *My Stephen Crane*, ed. Edwin H. Cady. Syracuse, New York: Syracuse University Press, 1958.

This memoir is based upon a typescript entitled "Stephen Crane: A Personal Record," which was acquired in 1953 by the Syracuse University Library as part of the collection of Crane letters, manuscripts, and photographs in the possession of the American painter Corwin Knapp Linson. Crane and Linson were introduced to one another in the winter of 1892–1893 by Linson's cousin, Louis Senger of Port Jervis, one of the men with whom Crane shared the camping experiences depicted in his Sullivan County sketches. Their personal relationship lasted until March, 1897, when Crane went to Greece as a war correspondent, but their closest associations were in the crucial years during which Crane wrote *The Black Riders* and *The Red Badge of Courage* and revised the first edition of *Maggie*. In the spring of 1894 Linson accompanied Crane on a trip to Scranton, Pennsylvania as the illustrator of an article on conditions in the coal mines which Crane wrote for S. S. McClure's new magazine. Linson's disjointed, impressionistic account of these years sheds little light upon the obscurity which surrounds Crane's early literary career, but there are intimate recollections of the impoverished Bohemian life he shared with magazine illustrators and medical students in Manhattan tenements and with the "Indians" of the old Art Students' League building whose hand-to-mouth existence he would depict in *The Third Violet*.

Linson's manuscript was written and revised over a period of many years. A sketchy outline appeared under the title "Little Stories of 'Steve' Crane," *Saturday Evening Post*, CLXXV (April 11, 1903), 19–20, but the major revisions occurred after the publication of Thomas Beer's biography in 1923 brought the name of Stephen Crane back into prominence. Linson's narrative structure was chaotic, and Cady was obliged to recognize the material into a coherent chronological order, to resolve major discrepancies, and to excise irrelevant material. Despite this careful editing, Linson's account still suffers from episodic structure, lacunae, and digressions. He is consistently wrong about Crane's age, and the chronology which he provides for the composition of Crane's books is very doubtful. There are some valuable observations about the origins of Crane's impressionistic style and the inspiration for *The Red Badge of Courage*. Linson denies that Crane's concern with color was the result of his association with painters and believes that his color sense was not contrived but integral to his vision. (This may be true, but we should also keep in mind that Crane's self-conscious use of color in his early books was part of a literary program.) It was in old copies of the *Century Magazine* found in Linson's studio that Crane first read the series of articles entitled "Battles and Leaders of the Civil War." Later he borrowed the separately published volumes containing these articles from Mrs. Olive B. Armstrong and derived from them the details of the Battle of Chancellorsville which form the realistic background of *The Red Badge of Courage*.

14. Solomon, Eric. *Stephen Crane in England: A Portrait of the Artist*. Columbus, Ohio: Ohio State University Press, 1964.

Unlike Henry James or the expatriates of the Lost Generation, Stephen Crane was an involuntary exile during the final three years of his life. Difficulties with the New

York City police and his illicit alliance with Cora made further residence in America impractical. Crane was attracted to England not only because of the adulation with which *The Red Badge of Courage* was received by London reviewers but because of the sophisticated circle of authors who had settled in Surrey within easy reach of the homes he successively occupied at Ravensbrook in Oxted and then at Brede Place. Solomon examines Crane's literary relationships with this group of writers, particularly H. G. Wells, Ford Madox Ford, Henry James, and Joseph Conrad.

Wells, like Edward Garnett, admired Crane's artistry and considered him a great master of English prose, although he deplored his apparent ignorance of scientific, social, and political matters. Ford, whose literary antecedents were Flaubert and Turgenev, also praised the economy and design in Crane's work which allied him with James and Conrad in opposition to the inclusive, rambling tradition of the English novel. Crane's association with James was based upon a mutual interest in the Civil War and the fact that Crane was becoming increasingly concerned with fiction as an art. Conrad was piqued by suggestions that he imitated Crane's technique but recognized the similarities in their approaches to questions of structure, point of view, and subject matter. Crane believed Conrad to be the finest writer of his generation, and Conrad's admiration for Crane was expressed in letters, essays, and memoirs.

This book offers a concise yet detailed discussion of Crane's literary relationships with the masters of English prose who were his friends in England. Little new information is given, since Solomon's sources, primarily letters and personal recollections by Garnett, Ford, Wells, Joseph and Jessie Conrad, and others, are well known to Crane scholars. Perhaps because Crane's relationships with them were more personal than literary, scant attention is paid to his close association with other expatriate writers such as Harold Frederic and Robert Barr who completed the posthumous *The O'Ruddy*. Solomon maintains that Crane shifted his allegiance from William Dean Howells and Hamlin Garland to the English writers, because he became more interested in the aesthetics rather than the ideology of literature, and it is true that the best of his later fiction is more carefully structured than his earlier. But Crane was always more concerned with technique than with ideas, and most of his literary principles were established before he decided to settle in England. A good number of Crane's opinions about English and Continental writers quoted by Solomon are derived from Thomas Beer's undocumented biography, and some of them may well be apocryphal.

15. Stallman, R. W. *Stephen Crane: A Biography*. New York: George Braziller Inc., 1968.

Virtually all the known facts about Stephen Crane are brought together in this book, which will probably remain the definitive biography for many years to come. Whenever possible, Stallman allows Crane to tell his own story through relevant material in his fiction and poetry and, more frequently, through his journalism.

This method conveys a sense of immediacy, but extended summaries of the minor creative writing and travel and war correspondence often clog the narrative and inordinately swell the bulk of the volume. Crane's self-portrait is counterpointed by the perspectives of literary friends and acquaintances: Hamlin Garland, William Dean Howells, Richard Harding Davis, Joseph Conrad, Ford Madox Ford, Henry James, and many others. Their testimony, at times contradictory, is tested and reconciled in the alembic of Stallman's comprehensive knowledge, acquired in the course of over twenty years as the dean of Stephen Crane studies. What is missing from the book is an emotionally satisfying portrait of Stephen Crane, the man as artist. The externals of his life have been assembled and exhaustively scrutinized, but the personality that created the literary works for which we admire him continues to elude us.

The scholarly quality of this monumental biography is generally high, although there are an unfortunate number of minor errors. Sporadic documentation and the absence of an adequate bibliography sometimes preclude recognition of the work of previous scholars and critics. Analyses and evaluations of Crane's most important works of fiction (there is relatively little criticism of the poetry) are concise and perceptive. Stallman has modified but not abandoned his controversial interpretation of *The Red Badge of Courage* as a Grail quest in which Jim Conklin assumes the role of sacrificial God (cf. Entry 80), and he now concedes that the religious imagery of the novel does not follow a consistent allegorical pattern. *The Red Badge* is a study in human conceit which begins with motifs of change and growth but ends in self-deception. The final image of the golden sun gleaming through leaden rain clouds recapitulates the despair-hope contrast of the first chapter. This circular design with its ironic implications, Stallman emphasizes, is paralleled in "The Open Boat," which ends as it begins with the contrast of hope and despair. In "The Blue Hotel" the device of contradictory endings is less effective, since they negate one another and thus ruin the artistic unity of the story. One may accept Stallman's judgment that "Death and the Child" is vitiated by its sentimentality, but "The Monster" is undervalued when it is viewed primarily as "an appeal for brotherhood between white and black" (p. 334). The novelette deserves to be grouped among Crane's masterpieces. It is a trenchant social satire as well as a study in a peculiarly American type of self-fulfillment and simultaneous alienation, an ironic revelation of small-town narrowness and hypocrisy which reflects the "revolt from the village" tradition of Harold Frederic's *The Damnation of Theron Ware* and anticipates Sinclair Lewis' *Main Street*.

V. Criticism

Books:

16. Cady, Edwin H. *Stephen Crane.* New York: Twayne Publishers, 1962.

Since Crane's ideas and artistic practices have been variously categorized as realistic, naturalistic, symbolistic, impressionistic, and even romantic by small but militant groups of scholars, Cady feels it essential to present a pluralistic view of the man and his work. The first three chapters of this book survey Crane's life, literary career, and controlling ideas in terms of Cady's previous study of *The Gentleman in America* (1949) and his edition of *Stephen Crane's Love Letters to Nellie Crouse* (1954). John Berryman's portrait of Crane as a sensitive, compulsive personality driven by neurotic fixations is decisively rejected. Instead, Crane is seen as a defaithed Christian gentleman, the renegade scion of an aristocratic and evangelical New Jersey family. In an attempt to adopt transmuted Christian ideals to American conditions he replaced the God of his fathers with a neoromantic dedication to athletics and the conquest of the natural environment. As an artist he was an "apprentice sorcerer" who experimented with a number of literary theories but did not live long enough to settle upon any one of them. The last three chapters discuss Crane's writings against the background of the prevailing literary movements of his time. Cady condemns mythological and symbolistic readings of Crane's work which ignore both evidence and common sense. His own view is more balanced and takes into account the importance of the social and intellectual milieu in which Crane's art was created. There are perceptive studies of the early fiction and *The Red Badge of Courage*. The poetry and later work are discussed more briefly but with equal acumen. The annotated bibliography at the end of the volume is also valuable.

One does not wish to cavil with so excellent a book, but Cady's insistence upon "the intrinsically aristocratic *and* Christian qualities of Crane's vision" (p. 78) is almost as restricted an interpretation of Crane's point of view as Berryman's and seems to lack adequate foundation. It is based to some extent upon the inflated idealism of the Nellie Crouse letters in which Crane vainly attempted to convince a vapid and thoroughly conventional young beauty with whom he was desperately in love of his respectability and ambition. Cady stresses Crane's compassion, a quality which he did not identify with Christianity, as witness the harsh indictment of Christian hypocrisy and lack of human sympathy in *Maggie*, *The Black Riders*, and *George's Mother*. At the same time, Cady understates Crane's naturalism. While it is true that the central characters in *Maggie* do make choices, these choices are conditioned by their physical and social environment. It is also true that Crane cut most of the explicit naturalistic formulas which appear in the manuscript of *The Red Badge* out of the published novel, but this does not necessarily mean that he repudiated the naturalistic point of view as Cady believes. The excisions indicate rather that Crane removed bombastic abstract statements of naturalistic concepts which were already explicit in the action of the novel. Another excellent short survey of Crane's literary career is Jean Cazemajou's monograph, *Stephen Crane*. University of Minnesota Pamphlets on American Writers, No. 76 (1969).

17. Gibson, Donald B. *The Fiction of Stephen Crane*. Carbondale, Illinois: Southern Illinois University Press, 1968.

If John Berryman's biographical identifications of incest motifs and mother surrogates (Entry 11) are excepted, Gibson's is the first book-length study of Crane's fiction that utilizes insights derived from depth psychology in explicating the central concern of his novels and short stories, the adaptations of the individual to his natural and social environment. Gibson examines the growth of ego-awareness in Crane's protagonists, applying, often rather superficially, the basic formulations of Erich Neuman's Jungian study, *The Origins and History of Consciousness* (Bollingen Series, XLII. New York: Pantheon Books, 1954).

Gibson's concentration upon the psychological implications of the struggle between man and his environment in Crane's work sometimes results in tendentious and misleading readings, and he betrays an insensitivity to Crane's dramatic irony, especially in *Maggie* and *The Red Badge of Courage*. His analysis of "The Blue Hotel," based upon an earlier essay (Entry 91) helps to reconcile the logical discrepancies between the Swede's apparently psychotic death wish and the Easterner's final statement of moral complicity. "The Monster," also a story about human responsibility, is inappropriately grouped by Gibson with Crane's minor novels, since it is, properly speaking, neither minor nor a novel. While Gibson realizes that *The Third Violet* and *Active Service* are little more than commercial potboilers, he inexplicably praises the humor of the posthumous *The O'Ruddy*, and he mistakenly believes that Crane was the author of only one fourth of the book. But a number of analyses of the prose style of this tedious picaresque satire agree that Crane wrote almost two thirds of the novel (cf. Entry 3, pp. 93–94). Gibson's casualness in this matter is unfortunately indicative of the general level of his scholarship, and factual information in this book should be used with extreme caution.

The most crucial problem in Crane's fiction is the attainment of identity by his protagonists, and Gibson equates this with the development of ego-awareness and the simultaneous undermining of the domination of the unconscious. This theme is most clearly evident in those works Gibson considers Crane's best: *The Red Badge of Courage*, "The Open Boat," "The Bride Comes to Yellow Sky," and "The Blue Hotel." One would not quarrel with this estimate but might be inclined to widen its scope. At times, Gibson's concern with the development of consciousness in Crane's protagonists causes him to undervalue those works in which this theme is subordinated to others, and this includes not only Crane's best East Side and Bowery tales but also "Death and the Child," "The Five White Mice," and some of the Spanish–American War stories of *Wounds in the Rain*.

18. Solomon, Eric. *Stephen Crane: From Parody to Realism*. Cambridge, Mass.: Harvard University Press, 1966.

Parody was an important form of American humor in the nineteenth century, and Solomon contends that Crane adapted the conventions of the subliterature of his time to create parodic equivalents of popular fiction. Thus, *Maggie* and *George's Mother* reverse sentimental attitudes toward the poor found in dime novels by burlesquing the familiar characters and themes of such stories. *The Red Badge of Courage* is more complex, but here also Crane uses parody in satirizing the qualities of the war hero. Solomon finds little parody in *Wounds in the Rain* and the "Spitzbergen Tales," and he admits that *The Third Violet* and *Active Service* apparently accept rather than deny the clichés of romantic fiction. "The Open Boat" is not essentially a parody either. While the *Whilomville Stories* mock the stereotypes of idyllic childhood, "The Monster" exposes the hypocrisies beneath the nostalgic view of the small town. Crane's stories of the West caricature the legends of the cowboy and the gunfighter but still manage to recreate them.

This is the first book-length study devoted entirely to Crane's fiction, and it is eminently readable. There are some discerning analyses of Crane's novels and short stories and many provocative comments. But occasionally Solomon's thesis wears very thin. We may accept the conclusion that "Crane's major fiction often commences in parody and concludes in creativity." At least at times, "In his best work parody and realism become one" (p. 282). Yet, Crane surely does not consistently imitate the norms of popular literature, and there is little evidence that he was ever aware of doing so. His characteristic technique rather is to deflate romantic misconceptions about environments like the slums, war, the sea, small towns, and the West through ironic reversal of accepted attitudes and characterizations; this is not parody, strictly speaking. There is also some overstatement in Solomon's insistence upon the development of the idea of social complicity in Crane's fiction, particularly in "The Open Boat," *The Red Badge of Courage*, and "The Blue Hotel." The protagonists of these stories never really abandon their egocentricity, and it is the very self-deception which causes them to feel that they have achieved viable relationships with their fellows that constitutes the essence of Crane's irony. Solomon utilizes poems from *The Black Riders* and *War is Kind* as epigrams for some of his chapters, but unfortunately he makes virtually no attempt to integrate the poetry with his discussion of the fiction.

General Essays:

19. Chase, Richard, ed. *Stephen Crane: The Red Badge of Courage and Other Writings*, Boston: Houghton Mifflin Company, 1960. The Introduction appears also in the Riverside Edition of *The Red Badge of Courage* (1960).

In addition to *The Red Badge of Courage*, this edition includes the best of Crane's shorter fiction—*Maggie, George's Mother*, "The Veteran," "A Mystery of Heroism," "An Episode of War," "The Blue Hotel," "The Bride Comes to Yellow Sky," "The Open Boat" (with Crane's newspaper version of the sinking of the *Commodore*), "The Monster"—and a small selection of Crane's poems. The texts have been collated with first and other early editions to correct numerous errors which have crept into these frequently reprinted works. Since Chase prefers to present the writer's final product rather than his workshop, words, phrases, and passages which Crane cancelled in the final holograph manuscript of *The Red Badge* or excluded from the first American edition have not been restored. In his introduction Chase characterizes Crane as one of the first truly modern American writers, a precursor of the novelists and poets of the twentieth century. At the same time, his books reflect the literary spirit of the 1890's and serve as a link between the writers of the Gilded Age and those of later generations. Carrying on a distinction established in his *The American Novel and Its Traditions* (1957), Chase describes Crane as a "romancer" rather than a novelist, but he disagrees with those who attempt to relate Crane to classic American writers by reading symbolic patterns and constructs into his work. Above all, Chase sees Crane as an ironist who interprets the human situation in terms of the contrast between man's idealization of himself as a rational creature in control of his destiny and man's actual situation, circumscribed by cosmic and social forces and by his own instincts and illusions.

Few essays maintain as balanced a critical perspective toward Crane's work as the introduction to this collection. Chase groups Crane among the naturalists but points out that his naturalism involves less detailed social observation and is more poetic and abstract than that of Norris or Dreiser. Crane was not a consistent mythmaker or symbolist, and Chase is probably correct in concluding that *The Red Badge of Courage* is episodic in construction, achieving whatever unity it possesses through the repetition of key moods or images rather than the clear development of plot, theme, or character. In his shorter fiction, however, Crane often demonstrated strict control over structural and thematic elements.

One may also agree with Chase that the material which Crane deleted from *The Red Badge* is generally inferior, particularly Henry Fleming's extended philosophical speculations which are inappropriate to the thought of an ignorant farm boy and would have destroyed sympathy for him as a character. On the other hand, many of the passages restored in brackets and footnotes by other editors help to clarify Crane's artistic methods and explain the development of the novel. They are extremely important to the scholar if not to the general reader.

20. Colvert, James B. "Structure and Theme in Stephen Crane's Fiction," *Modern Fiction Studies*, V (Autumn, 1959), 199–208.

Colvert explains that in Crane's best fiction structure is usually defined by the juxtaposition of two ironically divergent points of view: the deluded and circum-scribed vision of the main characters and the more expansive, realistic perspective of the narrator. Typically, the Crane protagonist is trapped within the confines of his prejudices and false pride, but to the omniscient narrator his incompetence and futility are evident. From this structural tension arises Crane's most familiar theme, the collapse of human vanity under the stress of experience. Crane concen-trated upon the absurd world of his characters' illusions, and irony became his favorite mode of expression. His antiheroes, like the "little man" of the Sullivan County sketches or the characters of *Maggie*, never transcend their egotistical self images. Only those few individuals, such as the correspondent of "The Open Boat," who can learn to adjust their inner worlds to external reality survive to interpret their experiences.

The double perspective which focuses attention upon the distance between the narrator and his subject is an important structural pattern in Crane's fiction. Colvert's lucid essay demonstrates the significance of this dual outlook as a thematic device as well. The development of the typical Crane story is not continuous but consists of an accretion of situations in which the pathetic, false world of illusions created by the characters is demolished by the real world which baffles and frustrates them. The theme of the futility of human pretensions is implicit in this structure. Colvert's essay is basic to an understanding of Crane's fictional methods.

21. Dickason, David H. "Stephen Crane and the *Philistine*," *American Literature*, XV (November, 1943), 279–287.

The first issue of Elbert Hubbard's whimsical periodical, the *Philistine*, appeared in June, 1895 with an endorsement of Crane's recently published book of poems, *The Black Riders*, and a reprinting of "I saw a man pursuing the horizon." More than a dozen of Crane's poems and seven of his short stories and sketches appeared in subsequent issues of the *Philistine*, most of them for the first time. Prominent among the poems are "The chatter of a death demon from a tree top," "The Blue Battalions," and "I stood upon a high place." The prose pieces include the "Tommie" stories, "A Great Mistake," and "An Ominous Baby," and the Bowery sketch, "The Men in the Storm," which had previously been published in the *Arena*. In December, 1895, shortly after the publication of *The Red Badge of Courage*, the

Society of the Philistines honored Crane with a dinner at their headquarters in East Aurora, New York. Dickason neglects to mention the fact that this banquet degenerated into a drunken farce during which Crane was ridiculed. The May, 1896 issue of the *Roycroft Quarterly* was a momento to the Philistine dinner with the title "A Souvenir and a Medley: Seven Poems and a Sketch by Stephen Crane." It was a reprint with additions of a booklet which had been presented to the dinner guests.

Dickason's essay is a competent summary of Crane's five-year literary relationship with the author of "A Message to Garcia." Elbert Hubbard publicized Crane's poems at a time when they met with derision in many respectable quarters. He kept Crane in the public eye with frequent reviews, anecdotes, and banter, although it is possible that Crane's association with the pretentious "Fra Elbertus" and the hyper-aesthetic Roycrofters did as much harm as good to his reputation. Dickason seems to believe that Hubbard's motives were largely altruistic, but the editor of the *Philistine* was himself seeking publicity for the new periodical through which he hoped to achieve literary fame. This is indicated by Hubbard's exploitation of the Philistine Society dinner for which he printed three souvenir pamphlets. Hubbard liked to think of himself as an iconoclast and a champion of the contemporary in literature, but he was occasionally uneasy about Crane's unconventional prose and poetry. In time the *Philistine* acquired a reputation for harsh satire, and even though Hubbard never actually abused Crane in print, his attitude toward the young writer's work was often equivocal and even derisive.

22. Ellison, Ralph. Introduction to *The Red Badge of Courage and Four Great Stories by Stephen Crane*. New York: Dell Publishing Co., 1960. Reprinted in *Shadow and Act*. New York: Random House, 1964, pp. 60–76.

A number of recent critics have attributed Crane's obsessive interest in the moral questions of cowardice and heroism, inner emotion and external behavior, and the relationship of the individual to himself and to the universe to the tensions of his fundamentalist Methodist background. Ellison recognizes the personal basis of Crane's spiritual probings but relates them also to the social problems of the age in which Crane lived and wrote. While the setting of *The Red Badge of Courage* is in the Civil War, its issues involve the civilization of Reconstruction America. The impressionistic style and episodic development of the novel convey the discontinuity and isolation of an individual who attempts first to secede from an unacceptable society and then to live within it while retaining some degree of integrity. *The Red Badge*, Ellison believes, deals with the invasion of the private life and the failure of post-bellum society to live up to the ideals for which it fought. "The Open Boat" also explores the capacity of the individual for physical and moral courage. The theme of this story is that true humanity is attained only through immersion in the dangerous seas of experience. "The Bride Comes to Yellow Sky" stresses the need for awareness of the realities of regional evolution. Inability to understand the rapidity of American social change kills the Swede of "The Blue Hotel," although, as in "The Monster," the failure of communal charity is also partly responsible.

Much of Crane's work is concerned with the interaction of the individual and society, but Ellison cites little evidence either from *The Red Badge of Courage* or the short stories to demonstrate the specific involvement of these works with the social issues of the 1890's. His examination of the role of the Negro characters in Crane's work is engaging and focuses on a dimension seldom mentioned. Most of Crane's Negroes are stereotyped figures like Black John in "Billy Atkins Went to Omaha" who shines shoes to make money for gingerbread, the clownish Peter Washington and Alek Williams of the Whilomville Stories, or the dancing teamster in *The Red Badge*. In "The Bride Comes to Yellow Sky" Marshal Potter and his wife are cajoled and bullied by two Negroes, a Pullman car porter and a waiter in the dining car. Ellison interprets Crane's comment that "historically there was supposed to be something infinitely humorous in their situation" not only as a reference to the newly married status of the couple but as a sardonic allusion to the complexities of a situation in which the marshal, confronting the reality of the Negro, finds himself as helpless as Scratchy Wilson. "The Monster" is, of course, a more serious statement upon the Negro question and American civilization in general, for in this story Dr. Trescott loses his practice and his social status by assuming human responsibility toward the Negro.

23. Garland, Hamlin. "Stephen Crane: A Soldier of Fortune," *Saturday Evening Post*, CLXXIII (July, 28, 1900), 16–17. Reprinted in *Stephen Crane: Letters* (Entry 9), pp. 299–305.

Crane's meeting with Hamlin Garland at Avon-by-the-Sea in the summer of 1891 was a highly significant factor in his development toward the practice of literary impressionism. Garland was delivering a course of lectures at the Seaside Assembly, and in his capacity as shore correspondent for the New York *Tribune* Crane reported Garland's talk on Howells in the August 18 issue of the newspaper. At the time of these lectures Garland was America's leading advocate of impressionism in painting and literature and was already formulating the essays he would publish in the *Arena* in 1892 and 1893 and eventually incorporate into *Crumbling Idols* (1894). In this first account of his relationship with Crane, Garland misdates their initial meeting and subsequently confuses other dates (see Entry 37). It was in the early months of 1894, not in the spring of 1893 as Garland remembers, that Crane was a frequent visitor to the Harlem apartment which Garland shared with his brother Franklin. Here Crane showed Garland the first draft of *The Red Badge of Courage*, which cost Garland fifteen dollars to read, for he gave Crane that sum in order to redeem the last half of the manuscript from the typewriter agency. Crane also brought to the apartment some of the poems which were to go into *The Black Riders*. He amazed Garland by apparently drawing off one of the poems at a moment's notice, maintaining that they come into his mind in some mysterious fashion. Garland, with his enthusiasm for psychial phenomena, was all too willing to believe that the composition of the poems, as well as *The Red Badge*, was an automatic process. In turn, Crane, who was aware of Garland's gullibility in such matters, probably enjoyed deluding him into the belief that these works were the products of direct and painless inspiration.

Garland left three other accounts of his relationship with Crane: *Yale Review*, N.S. III (April, 1914), 494–506; *Bookman*, LXX (January, 1930), 523–528; *Roadside Meetings* (1930), pp. 189–206. Like this one, they are distorted and unreliable. A number of shorter unpublished versions add little. Garland became a conservative in his later years. He disapproved of Crane's expatriation and considered his life at Brede Place affected and disreputable. After Crane's death he became increasingly disturbed by the false rumors which circulated about his young friend's alleged immorality and opium addiction. Garland did not want to be associated with what he considered the shady side of Crane's Bohemian life. Therefore, in his recollections he intentionally understated his relationship with Crane and telescoped their many meetings into a few in order to obscure their close association between 1891 and 1895 and the fact that for a time he had actually functioned as Crane's literary mentor. When Wilson Follett edited Crane's *Work*, he chose not to publish Garland's introduction to one of the volumes because of its extreme inaccuracy. Yet, Garland's memoirs are an important record of Crane's first and perhaps most influential literary friendship.

24. Geismar, Maxwell. "Stephen Crane: Halfway House," in *Rebels and Ancestors: The American Novel, 1890–1915*. Boston: Houghton Mifflin, 1953, pp. 69–136.

Maxwell Geismar is a literary historian and critic who writes with the skill of a novelist, but his Freudian predilections at times lead him into monolithic interpretations, and consequently he considers Crane's fiction and poetry little more than literary projections of unresolved Oedipal conflicts. Geismar follows John Berryman's thesis (Entry 11) that Crane's career exemplifies the "prostitute complex" in which "the hero of infancy, in attempting to 'save' a fallen woman—an emotional pattern which was recurrent in Crane's career—was in fact reclaiming a fallen mother-symbol from the sexuality of the marriage relationship itself" (p. 115). Thus *Maggie* reveals Crane's youthful war with authority, while *The Black Riders* expresses childish tantrums rather than adult dissent. *The Red Badge of Courage* is a Christian allegory with mythic and naturalistic overtones emphasizing Crane's deep-seated conviction of sin and need for redemption. As a result of his unconscious Oedipal desires, Crane punished himself with symbolic castration in "The Monster" and symbolic death in "The Blue Hotel." This also explains why his war stories are obsessively concerned with mutilation and the relationship of the living to the dead. Geismar finds a return to conformity with accepted values in Crane's later writings, particularly the chauvinistic *Wounds in the Rain*, which he feels represents an ultimate failure to attain artistic maturity.

The reading of literature as spiritual autobiography, if it is pursued literally and exclusively, does violence both to life and to art. Crane's achievement cannot adequately be explained by an approach which views his work solely as an expression of childhood traumas and neurotic conflicts, although these are often reflected in his writings. In reality, Crane had strong emotional attachments to conventional women like Nellie Crouse as well as to discredited ones like Cora Taylor. There is little reason to believe that he thought of respectable women as unattainable or that his fictional heroes, such as Hawker of *The Third Violet* and Coleman of *Active Service,* turn to them because of a sense of guilt for actually desiring their courtesian counterparts. Geismar's analysis of the thematic development of Crane's work is stimulating and even challenging, but he virtually ignores the author's stylistic complexity and structural skill. Instead, Crane's works are evaluated in terms of how closely they conform to the Oedipal drama which Geismar insists pervades Crane's fiction and poetry. Therefore, "The Open Boat," which apparently cannot easily be accommodated to this thesis is dismissed as a conventional adventure story. On the other hand, Geismar is one of the first critics to recognize the artistic perfection and emotional complexity of "Death and the Child."

25. Gibson, William M., ed. *Stephen Crane: Selected Prose and Poetry.* New York: Rinehart & Co., 1950; Revised Edition, *The Red Badge of Courage and Selected Prose and Poetry.* New York: Holt, Rinehart and Winston, 1956; Third Edition, 1968.

The almost simultaneous publication of this anthology, the first significant collection of Crane's work since Mark Van Doren's *Twenty Stories* (1940), with John Berryman's Freudian biography (Entry 11) initiated the current revival of interest in Crane and did much to define what has come to be considered the best of his writings. Reserving *The Red Badge of Courage* for the second edition, Gibson reprinted *Maggie,* "The Open Boat" with "Stephen Crane's Own Story" of the sinking of the *Commodore* from the New York *Press,* "The Bride Comes to Yellow Sky," "The Monster," "The Blue Hotel," a small number of poems, and a revealing interview with William Dean Howells, "Fears Realists Must Wait."

Gibson's initial selection was an act of criticism, and the growth of this anthology in its two revisions is interesting to observe, since it reflects an expanding awareness of what is relevant in Crane's work. The second edition added "The Men in the Storm," "The Five White Mice," "The Price of the Harness" (with the New York *World* dispatch "Regulars Get No Glory" which was its journalistic predecessor), "An Episode of War," as well as *The Red Badge* and its sequel, "The Veteran." The introduction and textual note were also revised and expanded in the 1956 edition. In the third edition Gibson adds *George's Mother* to what he rightly considers the best of Crane's fiction and also other important New York City tales and sketches such as "An Experiment in Misery," "A Desertion," "A Dark Brown Dog," and "When Every One Is Panic Stricken," an impressionistic account of a fire which

Crane fabricated and published in the *Press* as a news report. Crane's journalism is represented by a number of other selections, the most notable of which are "In the Depths of a Coal Mine" and "Nebraskans' Bitter Fight for Life." A new section, "Sullivan County and Whilomville," reprints the most interesting of Crane's tales about children and the small town, while "A Mystery of Heroism," "Death and the Child," and "War Memories" enhance the section about war. In order to illustrate the relationship of Crane's poetry to his prose, Gibson includes the five "Legends," curious symbolic epigrams that appeared in the *Bookman* in 1896.

The introduction to this volume remains one of the most perceptive concise estimates of Crane's total achievement. Gibson was among the first to recognize Crane as a complex, multivalent writer, an impressionist and symbolist as well as a pioneer realist and naturalist. Crane is viewed as a master of prose style, in Thomas Wolfe's terms, "a taker-outer" like Flaubert rather than "a putter-inner" like Shakespeare, Cervantes, or Dostoevski. Gibson emphasizes that even *Maggie*, the most deterministic and doctrinaire of Crane's novels, is tightly structured with paired and contrasting chapters and three symbolic beer hall scenes. In *The Red Badge of Courage*, however, Gibson feels that the naturalistic episodes conflict with the maturation theme, and thus the conclusion of the novel lacks verisimilitude. Later stories such as "The Open Boat," "The Monster," "The Bride Comes to Yellow Sky," and "The Five White Mice" reveal Crane's growing virtuosity as a satirist and an ironist. In poetry Crane was an innovator and a precursor of the Imagists, and his rebellion against the social and religious mores of his time is more evident than in his fiction. Gibson's analysis of the revisions in *Maggie* differs markedly from that of R. W. Stallman (Entry 67), and he argues that the omission from the 1896 edition of the passage in the syncopated Chapter XVII in which Maggie encounters "a huge fat man in torn and greasy garments" improves the logic and unity of the book.

26. Griffith, Clark. "Stephen Crane and the Ironic Last Word," *Philological Quarterly*, XLVII (January, 1968), 83–91.

Formally considered, Crane's most important works of fiction appear to be maturation stories in which a protagonist confronts challenges and emerges from his ordeal strengthened or more insightful. But Griffith strikes through this deceptive structural framework to what is revealed by closer observation, "that the character has stood still, or, alternatively, that his new-found knowledge is somehow fraudulent and thus becomes the basis upon which he predicates even grosser errors" (p. 86). At the conclusion of "The Open Boat" the men seek a less ego-deflating interpretation of their experiences than the indifference or hostility of nature to their survival demonstrated upon the sea. The smug naturalistic formula of the Easterner at the end of "The Blue Hotel" ignores the reality that the Swede sought and found his murderer (cf. Entries 91 through 94). In *The Red Badge of Courage* Henry Fleming's final self-deceptions indicate how little he actually learned in battle.

This is one of the most valuable as well as best-written of the many essays concerned with Crane's narrative technique. Like James Colvert's "Structure and Theme in Stephen Crane's Fiction" (Entry 20), it demonstrates that the ironic vision is central to Crane's creative method. Griffith refutes not only the critics who interpret Crane's best stories as simple initiations into knowledge but also those who recognize the author's consistently sardonic point of view but consider it evidence of his emotional detachment. Griffith explains that Crane's irony underscores his compassion. In a naturalistic universe men need illusions to preserve their sanity. Crane does not blame or laugh at them for rationalizing their behavior and its implications, since self-deception is integral to the human condition. For a negative evaluation of Crane's ironic perspective, see Joseph X. Brennan "Stephen Crane and the Limits of Irony," *Criticism*, XI (Spring, 1969), 183–200.

27. Gullason, Thomas A. "Stephen Crane's Private War on Yellow Journalism," *Huntington Library Quarterly*, XXII (May, 1959), 201–208.

For the greater part of his adult life Crane functioned as a journalist as well as a creative writer. During the summer months from 1888 through 1892 he assisted his brother Townley in reporting shore news at Asbury Park for the New York *Tribune*. During the next two-and-a-half years he was a free lance reporter in New York, contributing items to the *Sun, Press, Journal,* and *World*. In the spring of 1895 he travelled through the West and into Mexico for Irving Bacheller's infant newspaper syndicate, and in the fall of 1896 he undertook the journey to rebellion-torn Cuba which ended in the sinking of the *Commodore*. From 1897 to 1900 Crane served as a foreign correspondent in Greece, Cuba, and England. In these later years he had among his employers William Randolph Hearst of the *Journal* and Joseph Pulitzer of the *World*, the chief practitioners of yellow journalism and jingo propaganda. Nevertheless, Gullason points out in this essay, Crane retained his integrity and his devotion to the ideal of honest reporting.

Crane never wrote an extended criticism of the sensational journalism of the 1890's, but Gullason cites many instances in which he attacked the irresponsible practices of the press in his fiction and poetry. In *The Red Badge of Courage* and "The Monster" newspapers are shown to be distorters of facts. The editor of the *Eclipse* in *Active Service*, who Gullason feels may have been modeled upon William Randolph Hearst, plans to stimulate circulation by sending a military expedition to Cuba, and other characters in the novel suffer from the corrupting influence of yellow journalism. In Crane's Cuban sketches the ignorance and triviality of war correspondents are exposed, while editors are condemned for insisting that prosaic events be presented as tales of heroism or tragedy to satisfy the demands of a sensation-hungry public. Crane's most explicit statement upon the evils of yellow journalism is the title poem in *War Is Kind* which characterizes the newspaper as "a collection of half-injustices." He was, however, convinced that honest reporting was a vital public service and avoided sensationalism in his own work. For other discussions of Crane's newspaper career, see Victor A. Elconin, "Stephen Crane at Asbury Park," *American Literature*, XX (November, 1948), 275–289; and Joseph Kwiat, "The Newspaper Experience: Crane, Norris and Dreiser," *Nineteenth-Century Fiction*, VIII (September, 1953), 99–117. For Crane's reporting of political and military events, see Thomas A. Gullason, "Stephen Crane: Anti-Imperialist," *American Literature*, XXX (May, 1958), 237–241; and entries 5 and 7.

28. Gullason, Thomas A. "Thematic Patterns in Stephen Crane's Early Novels," *Nineteenth-Century Fiction*, XVI (June, 1961), 59–67.

Similarities between the subject matter and technique of *Maggie* and *George's Mother* are evident, but Gullason convincingly shows that the two Bowery tales are thematically united with *The Red Badge of Courage* in a trilogy which reflects Crane's own youthful personality conflicts. The predominant themes of the early stories are ideals versus realities, religious crises involving the mother, and the relationship of fear to cowardice, courage, conflict, or war. Maggie, Henry Fleming, and George Kelcey are dreamers and idealists betrayed by their illusions into brutal confrontations with reality which end disastrously for all except Henry who makes an uneasy compromise with the world. Gullason stresses that the religious theme is also integral to the three novels. Each protagonist is deceived by the hope of a spiritual solace, proffered in a number of ways but primarily by three ineffectual maternal figures. Mary Johnson, Mrs. Fleming, and Mrs. Kelcey mouth pious phrases but invariably fail their children at crucial moments. Fear is pervasive in the three books, and at least one character in each is concerned with the moral question of courage and cowardice. Combat terms and animal imagery are used to describe encounters in civilian life as well as in war.

The thematic patterns of Crane's early fiction, capably delineated by Gullason in this essay, reveal that his work had emotional as well as literary antecedents. When *The Red Badge of Courage* first appeared in the autumn of 1895, a number of reviewers took it for granted that the author was a veteran of battle, and in a figurative sense this assumption was correct. The severe religious conflicts and identity struggles of Crane's youth caused him to view social situations in terms of the terror and violence of war. Fear, rage, and loneliness are the central emotions of the Sullivan County sketches in which battle has become a metaphor of life. In *Maggie* tenement women rage and tear at each other in frenetic quarrels, and Jimmie and Pete engage in an atavistic brawl over the question of Maggie's honor. After the riotous party in *George's Mother*, Bleeker's room "resembled a decayed battlefield," like Maggie's apartment after her parents' destructive fights. The religious theme discussed by Gullason (the protagonists are duped or disillusioned in their search for spiritual help) has its origins in Crane's youth in a rigid Methodist household where pleasure was equated with evil and the God of wrath stressed at the expense of the God of mercy (cf. Entry 47). It should be mentioned that the significant passage in *The Red Badge of Courage* cited by Gullason in which Henry Fleming's mother offers him a Bible as a guide in the spiritual wilderness appears in the manuscript but not in the published novel.

29. Gullason, Thomas A. "The Jamesian Motif in Stephen Crane's Last Novels," *Personalist*, XLII (Winter, 1961), 77–84.

Modern criticism has rejected Crane's last novels—*The Third Violet* (1897), *Active Service* (1899), and *The O'Ruddy* (1903)—but Gullason reminds us that they were well received at the time of their initial publication. He suggests that these books do not show a decline in Crane's talents but a change in his fictional direction toward experimentation with the Jamesian motif of social classes in conflict. The novels probe the tensions between the wealthy and educated and the poor but "natural aristocrat" whom Crane praises in his letters to Nellie Crouse. The protagonists are determined lower-class characters who overcome all social obstacles to wed rebellious heroines of the upper class. "In the last novels, then, Stephen Crane consistently debunks high society for its arrogance, greed, hypocrisy, and narrow-mindedness; his sympathies are with the lower classes. And he looks toward a brave new world" (p. 83).

Gullason describes the similarities in the motifs of these books and indicates that Crane was attempting to master the technique of the novel of manners, but the implication that they were successful as works of fiction is unjustified. *The Third Violet* is perhaps the most engaging, but its episodic plot, fragmented scenes, and failure to resolve realistically the problems of class tensions and Bohemianism versus respectability are fatal deficiencies. Almost identical faults ruin *Active Service* (also hampered by stiff, wooden dialogue), a commercial potboiler written at the insistence of Harold Frederic who convinced Crane that a popular adventure novel would save him from financial ruin. The posthumous *The O'Ruddy* is a tedious picaresque romance intended to burlesque the swashbuckling *genre* admired by readers of Robert Louis Stevenson.

30. Hoffman, Daniel G., ed. *The Red Badge of Courage and Other Stories by Stephen Crane*. New York: Harper & Brothers, 1957.

Restricted to Crane's writings about war, this collection includes *The Red Badge of Courage* (without manuscript variants), "The Veteran," "A Mystery of Heroism," "An Episode of War," and two short essays: Crane's review of Ouida's *Under Two Flags* ("Ouida's Masterpiece"), not previously reprinted, and an unpublished Decoration Day article found in manuscript in the Columbia University Crane Collection, entitled by Hoffman "The Gratitude of a Nation." Hoffman's introduction takes a sensible position toward the vexing problem of the sources of *The Red Badge* and explores the possibility of indirect influences from Crane's military and religious heritage as well as literary predecessors such as Zola's *La Débâcle*, Kipling's *The Light That Failed*, and Tolstoy's *Sevastopol*. Crane's choice of the psychology of fear as his central subject is placed in the context of the concern with individualism and death traditional in the American novel. Hoffman's analysis of the themes and characters of *The Red Badge* is based upon the theory of a Christian redemption allegory first advanced by R. W. Stallman. Although Hoffman recognizes that the question of whether or not Henry Fleming becomes a hero or attains salvation is never decisively resolved in the novel, he defines Henry's character through his mother's Christian humility, Jim Conklin's Christ-like sacrifice, and Wilson's transformation from a loud to a humble soldier.

The crux of Hoffman's interpretation is the assertion that "Jim's appearance in *The Red Badge* is both symbolically and literally a Second Coming" (p. xix). Henry Fleming attempts to follow this Jesus surrogate, but not even witnessing the death of Jim or experiencing the purifying fire of battle makes him worthy of regeneration. According to Hoffman, Henry undergoes no permanent spiritual change either through Jim Conklin's death or through his battle experiences, but "Wilson, the loud soldier, has been truly converted by his. It is Wilson's role to show Henry that such conversion is possible, and to show us how far short of it Henry remains to the end" (p. xxiii). We are, however, entitled to ask in what way Conklin is a Christ surrogate if his "sacrifice" has no lasting effect upon the subsequent moral development of Henry Fleming and if Wilson experiences conversion prior to his death. With the exception of this inconsistency, Hoffman's analysis of *The Red Badge* is essentially sound, and there are some enlightening comments about Crane's ambiguous world view and metaphorical prose style. Two minor errors should be corrected. Hoffman mangles by misquotation the well-known wafer image with which Crane underscores Jim Conklin's death, "The red sun was pasted in the sky like a wafer," and he repeats Stallman's mistaken attribution to Crane of the remark that Tolstoy's morality was "simply that of Christ." This statement was never made by Crane but appears in a letter from William Dean Howells to Curtis Brown. See Brown's *Contacts* (New York, 1935), p. 294.

31. Johnson, George W. "Stephen Crane's Metaphor of Decorum," *PMLA*, LXXVIII (June, 1963), 250–256.

With other adventurous young men of his generation, Crane shared the need to be simultaneously unconventional and respectable, barbarous and docile, and like them he ritualized in sports and war the desire to be savage within the rules of gentlemanly decorum. The question of proper conduct in a chaotic universe, the "metaphor of decorum," became an important concern of Crane's fiction. In the war stories Johnson finds a development from the integration of ferocity into the society of the regiment in *The Red Badge of Courage*, through a more ironical view of docility and acceptance in "A Mystery of Heroism," to a final metaphor of man's suspension between a frightening, unknowable world and incongruous social ceremonies in "An Episode of War" and "The Upturned Face." Civilian society also is defined by its ability to accept incongruities. Dr. Trescott of "The Monster" discovers that his humanity paradoxically makes him unacceptable to the community. In "The Bride Comes to Yellow Sky" two doomed conventions—the romance of the honeymoon and the ceremony of the gunfight—have a final moot confrontation. "The Blue Hotel" similarly illustrates the futility of man's efforts to create order from the wilderness of his experience. The Swede is murdered while attempting social integration, and the Easterner remains deluded in the belief that he might have controlled the situation.

This is a complex and closely structured essay. Johnson's own fondness for metaphor and verbal abstraction sometimes obscures his meaning, but his delineation of the experiences of the typical Crane protagonist is very accurate. In Crane's fiction the efforts of the individual to integrate his experience within social conventions is often fordoomed, and he becomes the victim if institutions which he cannot comprehend or control. Man desires and even needs social restraints to confine the excesses of his imagination, but within them he experiences a loss of identity like Henry Fleming of *The Red Badge* or finds himself a silent collaborator in murder like the Easterner of "The Blue Hotel." Crane's anti-hero is caught in a constant state of tension between the terrors of isolation and the price of the harness of civilization, and any choice may spell disaster. In his art as in his life Crane attempted to harmonize the contradictions between the individualistic life of action and the settled conventions of the world. For another point of view toward Crane's concept of the relationship of the individual to his society, see Entry 40.

32. Katz, Joseph, ed. *The Portable Stephen Crane.* New York: Viking Press, 1969.

This compact and attractive anthology offers authoritative texts of *The Red Badge of Courage, Maggie* (the 1893 edition), *George's Mother*, nineteen of Crane's best tales and sketches, and a judicious selection of his poetry. Each of the book's five sections contains major works representative of a particular aspect of Crane's career and letters, stories, sketches, and journalism which complement and illuminate them. The bibliographical and textual notes are extremely reliable.

Katz's excellent introduction demonstrates how throughout the range of Crane's career his works can be grouped according to recurrent settings, themes, characters, and points of view. Taken as a whole, Katz concludes, Crane's writings record "an acutely ironic perception of man caught between the claims of the past and the demands of the present, between the stated and the tacit, among all of the conflicting forces that define the human condition" (p. xx).

33. Labor, Earle. "Crane and Hemingway: Anatomy of Trauma," *Renascence,* XI (Summer, 1959), 189–196.

Although Hemingway's hunting story, "The Short Happy Life of Francis Macomber," appears to offer more situational and thematic parallels to *The Red Badge of Courage*, it is *A Farewell to Arms* that has been most frequently compared to Crane's novel. Labor feels, however, that the difference between the two books are more significant than the much-discussed resemblances and that *The Red Badge* is clearly "dated" as a nineteenth-century novel by the fact that Henry Fleming is able to resolve a problem that for Hemingway's Frederick Henry, an extremely modern protagonist, has become insoluble. Fleming has spent his childhood in an ordered environment, and his physical and psychic wound is received at an age when he is mature enough to prevent it from destroying him completely. But Frederick Henry, whose avatar is the Nick Adams of *In Our Time*, is a victim of early traumatic shock which has left him with a spiritual callous and precludes an easy social adjustment. Labor points to Crane's metaphor of the "moving box" of the regiment in which Henry Fleming finds himself enclosed as implying a structured social pattern limiting the extent of Fleming's confusion so that in the end he is able to recover from his wound and to rejoin his society. Hemingway's hero, on the other hand, is unable to find spiritual remedies to ease his pain and can never adjust to a world in which all definitive values have been lost.

Ernest Hemingway expressed his admiration of Crane's fiction in *Green Hills of Africa* (1935) and in his anthology, *Men at War* (1942), reprinted *The Red Badge of Courage* in its entirety as one of the war stories which had most impressed him. The emotional affinity between Crane and Hemingway, as well as the striking similarities in their careers, aesthetic credos, and literary styles, has long been recognized, Philip Young expresses it best in his statement that "Crane's whole dark view of existence, of men damaged and alone in a hostile, violent world, of life as one long war which we seek out and challenge in fear and controlled panic—it is all an amazing forecast of Hemingway" (*Ernest Hemingway* [1952], p. 163). Clearly, Labor has very much exaggerated the differences in the attitudes of the two writers toward the alienating effect of traumatic shock. He regards Henry Fleming's adjustment to the regiment which represents his society as complete, ignoring the many passages in the novel which suggest that it may be self-delusive and temporary. A number of Crane's protagonists such as the lieutenant of "An Episode of War" and Peza of "Death and the Child" resemble Hemingway's shattered heroes in that they can never recover from their physical and emotional wounds. Henry Fleming and Frederick Henry are alike in that they are both sensitive men in a world given over to confusion and violence. They are representative of a large group of modern fictional soldiers, the questioning and disillusioned protagonists of Barbusse, Remarque, and Dos Passos, whose lack of inner conviction and commitment to the common goal causes them to recoil from the incredible butchery of war and to seek a separate peace.

34. Liebling, A. J. "The Dollars Damned Him," *New Yorker*, XXXVII (August 5, 1961), 48–60, 63–66, 69–72.

Not only tuberculosis but poor medical advice, overwork, and anxiety about money brought about Crane's untimely death. Unlike Melville, who virtually abandoned literature for a sinecure in the New York Custom House when he realized that he could not live by his pen, Crane insisted upon remaining a writer to the end. Despite his Bohemianism, he had a bourgeois sense of responsibility, engendered, Liebling believes, by his minister father and nurtured by his grasping lawyer brother. Crane's last eighteen months were spent in a struggle for financial independence, but he died owing more than five thousand dollars. In order to satisfy his creditors he was forced to produce inferior hackwork which was easy to write and sold readily. Liebling disagrees with Thomas Beer's opinion that Crane lacked the capacity to improve and R. W. Stallman's contention that his death at twenty-eight was no loss to literature because his genius had been exhausted (Entry 43). Instead, poverty, debt and illness, compounded with a middle-class need for financial stability were responsible for Crane's literary decline. The quality of his work had improved greatly between 1893 when he wrote *The Red Badge of Courage* and 1897 when he wrote "The Open Boat," and in affluence and health he might have gone on to create even more important fiction.

Written in an informal journalistic style, this essay presents an extremely readable account of Crane's final years in England. The fact that Crane was able to compose "The Bride Comes to Yellow Sky," "The Blue Hotel," and "The Monster" in these years makes it evident that his talents were not depleted and that he could have continued to develop as an artist if it had not been necessary for him to grind out stories and sketches for magazines. One must, however, resist the conclusion, broadly implied in this essay, that it was a Philistine society that does not reward the artist adequately for his labors which was responsible for Crane's desperate financial situation and not Cora's, and perhaps his own, prodigality.

Liebling makes interesting incidental comments upon John Berryman's Freudian speculations (Entry 11) and upon the literary background of *The Red Badge of Courage*, which he believes to be in the oral reminiscences and written memoirs of Civil War veterans. Popular magazines, *Harper's* and *Leslie's* in particular, contained a large number of eyewitness accounts of battle, including articles by John W. De Forest which were first published in *Harper's* at intervals from 1864 to 1868 and later collected with other De Forest items as *A Volunteer's Adventures* (1946).

35. Morgan, H. Wayne. "Stephen Crane: The Ironic Hero," in *Writers in Transition: Seven Americans*. New York: Hill and Wang, 1963, pp. 1–22.

As a social historian rather than a literary critic, Morgan is concerned primarily with the role of the writer as a spokesman for the cultural changes which accompanied post-bellum America's evolution from a stratified agrarian into a democratic urban society. Little is said about Crane's contribution to this transition other than the commonplace that he was a pioneer of the emerging literary realism and naturalism which would eventually triumph over the sentimental idealism of the genteel tradition. This essay is an appreciation rather than an analysis of Crane's fiction, and there is no discussion of the poetry. Attention is directed to the writer's personal philosophy rather than to his artistry. Questions of courage or heroism are seen as central to Crane's work. These internal qualities serve as the measure of man's ability to surmount the environmental forces which limit or threaten him. Courage requires the temporary suspension of selfish motives, and this moral stance gives the individual the dignity which allows him to challenge the power of fate and to affirm his identity.

Despite some minor errors of fact and misquotations, this essay is a fairly satisfactory summation of Crane's career as a writer of fiction, but the advanced student will find no new information or insights here. The perspective of the book as a whole is historical, but Crane is only vaguely related to the social, political, or intellectual currents of his era. Some of Morgan's few critical comments are based upon erroneous assumptions. Crane was not an "undisciplined artist" who "wrote easily" (p. 2) but a self-conscious experimenter with style and structure. Joseph Brennan's painstaking analysis of *Maggie* (Entry 62) demonstrates that the novelette is not "poorly developed" (p. 6) and lacking in finish as Morgan believes. The reading of *The Red Badge of Courage* as a redemption story in which Henry Fleming's return to the battlefield and subsequent bravery are motivated by moral convictions is unsupported by the text of the novel. Morgan quotes, seemingly without comprehension of Crane's irony, the comment that Henry "had slept and, awakening, found himself a knight," indicating that his bravery is an unconscious emotional reaction, very much like his earlier cowardice, and that the ethical value assigned to it by society is entirely arbitrary.

36. Øverland, Orm. "The Impressionism of Stephen Crane: A Study in Style and Technique," *Americana Norvegica: Norwegian Contributions to American Studies*. Philadelphia: University of Pennsylvania Press, 1966, I, 239–285.

Recent commentator's upon Crane's style, as well as reviewers and critics in his own day, often describe his literary technique as impressionistic. Crane never formulated his aesthetic credo, but random statements indicate that he tended to equate his personal vision with reality in the manner of the French impressionist painters and their counterparts in literature. Øverland does not find structural patterns in Crane's novels ōther than "a simple succession of fragmentary episodes" (p. 252), corresponding with the impressionists' view of experience. Crane minimizes the elements of auctorial comment and narrative in his fiction. The world he depicts is rendered almost entirely through the limited and often distorted perspectives of his characters and is defined by the impressions that at any given time are conveyed to them through their senses.

Other important impressionistic aspects of Crane's style are the equation of personal appearance or movements with states of mind; "substitutionary" speech, which makes no clear distinction in what is said, thought, or reported; confused relationships between objects or phenomena; synecdoche in description of persons, places, or events; extensive use of personification, animation, similes, rare and bizarre imagery, onomatopoeia; and a number of purposeful grammatical confusions.

Øverland does not explain the origins of Crane's impressionism but points to his friendship with Hamlin Garland and William Dean Howells, both of whom were familiar with European literary movements, and his early association with artists and illustrators in New York studios. The influence of Garland, who equated his "veritism" with impressionism seems particularly important in this regard (cf. Entry 37). Øverland's study of Crane's literary impressionism is instructive and complete with the singular exception that he devotes scant attention to the most striking and most frequently mentioned impressionistic criterion of Crane's style, the pervasive use of color imagery both in realistic description and metaphorically. In his stress upon Crane's episodic method of presentation, Øverland ignores thematic principles of structure in the novels. For a discussion of Crane's impressionistic experiments with point of view, see Rodney O. Rogers, "Stephen Crane and Impressionism," *Nineteenth-Century Fiction*, XXIV (December, 1969), 292–304.

37. Pizer, Donald. "The Garland–Crane Relationship," *Huntington Library Quarterly*, XXIV (November, 1960), 75–82.

In recounting the personal relationship between Crane and Hamlin Garland, Pizer corrects the garbled chronology of Garland's four contradictory memoirs (cf. Entry 23). Garland placed his most significant meetings with Crane in the spring of 1893, but they actually occurred early in 1894 when Crane brought manuscripts of some of his poems and *The Red Badge of Courage* to the Harlem apartment that Garland shared with his actor brother, Franklin. In his *Saturday Evening Post* article (Entry 23) Garland recalled that at the time of their intimate association Crane visited the apartment three or four times a week, but in subsequent memoirs he tended to describe his friendship with Crane as casual and sporadic.

Pizer clearly and accurately determines the proper sequence of time and events in an important literary relationship. In an earlier study ("Romantic Individualism in Garland, Norris, and Crane," *American Quarterly*, X [Winter, 1958], 463–475) he discusses the influence of Garland's realism and localism upon Crane's literary theories. The probable influence of Garland's strong advocacy of impressionistic techniques in the arts upon the development of Crane's style is discussed by Stanley Wertheim in "Crane and Garland: The Education of an Impressionist," *North Dakota Quarterly*, XXXV (Winter, 1967), 23–28. Garland's articles on impressionism appeared in the *Arena* and the *Forum* during the crucial years of his friendship with Crane. They stressed experimentation, modernism, and a subjective conception of truth in art. The impressionist painters were lauded for their emphasis upon the emotional effects of color and for their efforts to reproduce objects in the external world in the precise manner in which they impress the beholder. These theories probably had some influence upon the techniques Crane employed in *Maggie* and in *The Red Badge of Courage*, especially the metaphorical use of color, the subjective point of view, and the intertwined patterns of personification and machine and animal imagery. Garland made only occasional use of impressionistic techniques in his own fiction, although in the 1890's he experimented with impressionistic sketches highly imitative of Crane. For an essay describing these sketches which denies that Garland may have led Crane to impressionism, see James B. Stronks, "A Realist Experiments with Impressionism: Hamlin Garland's 'Chicago Studies,'" *American Literature*, XXXVI (March, 1964), 38–52.

38. Pratt, Lyndon Upson. "The Formal Education of Stephen Crane," *American Literature*, X (January, 1939), 460–471.

Pratt considers Stephen Crane's formal education to have been extensive, but it was actually scanty and desultory. Crane first enrolled in Claverack College and Hudson River Institute, a preparatory school and junior college in lower New York State, in January 1888. He pursued an academic course of study, wrote occasionally for the school magazine, *Vidette*, and was a lieutenant of cadets in the military regiment, being promoted to captain shortly before he left Claverack to enter Lafayette College in the autumn of 1890. At Lafayette Crane pledged Delta Upsilon Fraternity, played baseball, and received passing grades in only two of the four subjects he studied. He transferred to Syracuse University in January 1891 and spent two terms (the equivalent of one modern semester) enjoying fraternity life, playing on the varsity baseball team, and receiving only a single grade, an A in English literature. When he left Syracuse in June, 1891, he was only nineteen years old, and his experiences with formal education had come to an end.

Subsequent biographical research has added relatively little to Pratt's concise account of Crane's schooling. Thomas A. Gullason describes the two and a half years Crane spent at Pennington Seminary (1885–1887) where his father had been principal from 1849 to 1858 in "The Cranes at Pennington Seminary," *American Literature*, XXXIX (January, 1968), 530–541. Pennington was greatly concerned with training young men for the Methodist ministry, and Crane transferred to Claverack for this reason and because Claverack had a military training program. But he was to leave Claverack also after completing only two and half years of the four-year course, because his brother William convinced him that the profession of a soldier, for which he was preparing himself, would be impractical (cf. Stanley Wertheim, "Why Stephen Crane Left Claverack," *Stephen Crane Newsletter*, II [Fall, 1967], 5). Further details about Crane's education may be found in Harvey Wickham, "Stephen Crane at College," *American Mercury*, VII (March, 1926), 291–297; Claude Jones, "Stephen Crane at Syracuse," *American Literature*, VII (March, 1935), 82–84; Entry 57.

39. Rahv, Philip. "Fiction and the Criticism of Fiction," *Kenyon Review*, XVIII (Spring, 1956), 276–299.

The section of this essay concerned with the writings of Stephen Crane is largely an attack upon R. W. Stallman's application of "new critical" techniques originally utilized in the analysis of poetry to works of fiction such as *The Red Badge of Courage* and "The Open Boat" (cf. Entries 43 and 80). Rahv charges that Stallman's predilection for symbolism and mythic patterning leads him to distort the famous wafer image in the final sentence of Chapter IX of *The Red Badge* in order to accommodate it to his interpretation of the novel as a Christian redemption allegory. While Joseph Conrad recognized Crane's faculty of distinguishing a scene through an unusual simile, "Conrad's remark has the aptitude of close critical observation, whereas Mr. Stallman's far-fetched religious exegesis is mere *Zeitgeist* palaver" (p. 284). Similarly, the phrase "cold, comfortable sea-water" in "The Open Boat" is not a poetic paradox as Stallman affirms but a mere statement of fact in the context of the story. Rahv observes that such distortions are typical not only of Stallman's critical methods but of mythological-symbolistic critics in general. Rahv does not exclude symbolism from fiction, but he insists that the symbolic import of a novel can be nothing more than its larger meaning beyond the specific situation it depicts. The novel is primarily a representation of reality, and symbols have meaning only within its total context. They should not be isolated as clues to the ostensible hidden meaning of the text. Norman Friedman expresses a similar point of view in his assertion that the modern tendency to read literary works in terms of imagery, symbolic associations, and archetypal structures is largely responsible for the overvaluation of *The Red Badge of Courage*, which is essentially a realistic study of the Civil War ("Criticism and the Novel," *Antioch Review*, XVIII [Fall, 1958], 343–370).

In his capable rejoinder, "Fiction and Its Critics: A Reply to Mr. Rahv," *Kenyon Review*, XIX (Spring, 1957), 290–299. Stallman contends that except in the degree of compression, poetry and prose do not differ fundamentally in their use of verbal means. The poem being more restricted in scope than the novel necessarily employs language more intensely. Other linguistic distinctions between the novel and the poem are arbitrary, and style is of paramount importance in both *genres*. Stallman defends his symbolistic readings of *The Red Badge* and "The Open Boat," charging in turn that Rahv has attacked his interpretations on the basis of single images taken out of context.

One may have serious reservations about Stallman's methods of analysis, but it must be conceded that Crane, like James and Conrad, cannot be read on a realistic level alone. Meaning in his fiction is often dependent upon a style that is predominantly metaphorical and indirect, utilizing symbols, recurring motifs, and ambiguity of meaning in a manner which makes multi-level criticism essential to a proper understanding of his art. The very fact that the controversy over the fictional method of *The Red Badge*—symbolistic, naturalistic, or realistic—has never been resolved indicates Crane's true complexity.

40. Schneider, Robert W. "Stephen Crane: The Promethean Protest," in *Five Novelists of the Progressive Era*. New York: Columbia Press, 1965, pp. 60–111.

As an historian engaged in the study of that generation of Americans which reached maturity during the 1890's, the dawn of the Progressive era, Schneider has chosen to examine literary subjects, because he believes that writers have generally been more successful than other intellectuals both in reflecting and transcending the values of their time. The Progressive era, like other historical periods, was not characterized by a complete shift in philosophical orientation but by a conflict between the traditions of the past and the scientific speculations about the future of man's relationship to nature and to society. Schneider finds a tension in Crane's writings between his view of man as isolated and insignificant in a world he never made and his simultaneous insistence upon the importance of the human struggle, although ultimate defeat is inevitable.

Crane expressed indignation over social, economic, and cosmic injustice, but he refused to resign himself completely to scientific determinism. For this reason, Schneider believes, Crane expressed belief in a merciful indwelling God and in relative freedom of the will. In social situations, he saw individuals as limited not so much by the external forces of the environment as by their own inner weaknesses. Despite his essentially tragic view of life, Crane felt that man could endure if not prevail through the practice of those Christian virtues of honesty, justice, kindness, and truth which were the basic elements in his father's New Testament theology. Thus, Schneider points out, while Crane rebelled against the naturalistic meliorism of Spencer and Zola and the optimism of the Progressive social thinkers of his generation, he retained an essentially religious faith in an ethical code which emphasized engagement in the Promethean struggles of existence without hope of any other victory than the attainment of a tragic dignity.

Because of the significance accorded to the natural or social environment in Crane's writings and the frequent emphasis upon the futility of life, he has often been dismissed as a mere naturalistic determinist and a pessimist. Like Edwin H. Cady, with whom he fundamentally agrees (cf. Entry 16), Schneider examines the complexity of the philosophical and social thought which is revealed through Crane's fiction and poetry. He argues that the conviction expressed in Crane's work that nature is inherently neither benevolent nor hostile to man but flatly indifferent and that the universe is meaningless is incompatible with the determinism of philosophical and literary naturalism. Probably too much stress is placed upon what Schneider considers Crane's belief in freedom of the will and his espousal of the heroic ideal. Unlike the social reformers of the Progressive era, Crane did not deny the evil in man's nature, but he shared with the Progressives the belief that the individual can gain dignity through involvement in the battle against cruelty and injustice. Schneider understates Crane's naturalistic stance, particularly in his early writings, but relates his work to the social thought of the "mauve decade" much more cogently than Larzer Ziff's facile and erroneous generalization in *The American 1890s* (Viking Press, 1966, pp. 185–205) that Crane's fiction failed to bridge the gap between his imagination and reality and that he died before he could come to grips with the problems of his day.

41. Shroeder, John W. "Stephen Crane Embattled," *University of Kansas City Review*, XVII (Winter, 1950), 119–129.

With the exception of one brilliant naturalistic story, "Death and the Child," Shroeder believes that Crane's adherence to the principles of literary naturalism is usually responsible for his artistic shortcomings. Whenever he wrote primarily to point up a naturalistic moral, Crane's creative powers flagged, and it was only when he transcended the limitations of pessimistic determinism that he rose to the level of excellence. In his best work, Shroeder maintains, Crane addressed himself to the problem of salvation, which is the theme of the greatest American fiction. Salvation is not completely realized in *The Red Badge of Courage*, since there is a confusion as to whether the protagonist has survived by descending to the level of a beast in battle or by merging his identity in the mystic brotherhood of humanity. But in "The Monster" and "The Open Boat" the vagaries and inconsistencies of Crane's vision have been resolved and he opposes "the subtle brotherhood of men" to the indifference of nature and society. Shroeder concludes that these two stories represent an advance in Crane's art from the partly realized achievement of *The Red Badge* and, with "Death and the Child," are his most significant works.

Heredity and environment circumscribe the lives of characters in Crane's tales of the New York slums. Yet, they are free to make ethical choices within their limitations but are prevented from doing so by moral cowardice, an inability to discard their illusions and come to terms with the actual conditions of their lives. Crane's naturalism is quite complex, and Shroeder does not examine the naturalistic components of the Bowery tales. His comments upon those tales he finds are unsatisfactory because they are written around naturalistic tags and are extremely tendentious. "The Blue Hotel," for example, "exists, mostly, for the convenience of a statement which every critic likes to quote when displaying Crane's Naturalism at large" (that is, the final speech of the Easterner), and "A Mystery of Heroism" is "devoted, in its conclusion, to the accidental overturning (the Universe doesn't care!) of a pail of water that a soldier has ventured his life to draw" (p. 122). This is distortion by oversimplification, and Shroeder's insistence that the only significant works of literature are those which concern themselves with the problem of salvation seems completely arbitrary.

42. Solomon, M. "Stephen Crane: A Critical Study," *Masses and Mainstream*, IX (January, 1956), 25–42; (March, 1956), 31–47.

The critical perspective of this essay is circumscribed in a monolithic framework which reduces Crane's writings from works of art to statements of social protest against the institutions of capitalistic American society. Thus, *Maggie* rejects the illusion of social mobility and the gospel of wealth and, with *The Red Badge of Courage*, is "a central attack on the 'dog-eat-dog' philosophy of American life during the rule of the 'Robber Barons'" (January, p. 38). The theme of brotherhood, suggesting class solidarity, unites Crane's most important short stories. In "The Open Boat" the shipwrecked men learn the importance of discipline and comradeship when confronted with the threat of annihilation. "The Blue Hotel" highlights "the terrible desolation of a stranger in distress who needs sympathy and finds death because society measures relationships in terms of false pride and cash value" (March, p. 38). The central theme of "The Monster" is an appeal for brotherhood among races. Solomon concedes that Crane did not join Twain and Howells in condemning American military intervention in Cuba and the Philippines but contradicts himself with the assertion that "The Price of the Harness" is Crane's greatest story because it shows him as "an opponent of this imperialist war, as an artist who cries out against its waste of life and ravagement of youth" (March, p. 46).

The importance of this essay is largely that it presents the only extended Marxist critique of Crane's work in English. "M. Solomon" is probably a pseudonym, since investigation has failed to disclose his identity. It should be evident that Crane's themes cannot readily be adapted to the dogmas of Marxist social realism without a great deal of distortion. In *The Red Badge of Courage*, for example, Henry Fleming bolts from the firing line in a blind moment of terror but later considers himself a victim of cosmic hostility. Solomon accepts Henry's rationalizations as Crane's point of view, completely ignoring the irony of the situation, and obtusely insists that Henry deserted because "war wrenches young people out of their path of life, thwarting their aspirations for work, education, love, marriage, family, self-development. Because it sets brother against brother, destroys the home, the land, the culture" (January, p. 38). Crane believed that man was capable of exerting only a limited degree of control over his institutions and traditions, but while he protested against poverty, war, and social prejudice, he felt that the cause of these evils was rooted in the human psyche as well as in external conditions.

43. Stallman, Robert Wooster, ed. *Stephen Crane: An Omnibus.* New York: Alfred A. Knopf, 1952.

Three of Crane's novels—*Maggie, The Red Badge of Courage,* and *George's Mother*—ten of his short stories, sixteen poems, and a generous selection of letters appear in this extremely influential anthology. In the general introduction and in the provocative short introductions which precede each section of the book, Crane's achievement is revaluated from an aesthetic and analytical rather than an historical point of view, although the biographical circumstances surrounding the publication of the works are not neglected. Crane subscribed to Garland's "veritism," Howells' social realism, and his own personal cult of experience, but Stallman emphasizes that his greatest fidelity was to an inward vision. Crane's art does not imitate reality but is impressionistic and symbolic in the manner of Joseph Conrad and Henry James. "A great stylist, Crane puts language to poetic uses, which is to use it reflexively and symbolically. *The works that employ this reflexive and symbolic language constitute what is permanent of Crane*" (p. xlv).

One of the most important features of this book is a collation of the holograph manuscripts of *The Red Badge of Courage* and the reproduction, for the first time in an American edition, of critically significant variants from both the final manuscript and an earlier draft of the novel. Lapses in the pagination of the completed manuscript indicate that Crane removed a total of fifteen pages before sending the loose sheets as a gift to Willis Brooks Hawkins in January, 1896. Among these pages was an entire chapter, Chapter XII, which Crane expunged from the novel and then renumbered Chapter XIII as XII. Three pages of the shorter fragmentary manuscript (found on the reverse of fifty seven of the sheets of the completed version) contain a portion of this expunged chapter and are reproduced in *Omnibus*. Five more pages of the original Chapter XII have subsequently been discovered and are in the possession of various libraries. These five pages are brought together by Stallman in the Signet Classic edition of *The Red Badge of Courage* (1960). Stallman's controversial introduction to the Modern Library edition of the novel (Entry 80) appears revised and expanded in *Omnibus*, and here the inconsistencies of his interpretation of Henry Fleming's experience of war as a Christian redemption allegory become even more apparent. For example, after a breathtaking account of how "Henry's regeneration is brought about by the death of Jim Conklin his friend since childhood [who] is intended to represent Jesus Christ" (p. 199), we find some pages later the statement that "Henry Fleming recognizes the necessity for change of heart but wars against it, and at the end he is the same Henry Fleming. He has undergone no change, no real spiritual development" (p. 221).

44. Stein, William Bysshe. "Stephen Crane's *Homo Absurdus*," *Bucknell Review*, VIII (May, 1959), 168–188.

An existential estrangement, a sense of the absurd springing out of the irrationality of human experience, Stein explains, is the vision of reality which constitutes Crane's world view. Crane's protagonists experience what Sartre called the triumph of the absurd. Henry Fleming of *The Red Badge of Courage* and the correspondent of "The Open Boat" are lost in a universe seemingly devoid of purpose. In "The Monster" Dr. Trescott's attempt to extend human compassion paradoxically ends in his alienation from society, while in "The Blue Hotel" the Swede is destroyed by his imposition of a distorted concept of order upon the chaos of existence. Crises of identity also occur in *Maggie, George's Mother*, "The Five White Mice," and "A Mystery of Heroism." The central characters in these stories are confronted with their inability to give meaning to experience or to define their relationship to society. "Like Kierkegaard and Kafka," Stein comments, "Crane finds the absurd in every walk and in every stage of life. It manifests itself in the contradictions of social experience independent of class and position" (p. 182). In such stories as "The Bride Comes to Yellow Sky" and "The Five White Mice" Crane's pessimism is somewhat relieved by a seriocomic attitude toward existential absurdity.

The "cloud of despair" in Crane's work "that shrouds the noblest efforts of man under a blanket of futility" (p. 188) is overemphasized in this essay. Nevertheless, this is a profound study of Crane's sensibility which combines critical acumen with an eloquent prose style. Stein's cogent thesis that Crane was a precursor of Sartre and Camus who anticipated the basic premises of existential philosophy reinforces the current evaluation of him as the most modern of late nineteenth-century American authors. Crane's high reputation is in no small measure owing to the fact that alienation based upon recognition of the absurdity of experience has become the most pervasive of our intellectual realities, and he was among the first to record its impact.

45. Walcutt, Charles C. "Stephen Crane: Naturalist and Impressionist," in *American Literary Naturalism: A Divided Stream*. Minneapolis: University of Minnesota Press, 1956, pp. 66–86.

Walcutt considers Crane's works more uncompromisingly naturalistic than those of any other American writer. "Crane is the Christopher Marlowe of American naturalism—and we have had no Shakespeare" (p. 67). *Maggie* illustrates that the freedom of individuals is as much limited by their illusions and superstitions as by their external environment. "The Blue Hotel" reveals how a sequence of events may occur despite the best efforts of individuals to prevent them. In *The Red Badge of Courage*, to which Walcutt devotes the greatest amount of space, Crane makes us see his protagonist as an emotional puppet, completely under the control of circumstances. The concluding paragraphs of the novel, in which Henry Fleming speculates upon the degree of maturity he believes he has achieved, are interpreted as merely the climax of his self-delusion. In "The Monster" also, individuals find themselves entangled in a web of inextricable circumstances. Walcutt concedes that in "The Open Boat" the virtues of courage and brotherhood are able to endure briefly.

Naturalistic elements unquestionably loom large in Crane's fiction. *Maggie* depicts the isolation of the individual in a world bounded by the tenement, the sweatshop, and the mission. The protagonist of *The Red Badge of Courage* is plunged into the insane brutality of battle and under its pressures descends to the level of a beast. Survival amid the ranging seas of "The Open Boat" is a matter of chance. In all these stories the delusions of the characters further limit their ability to come to terms with reality.

But orthodox naturalistic fiction usually features characters who are somewhat below average in intelligence like Zola's Nana or Norris' McTeague. These persons are hampered by an inherited or acquired defect and crushed by the overwhelming forces of their environment. Crane's stories. on the other hand, are psychological studies which concentrate upon internal responses to the external world. Characters like Henry Fleming and the correspondent of "The Open Boat" are intelligent and resourceful; they do not degenerate but emerge strengthened from their ordeal. Walcutt unaccountably ignores stories like "Death and the Child" and "The Price of the Harness" which would have more clearly supported his point of view. See also Winifred Lynskey, "Crane's *The Red Badge of Courage*," *Explicator*, VIII (December, 1949), Item 18.

46. Weimer, David R. "Landscape of Hysteria: Stephen Crane," in *The City As Metaphor*. New York: Random House, 1966, pp. 52–64.

William Dean Howell's *A Hazard of New Fortunes* (1890) preceded *Maggie* by three years as a pioneer study of the confrontation between the individual and the chaos of American city life. Yet Weimer considers *Maggie* and Crane's other Bowery tales superior to *A Hazard,* because Crane's city is real while Howells' is merely picturesque. This sense of reality is conveyed in Crane's war as well as city fiction and is based upon a correspondence between emotional disturbances within his characters and disorders in the military or urban worlds to which they are compelled to adjust.

Fantasies and distortions in the minds of the protagonists of stories such as *The Red Badge of Courage* and "An Incident of Heroism" parallel the irrationalities of the world at war, while the disoriented persons and places of *Maggie* and *George's Mother* interact to form a "landscape of hysteria" (the phrase is Charles Walcutt's, Entry 45, p. 69). Weimer suggests but fails to explain that this reflexive distortion is an aspect of Crane's expressionistic as well as impressionistic style, in which the external world is abolished as an entity and exists only as the extension of a particular point of view. Weimer does not find connectedness of disturbed minds with disturbed environments in stories that do not have war or city settings. In some of these, however, like "The Open Boat" or "The Blue Hotel," the propinquity of irrational persons and places—the enormous waves and the terrified correspondent, the whirling snowstorm and the frenzied Swede—seems most obvious.

47. Wertheim, Stanley. "Stephen Crane and the Wrath of Jehova," *Literary Review*, VII (Summer, 1964), 499–508.

John Berryman and Daniel Hoffman (Entries 11 and 101) suggest that Crane's mother and the Peck family held more narrow and condemnatory religious views than those of Stephen's father, Jonathan T. Crane. But although the Reverend Dr. Crane had forsaken Calvinistic determinism and had accepted the Arminian position that salvation may be achieved through the faith of the individual, the distinction between the justified and the unregenerate remained sharp in his theology, and he had by no means given up the fiery pit. The elder Crane's antipathy for sensual indulgence was embodied in four books condemning the most innocent amusements as machinations of the Devil which his libertine son retained in his library until his death.

The theme of revolt against the father is exemplified more clearly in Stephen Crane's life and work than in any other American writer. But despite his rejection of repressive orthodoxy, Crane could not rid himself of the dilemma of religious conscience. His rejection of the moral code embodied in the manuals of piety compiled by his father was essential, but it left him with a feeling of loneliness in a hostile universe which found expression in all his writings. With his personal sense of alienation from his ethical and religious roots as well as from the materialistic, self-assertive spirit of his generation, Crane became the analyst of the terrified soul, and isolation in the face of danger and possible death is the characteristic situation of his protagonists. The "eels of despair" which lay wet and cold against the back of the New York Kid in the story of "The Five White Mice," the quaking apprehension of the wild-eyed Collins of "A Mystery of Heroism," "mad from the threats of destruction," and Henry Fleming's anxieties about his courage in *The Red Badge* were familiar states of mind to the minister's son from New Jersey whose emotional life was dominated by fear and loneliness.

48. West, Ray B., Jr. "Stephen Crane: Author in Transition," *American Literature*, XXXIV (May, 1962), 215–228.

The focus of this essay is at times somewhat blurred, but for the most part it deals with the development of the theme of social complicity in Crane's fiction. West views Crane as a transitional figure whose attitude toward human relationships, ostensibly the preoccupation of his work, underwent a gradual shift from the simple reformist concerns of the literary naturalists to an awareness of the importance of the social structure. Simultaneously, there was a parallel refinement of his technique "from the rugged 'veritism' of *Maggie* to the ironic symbolism of 'The Blue Hotel'" (p. 227). Crane constantly stressed the importance of nature, but the fate of his characters is decided by their involvements with others. While *Maggie* explored the evils of society, society itself became the subject of *The Red Badge of Courage*. In the war novel not natural but human turmoil threatens man. The point is developed in "The Open Boat" where nature is shown to be indifferent despite its power, but the rewards of comradeship in the face of danger are evident. "The Bride Comes to Yellow Sky" is a minor comedy of manners, and in "The Blue Hotel" the Swede is destroyed because of his ignorance of the social conventions which protect the other characters.

One may agree with West that man's relationship with his fellows is an important concern in Crane's fiction, but the primacy of the theme of social complicity and the course of its development in his writings as a whole are by no means clear. Actually, Crane's preoccupation throughout his work remained with the isolation of the individual in a hostile or indifferent universe. This is true of his early fiction and poetry as well as of later stories like "Death and the Child" and "A Mystery of Heroism." West's evidence for Crane's increasing concern with the mores and manners of society is selectively chosen, but it is curious that he devotes no attention to "The Monster" and the stories of *Wounds in the Rain* as studies of the codes of conduct which govern human relationships. At the same time, it seems superfluous to provide a detailed plot summary of a story as well known as "The Blue Hotel" in an essay appearing in a journal intended primarily for specialists in American literature.

49. Westbrook, Max. "Stephen Crane's Social Ethic," *American Quarterly*, XIV (Winter, 1962), 587–596.

Literary histories often describe Crane as the first American naturalist and characterize his fiction as representative of pessimistic determinism in literature. Westbrook maintains that while Crane emphasizes the role of environment in shaping men's lives he does not adopt an entirely deterministic ethic but holds his characters responsible for what he calls their "quality of personal honesty." Thus, in the moral structure of Crane's fiction, men are not accountable for the situations in which circumstances have placed them, but they are responsible for the decisions they make within the limits of their insight. Maggie's life may have been shaped by her environment, but within that environment are individuals who have ignored ethical obligations of which they are very much aware. Similarly, in "The Blue Hotel" there is an implicit condemnation of Scully, Johnnie, the cowboy, and the Easterner, because each of them has failed in some way to assume moral responsibility for the Swede and has contributed to the death of a deluded but innocent man.

In this penetrating study of Crane's social ethic, nineteenth-century naturalism and individual insight and freedom are shown to be to a small but significant extent compatible with one another. Westbrook stresses that Crane's philosophical stance is not absolutist and does not demand an exclusive choice between free will and determinism. Environment in Crane's action is, as he himself put it, "a tremendous thing" which "may shape lives regardless," but individuals retain the responsibility for making ethical decisions and acting upon them within the limits of their insights and capacities. In *Maggie*, "The Blue Hotel," "The Open Boat," and "The Monster," Crane implies that men should assume the burdens of moral involvement, although their efforts to triumph over their physical and social environments may be doomed to partial or complete failure. Westbrook has also examined Crane's attitudes toward freedom of will, universal values, and social ethics in "Stephen Crane: The Pattern of Affirmation," *Nineteenth-Century Fiction*, XIV (December, 1959), 219–229, and "Stephen Crane and the Personal Universal," *Modern Fiction Studies*, VIII (Winter, 1962–1963), 351–360.

Sources and Influences:

50. Åhnebrink, Lars. *The Beginnings of Naturalism in American Fiction*. Uppsala, Sweden: A. B. Lundequistska Bokhandeln, 1950. Reprinted, New York: Russell & Russell, 1961.

External evidence for Crane's reading of European literature is extremely scanty. There are few references to writers or books in Crane's works, and his extant letters mention European authors other than Tolstoy largely to deny their influence upon him. Statements by Crane's acquaintances are contradictory but show a tendency to deny his indebtedness to literary sources. Most of the information usually cited by scholars regarding Crane's reading comes from Thomas Beer's completely undocumented biography (Entry 10), and the originals of letters quoted by Beer in which Crane expresses his opinions of books by Flaubert, Balzac, Zola, and others have unfortunately disappeared.

Åhnebrink's well-documented study explores the emergence of naturalistic techniques and themes in Crane's work, as well as in the fiction of Hamlin Garland and Frank Norris, with particular attention to European influences. Through extensive parallels, it is shown that *Maggie* may have been indebted to Zola's *L'Assommoir* and that Zola's war novel, *La Débâcle*, could have served as a model for some aspects of structure and tone and for certain episodes in *The Red Badge of Courage*. Parallels between *The Red Badge* and Tolstoy's *Sevastopol* are drawn to demonstrate that Tolstoy was influential in shaping Crane's concept of war and his use of an unromantic hero. Åhnebrink also finds a number of similarities of character and theme between *George's Mother* and Turgenev's *Father and Sons* and believes that Crane may have derived some inspiration for "The Monster" from Ibsen's *An Enemy of the People*.

Åhnebrink's scholarship is exacting, and he makes many original and interesting observations, but he often falls into the error of assuming that parallels between books necessarily indicate the influence of one author upon the other. Most of the parallels between *The Red Badge of Courage* and *La Débâcle* and *Sevastopol* arise from basic similarities in the themes, characters, and incidents of realistic war fiction. *The Red Badge* resembles *La Débâcle* and *Sevastopol* in illustrating the waste and bloodshed of war and its lack of glamor. Crane, like Zola and Tolstoy, depicted an unheroic type of soldier who is a follower rather than a leader and who displays none of the high-flown patriotism of the conventional war hero. Both *La Débâcle* and *Sevastopol* contain descriptions of life in camp and field which could have provided source material for *The Red Badge*, but such details might also have been derived from many other works of fiction or from personal chronicles written by veterans of the Civil War. The parallels between *Maggie* and *L'Assommoir* are a good deal more impressive. It is possible that Crane read Zola's study of the Paris slums and was stimulated by it, but it is even more likely that the literary sources of *Maggie* are to be found in the mass of social literature on slum life produced by Americans after the Civil War (see Entries 53 and 95). Resemblances between Crane's work and Turgenev's and Ibsen's seem to be coincidental.

51. Anderson, Warren D. "Homer and Stephen Crane," *Nineteenth-Century Fiction*, XIX (June, 1964), 77–86.

As Anderson concedes, few if any direct borrowings from Homer appear in *The Red Badge of Courage*, and there are only a small number of rather conventional allusions which may be identified with the Greek poet. Yet, this essay attempts to prove that Crane consciously followed Homeric and Vergilian precedent in the composition of the war novel. Particular images and incidents in *The Red Badge* seem to echo the *Iliad*, but it is admitted that this may be coincidental. The most striking similarity Anderson finds between Crane and Homer is in the use of similes, particularly those which compare men at war with animals. Crane's assessment of war in *The Red Badge* is distinctly antiheroic, reflecting the naturalistic doctrine that in battle man descends to the level of the beast rather than the classical attitude that bravery represents excellence. But the brotherhood of heroes is extolled in "The Clan of No-Name," and here Crane allies himself with traditions that reach back to Hector and Achilles.

Jonathan T. Crane was a student of the classics, and some Homer and Virgil would be almost inevitable in the reading of a minister's son in the nineteenth century. Yet, few of the parallels cited by Anderson reveal that Crane's knowledge of the classics was more than cursory. Comparison of the actions of men to those of animals is a conventional technique in naturalistic fiction and frequently utilized by American naturalists such as Frank Norris and Jack London. It is surely more logical to assume that they as well as Crane derived their animalism from the works of Zola and his followers than from so remote a source as Homer. Furthermore, animal similes and metaphors in *The Red Badge* are not used as they are in Homer to illustrate man's oneness with the animal creation but follow a pattern which reflects Henry Fleming's changing perception of reality; see Mordecai and Erin Marcus, "Animal Imagery in *The Red Badge of Courage*," *Modern Language Notes*, LXXIV (February, 1959), 108–111. Loosely speaking, there may be epic "machinery" in the novel—set speeches, choral responses, interaction between man and god-like nature—but when Anderson asserts that "A classicist will find repeated resemblances to Achilles in Crane" or suggests that the division of *The Red Badge* into twenty-four chapters "hints at the traditional division of *Iliad* and *Odyssey* into twenty-four books each" (p. 78) he is defining the classical parallels much too narrowly.

52. Colvert, James B. "The Origins of Stephen Crane's Literary Creed," *University of Texas Studies in English*, XXXIV (1955), 179–188.

Colvert rejects the assumption that Crane's art was the spontaneous outgrowth of innate genius or that he was indebted to nineteenth-century French and Russian naturalism for the origins of the literary creed which he projected into his work after 1892. In view of Crane's known enthusiasm for Rudyard Kipling in the early nineties, it is probable that he read *The Light That Failed* (1890) during the spring semester of 1891 at Syracuse University. Colvert suggests that a remarkable kinship in temperament exists between Kipling's protagonist, Dick Heldar, and Crane's own personality and that Dick's ideas about art were a strong influence upon Crane at the time when he was formulating his own literary beliefs. Heldar is an impressionistic painter and war illustrator who seeks the truth about life on the sands of the Sudan and in the slums of London. He is enthusiastic about color and uses it to evoke emotional responses. Like Heldar, Crane believed that the artist's material should be drawn from personal experience and that all experience, even if it is ugly or unpleasant, must be truthfully reported.

The most striking evidence that Crane knew *The Light That Failed* at the time of the composition of *The Red Badge of Courage* was first brought out in Scott C. Osborn's note, "Stephen Crane's Imagery: 'Pasted Like a Wafer,'" *American Literature*, XXIII (November, 1951), 362. At one point Kipling refers to the reflection of the sun as "a blood-red wafer, on the water," which strongly resembles Crane's image at the end of Chapter IX of *The Red Badge*, "the red sun was pasted in the sky like a wafer" (Colvert misquotes this image, as do many other commentators. It is probably the most frequently misquoted image in American literature). However, with the exception of general similarities such as the use of impressionistic imagery and a keen sense of the ironic, there are no other significant correspondences between *The Light that Failed* and *The Red Badge*. Kipling's book contains some battle description, but it is not at all specific. The resemblances that Colvert finds between Kipling's literary creed and Crane's confirm the strong hold of the English writer upon Crane's youthful imagination, although the use of color and fidelity to experience were advocated by a number of impressionists and realists at the end of the nineteenth century. Despite Crane's early rejection of him as a literary mentor, Kipling remained one of his lifelong favorites. There were thirteen of Kipling's books in Crane's library at Brede Place, but there was not one by Stendhal, Flaubert, Tolstoy, or Zola.

53. Cunliffe, Marcus. "Stephen Crane and the American Background of *Maggie*," *American Quarterly*, VII (Spring, 1955), 31–44.

Many literary historians have assumed that Crane read Zola's *L' Assommoir* before he wrote *Maggie* and was very much influenced by the French novelist's study of the Paris slums. Cunliffe admits that Crane's book resembles Zola's in that both deal frankly and pessimistically with human experience and reveal the overpowering effect of environment upon the city poor, but he maintains that the most obvious antecedents for *Maggie* are to be found not in Paris but in New York. Nineteenth-century American social reformers wrote voluminously about the evils of life on the Bowery and the lower East Side. Crane could have learned more details about the slums and prostitutes by reading books such as Charles Loring Brace's *The Dangerous Classes of New York* (1872) and Thomas DeWitt Talmage's *The Night Sides of City Life* (1878) than from *L' Assommoir*. Through these and other late nineteenth-century books and articles, Cunliffe shows that the factual and situational backgrounds of *Maggie* may have been drawn from popular social literature of the day.

Crane sketched out a preliminary draft of *Maggie* before beginning his exploration of the New York slums in the autumn of 1891, but the completed novelette is more indebted to his experiences as a reporter than to literary sources. Cunliffe is, however, justified in assuming that if the background for *Maggie* is to be found in books, the genteel American social-protest literature of the time offers even more convincing parallels than *L' Assommoir*. Comparison of Crane's artistic rendering of the life of the slums in *Maggie* and in his other New York sketches with the work of reformers like B. O. Flower, James McCabe, and other writers in the *Arena*, the *Century*, and the *Nation* is very revealing (cf. Entry 95). Thomas A. Gullason points out some close parallels between *Maggie* and Jacob Riis' *How the Other Half Lives* (1891) in "The Sources of Stephen Crane's *Maggie*," *Philological Quarterly*, XXXVIII (October, 1959), 497–502. Stanley Wertheim evaluates the relationship between reform literature and Crane's Bowery novelettes in the Introduction to *Studies in Maggie and George's Mother*. Columbus, Ohio: Charles E. Merrill Co., 1970.

54. Hough, Robert L. "Crane and Goethe: A Forgotten Relationship," *Nineteenth-Century Fiction*, XVII (September, 1962), 135–148.

Crane's interest in the emotional impact of color imagery may have been heightened by his reading a translation of Goethe's *Farbenlehre* while he was still a student at Syracuse University in 1891. Goethe's treatise is primarily scientific and technical, but one short section entitled "Effect of Color with Reference to Moral Associations" delineates the possible aesthetic uses of color. Hough compares and contrasts Goethe's remarks in this section with Crane's use of Color imagery, particularly in *The Red Badge of Courage*. He concludes that Crane's metaphorical adaptation of colors to various states of mind may well have been suggested by Goethe who also associated specific colors with particular feelings and realized that the juxtaposition of contrasting or complementary colors could produce powerful emotional effects.

This is a well-documented essay, but Crane's metaphorical use of color cannot be attributed to any one isolated influence. His intense interest in the emotional effects of color was at once primitive and instinctive and an aspect of the impressionism of his time. Goethe's symbolic associations for particular colors were, like Crane's largely conventional. As Hough exemplifies them, for both writers yellow in its pure state suggests gaiety or excitement but when sullied or pale connotes ugliness or death; red almost always stands for violence, anger, or other heightened emotions. That light and color against darkness or the contrast of colors may produce startling effects is also common knowledge which Crane might readily have derived from observation or from the literary theories of Hamlin Garland whose writings on aesthetics he began to read only shortly after he read Goethe. Cf. Entries 23, 37, and 85.

55. Kindilien, Carlin T. "Stephen Crane and the 'Savage Philosophy' of Olive Schreiner," *Boston University Studies in English*, III (Summer, 1957), 97–107.

Hamlin Garland first suggested the thematic similarity between Crane's curious verse epigrams and the "savage philosophy" of the South African feminist writer Olive Schreiner. While Garland was probably thinking of her autobiographical novel, *The Story of an African Farm* (1883), which resembles Crane's poetry in its cosmic pessimism, iconoclasm, and distinction between internal and external religion, Kindilien's study is focused primarily upon the correspondence between Miss Schreiner's volume of didactic prose allegories, *Dreams* (1891), and the poetry of *The Black Riders* and *War Is Kind*. The basic resemblance is in the motif of a symbolic journey through a wasteland described as a dark place to the mountains which are bathed in light. Kindilien also describes verbal echoes and themes and situations in *Dreams* which may have inspired Crane.

The author of this study probably did not have access to the typescript of Corwin K. Linson's memoirs (Entry 13) where there is substantiating evidence for his assumption that Crane was familiar with the works of Olive Schreiner. Linson recalls that Crane read *The Story of an African Farm* and was impressed with Miss Schreiner's artistry and good sense. He may have had her allegories in mind when he conceived his poems, but it is more probable that he intended to write ironic commentaries upon Biblical parables and statements. From Miss Schreiner's *Dreams* Crane could have derived his technique of personifying abstract qualities and emotions and his characteristic imagery of mountains and valleys, the sea, gardens and deserts, although these are also typically Biblical. Kindilien cites a substantial number of parallels of theme and imagery between Olive Schreiner's prose and Crane's poetry, but since he provides few extended quotations from Miss Schreiner's novel or sentimental fables, it is difficult for the reader to determine the extent of her influence on Crane without consulting them.

56. Kwiat, Joseph J. "Stephen Crane and Painting," *American Quarterly*, IV (Winter, 1952), 331–338.

Crane was personally acquainted with graphic artists during his early years in New York. Most of the inhabitants of the old Art Students' League building on East Twenty-Third Street where he lived in the winter of 1893–1894 were young men struggling to attain reputations in the arts. This setting and several of these men appear in *The Third Violet* and in one or two of Crane's newspaper sketches. Kwiat attempts to demonstrate that Crane's impressionism was an outgrowth of his relationship with painters and that he made use of their artistic methods in early sketches for the New York *Tribune* and in later stories such as "An Experiment in Misery" and "The Pace of Youth." It is also suggested that Crane formulated his own artistic principles by analogy with his knowledge of the aesthetic problems of the painter and that, as he indicated in "War Memories," he was attempting to do in thought what the French impressionists did in color.

Few of Crane's studio associates mentioned by Kwiat were actually painters. R. G. Vosburgh, Nelson Greene, Frederick Gordon, W. W. Carroll, and Edward S. Hamilton were undistinguished illustrators. David Ericson did not begin painting until after his association with Crane had ended. Corwin K. Linson, who was more closely associated with Crane in the years of his literary apprenticeship than any other artist denied emphatically that Crane's color sense depended upon a knowledge of painting (*My Stephen Crane*, Entry 13, p. 46). Kwiat insists that one cannot differentiate sharply between painters and illustrators in the late nineteenth century. But the major American magazines and newspapers of the 1890's did not use color illustrations, and the effect of the impressionistic method depends almost entirely upon the diffusion and shading of colors. Finally, the density of color imagery in many of the Sullivan County pieces is almost as great as in *The Red Badge of Courage*, and they were written before Crane became involved with graphic artists other than his sister Mary Helen who taught art classes in Asbury Park and his childhood friend Phebe English who was an amateur painter.

57. O'Donnell, Thomas F. "John B. Van Petten: Stephen Crane's History Teacher," *American Literature*, XXVII (May, 1955), 196–202.

A possible connection between *The Red Badge of Courage* and Claverack College, the preparatory school which Crane attended, lies in the fact that the professor of history and elocution at the school was the Reverend General John B. Van Petten, a known raconteur of Civil War stories. In a previous essay, Lyndon U. Pratt pointed out that Van Petten, as chaplain of the 34th New York Volunteers (a number suggestive of Henry Fleming's fictional 304th Regiment) had witnessed the retreat of that regiment at the Battle of Antietam and may have spoken of this experience to his military-minded young charges at Claverack, thus providing a source for some of the incidents in *The Red Badge* ("A Possible Source of *The Red Badge of Courage*," *American Literature*, XI [March, 1939], 1–10). O'Donnell corroborates Pratt's argument with further details of Van Petten's military career. After the Battle of Antietam Van Petten became Lieutenant Colonel of the 160th New York Volunteer Regiment and was subsequently appointed its permanent commander. In his new post Van Petten was no longer a chaplain but a combat officer, and again, at the battle of Winchester, he witnessed a rout and saw foot soldiers running in terror from the enemy. O'Donnell feels that Crane, as a student in Van Petten's history class, would have listened intently to the General's accounts of the bloody battles at Antietam and Winchester.

Van Petten was an eyewitness to the panic of American soldiers on a battlefield, but it seems unlikely that as a Union general, a minister of the Gospel, and a teacher of American history he would enlarge upon this topic before boys in whom he was attempting to instill the virtues of fortitude and patriotism. There is little to substantiate his influence upon *The Red Badge*. What is more probable (as O'Donnell shows in a subsequent essay) is that Van Petten introduced Crane to the writings of John W. De Forest, with whom he had been comrades-in-arms in western Louisiana during the spring of 1863 and again at the Battle of Winchester in the autumn of 1864. De Forest was the author of a number of autobiographical battle accounts in *Harper's Magazine*. some of which were incorporated into his novel, *Miss Ravenel's Conversion* (1867). The articles and the novel present a subjective portrayal of the ghastly details of battle and the agony of the field hospital. *Miss Ravenel's Conversion* is also the first American war novel in which a central character confesses to fear and individual soldiers are described fleeing in panic from the front lines. Crane could have learned a great deal about the emotions of men at war from it. See Thomas F. O'Donnell, "De Forest, Van Petten, and Stephen Crane," *American Literature*, XXVII (January, 1956), 578–580.

58. Osborn, Neal J. "William Ellery Channing and *The Red Badge of Courage*," *Bulletin of the New York Public Library*, LXIX (March, 1965), 182–196.

Through parallels between William Ellery Channing's 1816 sermon on "War" and *The Red Badge of Courage*, Osborn tries to show that Channing's attacks on military courage as a virtue were an important influence upon the theme of Crane's war novel. Evidence from other discourses of Channing and Crane's short stories and poems is cited when considered relevant. Channing and Crane both debunked military courage, which they considered the outgrowth of ignorance and barbarism. Universal Christianity was Channing's remedy for the evils of war, although, like Crane, he realized that historically religion had failed to maintain peace. Both writers felt that the continuance of war in Christian civilizations depended upon wrong concepts of heroism and glory, and both insisted upon the primacy of intellect and conscience in the conversion to the gospel of peace.

Osborne acknowledges that the evidence for Channing's influence upon Crane is entirely inferential, and the "parallels" offered in this essay are for the most part so inexact that they are little more than vague similarities in attitude. Crane never mentioned Channing in his writings or letters, and it is highly improbable that he would have devoted close study to the works of a Unitarian minister whose temperament and concerns were so foreign to his own. General similarities between the ideas of the two writers about the nature of courage and war do not in themselves indicate the influence of one upon the other, particularly when these speculations are neither original nor profound.

59. Solomon, Eric. "Another Analogue for 'The Red Badge of Courage,'" *Nineteenth-Century Fiction*, XIII (June, 1958), 63–67.

Joseph Kirkland's *The Captain of Company K* (1891) is noteworthy in the development of realistic American fiction, because it is one of the first of our war novels in which a high-minded hero not only fails to lead his men to a glorious victory but actually trembles with fear and makes every effort to avoid the fighting. We do not know whether Crane read *The Captain of Company K*, but it is possible that the novel was recommended to him by Hamlin Garland who had encouraged Kirkland to develop his realistic fiction. Solomon shows that Kirkland's protagonist, William Faregon, follows the same path of development as Henry Fleming, beginning with pride and passing through doubt of his courage, acute fear before the first experience of battle, unnoticed cowardice, and final bravery as he becomes a veteran. He is almost as introspective as Henry and frequently broods about the brutality of war and the indifference of nature. In contrast to the romantic hero of conventional war fiction, Faregon is very much afraid of being wounded or killed. Like Henry he is accidentally wounded, and upon rejoining his company he is asked whether he has been hit by a bullet; in contrast to Henry he refuses to gain the respect of his fellows with an accidental injury and does not take credit for a combat wound.

Solomon believes that Kirkland's novel and other late nineteenth century American works of fiction should be considered as analogues to *The Red Badge of Courage* rather than as sources. Yet, Crane could have learned as much about the feelings of men in battle from De Forest's *Miss Ravenel's Conversion*, Bierce's *Tales of Soldiers and Civilians*, or *The Captain of Company K* as from books by Stendhal, Flaubert, Tolstoy, or Zola. It seems reasonable to assume that he would more easily find inspiration in books dealing with the American Civil War and with a character type into which he could project his own protagonist than in novels having their setting in France, Russia, or Carthage. With the possible exception of Bierce's *Tales*, however, we cannot conclude with certainty that Crane was influenced by any single work of American war fiction, although there is sufficient evidence to indicate that his general conception of the development of an unsophisticated youth into a veteran through immersion in battle was an outgrowth of his familiarity with autobiographical Civil War narratives (see Entry 60).

60. Webster, H. T. "Wilbur F. Hinman's *Corporal Si Klegg* and Stephen Crane's *The Red Badge of Courage*," *American Literature*, XI (November, 1939), 285–293.

By the time that Crane came to write *The Red Badge of Courage* there were literally thousands of personal memoirs of the Civil War, often semi-fictional in nature, which traced the adventures of a recruit from the time of his enlistment through the battles of the Army of the Potomac or the Army of the Cumberland. Webster describes many similarities of conception and factual details between *The Red Badge* and one of these fictionalized chronicles, Wilbur F. Hinman's *Corporal Si Klegg and His "Pard"* (1887). Each book shows the development of a farm boy from a recruit into a battle-hardened veteran. Among parallels of incident it is noted that after their enlistment both Henry Fleming and Si go through a period of training that largely dispels their romantic notions of war. Each boy has a tall soldier as a companion. Si finds it necessary to dispose of certain superfluous articles during his first long march, while Henry and his comrades completely discard their knapsacks on their way to battle. The night before the first encounter with the enemy both lie awake and doubt their courage, but each later distinguishes himself by seizing a flag from a falling standard bearer.

These parallels are impressive, but Webster apparently failed to realize that *Corporal Si Klegg* exists in a tradition of semi-autobiographical Civil War narratives and that the incidents embodied in it are commonplaces of such accounts. These narratives usually emphasize the "development" theme, depicting the transformation of a young man from a raw recruit into a veteran. By 1890 many examples of the *genre* such as Frank Wilkeson's *Recollections of a Private Soldier in the Army of the Potomac* (1887) and Warren Lee Goss's *Recollections of a Private* (1890) were enjoying popularity with both juvenile and adult readers (see C. E. Dornbusch, *Regimental Publications and Personal Narratives of the Civil War: A Checklist*, New York Public Library, 1961–1967). Crane, with his lifelong interest in war and in the lives of soldiers, would undoubtedly have read and remembered more than one of them. *The Red Badge of Courage* is an outgrowth of this autobiographical tradition, but one need not assume, as Webster does, that any one chronicle served as a direct source. Marvin Klotz mentions two other Civil War narratives in "Crane's *The Red Badge of Courage*," *Notes and Queries*, VI (February, 1959), 68–69.

Maggie, George's Mother, and The Monster:

61. Brennan, Joseph X. "The Imagery and Art of *George's Mother*," *College Language Association Journal*, IV (December, 1960), 106–115.

The rendering of experience through the consciousness of central characters while the omniscience and objectivity of the narrator are retained is characteristic of Crane's impressionistic method. Brennan finds a pattern of evolvement in the imagery of *George's Mother* from the conflict of romantic illusions to a final struggle between harsh realities. At the beginning of the novelette both George and his mother visualize his destiny and the obstacles confronting him in terms of heroic-chivalric movements and settings. George's dream world is shattered when he is spurned by Maggie Johnson, who has become the fair princess of his imagination, and he seeks solace in debauchery. The struggle between mother and son becomes representative of the opposition between the church and the hedonistic modern world, between the old morality and license. The failure of the church to convert George, prefigured by the symbolic placing of the little chapel, "humbly between two towering apartment houses" and confronted by the brilliant lights and roaring noises of a city street, transposes the struggle between his mother and himself into a final battle of faith against nihilism. The defeat of Mrs. Kelcey's dreams and her death precipitates George's awakening into a world of terrifying reality, symbolized by the inexorable ticking of a nickle-plated clock upon the kitchen shelf.

William Dean Howells praised the artistry as well as the honesty and compassion of *George's Mother* in his review of "New York Low Life in Fiction" for the New York *World* (July 26, 1896, p. 18), but no critical exegesis of the novelette appeared from the time of its publication in 1896 until this essay. Brennan shows incisively that *George's Mother* is at once more realistic and convincing and more psychologically penetrating than *Maggie* and that it deserves to be reclaimed from the neglect into which it has inexplicably fallen. Crane's own mother was, like Mrs. Kelcey, a strong-willed, moralistic woman, a member of the W.C.T.U. who struggled vainly to keep her Bohemian youngest son within the church. Significantly

George's Mother was first entitled "A Woman Without Weapons." Brennan's study reveals that from these autobiographical fragments Crane constructed one of his most artful works of fiction. The theme of *George's Mother*, the shattering of man's romantic illusions through involvement with reality, is prevalent in much of Crane's work, and here it is treated with a pathos which never degenerates into sentimentality. The relationship between mother and son is explored through an elaborately evolving image pattern, but the sense of immediacy and reality is not violated. See also Maurice Bassan, "An Early Draft of *George's Mother*," *American Literature* XXXVI (January, 1965), 518–522 and Agnes M. Jackson, "Stephen Crane's Imagery of Conflict in *George's Mother*,"*Arkansas Quarterly*, XXV (Winter,1969), 313–318.

62. Brennan, Joseph X. "Ironic and Symbolic Structure in Crane's *Maggie*," *Nineteenth-Century Fiction*, XVI (March, 1962), 303–315.

Maggie has received widespread recognition as a landmark of literary naturalism and has been the subject of a number of good general evaluations, but this essay offers the first extended analysis of the novelette as a work of art. Brennan focuses attention upon the ironic and symbolic structure of the book. Crane's structural method in *Maggie* consists primarily of ironic inversions of single terms and the interlinking of situations and chapters through the ironic inversion of a significant phrase or circumstance. Chapters XV and XVI, for example, are connected by the fact that Jimmie's callous repudiation of Hattie anticipates and is a parody of Pete's rejection of Maggie. Chapter XVII, in which Maggie's decline is symbolically telescoped, is closely related to the following chapter in which Pete's degeneration is also shown to be inevitable. The central irony of the novelette, from which all the particular ironies emanate, is the condemnation of a woman by the very society that has destroyed her.

Brennan's detailed analysis of the structure of *Maggie* shows that Crane was from the beginning a careful and deliberate artist. This essay also explores minor symbolic patterns in the novelette such as the relationship between Jimmie's ambivalent attitudes toward fire engines and toward his mother and the emotional significance of the lambrequin and blue ribbons with which Maggie attempts to make her home more cheerful. Attention is directed to the thematic significance of these symbols and their contribution to the total meaning of the book. See also Janet Overmyer, "The Structure of Crane's *Maggie*," *University of Kansas City Review*, XXIX (October, 1962), 71–72.

63. Fitelson, David. "Stephen Crane's *Maggie* and Darwinism," *American Quarterly*, XVI (Summer, 1964), 182–194.

Fitelson identifies the ideology of *Maggie* with a rigorous Darwinistic determinism. The Darwinism of the novelette does not resemble the evolutionary meliorism of nineteenth-century social reformers or the optimistic assurances of the apologists for the robber barons that their business methods would result in the survival of the fittest. Instead, *Maggie* presents a pessimistic atavism in which the struggle for existence occurs on an animal level, and violence is the predominant form of communication. All of the characters are aware of the absolute value of survival. Fitelson believes that Maggie's downfall is attributable to a dual vision which causes her to engage in futile dreams of escape to a world of beauty and compassion, despite the fact that she understands the need for struggle in the actual world.

It is unlikely that Crane read Darwin's *The Origin of Species* or even the writings of the social Darwinists, but the survival of the fittest was an idea firmly implanted in the popular consciousness by the end of the nineteenth century, and Crane could not have escaped exposure to the Darwinian world view. Fitelson places a great deal of emphasis upon Maggie's vision of a more beautiful world, but in the novelette this is evident only in a few pathetic incidents. Moreover, he insists that she commits suicide because she "has retained a fatal measure of her vision of the other world, and it now appears to her unreasoning consciousness that escape to it can be accomplished only by means of a forcible exit from the actual one" (p. 193). However, Chapter XVII, in which Maggie descends to the river, does not describe a single incident but is a syncopated account of her entire career as a prostitute. She begins successful and well-dressed in the Tenderloin district of the city but is gradually debased to a point where she can solicit only the most depraved denizens of the waterfront. In Darwinian terms, she loses the struggle for survival, and she drowns herself because she is unable to endure further degradation.

64. Hafley, James. "'The Monster' and the Art of Stephen Crane," *Accent*, XIX (Summer, 1959), 159–165.

Little critical attention has been given to Crane's Whilomville novelette, "The Monster." Hafley, who is among the first to apply the methods of textual analysis to the work, believes that it is primarily concerned with "an examination of American values conducted largely in terms of a paradoxical handling of the appearance-reality motif" (p. 159). The central action of the story consists of losing face, Henry Johnson having literally lost his face in the struggle to rescue Dr. Trescott's young son from a burning house. But Hafley explains that those who lose face in the story ultimately save face, while those who attempt to retain a frigid respectability are dehumanized. The face-saving images are intermingled with light-darkness and impression-fact contrasts which reinforce Crane's point that moral and social values cannot be reconciled. Both Henry and Dr. Trescott attain personal fulfillment in acts of social responsibility, but paradoxically their acceptance of such responsibility destroys their position in society. Crane's heroes often express individuality through social acts which leave them isolated but aware of their manhood.

In this illuminating essay, Hafley stresses the skillful patterning and thematic richness of "The Monster." The novelette does not lack unity, as a number of previous commentators have assumed. It is a well-developed social satire in which the ambiguity of the monster symbol becomes apparent as it is gradually transferred from the mutilated but saintly Henry Johnson to the collective citizenry of Whilomville. For a short but penetrating explication of the symbols of the story, see Thomas A. Gullason, "The Symbolic Unity of 'The Monster,'" *Modern Language Notes*, LXXV (December, 1960), 663–668.

65. Pizer, Donald. "Stephen Crane's 'Maggie' and American Naturalism," *Criticism*, VII (Spring, 1965), 168–175.

Critics have noted that Maggie, who "blossomed in a mud puddle," remains curiously innocent despite the degradations forced upon her by her environment (cf. Entry 16, p. 110). In this essay, a portion of his book, *Realism and Naturalism in Nineteenth-Century American Literature* (1966), Pizer develops this point in order to identify Crane's uniqueness in the continuous tradition of American naturalism. According to Pizer, *Maggie* is primarily a study in the false application of abstract, middle-class values to the amoral environment of the animalistic slum world. Despite the chaos of their existence, the Johnsons and Maggie's lover Pete uphold an ethic of responsibility. Maggie is not destroyed by her physical environment, the tenement, and the sweat-shop, but by the hypocritical morality of the slums. Thus, "Crane's focus in *Maggie* is less on the inherent evil of slum life than on the harm done by a false moral environment imposed on that life" (p. 174). This stress on social values in the novelette allies Crane's naturalism with the critical realism of William Dean Howells and at the same time illustrate Crane's individuality within naturalistic conventions.

The main argument of this essay, that *Maggie* is an attack upon smug self-righteousness and the application of unrealistic moral imperatives to the atavistic world of Devil's Row, is well supported by examples from the novelette. Pizer singles out the melodramatic attempts of the characters to project themselves into virtuous roles: In dance hall and theater scenes the Bowery audience applauds idealistic values unrelated to their own conditions of existence. Attempting to gain social approval, Mary Johnson and Jimmie assume sanctimonious postures and express their abhorrence of Maggie's degradation. The mission or church, like the theater, adopts moral postures which ignore the nature of its congregation. One should also remember David Fitelson's point (Entry 63) that beneath these postures no true distinction between right and wrong action exists in the Darwinian world of the novelette other than an unconscious approval of those actions which insure survival. Cf. Malcolm Bradbury, "Romance and Reality in *Maggie*," *Journal of American Studies*, III (July, 1969), 111–121.

66. Pizer, Donald. Introduction to *Maggie: A Girl of the Streets*. San Francisco: Chandler Publishing Co., 1968.

This introduction to an attractive facsimile edition of the 1893 *Maggie* (bound in paper as was the original) presents an intelligent discussion of the novelette's biographical and historical backgrounds and its relevance as a work of art. *Maggie* marks a transitional phase, both in Crane's career and in the fiction of the 1890's. It reveals the tensions of Crane's conflicting postures as Bohemian rebel and as a practitioner of the Strenuous Life. Pizer explains that while Crane accepted the tenets of environmental determinism, *Maggie* is not a document in the literature of social reform but an ironic comment on "the relationship of self-satisfying moral and romantic roles to the actualities of experience" (p. XXVI, cf. Entry 65).

Crane probably did sketch out a story about a prostitute while he was a student at Syracuse University in the spring of 1891, but Pizer concludes that *Maggie* as we know it was written almost entirely in the autumn and winter of 1892–1893, after Crane had absorbed William Dean Howells' theory of literary realism as enunciated and embellished by Hamlin Garland and had personally experienced life on the Bowery. In his attempt to resolve conflicting accounts of the composition of *Maggie*, Pizer ignores the probability that Garland saw an intermediate manuscript of the novelette before it appeared as a privately-printed book. This is a controversial question, and there is some confusion in Pizer's dating and interpretation of an important note from Garland to Richard Watson Gilder, editor of the *Century*. Garland recommended *Maggie* for publication in the *Century*, and the note probably concerns the penultimate and final drafts of *Maggie* and not a manuscript of *The Black Riders* for which Crane putatively substituted *The Red Badge of Courage*. See Stanley Wertheim, "Garland, Gilder and Crane: The Saga of March 23rd.," *Stephen Crane Newsletter*, III (Winter, 1968, pp. 1–3 and Spring, 1969, p. 1).

67. Stallman, Robert W. "Stephen Crane's Revision of *Maggie: A Girl of the Streets*," *American Literature*, XXVI (January, 1955), 528–536.

Maggie was first privately printed by Crane under the pseudonym of Johnston Smith in March, 1893. It remained almost entirely unnoticed and was not formally published until 1896, when the success of *The Red Badge of Courage* had assured a reading public for Crane's fiction. Stallman collates these first two editions of the novelette and shows that when Crane revised *Maggie* for publication by Appleton, he excised much blasphemy and profanity which violated nineteenth-century standards of decorum. The syntax, orthography, and punctuation of the book were corrected, so that stylistically the 1896 version is in many ways an improvement. However, a great deal of forceful and picturesque language was lost. The style was somewhat emasculated through the substitution of relatively weak exclamations for the numerous swear words, and a number of striking descriptive phrases were flattened. In Chapter XVII, where Maggie descends to the river, an encounter with "a huge fat man in torn and greasy garments" was omitted. Stallman believes that this passage deserves to be reincorporated into future editions of the novelette because of its artistic relevance to what precedes and follows it.

Stallman's account of the similarities and differences between the privately printed 1893 *Maggie* and the first American edition published by Appleton is a comprehensive and accurate synopsis of more than 300 variants. The excision of the leering fat man in the symbolic chapter which culminates in Maggie's suicide is obviously the most significant change which Crane made. Stallman feels that this passage should have been retained, because the fat man's attribute of "dead jelly fish" anticipates and prepares for Maggie's death by drowning. William M. Gibson, on the other hand, considers the omission of this passage an artistic necessity, since it would have destroyed the unity of the chapter by implying that Maggie might accept the disgusting fat man (Entry 25, Third Edition, pp. xxi–xxii). Gibson points out that in the revised text of the novelette, Maggie ignores both the "man with blotched features" and "ragged being with shifting bloodshot eyes and grimy hands," indicating clearly that she will not allow herself to sink to the level of soliciting such depraved individuals. By cutting her dialogue with these last two men and omitting the encounter with the fat man altogether, Crane removed the ambiguity that the original version introduced and underscored Maggie's decision to drown herself rather than endure greater shame. For a persuasive counterargument which stresses that Crane's revisions, made at the demand of Appleton's agent, Ripley Hitchcock, violated the artistic integrity of the novelette, see Joseph Katz, "The *Maggie* Nobody Knows," *Modern Fiction Studies*, XII (Summer, 1966), 200–212. Katz has produced a facsimile edition of the original *Maggie* (Scholars' Facsimiles and Reprints, 1966). A number of paperback editions of the 1893 version are also now available. Cf. Entry 66.

68. Stallman, Robert W. "Crane's 'Maggie': A Reassessment," *Modern Fiction Studies*, V (Autumn, 1959), 251–259.

Maggie retains its impact as literature despite the fact that it is a sentimental melodrama and is very much outdated as a social study. The explanation for this paradox, Stallman concludes, is that *Maggie* is a work of art as well as an exemplar of literary naturalism. The theme of the novelette is that human lives are shaped by their environment, which in this instance is composed of cowardly individuals and corrupt social institutions such as the church, the mission, the factory, and the saloon. Stallman asserts that *Maggie* has a definite structure in which each part is integral to the meaning of the whole but feels that the episodes and images are related by alternations of contradictory moods rather than by logical patterns. As in Flaubert's *Madame Bovary*, romantic sentiments, hopes, and illusions are shattered by realities.

The analogy Stallman draws between *Maggie* and *Madame Bovary* is suggestive in that both books reveal the contradictions between illusion and reality, but it should be understood that the ironic perspectives of Flaubert and Crane are very different. Flaubert identifies with his heroine and gives her a certain amount of sympathy, while Crane remains clinically detached from Maggie who is only a shadowy cipher. Stallman devotes little attention to the formal structural devices in the novelette such as the declining order in the quality of the beer halls to which Pete takes Maggie, the pattern of gestures of withdrawal and revulsion with which the inhabitants of the Bowery world reject one another, parallel incidents and chapters, and the symbolic telescoping of Maggie's decline and suicide in Chapter XVII.

The Red Badge of Courage:

69. Cox, James T. "The Imagery of 'The Red Badge of Courage,'" *Modern Fiction Studies*, V (Autumn, 1959), 209–219.

Critics who emphasize the naturalistic aspects of *The Red Badge of Courage* focus attention upon the irony of the novel. Cox finds that the naturalism of *The Red Badge* closely parallels that of "The Blue Hotel." In both works the energy of all life ultimately originates from the heat of the sun, which plays a metaphorical and philosophical role in the war novel, and all men are engaged in a perpetual struggle for survival that places them in a hostile relationship to their environment. Cox believes that Crane ironically compares the heroes of both stories with Jesus Christ, but he feels that the religious imagery of *The Red Badge* has been misinterpreted by R. W. Stallman and agrees with Bernard Weisberger (Entry 83) that the symbolism of Christian conversion in the novel is negative. "In the ironic resemblances of Conklin to Christ, Crane is perhaps naively, but clearly and powerfully saying that in this red world Jesus Christ is a grim joke" (p. 217). The truth that Henry Fleming comes to realize after his experience of battle is that selfless heroism paradoxically emerges through egocentric animal selfishness. Cox makes a careful examination of the interacting patterns of sun and smoke symbolism, nature and color imagery, and machine and animal metaphors through which Crane develops the themes of the novel.

Cox's approach to *The Red Badge of Courage* as a complex work of art is essentially correct, although one may at times disagree with his specific applications of the technique of close textual analysis. In the examination of the sun imagery of the novel for example, Cox identifies the mounted general whom Henry Fleming encounters after his flight from the ranks with the sun, largely because the general is described as beaming upon the earth "like a sun." Even more arbitrarily, he describes Henry's red badge as "seed and sign of this same sun" (p. 213). Rather than determining the conditions of human existence, as Cox insists, the sun seems to function in very much the same way as the other nature imagery of the novel in that the various states in which it appears reflect Henry's shifting conception of reality. Cf. Entry 81.

70. Crews, Frederick C. Introduction to *The Red Badge of Courage*. Indianapolis: Bobbs-Merrill Co., 1964.

Crews discusses *The Red Badge of Courage* as a work of the not-so-gay 1890's and maintains that the tone of the novel was influenced by disillusionment with cultural values and individual virtues in an era of economic and social upheaval. Despite *The Red Badge's* oblique contemporaneity, 1895 was an inauspicious year in which to publish a realistic study of the Civil War. The romance was the most popular form of reading matter, and Crane was forced to contend against the established conventions of the genteel tradition. To illustrate the extent of Crane's realism Crews provides an account of the circumstances of the Battle of Chancellorsville and, like Harold Hungerford (Entry 75), concludes that Crane strove for historical authenticity and deliberately chose a battle that would exemplify the futility of war.

Crews refuses to view *The Red Badge* as a simple maturation story and stresses the almost consistent irony with which Henry Fleming is treated for the greater part of the novel. Henry's return to the battlefield is involuntary, and his "courage" is forced upon him by the conditions of battle; in the grip of animalistic feelings he becomes a hero. His final visions of harmony with nature are still naive, but he has at least learned the futility of his childish tirades against the order of the universe. Crews supplements his introduction with a Crane chronology, a selective bibliography of critical studies of *The Red Badge of Courage*, and maps of the Chancellorsville campaign on the three days of the battle.

Crews avoids the exclusiveness which has plagued much Crane scholarship through his critical competence and the realization that *The Red Badge* is a complex work which resists categorical definitions. Analysis of the structure and themes of the novel has often been partial and thesis-ridden, obscuring the technique of ironic paradox whereby Crane synthesized realistic, naturalistic, and symbolic approaches. Above all, Crews sees Crane as an ironist who stood apart from his work and allowed the reader to realize for himself the full ambiguity of human experience. There is perhaps an overemphasis in this essay upon the significance of Crane's use of the setting and tactics of the Battle of Chancellorsville. Crane was interested not in group but in individual psychology, and despite his realism he ignored the political and social questions of the Civil War. *The Red Badge* contains no mention of the name of a single Union or Confederate leader and does not attempt to deal with the attitudes of the soldiers toward the cause for which they are fighting. Indeed, the primary relevance of the war setting is its symbolic use in enforcing Crane's theme that the essence of all life is battle.

71. Fryckstedt, Olov W. "Henry Fleming's Tupenny Fury: Cosmic Pessimism in Stephen Crane's *The Red Badge of Courage*," *Studia Neophilologica*, XXXIII (1961), 265–281.

The holograph manuscripts of *The Red Badge of Courage* contain a number of passages of self-posturing in which Henry Fleming considers himself to be the victim of a naturalistic universe operating under a relentless law which insures the survival of the fittest. Most of these passages were excluded from the text of the first American edition, presumably because Crane abhorred preaching in art and preferred the thematic implications of his story to arise from the action itself. Fryckstedt suggests that in the excised manuscript material relating to Henry's revolt against the universe Crane is not merely deriding the presumptions of his central character but is also taking a detached and ironic point of view toward what is essentially his own philosophical position. The satire notwithstanding, Henry's convictions are close to those of the author. He is expressing the perspective which emerges from the best of Crane's fiction and poetry, and his seemingly absurd rationalizations echo the tragic plight of helpless man in an indifferent universe.

Poems in *The Black Riders*, composed almost simultaneously with *The Red Badge of Courage* or shortly afterwards, in which the individual appears as the puny victim of a wrathful and cruel Jehova give strong support to the position enunciated in this essay. Fryckstedt is a sensitive as well as a perceptive critic and understands that the themes of protest and despair are conveyed through the moods of the novel as well as through Henry Fleming's more explicit "tupenny fury." The horrors of battle are depicted with a ghastly sardonic humor which evokes pity for the helpless and insignificant soldiers victimized by gigantic, seemingly impersonal forces. In this way, Henry's impotent rage and defiance are related to the plight of all men and are given universality.

72. Greenfield, Stanley B. "The Unmistakable Stephen Crane," *PMLA*, LXXIII (December, 1958), 562–572.

Some well-known commentaries on *The Red Badge of Courage*, Greenfield points out, contain factual errors, quotations taken out of context, and serious distortions of meaning. R. W. Stallman's controversial analysis of the novel (Entries 43 and 80) is particularly vitiated by these flaws. Greenfield shows that a more accurate interpretation of *The Red Badge* may be achieved if the novel is examined in conjunction with "The Open Boat" and "The Blue Hotel." Crane's complex moral vision does not grant exclusive sway over man's destiny to environment, tradition, free will, or chance. In the short stories both volitional and deterministic views of human behavior are presented, and although they are given almost equal importance, neither is granted ultimate victory. A similar purposeful ambiguity is evident in *The Red Badge of Courage*. The soldiers in the novel make free ethical choices, but their reactions are to a large extent instinctive or conditioned by circumstances. Furthermore, in a universe in which chance plays a part the effectiveness of moral action is always uncertain.

This essay presents a sophisticated approach to Crane's aesthetic perspective and technique and makes an impressive attempt to reconcile the naturalistic and volitional points of view toward Crane's best known short stories and *The Red Badge of Courage*. Yet, in his analysis of the war novel, Greenfield does not account satisfactorily for the decided growth in moral development that he finds in Henry Fleming or for the paradox which emerges from this interpretation—that Henry becomes a responsible human being through the process of losing his human qualities in order to act as an animal in battle. A more detailed study of the "doubleness" in point of view and style that is largely responsible for the thematic complexity of

The Red Badge may be found in Robert C. Albrecht's "Content and Style in *The Red Badge of Courage*," *College English*, XXVII (March, 1966), 487–492.

73. Hart, John E. "*The Red Badge of Courage* as Myth and Symbol," *University of Kansas City Review*, XIX (Summer, 1953), 249–256.

As a primitive culture achieves sophistication, the physical embodiments of initiation ceremonies celebrating the passage of children into adult society are gradually replaced by symbolic interpretations, and ritual is elaborated into myth. The initiate is transformed into a representative hero whose journey symbolizes the struggle of his people toward cultural maturity, and his path follows the formula of the initiation ritual—separation, initiation, and return. Hart believes that *The Red Badge of Courage* embodies this traditional mythical formula and that its meaning is developed through symbolism, the language of myth. Henry Fleming's inability to face the battle monsters or to identify with his comrades symbolizes a spiritual and physical impotence which only a rebirth of identity can resolve. This spiritual resurrection is finally achieved, after many trials, in the climatic episode in which Henry is wounded by the rifle butt of a fleeing Union soldier. Despite the irony implied in such a wound, Hart insists that it represents an initiation of blood which enables Henry to atone for his cowardice and return to the regiment, not as an isolated individual but as a member. Through atonement and rebirth he becomes a hero who faces the dragons of war with fortitude.

In *The Hero with a Thousand Faces* (1949), Joseph Campbell, whom Hart cites, defines the mythological quest as the tale of a hero who ventures forth out of the world of common reality into the realm of supernatural wonders and there combats and wins a decisive victory over fabulous forces. The hero returns from this adventure with the ability to bestow benefits upon his fellow men. Clearly, *The Red Badge of Courage* lacks these essential attributes. But fragmentary mythic patterning may be found in the novel, although Hart overstates the case by maintaining that "the construction of the story, its moral and meaning, its reliance on symbol follow in detail the traditional formula of myth" (p. 249). Crane's protagonist is an uninitiated youth who is separated from the warm security of his home and childhood fantasies and is brought to the threshold of life symbolized by a world at war. The tests he must face are those of endurance and loyalty to comrades, and the reward consists of achieved security within the conventions of society, or, in anthropological terms, initiation and tribal acceptance. But Henry Fleming lacks the moral fortitude and high purpose of the mythological hero, He is no dragon slayer, no Perseus, Siegfried, or Saint George. His greatest enemies are within—the monsters of fear, self-doubt, and delusion, and, at best, he gains only a partial and ambiguous victory over them.

74. Howarth, William L. "*The Red Badge of Courage* Manuscript: New Evidence for a Critical Edition," *Studies in Bibliography*, XVIII (1965), 229–247.

A variorum text of *The Red Badge of Courage* might be established through a collation of Appleton's first edition of 1895 with the two drafts of the manuscript of the novel in the Barrett Collection at the University of Virginia's Alderman Library. The completed draft of the novel, which is 176 pages long, contains fragments of an earlier version on the reverse of 57 of the leaves. Howarth ingeniously reconstructs Crane's process of composition by distinguishing among five different types of paper that he used and noting the order of their appearance in the manuscript as well as tracing the actual changes in the text. The two manuscript drafts reveal seven different states of writing. Crane revised the truncated early draft only once after its first composition, but the completed version of the novel underwent three revisions by Crane and some final corrections by an editor or typist which consist of grammatical and typographical emendations within the text and a few marginal notations.

Crane's revision of *The Red Badge* was methodical, but Howarth does not find it to have been particularly thorough. The completed manuscript was based upon the unfinished draft which was transcribed with extensive changes and then expanded. In his revision of this final version Crane made about 80 per cent of the several hundred name changes from specific to anonymous characters which appear in the first edition, but there are some pages in which this was entirely neglected. Crane also normalized the dialect of Henry Fleming and Wilson throughout the text. He was inconsistent in revising the speech patterns of Henry's mother, Conklin, and the lieutenant and did not proceed in this beyond Chapter III. Other major revisions include the cancellation of descriptive passages and the complete removal of the bombastic Chapter XII. Five manuscript pages of this expunged chapter have been recovered and are held in various libraries; three others may be found in the early unfinished manuscript (cf. Entry 43).

Howarth concludes that the final holograph and not a lost typescript was used as copy for the typesetting; thus the variants from the manuscript which appear in the first edition are "obviously non-authorial," and "a thorough collation of both drafts and the 1895 edition would provide a complete history of the novel's revision" (p. 246). Howarth does not explain satisfactorily why he thinks it impossible that Crane introduced these variants into the proof sheets, which he is known to have corrected, but in most respects this is a brilliantly executed technical essay and one that will be indispensable to the Crane scholar until a variorum edition of *The Red Badge of Courage* is published. Discussions of the interrelationships of manuscript, newspaper versions, and first published edition of the novel may be found in Joseph Katz's introductions to his reprints of the New York *Press* appearance of *The Red Badge* on December 9, 1894 (Scholars' Facsimiles & Reprints, 1967) and Appleton's 1895 edition (Charles E. Merrill Publishing Co., 1969).

75. Hungerford, Harold R. "'That Was at Chancellorsville'; The Factual Framework of *The Red Badge of Courage*," *American Literature*, XXXIV (January, 1963), 520–531.

Since *The Red Badge of Courage* is primarily an internal narrative centered upon changing emotional states, little attention is devoted to tactical and circumstantial matters of war. The occasional descriptions of places and events given, however, follow closely the details of the Battle of Chancellorsville. Crane never identified the setting of the battle within the novel (except for Henry Fleming's sardonic "quotation from newspapers," drowned out by the roar of guns, "'All quiet on the Rappahannock'"), but his contemporaries were very much aware of the fact that Chancellorsville was intended, and Crane himself made this explicit in a short story, "The Veteran" (1896). Hungerford's essay demonstrates in detail how Crane utilized the events of the Battle of Chancellorsville as the setting for *The Red Badge.* Although no specific Union regiment may be identified with Henry Fleming's 304th New York, broad parallels may be drawn with the movements and activities of many regiments in the Second Corps, which was near the center of the Union line. Hungerford shows that certain episodes in the novel are readily identified with actual incidents at Chancellorsville. Henry Fleming probably received his head wound during the disastrous rout of the Eleventh Corps, and the retreat of the Union forces toward the Rappahannock River with which *The Red Badge* ends corresponds to the concluding events of the Chancellorsville campaign.

The parallels delineated in this essay between the incidents depicted in *The Red Badge of Courage* and the events of the Battle of Chancellorsville reinforce the view that Crane was consistent in the practice as well as the advocacy of circumstantial realism. Most likely, Crane derived the factual details incorporated into the novel from the bound volumes of Century's *Battles and Leaders of the Civil War* (1888), which he borrowed from Mrs. Olive Armstrong in the spring of 1893, and he may have gone to Fredericksburg, Virginia in May to visit the battlefield. *Battles and Leaders* describes the strategy of the Chancellorsville campaign in detail. An eyewitness report by John L. Collins, a trooper in the Eighth Pennsylvania Cavalry, contains an impressionistic account of the rout of the Eleventh Army Corps by Stonewall Jackson's forces. General Howard's efforts to rally his troops is portrayed in a half-page illustration in Collins' narrative, and there are striking similarities between Crane's and Collins' description of a hatless general vainly attempting to halt the flight of a mob of demoralized soldiers. Several other illustrations in *Battles and Leaders* must have been extremely suggestive to Crane. One sketch shows the right wing of the Union army crossing the Rappahannock in long snake-like columns over a pontoon bridge. In another illustration a private of the Eleventh Corps is seen fleeing from the enemy as an officer attempts to drive him back to the firing line with the flat of his sword. The plank road mentioned in *The Red Badge* appears in several illustrations and so does the tangled, thicket-ridden countryside around Chancellorsville.

76. Klotz, Marvin. "Romance or Realism?: Plot, Theme, and Character in *The Red Badge of Courage*," *College Language Association Journal*, VI (December, (1962), 98–106.

Klotz rejects both the symbolistic and naturalistic readings of *The Red Badge of*

Courage and considers the novel to be a realistic study of ordinary men at war. Its theme is the essential sameness of human behavior. Henry Fleming is the epitome of the common man and shares the anonymity of his comrades. Unlike the hero of romantic fiction, his personality is not neatly formulated and mechanically exemplified but is developed in the stress of experience. Henry's chivalric conceptions of war, initial courage, and panicky flight, as well as his heroism on the second day of battle, depict the motivations and reactions of the common soldier realistically for the first time in American war fiction. While Klotz does not ignore the irony at the conclusion of the novel, he discounts the importance that some critics have attributed to it and stresses that Crane's sympathy with the rationalizations of ordinary men prevented him from judging Henry's foibles. This sympathy with humanity is rarely found in nineteenth-century war fiction, and Klotz feels that it is the most realistic attribute of the novel.

This is an intelligent delineation of the essential realism of *The Red Badge of Courage*, but the statement that the book has "an unequivocally happy ending" (p. 100) is surely an oversimplification. A number of critics have remarked that the conclusion very much resembles the opening chapters in that Henry Fleming's longing for "soft and eternal peace" is as immature and unrealistic as his earlier romantic visions of broken-bladed glory. There is a quantitative lessening of the irony as the novel draws to a close, but Crane still views his protagonist as a deluded youth, a victim of self-deception who has failed to resolve the contradictions in his thoughts, feelings, and actions. There seems to be a mocking quality rather than a deep human sympathy in Crane's treatment of Henry's later musings. His happiness is based upon a feeling of superiority to his comrades rather than an empathy with them, and his pride is restored through a false evaluation of his spurious red badge of courage. "He had performed his mistakes in the dark, so he was still a man." Crane does not allow Henry to realize the absurdity of his final position, but his self-satisfaction is a sham which illustrates the conceit of man at which Crane marvelled in "The Blue Hotel."

77. LaFrance, Marston. "Stephen Crane's *Private Fleming: His Various Battles*," in *Patterns of Commitment in American Literature*, ed. Marston LaFrance. Toronto: University of Toronto Press, 1967, pp. 113–133.

"Private Fleming: His various battles" appears as the original title (crossed out) in the manuscript of *The Red Badge of Courage*. "Battles" in this sense may be internal as well as external, and LaFrance considers the novel essentially the inner narrative of an imaginative and sensitive person's striving for self-knowledge and moral growth amid the vicissitudes of experience. Crane's stress upon personal honesty as the only certain way to realize one's individuality in a formless and amoral universe found embodiment in the developing personality of Henry Fleming. The central subject of *The Red Badge* is "the weak mental machinery as it labours under the stress of some emotion, usually fear, to perceive correctly an area of reality which is not yet within the compass of the protagonist's experience" (p. 115). Realization and acceptance of limitations and the ability to fulfill one's commitments within them is, LaFrance contends, Crane's implicit definition of maturity.

Henry's private battles toward self-awareness and a balanced view of the external world are carefully set forth in this essay. Yet, LaFrance tends to be highly selective, and at times exclusive, in the passages he cites to illustrate the course of the protagonist's mental debates in his development toward maturity. Continuous suggestions in the novel, particularly in the final chapter, that authentic self-knowledge is beyond human realization and that Henry's belief that he has become a complete man is a delusion are dismissed too lightly. It is indeed puzzling that while LaFrance considers Crane primarily an ironist, one who maintains a double vision of reality, he is unable to find even a trace of such irony in the ambiguous concluding paragraphs of *The Red Badge of Courage* which describe Henry Fleming's change of soul. But, as Clark Griffith puts it, "if Henry succeeds in fooling himself (and, apparently, some of his critics), Stephen Crane knows better" (Entry 26, p. 89).

78. Marcus, Mordecai, "The Unity of *The Red Badge of Courage*," in *The Red Badge of Courage: Text and Criticism*, ed. Richard Lettis, *et al.* New York: Harcourt, Brace & Co., 1960, pp. 189–195.

The greatest critical problem in the thematic and structural analysis of *The Red Badge of Courage* remains the question of whether the novel is a maturation story or an ironic study in self-delusion. Marcus believes that the discrepancies in the unity of the book are caused by Henry Fleming's sudden and inexplicable insight into his behavior, the departure from naturalism which this entails, and the irony with which Henry is still treated in the final chapter. Whatever unity exists in *The Red Badge* is achieved through repetition of images, ideas, and actions; the protagonist's changing relationships to himself and to others; and the patterns of dramatic irony and irony of manner. Marcus acknowledges that the courage which Henry shows on the second day of battle is chiefly instinctual. Yet, he concludes that the excisions from the manuscript of the novel reveal that although Crane vacillated between portraying a chastened and matured hero and one who is still deluded, his final choice "was to present a Henry who has accepted his place in the universe and thus become a man" (p. 194).

Marcus realizes that the theme and plot of *The Red Badge of Courage* are not well integrated and the conclusion is problematic. He does not attempt to reconcile the contradictions presented by the novel with a facile explanation. In view of the consistent counterpointing of instinctive behavior and self-delusion with which Henry Fleming has been treated in the course of the novel, his attainment of insight in the final chapter is difficult to accept. It is as poorly motivated as his bravery in battle after his return to the regiment or as Wilson's precipitous transformation from a loud soldier into a humble one. Somehow, the experience of war has been a death and rebirth of the understanding for Henry, but Crane wavered in his decision whether or not to show growth of any type in his protagonist. A number of the passages excised from the final chapter of the manuscript, as well as some remaining in the published text, reveal strong irony of manner in Henry's concept of self and his relationship to others and to the universe.

79. Solomon, Eric. "The Structure of 'The Red Badge of Courage,'" *Modern Fiction Studies*, V (Autumn, 1959), 220–234.

Interpretations of *The Red Badge of Courage* as a Christian redemption allegory or as spiritual autobiography are rejected by Solomon who examines the novel as a realistic war story with a maturation theme. This essay delineates a threefold development in the pattern of growing and realized maturity. Crane first portrays the psychological journey of his protagonist from a foolish romantic pride, through depths of fear, to a realization of his place in the military scheme. When Henry Fleming rejoins his comrades, this cycle is repeated as the untried regiment undergoes its collective test of fear and the recapture of confidence in battle. Finally, the regiment and Henry unite to function no longer as initiates but as veterans. Solomon recognizes Crane's ambiguous attitude toward his hero throughout the novel but discounts all ironic readings of the concluding chapter and insists that Henry Fleming, through his participation in this threefold journey, emerges as a mature individual and member of society.

In view of the ironic attitude with which Crane treats Henry in the greater part of the novel, and which he does not abandon in the last chapter, the pattern of advancing maturity does not appear to be as straightforward as Solomon describes it. Crane mitigated this irony somewhat by cancelling or expunging many manuscript passages of absurd self-posturing in which Henry considers himself the victim of a naturalistic universe operating in terms of a relentless law of the survival of the fittest. Without the philosophy of tooth and claw which Henry expounds in these extirpated passages, however, there is an apparent lack of motivation for his sudden transformation from cowardice to heroism which constitutes a serious flaw in the construction of *The Red Badge* and is largely responsible for the continuing critical disagreement over whether or not Crane has written a maturation story.

Thomas M. Lorch's "The Cyclical Structure of *The Red Badge of Courage*," *College Language Association Journal*, X (March, 1967), 229–238 more or less reiterates Solomon's concept of the structure of the novel as interlocking spirals of experience emphasizing the integration of the individual with his group as the touchstone of maturity. Lorch is less categorical than Solomon about Henry Fleming's final loss of heroic ideals, and he feels that the cyclical patterns suggest "that the problems inherent in the individual's relations to war, to society, and to his own illusions, are endless" (p. 238). See also John W. Rathbun, "Structure and Meaning in *The Red Badge of Courage*," *Ball State University Forum*, X (Winter, 1969), 8–16.

80. Stallman, Robert W. Introduction to *The Red Badge of Courage*. New York: Random House, 1951.

This important introduction, incorporated with some additions and variations into Stallman's Crane *Omnibus* (Entry 43), precipitated a ten-year controversy over the structure and themes of *The Red Badge of Courage*. Stallman characterizes the style of the novel as "prose pointillism" and the structure as an episodic grouping of contradictory moods which alternate between illusion and reality, fact and fantasy, coalescing finally into a single unified effect. Thematically, Stallman argues, *The Red Badge* is mythic and ritualistic, and its dominant symbolism is religious. The theme of the novel is that man's salvation lies in spiritual growth, which is attained by immersion in the flux of experience. The battle portrayed by Crane is symbolic of life at its most intense moments, and Henry Fleming's personal combat is against the change and growth that he stubbornly resists. Henry's redemption is brought about by the death of Jim Conklin, who, Stallman believes, represents Jesus Christ "in such descriptive details about him as his wound in the side, his torn body and his gory hand, and even in the initials of his name. . . ." He is depicted by Crane as the "devotee of a mad religion," and the wafer image at his death suggests the sacrifice celebrated in the communion (xxxiii–xxxiv).

However imaginative and stimulating it may be, this interpretation of Henry Fleming's story as a Christian redemption allegory cannot be sustained. Henry's dilemma is one of Christian conscience, and religious symbolism may be found in the novel, but it is most often used ironically to deny Christian values rather than to confirm them. As Stanley Greenfield has demonstrated (Entry 72), the coherence of Stallman's argument is greatly dependent upon the religious phrasing in his summary of the plot of *The Red Badge* which predisposes the reader toward an interpretation of spiritual transformation and the use of misplaced quotations from the text of the novel. Even more important, however, is the fact that the hypothesis of a sacrificial redemption story simply does not fit the facts of the plot. There is no integral connection between Jim Conklin's death and Henry's return to the battle-field, which is an accidental consequence of his ignominious wound. Henry neither repents nor receives absolution. As he marches away from battle, he feels less regret for his sins than fear that his initial cowardice may yet be detected. Furthermore, there is nothing godlike in the character of the tall soldier and nothing to suggest Christ beyond the initials of his name. To a greater extent than Henry Fleming, Jim Conklin is a hapless victim of war, not a sacrifice, but a casualty. At his death he does not show the stoic compassion of Christ but the confusion of a wounded and terror-stricken animal. Cf. Entry 39.

81. Stone, Edward. "The Many Suns of *The Red Badge of Courage*." *American Literature*, XXIX (November, 1957), 322–326.

The ever-changing image of the sun reveals the developing relationship of the protagonist of *The Red Badge of Courage* to the natural and moral universe. Stone

cites six instances in the novel in which the sun functions dramatically and symbolically rather than as a mere source of illumination. In Chapter II fear of the unknown,
appropriately symbolized by darkness, is dispelled by the rising sun. At the conclusion of Chapters V, VI, and XVII, the sun reflects in various ways Henry Fleming's
conviction that nature is flatly or perhaps even cheerfully indifferent to the struggles
of men. In the climatic scene at the end of Chapter IX, when "The red sun was pasted
in the sky like a wafer," Henry no longer views the sun as an unconcerned spectator
but as a malevolent symbol of nature's hostility and the seal of the brutal forces of
war. The sun is seen shining through leaden rain clouds in the final paragraph of the
novel, and this balanced image of light and darkness suggests a new equilibrium in
Henry's perspective. He now sees the sun neither as a sign of nature's indifference nor
brutal wrath but is able to accept the ambiguous symbol of an unpredictable future,
the alternating light and darkness of sun and cloud.

This short but thorough analysis reveals that the sun in *The Red Badge of Courage*
is an important symbolic index to the shifting emotional states of the protagonist.
Stone's interpretation of the disk-shaped sun image at the close of Chapter IX
is an implicit refutation of R. W. Stallman's contention that the red sun symbolizes
the wafer of the mass and that Henry blasphemes against this symbol of his faith
(Entry 80). The test of the novel at this point reads:

> The youth turned, with sudden, livid rage, toward the battlefield. He
> shook his fist. He seemed about to deliver a philippic.
> "Hell—"
> The red sun was pasted in the sky like a wafer.

It is clear that Henry's protest is directed not against the sun but against the battlefield
and the bestiality of war. The sun appears red at this moment, because it has assumed
the color of battle and is now the symbol of the violence and hostility of the universal
forces which Henry believes to be directed against him. For other discussions of this
controversial image, see Robert W. Stallman, "The Scholar's Net: Literary Sources,"
College English, XVII (October, 1955), 20–27; Eric W. Carlson, "Crane's *The Red
Badge of Courage*, IX," *Explicator*, XVI (March, 1958), Item 34; Entry 72; Cecil D.
Eby Jr., "Stephen Crane's 'Fierce Red Wafer,'" *English Language Notes*, I (December,
1963), 128–130.

82. Vanderbilt, Kermit and Daniel Weiss. "From Rifleman to Flagbearer: Henry
    Fleming's Separate Peace in *The Red Badge of Courage*," *Modern Fiction Studies*,
    XI (Winter, 1965–1966), 371–380.

Crane described *The Red Badge of Courage* as a "psychological portrayal of fear,"
and although Henry Fleming's fear of war is eventually dissipated, this does not occur
when he is a witness to the agony of Jim Conklin or during the initial charge on the
second day of battle when the rage and fury he directs against the enemy is motivated
by the same panic which caused his original cowardice. Vanderbilt and Weiss suggest
that at this point in the novel Henry has attempted two extreme forms of adjustment

toward his terror—a flight from danger and a flight toward it induced by a prefer-
ence for destruction to the pain of further apprehension. In the fourth charge of
Henry's battle career, the fear of death again almost overwhelms him until he gains
possession of the flag which he and Wilson wrench from the hands of a falling
standard bearer and endows it with magical qualities of divinity, invulnerability,
and maternity. In his still childish fantasies, the flag becomes a charm against danger
that allows him to return to the earlier delusion that war is a game in which he is
not a participant but a charmed spectator.

This is a highly original study of the psychological development of the young
protagonist of *The Red Badge of Courage* in which Henry Fleming's mental defences
and adaptions are subjected to close analysis. The authors conclude that Henry
fails to achieve social or spiritual growth, but through his concept of himself as a
standard bearer he returns finally to the delusional warmth and security of his
heroic fantasies. When he gives up his status as a rifleman to become a flagbearer,
his role is changed from an aggressive combatant to a curious spectator. Although
there is much in the novel to support this point of view, the evidence against it is
equally convincing. In Chapter XXIII Henry carries the flag forward in a bayonet
charge that results in the taking of prisoners, and here his mental attitude may
hardly be characterized as passive. He advances in a state of frenzy, "shrieking mad
calls and appeals," possessed by "a gigantic hatred" for the enemy, and plunging
"like a mad horse" at the Confederate banner. Such aggressive actions in the
penultimate chapter of the novel contradict the position maintained in this essay
that "Henry remains essentially the young Hamlet, the contemplative youth whose
responses to danger could never be hammered into the merciless reflexes of the
hardened veteran" (p. 379). For other studies of Henry Fleming's emotional development, see Entry 84 and John J. McDermott, "Symbolism and Psychological Realism
in *The Red Badge of Courage*," *Nineteenth-Century Fiction*, XXIII (December, 1968),
324–331.

83. Weisberger, Bernard. "*The Red Badge of Courage*," in *Twelve Original Essays
on Great American Novels*, ed. Charles Shapiro. Detroit: Wayne State University Press, 1958, pp. 96–123.

The maturation or initiation story is a tale in which a young protagonist passes
from ignorance of his own soul to self-discovery or from ignorance of the external
world to vital knowledge through immersion in a communal experience. Weisberger considers *The Red Badge of Courage* as an existentialist search for identity with
a maturation theme as well as a realistic story of the Civil War. Henry Fleming's
cowardice makes him aware of his psychic isolation and precipitates an intensely
introspective search for values. The wound he receives from the rifle butt of a
fleeing Union soldier brings him face to face with his own image, and this, Weisberger believes, is the first step in his redemption. Henry's redeemer, the man with

the cheery voice who leads him back to his regiment, functions as an almost supernatural guide in the wilderness. He is, however, no enlightened saint or prophet but also a wanderer, and he offers no clearly defined assurance of salvation. His gospel negates the Christian concept of conversion and implies that there are no ultimate purposes in existence. Henry acquires an antifaith, a realization that controlling values are unattainable in a world of cross purposes. Weisberger concludes that *The Red Badge* has contemporary appeal because it deals with the crisis of identity and employs modern fictional techniques such as symbolism, careful attention to environmental details, and the type of naturalism which dwells upon the isolation of the individual in an indifferent or malevolent universe.

Like the proponents of the theory that *The Red Badge of Courage* is an allegory of redemption, Weisberger assumes that Henry Fleming's wound serves as a blood atonement for his sin of cowardice and is a determining factor in motivating his return to battle and subsequent bravery. However, the youth does not rejoin his regiment voluntarily but is led back in a dazed and semiconscious condition by the man with the cheery voice. He neither accepts responsibility for deserting his comrades in the ranks nor for abandoning the dying tattered soldier. Instead, he resumes his place in the regiment on the strength of a dishonorably acquired wound, his ironic red badge of courage, and drifts into the insensate violence of war, fighting furiously in the grip of a blind rage that turns him into an animal. Weisberger correctly assumes that the only spiritual conversion in *The Red Badge* is a negative one, the reverse of the symbolic Christian redemption stressed by some critics. What Henry Fleming comes to understand is the futility of attempting to impose arbitrary schemes of order upon universal chaos.

84. Weiss, Daniel. "*The Red Badge of Courage*," *Psychoanalytic Review*, LII (Summer, 1965), 35–52; (Fall, 1965), 130–154.

Unlike Hemingway, Crane depended upon research and intuition rather than experience for his initial concept of battle. Nevertheless, Weiss affirms that the psychological processes of men at war are accurately realized in *The Red Badge of Courage*. Emotional rather than historical events occur in the novel which, in psychoanalytical terms, is a study in the anxiety defense mechanisms of its protagonist. Obsessed with a need to purge himself of fear, Henry Fleming attempts to adapt to a threatening reality. Unconsciously, the collective enfolding army and its assertive leaders are mother and father to him, and Jim Conklin is his "sibling ideal." Jim's death ends Henry's fantasy of immunity and forces him to accept the possibility of personal destruction. While his behavior as a fighter is infantile, the competition with Wilson for the flag shows that he has made basic interpersonal relationships. It represents the rivalry of brothers for parental love. Under the shelter of the flag, certain psychic imperatives are satisfied for Henry, and parental and sibling relationships are resolved.

Psychoanalysis of a literary character can at best be only suppositional, since the dynamics of personality are rendered static upon the printed page. But Weiss has overcome this limitation as well as possible and has shown that *The Red Badge of Courage* is true to unconscious as well as external reality. He has also wisely refrained from attempting to make psychoanalysis a substitute for literary criticism. For the reader unfamiliar with the terminology and approaches of clinical psychology, however, this complex study of fear and courage in battle may prove forbidding, particularly since Crane's novel is at times all but forgotten in lengthy passages of abstruse psychoanalytic speculation.

85. Wogan, Claudia C. "Crane's Use of Color in 'The Red Badge of Courage,'" *Modern Fiction Studies*, VI (Summer, 1960), 168–172.

Crane's spectacular use of color in *The Red Badge of Courage* was the aspect of his impressionism most frequently singled out for adverse criticism or parody by his contemporaries. Miss Wogan finds 235 uses of color words in the novel, but her count and her statistical breakdown are only approximately accurate. The predominant colors are blue, red, black, and gray, and more than two fifths of the color words are to be found in the first three and last three chapters of the novel. They are, for the most part, used in realistic descriptions: there are the blue and gray of uniforms, the red of campfires, the yellow and orange of sunlight, and the green of forests. Often colors serve metaphorical purposes, but Miss Wogan cautions that no single association can be applied to any one color. Thus red is predominately associated with war and rage and at times with both fear and courage. Green and brown are the colors of the earth and reflect the deceptive serenity of nature. Yellow usually illuminates the world of objective reality but when pale or sullied suggests death and decay. Blue is almost always employed functionally to describe the uniforms of the Union army, the color of the sky, or shades of smoke; at times it serves as the traditional metaphor of sadness and depressive states of mind. Black is the color of passion, while purple and gold often expose false heroics.

The rich sensuousness of Crane's impressionistic style owes much to both the realistic and metaphorical use of color imagery, and this essay presents a concise and informative analysis of an important stylistic component of *The Red Badge of Courage*. Miss Wogan does not comment upon the overuse of color in the novel which frequently results in bathetic effects and shows that Crane had not yet learned to discipline the juvenile enthusiasm for color which he displayed in some of his early New York *Tribune* sketches. Especially ineffective are the numerous and redundant color synesthesias describing "red cheers," "black curses," or "the red, formidable difficulties of war." Crane gradually toned down his literary impressionism, and in his later war stories the density of color imagery is much lower than in *The Red Badge of Courage* or the fiction written prior to 1895 (cf. Entry 97).

"The Open Boat":

86. Adams, Richard P. "Naturalistic Fiction: 'The Open Boat,'" *Tulane Studies in English*, IV (1954), 137–146.

Adams finds a thematic inconsistency in "The Open Boat" between the naturalistic assumption that the universe is flatly and coldly indifferent to the human situation and a romantic view of man and nature as bound together in an inextricable unity. The symbols of nature's unconcern are the tower on shore, described as "a giant, standing with its back to the plight of the ants," and "the high cold star on a winter's night" which reflects the cosmic chill toward the men in the dinghy. In contrast, the highly concentrated animistic imagery of the story indicates that nature is not indifferent but charged with feeling, and the pervasive color imagery (more concentrated here than is usual in Crane's later fiction) suggests a world of warmth opposed to the blackness of the star image. Adams also points out that although Crane's attitude toward human brotherhood is not as all-embracing as Melville's or Whitman's, the structure of "The Open Boat" follows the symbolic pattern of death and rebirth into the community of men characteristic of many romantic works. Such a development denies the defeat which almost invariably ends the struggle for survival in naturalistic fiction.

Unlike many of their European predecessors and contemporaries, American naturalists rarely followed the course of scientific determinism to an exclusively pessimistic conclusion. The same inconsistency which Adams finds in "The Open Boat" between the view that man is isolated in nature and that he is an integral part of the universal scheme is evident in Frank Norris' *The Octopus* and Theodore Dreiser's *Sister Carrie*. Crane hardly ever portrays the natural world with the benign feelings of the romantic poets, but neither does he stress its destructive aspects exclusively. Because of his antipathy for formal theories about the position of man in the universe, Crane refuses to take a doctrinaire philosophical stance (cf. Entry 87). At the conclusion of "The Open Boat" the survivors felt "that they could then be interpreters," but the ultimate meaning of their experience remains ambiguous. For a reading which considers the ending of the story an affirmation of insight, see Peter Buitenhuis, "The Essentials of Life: 'The Open Boat' as Existentialist Fiction," *Modern Fiction Studies*, V (Autumn, 1959), 243–250.

87. Colvert, James B. "Style and Meaning in Stephen Crane: *The Open Boat*," *Texas Studies in English*, XXXVII (1958), 34–45.

While Colvert does not entirely approve of R. W. Stallman's symbolistic reading of *The Red Badge of Courage* (Entry 80), he is wary of interpretations which ignore the predominately metaphorical and imagistic style of Crane's fiction. This style is ironic, characterized by indirection and ambiguity. Crane's central theme is man's futile struggle to unify the contradictions of experience presented by his faulty perception of reality. Colvert shows that in "The Open Boat" Crane maintains an ironist's ambivalence of attitude which rejects formal definitions. Nature appears to the men in the dinghy in different guises—cruel, and wrathful, picturesque, or merely indifferent. From the omniscient perspective of the narrator, no one of these attitudes necessarily excludes the others. At the conclusion of the story the correspondent is convinced that he has learned the truth about life through his experience, but he and his comrades remain merely "interpreters," and the ironic overtones of this final word accentuate Crane's distrust of all certainties.

This is the most balanced and perceptive of the essays about "The Open Boat", and Colvert's emphasis upon Crane's poetic use of language to evolve meaning is well placed. Crane's style is animated and impressionistic, evolving a universe in constant flux in which the differences between external reality and the individual's perception of that reality are blurred and elusive. It is, therefore, futile, as Colvert illustrates, to classify Crane as simply a realist, a naturalist, or an existentialist. In his most significant stories, such as "The Open Boat," he attains universality of meaning through this very resistance to dogmatic statement.

88. Day, Cyrus. "Stephen Crane and the Ten-Foot Dinghy," *Boston University Studies in English*, III (Winter, 1957), 193–213.

Day compares the factual framework of "The Open Boat" with the actual events which occurred from the time that the steamer *Commodore*, bound for Cuba with a cargo of arms for the rebels, foundered on the morning of January 2, 1897 until approximately twenty five to thirty hours later when a ten-foot dinghy with Stephen Crane among the survivors was beached at Daytona. The sources of information used are the newspapers of Jacksonville, New York, and other cities, and "The Open Boat" itself.

Despite its subtitle, "A Tale Intended to be After the Fact," Day feels that "The Open Boat" is a conglomeration of fact and fiction and maintains that the seas were not as high and dangerous as Crane described them and that he greatly exaggerated the physical hardships which he and his comrades endured in the dinghy. Under the circumstances, Captain Murphy's desertion of four men precariously afloat on a raft and three others marooned on the sinking steamer was ethically questionable, as was his failure to land the dinghy when it first reached shore on the afternoon of January second. Because Murphy waited sixteen to eighteen hours before daring the breakers, the opportunity to secure aid for the abandoned men was lost. Day believes that Crane felt guilty about his part in these desertions, and this is why in "The Open Boat" he magnified the dangers to which the men in the dinghy were exposed and obscured the facts in his dispatch to the New York *Press*. R. W. Stallman, on the other hand, reaffirms Crane's veracity in reporting the stormy conditions of the sea in "Journalist Crane in that Dinghy," *Bulletin of the New York Public Library*, LXXII (April, 1968), 261–277 and *Stephen Crane: A Biography* (Entry 15), pp. 550–551.

Whatever the height of the waves, Day's implication that Crane was in some measure responsible for Captain Murphy's conduct upon abandoning the ship or for his decision not to attempt a landing in the breakers on the afternoon of January second is unsubstantiated. Crane was a completely inexperienced sailor, and it is very doubtful that the Captain would have asked for or heeded his advice in matters of maritime ethics or seamanship. Equally questionable is Day's argument that in the light of his researches the artistic merits of "The Open Boat" must be revalued. Crane's story is a subjective portrayal of the feelings of men in danger of death by drowning, and in this regard it has verisimilitude. Whether or not it corresponds literally with the events as they occurred is aesthetically irrelevant. For other details of the factual background of "The Open Boat," see William Randel, "The Cook in 'The Open Boat,'" *American Literature*, XXXIV (November, 1962), 405–411.

89. Marcus, Mordecai. "The Three-Fold View of Nature in 'The Open Boat,'" *Philological Quarterly*, XLI (April, 1962), 511–515.

Many commentators have noted an apparent contradiction in the fact that "The Open Boat" depicts nature as simultaneously hostile and indifferent. Marcus explains that the thoughts of the characters in the story follow a progressive development. They view nature "first as malevolently hostile, then as thoughtlessly hostile, and finally as wholly indifferent" (p. 512). Crane remains true to human psychology in that the transitions from one attitude to another are gradual, and traces of the three views remain throughout the story. Through the interdependence of the men in the dinghy upon one another in the face of danger, there is a gradually deepening bond of human brotherhood which is the message of "the great sea's voice" and the meaning of their experience.

This is an insightful analysis of the successive attitudes of the central characters of "The Open Boat" toward their physical environment, which symbolizes for Crane the conditions of life itself. Marcus shows that the structure and major themes of the story evolve through the changing threefold view of nature in the minds of the men and particularly in the thoughts of the correspondent who is the auto-biographical protagonist of the story. One may not agree that the theme of "The Open Boat" is "that out of the experience of the pain inflicted by indifferent nature men learn to treasure brotherhood and life" (p. 515). Crane's conclusions are rarely so clear-cut or so moralistic. There is, after all, a significance in the fact that despite the brotherhood established among the men in the dinghy, they are unable to help one another at the most critical moment. In the death of the oiler is symbolized not only the tragic indifference of nature but the ultimate isolation of man.

"*The Blue Hotel*":

90. Cox, James T. "Stephen Crane as Symbolic Naturalist: An Analysis of 'The Blue Hotel,'" *Modern Fiction Studies*, III (Summer, 1957), 147–158.

Cox maintains that there is "an elaborately contrived symbolic substructure" underlying the surface realism of "The Blue Hotel" (p. 148). The central symbols of the story are the enormous stove in Patrick Scully's sitting room and the snow-storm that whirls around the hotel. While the stove represents the internally and externally directed hostilities of man, the snowstorm symbolizes the hostile environ-ment in which he exists. The whiteness of the snow is associated with fear and the red glow of the stove with violence, expressing Crane's realization of the struggle "both within man in the conflicting relationship between the elemental forces of fear and anger and outside in the conflicting relationship between this inner nature and his environment" (p. 151). Other symbolic contrasts which Cox finds in "The Blue Hotel" are between the animalistic nature of men in the West and the civilized inhabitants of the East, Scully as God and Scully as Satan, the hotel as heaven and the hotel as hell, Celtic and modern warfare, life as a game and life as conflict. What emerges from these paradoxes, Cox feels, is an uncompromising naturalism. Man is seen as devoid of free will, existing in an amoral, deterministic universe swept by forces over which he has no control.

Crane experimented with symbolism and made frequent use of the techniques of irony and paradox, but Cox attempts to impose a coherent symbolic pattern upon the impressionistic imagery of "The Blue Hotel." Metallic references to individuals as "bronzed," "iron-nerved," or "leaden-hued" are taken out of context and identi-fied with Scully's stove, which in turn becomes symbolic of man's inner nature. Scully is seen as God because his hotel provides santuary from the storm, he reads his newspaper "like an old priest," and he conducts his guests to wash basins which Cox identifies with baptismal fonts. The three quarters which the Swede offers Scully in payment for his board are assumed to be symbols of the trinity, because "in Scully's house the true God is money—god in three pieces" (p. 153). Examples could be multiplied, but the weaknesses of so arbitrary a critical approach are apparent.

91. Gibson, Donald B. "'The Blue Hotel' and the Ideal of Human Courage," *Texas Studies in Literature and Language*, VI (Autumn, 1964), 388–397.

Antithetical interpretations have been advanced to explain the speech of the Easterner in the concluding section of "The Blue Hotel." Some critics regard it as an affirma-tion of the necessity for human brotherhood, while others find a naturalistic outlook confirming the irresponsibility of the individual in a world he never made and cannot control. Gibson rejects the deterministic reading and refuses to discount the compli-city of the other characters in the Swede's death as being "tacked one." Although the Swede creates the circumstances which bring about his destruction, Gibson argues that the final section of the story complements what has gone before by revealing the extent to which others collaborated in the event. The Easterner's view is limited, since he fails to include the Swede himself among those responsible. But this does not mean that Crane considers the Swede to be an entirely innocent victim. The Swede's misguided courage is untempered with discretion, while the Easterner's failure to support the Swede's valid charges against Johnnie reveals that in his case discretion has replaced courage. Both have abnegated their roles as links in what Hawthorne called "the magnetic chain of humanity" and have contributed to the final tragedy. Therefore, Gibson believes that social consciousness and courage tempered with discretion in the face of evil are the central themes of the story.

This study makes a valuable contribution toward an understanding of the themes of "The Blue Hotel" by bridging the logical gap between the Swede's obvious responsibility for bringing about his own death and the Easterner's statement that "Every sin is the result of a collaboration." Gibson explains that Crane's hostile attitude toward the Swede, whom he depicts as utterly offensive, makes sympathetic judgment of him impossible. If the events of the story have convinced the reader that the Swede deserves his fate, he may resist the Easterner's interpretation of the affair. But all the characters were involved in the catastrophe, and the Easterner knows that his moral cowardice renders him particularly culpable. On the other hand, Gibson does not account for the stilted, hyperbolic tone of the Easterner's speech, which Crane may have intended as a burlesque either of literary naturalism or the doctrine of complicity itself (cf. Entry 93).

92. Gleckner, Robert F. "Stephen Crane and the Wonder of Man's Conceit," *Modern Fiction Studies*, V (Autumn, 1959), 271–281.

In "The Blue Hotel" Crane expresses wonder at the continued existence of human beings in a universe seemingly bent upon their destruction. Gleckner agrees with James T. Cox (Entry 90) that Crane's point of view in this story is uncompromisingly naturalistic but feels that it is essential to understand his attitude toward man's determination to endure in a hostile world. Crane does not deny man free will but believes that it is submerged and thwarted in the struggle for survival. The egocentric desire to control and its inevitable defeat forms the structural principle of "The Blue Hotel." In the opening scenes Scully manipulates his guests like a benevolent god, but the Swede with his anger and violence wrests control from him. Ironically, the Swede has created his own universe, the wild West of his imagination, and has conquered it. Yet, when he enters the saloon he encounters a gambler who also has pretensions to free will and a desire to control, and his conceit is punctured with a swift thrust of the gambler's knife. In turn, the gambler realizes that he too must relinquish control, and he returns home to await arrest. Gleckner considers the final dialogue between the Easterner and the cowboy a logical conclusion to what has gone before, since it reveals that the characters of the story all had some degree of responsibility for the death of the Swede, but no one of them could have exerted a final control over the situation.

Gleckner's astute interpretation of the structure of "The Blue Hotel" does much to resolve the controversy over whether the story is a naturalistic object lesson whose theme is enunciated in the final section or whether the cash-register legend upon which the dead Swede's eyes are fixed—"This registers the amount of your purchase"

—indicates that he has sought and deserved his death, making the conclusion super-fluous and contradictory. Gleckner shows that Crane, who despised theoretical and doctrinaire attitudes toward problems of freedom or fate, viewed the life of man as a confusion of cross-purposes and desires. The storm which sweeps around the Palace Hotel and through which the Swede marches exultantly to his death stands for the violent and mysterious forces which resist man's efforts to define and control his situation. In the debacle of human presumptions rational definitions of reality in terms of free will and determinism seem entirely futile. The true miracle is that humanity continues to exist at all, and "the wonder of man's conceit" is his persistent belief that he will ultimately control his physical and social environment. Cf. Robert Narveson, "Conceit in 'The Blue Hotel,'" *Prairie Schooner*, XLIII (Summer, 1969), 187.

93. Klotz, Marvin. "Stephen Crane: Tragedian or Comedian: 'The Blue Hotel,'" *University of Kansas City Review*, XXVII (Spring, 1961), 170–174.

This essay deplores unhistorical attempts to explicate Crane's impressionistic style in terms of the modern shibboleths of myth and symbolic patterns and to interpret his themes as abstruse philosophical statements whose meanings must be deciphered through textual analysis. Crane was neither a Christian allegorist nor a modern existentialist. He despised pretentious theorizing and scorned the dogmatization of ideas into systems. Klotz reminds us that Crane frequently employed sardonic humor to mock the absurdities of contrived theories and suggests that "The Blue Hotel" may be read as a deliberate parody of literary naturalism. To the bewilder-ment of the other characters in the story, the Swede insists upon being destroyed by his environment. The speech of the Easterner in the final section, if taken at face value, is a classical statement of the naturalistic position, but the mocking, hyperbolic language marks it as a ludicrous simplification and overstatement of a naturalistic determinism which reduces the complexity of life to a formula.

Klotz's interpretation of the final section of "The Blue Hotel" and its relevance to the structure and theme of the story is highly original. Most critics take the dia-logue between the Easterner and the cowboy quite seriously, either condemning it as superfluous moralizing or considering it the logical conclusion to a story which emphasizes the theme of social complicity that Crane derived from William Dean Howells. Actually, the Easterner's allegation that "'We, five of us, have collaborated in the murder of this Swede'" is bathetic, since the Swede had a compulsive drive toward self-destruction and made every effort to provoke his fellows into doing away with him. Crane often wrote seriously in the naturalistic vein, but it is possible that in "The Blue Hotel" he turned his irony against the deterministic aspect of naturalism and its animalistic concept of man. For an interesting counterargument which defends the sincerity of Crane's belief in social complicity, see Joseph N. Satterwhite, "Stephen Crane's 'The Blue Hotel': The Failure of Understanding," *Modern Fiction Studies*, II (Winter, 1956–1957), 238–241.

94. Sutton, Walter. "Pity and Fear in 'The Blue Hotel,'" *American Quarterly*, IV (Spring, 1952), 73–78.

Sutton reads "The Blue Hotel" as a naturalistic story embodying a pessimistic determinism which, since it operates in a social context and suggests a protest against man's predicament, is ultimately melioristic. The Easterner and the Swede are seen as twin projections of Crane's psyche. While the Swede represents human isolation and terror in the most primitive sense, the Easterner's basic fear is modified by his understanding of man's place in nature and his ability to empathize with others. Crane's apparent detachment is an artistic illusion created by his ironic technique and should not be interpreted as indifference to moral values. Unlike Mark Twain, Crane does not express human sympathy directly in his work, but the two writers are alike "in their employment of ironic understatement and hyperbole to satirize society's deviation from the scale of moral values for which they stand" (p. 77).

Naturalistic formulas are insufficient to explain Crane's attitudes toward the problem of social complicity in "The Blue Hotel." Sutton interprets the sardonic cash register legend that the Swede's death is a "purchase" as a naturalistic moral judgment later elaborated upon by the Easterner. Yet, the Swede's destruction is to a great extent self-impelled and only partially determined by his social and natural environment. As Sutton acknowledges, the Swede actually creates for himself the dangerous West which the other characters regard as an illusion. The contention that the Easterner represents and gives voice to Crane's human sympathy is also questionable. The Easterner remains a detached observer of the Swede's plight, and it is this very indifference for which he berates himself and the others at the conclusion of the story. He is, if anything, more callous than his fellows, because he withholds the vital knowledge that Johnnie was cheating which might have prevented the Swede's death. It is more likely that the meaning of the story is embodied in the cowboy's final anguished cry, "'Well, I didn't do anythin', did I?'" ironically indicating man's moral inadequacy in a chaotic and dangerous universe.

Social Studies and War Stories:

95. Bassan, Maurice. "Misery and Society: Some New Perspectives on Stephen Crane's Fiction," *Studia Neophilologica*, XXXV (1963), 104–120.

Social writers in the 1890's were actively investigating and commenting upon the city tramp and Bowery environment which are the subjects of Crane's "An Experiment in Misery," first published in the New York *Press* on April 22, 1894. Bassan examines the work of these writers, not primarily to find literary sources for Crane's story but to demonstrate Crane's involvement with the problems of vagrancy and poverty and the differences between his approach to these questions and those of his contemporaries. Cited as particularly significant progenitors of "An Experiment in Misery" are: Jacob Riis' *How the Other Half Lives* (1891) and Riis' other studies going back to the 1880's; Benjamin O. Flower's *Civilization's Inferno: Studies in the Social*

Cellar (1893); articles in the *Arena* (edited by Flower), the *Nation*, and the *Forum;* Josiah Flint's *Tramping With Tramps* (1899), extracts from which began to appear in the *Century* late in 1893; William Dean Howells' Altrurian studies published in *Cosmopolitan* between November, 1892 and September, 1894. These and a large number of other studies contained descriptions, sketches, and photographs of the Bowery lodging houses and their inhabitants.

The majority of the reformers had little sympathy for tramps and considered them responsible for their own degradation, but Crane, Bassan observes, takes an environmentalistic position in "An Experiment in Misery" and implies that the derelicts are victims of social disorientation. This brings him closer to the thought of the *Arena* radicals than to the moralistic conclusions of the more detached professional students of the problem and seems to contradict his often-quoted assertion that "the root of Bowery life is a sort of cowardice." Bassan identifies Crane's "Experiment" with the general social investigation prevailing during the economic depression of 1893, but it should be remembered that Crane had little interest in social reforms and considered his Bowery tales to be psychological analyses and realistic works of art. The resemblance of his descriptions of flophouses and slum environments to those of the social reformers, however, verifies the accuracy of his powers of observation.

96. Bassan, Maurice. "Stephen Crane and 'The Eternal Mystery of Social Condition,'" *Nineteenth-Century Fiction*, XIX (March, 1965), 387–394.

"An Experiment in Luxury," one of Crane's "Midnight Sketches." was first published in the New York *Press* on April 29, 1894 as a sequel to the better-known "An Experiment in Misery," which had appeared in the *Press* a week earlier. Bassan states that "An Experiment in Luxury" has not been reprinted since Crane's *Collected Work* in 1926, but the sketch may be found in Thomas A. Gullason's collection of Crane's short stories and sketches (Entry 2) and in Olov Fryckstedt's edition of the *Uncollected Writings* (Entry 5). More recently it has been included in *The New York City Sketches of Stephen Crane and Related Pieces* (Entry 8). "An Experiment in Luxury" has been given little critical attention, and Bassan believes that it should be studied not only for its intrinsic merits but because it provides another insight into Crane's attitudes about man's relationship to nature and to society.

Bassan points out that the youth in the second "Experiment" does not at all seem to have learned the social lesson that caused the youth in "An Experiment in Misery" to reach "certain convictions." In "An Experiment in Luxury" Crane's viewpoint shifts from economic determinism to philosophical nihilism as the youth realizes the truth of his friend's statement that "'Nobody is responsible for anything.'" Sheer chance and not cosmic injustice renders one man wealthy and another destitute. The rich are not responsible for social evils, since they are also creatures of circumstance. Bassan does not believe that the effect of the sketch is entirely pessimistic. Crane realizes that nature dispenses advantages and disadvantages through the medium of chance, although the youth's statement that this distribution is "'both strange and proper'" seems to correspond to the conventional view of the moral order of the universe. What "An Experiment in Luxury" does attempt to destroy is the pious social lie that poverty is a virtue and that wealth invariably renders its possessors unhappy.

97. Gullason, Thomas A. "The Significance of 'Wounds in the Rain,'" *Modern Fiction Studies*, V (Autumn, 1959), 235–242.

The fame of *The Red Badge of Courage* has caused Crane's Cuban war sketches to fall into relative obscurity. These were originally published in one volume, *Wounds in the Rain*, in 1900 but were redistributed in the twelve-volume edition of Crane's *Collected Work* (Entry 1). Impressionism was largely responsible for the success of *The Red Badge*. It gave to the novel an intensity and immediacy unparalleled in war fiction, but it also resulted in overwriting and rhetorical absurdities which did not escape the strictures of early reviewers. Crane insisted that the war novel was "all right"; yet, the stories and sketches written after he had personally experienced battle reveal that he discarded many impressionistic devices. The style of *Wounds in the Rain* is sparse and objective. Personification and the pathetic fallacy have practically disappeared, and the density of color imagery is very much reduced. Gullason suggests that the stories are unified by the words "wounds" and "rain." Each story deals with a particular "wound" or complaint which becomes apparent at the conclusion. Some of these "wounds" are tragic, but several stories such as "The Sergeant's Private Madhouse" and "The Second Generation" present essentially comic or satiric "wounds." The word "rain" is used, as it often is in Hemingway's fiction, to connote bleakness, agony, and the futility of war. Gullason emphasizes the unity and control that Crane achieved in these later war stories, indicating that his talent did not entirely fail him in the final years of his life.

As Gullason explains, Crane's experience as a correspondent for Hearst's New York *Journal* and Pulitzer's *World* was probably responsible for significant changes both in his attitude toward war and his prose style. Newspaper writing required an objective point of view and a concentration upon facts rather than impressions. It became necessary to replace pictorially conceived episodic structures with sustained chronological narratives. Crane also became interested in describing the life of the common soldier and sacrificed his subjective impressionism to this end. The prose style of *Wounds in the Rain* is terse, flat, and stripped of ornamentation. War has become the business of the professional soldier, and in the ranks there is no talk of fear or courage but merely an assumption of competency. These later stories are not popularized and superficial as some recent critics have inferred (cf. Entry 100). They resemble Crane's war dispatches in being less intense and less carefully executed than *The Red Badge of Courage*, but, splattered with mud and grime, they impart a more accurate sense of the monotony, the fatigue, the unglamorous nature of war.

98. Hagemann, E. R. "Crane's 'Real' War in His Short Stories," *American Quarterly,* VIII (Winter, 1956), 356–367.

In Crane's war stories the identity of individual soldiers is obscured and they become faceless and often nameless ciphers, almost indistinguishable from their comrades. Hagemann shows that when Crane does explore individuality in these stories it is to examine the lure of violence, the desire to kill which seems to take hold in all men once social inhibitions are removed. Crane also knew that soldiers in combat develop a hard protective shell which may temporarily blunt their morality but also serves to prevent the horrors of war from destroying their psychic balance. Not heroism but a sense of duty to oneself, comrades, and profession is the mark of an experienced soldier and leads to victory in battle. Hagemann also explores certain technical devices in Crane's war stories such as the tendency of soldiers to personify death as a presence on the battlefield or as a pagan god of destruction and a concern with the ruin of the natural environment in battle.

While Hagemann realizes that Crane did not fully comprehend the lure of violence before he had personally experienced battle, this essay tends to treat the war stories as a unit and does not clearly distinguish between the sentimental sketches of *The Little Regiment* and the tough realism of *Wounds in the Rain* or the sheer horror of the "Spitzbergen Tales" (cf. Entry 100). Many of the characteristics described by Hagemann—the anonymity of the soldiers, their emotional imperviousness, their professionalism—are much more prevalent in Crane's later war stories than in his earlier.

99. Osborn, Neal J. "The Riddle in 'The Clan': *A Key to Crane's Major Fiction?*" *Bulletin of the New York Public Library,* LXIX (April, 1965), 247–258.

"The Clan of No-Name" is prefaced by a cryptic riddle which Osborn believes not only illuminates the theme of the story but also asserts an affirmative Christian metaphysic and ethic in the face of what is apparently a naturalistic interpretation of the human condition. The second, third, and fourth lines of the riddle apply to the pessimistic events of the story and together with the fifth line ("Scorn hits strong because of a lie;") describe man's subjugation to overwhelming external forces, despite his illusions of autonomy and importance. The sixth and culminating line, however, proclaims the existence of a "mystic tie" superior to mechanistic determinism. The young lieutenant, Manolo Prat, chooses to die defending five insurgents trapped in a saucer-like hollow, because he recognizes the validity of a higher law, a spiritual bond which unites all men. This disinterested love and sacrifice contradicts and transcends naturalistic elements in the story such as the lonely death of soldiers, the scorn of cynical officers, and the infidelity of women.

Osborn finds variations on this naturalistic-idealistic conflict and the theme of human commitment in much of Crane's fiction. Both Maggie Johnson and the Swede of "The Blue Hotel" might have been saved from destruction if individuals had recognized the necessity of assuming responsibility for others. Dr. Trescott of "The Monster" obeys the law of human brotherhood to save the deformed Henry Johnson despite the opposition of natural and social forces. At the conclusion of *The Red Badge of Courage*, Henry Fleming feels guilty about his desertion of the dying tattered man, and in "The Open Boat" the cynical correspondent matures into a realization of the need for altruistic relationships among men. Osborn is correct in concluding that the question of ethical commitment is important in Crane's fiction, even if such commitment is usually shown to be futile in the conflict against natural and social hostility or indifference.

Sources cited in this essay as essential to Crane's development of the idea of human responsibility are Jonathan Townley Crane's *Popular Amusements* (1869), Henry M. Stanley's *In Darkest Africa* (1890), and essays by William Ellery Channing, but the parallels drawn from these works are very inexact and unconvincing.

100. Solomon, Eric. "Stephen Crane's War Stories," *Texas Studies in Literature and Language*, III (Spring, 1961), 67–80.

Earlier estimates of Crane's war fiction do not take sufficient account of a gradual development in the author's attitude toward war. Solomon finds that the short stories dealing with war fall into three distinct periods: Those published in *The Little Regiment* and *The Open Boat and Other Stories* either treat war in romantic-chivalric terms or continue the subjective psychological analysis of *The Red Badge of Courage*. Solomon feels that Crane's combat experience in Cuba destroyed his ability to create imaginative protagonists like Henry Fleming, Collins, or Peza, and consequently the stories of the middle period, collected in *Wounds in the Rain*, are "grim, inflexible sketches, totally lacking the tension and emotional complexity of his previous war fiction" (p. 74). Crane's final war stories, the "Spitzbergen Tales" which appear in the posthumous *Last Words*, reveal a return to the more balanced attitude held by the young novelist before he had actually experienced battle—that war has both positive and negative aspects, both excitement and horror.

Despite Solomon's failure to appreciate *Wounds in the Rain* this is a perceptive study not only of Crane's shifting attitude toward war but of the developing concept of the soldier in his fiction. Henry Fleming and Peza are typical of Crane's early protagonists who cannot distinguish between their heroic fantasies and the actual conditions of war. Isolated and unable to predict how they will adjust to the reality of battle, they find themselves lost in an undefined and dangerous universe. Crane's experiences in Cuba convinced him that war was neither as glorious as his heroes had imagined it to be before their trial by combat nor as terrifying as they found it in their first encounter with the enemy. The regular soldiers of *Wounds in the Rain*, typified by Private Nolan, are not untried adolescents but hardened veterans who have lost the capacity to be shocked and are surrounded by a protective shell of indifference. Henry Fleming was horrified by the sight of death, but when a lieutenant in "The Clan of No-Name" sees a corpse he is completely apathetic. In the

"Spitzbergen" tetralogy Timothy Lean, perhaps Crane's final ideal of the soldier, has become a stoic who looks upon war as a condition of life which must be confronted realistically.

Poetry:

101. Hoffman, Daniel G. *The Poetry of Stephen Crane.* New York: Columbia University Press, 1957.

Condemnation and parody were frequent critical responses to Crane's "lines" (he refused to call them poems) within his lifetime, and despite the acclaim now given to his fiction, revaluation of the poetry remains inconclusive. In this first book-length study of Crane's poetry, Hoffman capably utilizes manuscript material from the Columbia University Crane Collection and other sources, including seventeen previously unpublished poems, to prove that Crane was a skilled craftsman whose verses were carefully constructed and not, as Hamlin Garland believed, effortlessly drawn from his subconscious. Hoffman objects to the fact that anthologists continue to reprint the ironic epigrams and allegories of *The Black Riders* and slight the more complex longer poems. These nondiscursive symbolistic poems, such as "A man adrift on a slim spar," "Do not weep, maiden, for war is kind," and "The Blue Battalions," with their metaphoric expression of action and theme, represent for Hoffman Crane's highest achievement as a poet and mirror the best qualities of his fiction.

The themes of Crane's poetry—the relationship of the individual to God and nature; love; war; and social injustice—are each treated in a separate chapter of this book. Hoffman's approach to Crane's religious and love poetry is restricted by his somewhat modified acceptance of John Berryman's Freudian hypotheses (Entry 11). Thus, the brutal God of vengeance in *The Black Riders* is identified with the maternal Peck family, while the compassionate inner God is associated with Jonathan T. Crane's concept of divinity. Correlative religious themes, extending into *War is Kind* and new manuscript poems, are the irreconcilability of the humanistic and Christian traditions, the fallibility of the church, the brotherhood of man in sin, and the inscrutability of God. Again following Berryman, Hoffman maintains that the love poems reveal Crane's masochistic compulsion to rescue "sexually discredited" women older than himself. "Intrigue" and "The chatter of a death-demon from a tree-top" are analyzed to show the association of love with a sense of guilt and doom in Crane's verse; sexual consummation is equated with death and is imaged in terms of cowardice, desertion, and violence. Hoffman's chapters on the themes of war and social injustice are slight and somewhat vague, but in his excellent chapter on "Style, Sources, Symbols," he demonstrates the versatility of Crane's poetic techniques and their sources in Biblical parables, Olive Schreiner's *Dreams*, and Ambrose Bierce's *Fantastic Fables.* Hoffman believes that Emily Dickinson and Whitman had little influence upon Crane's thought or expression, and that resemblances between Crane's poetry and that of the *fin de siècle* Decadents and French symbolists are largely fortuitous. Perhaps not too appropriately, Crane's development from allegorist to symbolist is placed within the American tradition exemplified by Emerson, Hawthorne, and Melville. In a thoughtful final chapter, "Crane and the Poetic Tradition," Hoffman shows that Crane not only anticipated but in some ways transcended the aesthetics of the Imagists and pointed the way toward modern poetry. A technical analysis of Crane's poetics may be found in Henry Luedke's *The Democracy of Henry Adams and Other Essays* (Bern, Switzerland, 1950), pp. 111–122.

102. Katz, Joseph. "'The Blue Battalions' and the Uses of Experience," *Studia Neophilologica*, XXXVIII (1966), 107–116.

While Daniel Hoffman (Entry 101) groups "The Blue Battalions" among Crane's finest lyrical achievements, Harland S. Nelson (Entry 104) considers it a failure of ambitious poetic intention. Yet, both critics agree that this arcane poem, first printed in the June, 1898 issue of the *Philistine* and inexplicably omitted from *War Is Kind*, reveals an intense personal commitment not evident in the sardonic epigrams of Crane's first book of poetry, *The Black Riders*. Through a study of the physical characteristics of "The Blue Battalions" holograph in the Columbia University Crane Collection and a comparison of verbal and thematic parallels between the poem and Crane's Greco–Turkish War dispatches, Katz concludes that it was written in the one-year period from April, 1897 to April, 1898 and that its meaning is rooted in Crane's emotional reactions to his first experience of war at Velestino.

The convincing evidence and interpretation presented here does much to objectify the military imagery of armed and mounted men, clanging of swords, and ultimate triumph over foes which Hoffman and Nelson, the only previous commentators on the poem, read as symbolic of man's struggle against the miseries of existence and toward the attainment of truth and salvation. The empathy which these critics find in "The Blue Battalions" Katz shows to be the result of Crane's identification with the Greeks, who were, after all, Christians engaged in battle against the heathen, and his inability to conceive of the Turks as anything other than the forces of darkness—this accentuated by their black uniforms in contrast to the blue-clad Greek infantry. Crane's heartfelt desire for a Greek victory developed into a cosmic projection of the struggle and the apocalyptic vision in which the poem ends. This initial involvement in human tragedy, Katz believes, led Crane to a more general sympathy which is reflected in his subsequent work.

103. Miller, Ruth. "Regions of Snow: The Poetic Style of Stephen Crane," *Bulletin of the New York Public Library*, LXXII (May, 1968), 328–349.

Originally intended as the introduction to a concordance of Crane's poetry, this essay is more significant for its challenges to conventional assumptions than for relevant insights into the stylistic complexities of the poems themselves. Like most recent commentaries on Crane's poetry, it was written *contra* Daniel Hoffman (Entry 101) and disputes his claim that Crane at his best is a lyric poet who combines stark realism with sensuous awareness and a mastery of metaphorical expression. On the contrary, Miss Miller asserts, Crane is "a dramatic poet, a raconteur of disjunctive experiences, a monologist who effectively immobilizes his features into a stylized mask of indifference to those often violent, always outlandish events" (p. 329).

This definition seems to obscure more than it clarifies, and one may apply the same criticism to Miss Miller's explication of Crane's poetry that she charges against Hoffman's—that it demonstrates what the poetry is *not* rather than what it *is*. Thus, she shows that Crane is most often not emotionally involved in his poems; even when he is directly engaged, it is in a very small degree; he offers us only a limited insight into his emotions; in the love poems he remains detached; typically, he renders confrontations or encounters, but they are indecisive and limited in scope; his settings are barren; his diction is seldom original or unusual; his imagery is unimaginative; his wisdom is adolescent. Miss Miller leaves us wondering why anyone should bother to read Crane's poems at all.

104. Nelson, Harland S. "Stephen Crane's Achievement as a Poet," *Texas Studies in Literature and Language*, IV (Winter, 1963), 564–582.

Nelson acknowledges the comprehensiveness and lucidity of Daniel Hoffman's study of Crane's poetry (Entry 101) but disagrees with Hoffman's analytic criteria and his estimate of Crane's highest achievements in verse. Hoffman praises those poems which through their thematic and symbolic complexity make Crane seem almost modern, especially "The Blue Battalions," "Do not weep, maiden, for war is kind," and "A man adrift on a slim spar." Of these, Nelson considers the first forced and hollow, lacking the tension and restraint characteristic of Crane's best poetry; the second not a symbolic poem at all but a simple ironic anti-war statement; and the third owing its strength to indirection rather than metaphoric suggestion and its relevance to Crane's religious concerns. Nelson believes that Crane's best poems are those that spring from the Methodist heritage and express a secularized version of the Biblical view of man as basically corrupt and filled with self-love based on self-deception. Among these poems are "In a lonely place," "I stood upon a high place," "I was in darkness," and "The wayfarer/Perceiving the pathway to truth," some of the very allegories, epigrams, and parables which have been most frequently anthologized and which Hoffman considers inferior.

Since Crane's temperament was essentially ironic, he dealt with strong emotion through a mask of indirection. Nelson shows that this is particularly true of poems that make statements about God and religion or love. While Crane's denunciations of the wrathful Old Testament Jehova often take the form of invective, the gentle interior God he sets in opposition is weak and ineffectual. Love poems such as "Intrigue" and "Love walked alone" soon degenerate into sentimentality and pathos. Nelson effectively attacks the complex symbolic poems championed by Daniel Hoffman, but his defense of the ironic parables which he believes to be Crane's finest achievements in verse is less convincing. These are the poems "in which the content does not break through the restraint imposed by irony or symbol into a banal explicitness" (p. 581). But although complexity is not necessarily a virtue, control, simplicity, and indirection do not in themselves constitute good poetry, and for many critics the quality of Crane's eccentric epigrams and fables as works of art remains questionable.

105. Westbrook, Max. "Stephen Crane's Poetry: Perspective and Arrogance," *Bucknell Review*, XI (December, 1963), 24–34.

An apparent conflict between affirmative and deterministic points of view in Crane's poetry is reconciled by Westbrook's differentiation of two voices, the voice of perspective and the voice of arrogance which are often contrasted in dramatic dialogues such as "'Truth,' said the traveler" and "I saw a man pursuing the horizon." The voice of perspective is characterized by kindness, humility, and a realization of the multiplicity of truth, while arrogance is displayed by a narrow and aggressive dogmatism. Juxtaposition of these two value systems within the same poem allows Crane to assert humanistic values in the face of an indifferent or hostile universe and to suggest that elusive truth may only be approached through personal experience and cannot be established absolutely by dogma or tradition.

Westbrook shows that a single coherent value scheme lies behind Crane's dual vision. A large number of poems in *The Black Riders* and *War Is Kind* are dramatic dialogues in which two world views are enunciated. More often by inference than by direct statement, kindness and compassion with human suffering are shown to be on a higher ethical plane than a cynical or relentlessly deterministic outlook. This is especially evident in poems in which the brutal Old Testament Jehova is contrasted with a merciful interior God. "The God of many men" is ludicrous in his anger, "Fat with rage and puffing," but the inner God's soft eyes are "Lit with infinite comprehension." Poems which show men's arrogance and conceit are counterbalanced by others in which the honest and just strive for comprehension and perspective. These two seemingly contradictory points of view, Westbrook affirms, complement one another in Crane's poetry.

VI.   Bibliographical Index

The number in parentheses, at the end of each item, refers to the annotated entry of the same number.

Editions and Other Primary Materials:

Follett, Wilson, ed. *The Work of Stephen Crane*, 12 vols. New York: Alfred A. Knopf, Inc. 1925–1927. Reissued in 6 vols. New York: Russell & Russell, Inc., 1963.   **(1)**

Frryckstedt, Olov W., ed. *Stephen Crane: Uncollected Writings*. Uppsala, Sweden: Acta Universitatis Upsaliensis, 1963.   **(5)**

Gullason, Thomas A., ed. *The Complete Short Stories and Sketches of Stephen Crane*. Garden City, New York: Doubleday & Co., 1963.   **(2)**

Gullason, Thomas A., ed. *The Complete Novels of Stephen Crane*. Garden City, New York: Doubleday & Co., 1967.   **(3)**

Katz, Joseph, ed. *The Poems of Stephen Crane: A Critical Edition*. New York: Cooper Square Publishers, 1966.   **(4)**

Stallman, R. W. and Lillian Gilkes, eds. *Stephen Crane: Letters*. New York: New York University Press, 1960.   **(9)**

Stallman, R. W. and E. R. Hagemann, eds. *The War Dispatches of Stephen Crane*. New York: New York University Press, 1964.   **(7)**

Stallman, R. W. and E. R. Hagemann, eds. *The New York City Sketches of Stephen Crane and Related Pieces*. New York: New York University Press, 1966.   **(8)**

Stallman, R. W., ed. *Stephen Crane: Sullivan County Tales and Sketches*. Ames, Iowa: Iowa State University Press, 1968.   **(6)**

Biographies and Critical Biographies:

Beer, Thomas. *Stephen Crane: A Study in American Letters*. New York: Alfred A. Knopf, 1923.   **(10)**

Berryman, John. *Stephen Crane*. New York: William Sloane Associates, 1950.   **(11)**

Gilkes, Lillian. *Cora Crane: A Biography of Mrs. Stephen Crane.* Bloomington, Indiana: Indiana University Press, 1960. **(12)**

Linson, Corwin K. *My Stephen Crane,* ed. Edwin H. Cady. Syracuse, New York: Syracuse University Press, 1958. **(13)**

Solomon, Eric. *Stephen Crane in England: A Portrait of The Artist.* Columbus, Ohio: Ohio State University Press, 1964. **(14)**

Stallman, R. W. *Stephen Crane: A Biography.* New York: George Braziller Inc., 1968. **(15)**

Criticism:

Adams, Richard P. "Naturalistic Fiction: 'The Open Boat,'" *Tulane Studies in English,* IV (1954), 137–146. **(86)**

Åhnebrink, Lars. *The Beginnings of Naturalism in American Fiction.* Uppsala, Sweden: A. B. Lundequistska Bokhandeln, 1950. Reprinted, New York: Russell & Russell, 1961. **(50)**

Anderson, Warren D. "Homer and Stephen Crane," *Nineteenth-Century Fiction,* XIX (June, 1964), 77–86. **(51)**

Bassan, Maurice. "Misery and Society: Some New Perspectives on Stephen Crane's Fiction," *Studia Neophilologica,* XXXV (1963), 104–120. **(95)**

—————. "Stephen Crane and 'The Eternal Mystery of Social Condition,'" *Nineteenth-Century Fiction,* XIX (March, 1965), 387–394. **(96)**

Brennan, Joseph X. "The Imagery and Art of *George's Mother,*" *College Language Association Journal,* IV (December, 1960), 106–115. **(61)**

—————. "Ironic and Symbolic Structure in Crane's *Maggie,*" *Nineteenth-Century Fiction,* XVI (March, 1962), 303–315. **(62)**

Cady, Edwin H. *Stephen Crane.* New York: Twayne Publishers, 1962. **(16)**

Chase, Richard, ed. *Stephen Crane: The Red Badge of Courage and Other Writings.* Boston: Houghton Mifflin Co., 1960. **(19)**

Colvert, James B. "The Origins of Stephen Crane's Literary Creed," *University of Texas Studies in English,* XXXIV (1955), 179–188. **(53)**

—————. "Style and Meaning in Stephen Crane: *The Open Boat,*" *Texas Studies in English,* XXXVII (1958), 34–45. **(87)**

—————. "Structure and Theme in Stephen Crane's Fiction," *Modern Fiction Studies,* V (Autumn, 1959), 199–208. **(20)**

Cox, James T. "Stephen Crane as Symbolic Naturalist: An Analysis of 'The Blue Hotel,'" *Modern Fiction Studies,* III (Summer, 1957), 147–158. **(90)**

—————. "The Imagery of 'The Red Badge of Courage,'" *Modern Fiction Studies,* V (Autumn, 1959), 209–219. **(69)**

Crews, Frederick C. Introduction to *The Red Badge of Courage.* Indianapolis: Bobbs-Merrill Co., 1964. **(70)**

Cunliffe, Marcus. "Stephen Crane and the American Background of *Maggie,*" *American Quarterly,* VII (Spring, 1955), 31–44. **(53)**

Day, Cyrus. "Stephen Crane and the Ten-Foot Dinghy," *Boston University Studies in English* III (Winter, 1957), 193–213.   **(88)**

Dickason, David H. "Stephen Crane and the *Philistine*," *American Literature*, XV (November, 1943), 279–287.   **(21)**

Ellison, Ralph. Introduction to *The Red Badge of Courage and Four Great Stories by Stephen Crane*. New York: Dell Publishing Co., 1960. Reprinted in *Shadow and Act*. New York: Random House, 1964, pp. 60–76.   **(22)**

Fitelson, David. "Stephen Crane's *Maggie* and Darwinism," *American Quarterly*, XVI (Summer, 1964), 182–194.   **(63)**

Fryckstedt, Olov W. "Henry Fleming's Tupenny Fury: Cosmic Pessimism in Stephen Crane's *The Red Badge of Courage*," *Studia Neophilologica*, XXXIII (1961), 265–281.   **(71)**

Garland, Hamlin. "Stephen Crane: A Soldier of Fortune," *Saturday Evening Post*, CLXXIII (July 28, 1900), 16–17. Reprinted in *Stephen Crane: Letters* (Entry 9), pp. 299–305. **(23)**

Geismar, Maxwell. "Stephen Crane: Halfway House, in *Rebels and Ancestors: The American Novel, 1890–1915*. Boston: Houghton Mifflin, 1953, pp. 69–136.   **(24)**

Gibson, Donald B. "'The Blue Hotel' and the Ideal of Human Courage," *Texas Studies in Literature and Language*, VI (Autumn, 1964), 388–397.   **(91)**

—————. *The Fiction of Stephen Crane*. Carbondale, Illinois: Southern Illinois University Press, 1968.   **(17)**

Gibson, William M., ed. *The Red Badge of Courage and Selected Prose and Poetry*, 3rd Edition. New York: Holt, Rinehart & Winston, 1968.   **(25)**

Gleckner, Robert F. "Stephen Crane and the Wonder of Man's Conceit," *Modern Fiction Studies*, V (Autumn, 1959), 279–281.   **(92)**

Greenfield, Stanley B. "The Unmistakable Stephen Crane," *PMLA*, LXXIII (December, 1958), 562–572.   **(72)**

Griffith, Clark. "Stephen Crane and the Ironic Last Word," *Philological Quarterly*, XLVII (January, 1968), 83–91.   **(26)**

Gullason, Thomas A. "Stephen Crane's Private War on Yellow Journalism," *Huntington Library Quarterly*, XXII (May, 1959), 201–208.   **(27)**

—————. "The Significance of 'Wounds in the Rain,'" *Modern Fiction Studies*, V (Autumn, 1959), 235–242.   **(97)**

—————. "Thematic Patterns in Stephen Crane's Early Novels," *Nineteenth-Century Fiction*, XVI (June, 1961), 59–67.   **(28)**

—————. "The Jamesian Motif in Stephen Crane's Last Novels," *Personalist*, XLII (Winter, 1961), 77–84.   **(29)**

Hafley, James. "'The Monster' and the Art of Stephen Crane," *Accent*, XIX (Summer, 1959), 159–165.   **(64)**

Hagemann, E. R. "Crane's 'Real' War in His Short Stories," *American Quarterly*, VIII (Winter, 1956), 356–367.   **(98)**

Hart, John E. "*The Red Badge of Courage* as Myth and Symbol," *University of Kansas City Review*, XIX (Summer, 1953), 249–256.   **(73)**

Hoffman, Daniel G., ed. *The Red Badge of Courage and Other Stories by Stephen Crane*. New York: Harper & Brothers, 1957. **(30)**

—————. *The Poetry of Stephen Crane*. New York: Columbia University Press, 1957. **(101)**

Hough, Robert L. "Crane and Goethe: A Forgotten Relationship," *Nineteenth-Century Fiction*, XVII (September, 1962), 135–148. **(54)**

Howarth, William L. "*The Red Badge of Courage* Manuscript: New Evidence for a Critical Edition," *Studies in Bibliography*, XVIII (1965), 229–247. **(74)**

Hungerford, Harold R. "'That Was at Chancellorsville': The Factual Framework of *The Red Badge of Courage*," *American Literature*, XXIV (January, 1963), 520–531. **(75)**

Johnson, George W. "Stephen Crane's Metaphor of Decorum," *PMLA*, LXXVIII (June, 1963), 250–256. **(31)**

Katz, Joseph. "'The Blue Battalions' and the Uses of Experience," *Studia Neophilologica*, XXXVIII (1966), 107–116. **(102)**

—————. ed. *The Portable Stephen Crane*. New York: Viking Press, 1969. **(32)**

Kindilien, Carlin T. "Stephen Crane and the 'Savage Philosophy' of Olive Schreiner," *Boston University Studies in English*, III (Summer, 1957), 97–107. **(55)**

Klotz, Marvin. "Stephen Crane: Tragedian or Comedian: 'The Blue Hotel,'" *University of Kansas City Review*, XXVII (Spring, 1961), 170–174. **(93)**

—————. "Romance or Realism?: Plot, Theme, and Character in *The Red Badge of Courage*," *College Language Association Journal*, VI (December, 1962), 98–106. **(76)**

Kwiat, Joseph. "Stephen Crane and Painting," *American Quarterly*, IV (Winter, 1952), 331–338. **(56)**

Labor, Earle. "Crane and Hemingway: Anatomy of Trauma," *Renascence*, XI (Summer, 1959), 189–196. **(33)**

LaFrance, Marston. "Stephen Crane's *Private Fleming: His Various Battles*," in *Patterns of Commitment in American Literature*, ed. Marston LaFrance. Toronto: University of Toronto Press, 1967, pp. 113–133. **(77)**

Liebling, A. J. "The Dollars Damned Him." *New Yorker*, XXXVII (August 5, 1961), 48–60, 63–66, 69–72. **(34)**

Marcus, Mordecai. "The Unity of *The Red Badge of Courage*," in *The Red Badge of Courage*: *Text and Criticism*, ed. Richard Lettis, *et al.* New York: Harcourt, Brace & Co., 1960, pp. 189–195. **(78)**

—————. "The Three-Fold View of Nature in 'The Open Boat,'" *Philological Quarterly*, XLI (April, 1962), 511–515. **(89)**

Miller, Ruth. "Regions of Snow: The Poetic Style of Stephen Crane," *Bulletin of the New York Public Library*, LXXII (May, 1968), 328–349. **(103)**

Morgan, H. Wayne. Stephen Crane: The Ironic Hero," in *Writers in Transition: Seven Americans*. New York: Hill and Wang, 1963, pp. 1–22 **(35)**

Nelson, Harland S. "Stephen Crane's Achievement as a Poet," *Texas Studies in Literature and Language*, IV (Winter, 1963), 564–582. **(104)**

O'Donnell, Thomas F. "John B. Van Petten: Stephen Crane's History Teacher," *American Literature*, XXVII (May, 1955), 196–202. **(57)**

Osborn, Neal J. "William Ellery Channing and *The Red Badge of Courage*," *Bulletin of the New York Public Library*, LXIX (March, 1965), 182–196. **(58)**

————. "The Riddle in 'The Clan': *A Key to Crane's Major Fiction?*" *Bulletin of the New York Public Library*, LXIX (April, 1965), 247–258. **(99)**

Øverland, Orm. "The Impressionism of Stephen Crane: A Study in Style and Technique," *Americana Norvegica: Norwegian Contributions to American Studies*. Philadelphia: University of Pennsylvania Press, 1966, I, 239–285. **(36)**

Pizer, Donald. "The Garland-Crane Relationship," *Huntington Library Quarterly*, XXIV (November, 1960), 75–82. **(37)**

————. "Stephen Crane's 'Maggie' and American Naturalism," *Criticism*, VII (Spring, 1965), 168–175. **(65)**

————. Introduction to *Maggie: A Girl of the Streets*. San Francisco: Chandler Publishing Co., 1968. **(66)**

Pratt, Lyndon Upson. "The Formal Education of Stephen Crane," *American Literature*, X (January, 1939), 460–471. **(38)**

Rahv, Philip. "Fiction and the Criticism of Fiction," *Kenyon Review*, XVIII (Spring, 1956), 276–299. **(39)**

Schneider, Robert W. "Stephen Crane: The Promethean Protest," in *Five Novelists of the Progressive Era*. New York: Columbia University Press, 1965, pp. 60–111. **(40)**

Shroeder, John W. "Stephen Crane Embattled," *University of Kansas City Review*, XVII (Winter, 1950), 119–129. **(41)**

Solomon, Eric. "Another Analogue for 'The Red Badge of Courage,'" *Nineteenth-Century Fiction*, XIII (June, 1958), 63–67. **(59)**

————. "The Structure of 'The Red Badge of Courage,'" *Modern Fiction Studies*, V (Autumn, 1959), 220–234. **(79)**

————. "Stephen Crane's War Stories," *Texas Studies in Literature and Language*, III (Spring, 1961), 67–80. **(100)**

————. *Stephen Crane: From Parody to Realism*. Cambridge, Mass.: Harvard University Press, 1966. **(18)**

Solomon, M. "Stephen Crane: A Critical Study," *Masses and Mainstream*, IX (January, 1956), 25–42; (March, 1956), 31–47. **(42)**

Stallman, Robert W. Introduction to *The Red Badge of Courage*. New York: Random House, 1951. **(80)**

————. ed. *Stephen Crane: An Omnibus*. New York: Alfred A. Knopf, 1952. **(43)**

————. "Stephen Crane's Revision of *Maggie: A Girl of the Streets*," *American Literature*, XXVI (January, 1955), 528–536. **(67)**

————. "Crane's 'Maggie': A Reassessment," *Modern Fiction Studies*, V (Autumn, 1959), 251–259. **(68)**

Stein, William Bysshe. "Stephen Crane's *Homo Absurdus*," *Bucknell Review*, VIII (May, 1959), 168–188. **(44)**

Stone, Edward. "The Many Suns of *The Red Badge of Courage*," *American Literature*, XXIX (November, 1957), 322–326. **(81)**

Sutton, Walter. "Pity and Fear in 'The Blue Hotel,'" *American Quarterly*, IV (Spring, 1952), 73–78. **(94)**

Vanderbilt, Kermit and David Weiss. "From Rifleman to Flagbearer: Henry Fleming's Separate Peace in *The Red Badge of Courage*," *Modern Fiction Studies*, XI (Winter, 1965–1966), 371–380. **(82)**

Walcutt, Charles C. "Stephen Crane: Naturalist and Impressionist," in *American Literary Naturalism: A Divided Stream*. Minneapolis: University of Minnesota Press, 1956, 66–86.
(45)

Webster, H. T. "Wilbur F. Hinman's *Corporal Si Klegg* and Stephen Crane's *The Red Badge of Courage*," *American Literature*, XI (November, 1939), 285–293. **(60)**

Weimer, David R. "Landscape of Hysteria: Stephen Crane," in *The City As Metaphor*. New York: Random House, 1966, pp. 52–64. **(46)**

Weisberger, Bernard. "*The Red Badge of Courage*." in *Twelve Original Essays on Great American Novels*, ed. Charles Shapiro. Detroit: Wayne State University Press, 1958, pp. 96–123.
(83)

Weiss, Daniel. "*The Red Badge of Courage*," *Psychoanalytic Review*, LII (Summer, 1965), 35–52; (Fall, 1965), 130–154. **(84)**

Wertheim, Stanley. "Stephen Crane and the Wrath of Jehova," *Literary Review*, VII (Summer, 1964), 499–508. **(47)**

West, Ray B., Jr. "Stephen Crane: Author in Transition," *American Literature*, XXXIV (May, 1962), 215–228. **(48)**

Westbrook, Max. "Stephen Crane's Social Ethic," *American Quarterly*, XIV (Winter, 1962), 587–596. **(49)**

————. "Stephen Crane's Poetry: Perspective and Arrogance," *Bucknell Review*, XI (December, 1963), 24–34. **(105)**

Wogan, Claudia C. "Crane's Use of Color in 'The Red Badge of Courage,'" *Modern Fiction Studies*, VI (Summer, 1960), 168–172. **(85)**